BLINDSIDED

A Manager's Guide
to Crisis Leadership

2nd Edition

Bruce T. Blythe

Kristen Noakes-Fry, Editor

ISBN 978-1-931332-69-9 (Softcover)
ISBN 978-1-931332-70-5 (Hardcover)
ISBN 978-1-931332-71-2 (Ebook)

ROTHSTEIN PUBLISHING

a division of Rothstein Associates Inc

Brookfield, Connecticut USA
www.rothsteinpublishing.com

ISBN 978-1-931332-69-9 (Softcover)

ISBN 978-1-931332-70-5 (Hardcover)

ISBN 978-1-931332-71-2 (Ebook)

Library of Congress Control Number
(LCCN) 2014931038

a division of Rothstein Associates Inc

Philip Jan Rothstein, FBCI, Publisher
4 Arapaho Road
Brookfield, Connecticut 06804-3104 USA
203.740.7400 • 203.740.7401 fax
info@rothstein.com
www.rothsteinpublishing.com
www.rothstein.com

Keep informed of the latest crisis communication, crisis management,
and business continuity news.
Sign up for Business Survival™ Weblog: Business Continuity for Key Decision-Makers
from Rothstein Associates at www.rothstein.com/blog

Acknowledgments

No book, or career for that matter, can be successfully executed without the support of many people. I have been blessed with a truly wonderful support system. The worldwide network of professional consultants in our company is unsurpassed in their commitment to top quality services. The people we serve deserve no less than the best, and I am so proud to have you on our team. The management staff of my three companies, i.e., Crisis Management International, Crisis Care Network, and Behavioral Medical Interventions, are the finest with whom I have ever worked. My gratitude also goes to Pamela Porter for her contributions to this book, and for all she does for CMI. And to Norm Shockley: Even in your retirement, your influence has supported untold thousands of people. Thanks for twelve solid years. Your professionalism and ethics continue to light my career path.

For this 2nd edition in 2014, I would like to thank the CEO of my three US companies, Scott Alfieri, for initiating this updated version of *Blindsided*. Thanks also to Phillip Jan Rothstein and Kristen Noakes-Fry – and their whole team at Rothstein Publishing – for your assistance in directing me during the re-writing process.

In the original writing of this book in 2002, I had phenomenal support of the best, led by Robyn Freedman Spizman. Thank God for you, Robyn, and for your unwavering belief in me and this project. Evie Saks and Jonathan Lerner provided the support I needed every step of the way, and you know I could not have made it without you. A special thanks also to my literary agent, Meredith Bernstein, who made this book happen at lightning speed. And to Bill Brazell and Adrian Zackheim at Penguin Putnam for believing in this book and making it a reality.

James Kreindler, thanks for your input on Pan Am 103. Additional thanks to Jack Cox of Liberty Mutual, Chris Nelson of Target Corporation, and Joy Sever of the Reputation Institute for their valuable assistance. Gene Rugala, thanks for sharing the knowledge of the FBI Academy and for your friendship.

I want to acknowledge my wife, Becky, and my daughter, Alexandria, now a budding attorney. You two have given me the space to pursue my dreams, and I love both of you beyond words.

I also want to recognize all those executives we have helped before and during crises and the thousands of individuals who have been subjected to traumatic incidents and other crisis situations throughout my career. We have learned much together along the way. And I want to pay tribute to all those unsuspecting people who will be subjected to crises in the future. Hopefully, the contents and influence of this book will reach you and be helpful during your time of great need.

Last of all, I want to acknowledge you, the reader. If even one crisis is avoided, or the wellbeing of your organization or only a single person is protected, the value of the information in this book is priceless.

Bruce T. Blythe
Atlanta, Georgia

Dedication

This book is dedicated to

Alex Gross

As a holocaust survivor against unbelievable odds,
you have demonstrated amazing resiliency, forgiveness,
unselfish giving, and true enjoyment in humankind.

As a man whose wife was murdered,
you have shown how love can truly overshadow
fear, depression, and anger.

And as a parent who witnessed
the accidental death of your teenaged son,
you have deeply touched countless thousands of
children in schools across the nation.

You give us all hope.

What Business Leaders Are Saying About *Blindsided*

BLINDSIDED is a must-read for my editorial staff, an excellent reference on the topic of Crisis Management. As publishers of *Continuity Insights*, we rely on Bruce for his expertise on critical incidents in the workplace.

> Robert S. Nakao, Executive Publisher Continuity Insights

For more than 34 years as an Insurance and Risk Management professional, I have experienced countless traumatic, tragic workplace events within multiple organizations. I quickly learned that without traumatic crisis response expertise, my well-intended attempts had the potential to cause additional damage to affected personnel and to the reputation to the organization.

Bruce Blythe has successfully expanded on a book that during the past ten years has helped me develop my crisis leadership skills and a response program nationally recognized by peer Risk Managers and trade publications. With this new edition, Bruce brings forth additional concepts and tools based upon his extensive experience in the field of Crisis Leadership. *BLINDSIDED* is an invaluable leadership guide for improving your program and for planning, communicating, and executing aggressive, successful crisis management. Crisis response is all about the plan, the knowledge, and the practice. It is about doing the right thing and taking care of those traumatized. This book will provide leadership guidance for doing just that.

> David Theron Smith, Divisional VP, Risk Management
> Family Dollar Stores

BLINDSIDED offers practical, down-to-earth advice in dealing with crises. It is an excellent book which outlines step-by-step procedures on how to manage crisis situations and minimize fallout on organizations while keeping a moral compass. It is a must-have in any Crisis Manager's reading list and an essential companion to a Business Continuity Plan.

> Lyndon Bird Technical Director, Business Continuity Institute

Author's Preface to the 2ⁿᵈ Edition

Blindsided was originally published in 2002, soon after the tragedy of 9/11. Over a decade later, I began to write this 2ⁿᵈ edition to update the formidable lessons I have learned since that time into a balanced strategic and tactical crisis management approach to support you and every manager in your organization in becoming a better leader in times of crisis.

My commitment is to help you reduce your exposure to chaos and threat by guiding you as you analyze foreseeable risks and create a master plan for crisis response. These are lessons that have become essential for any organization.

I offer my thoughts as if I were sitting next to you at your desk, with real-world examples of what has worked – and not worked – in my 30 years of experience with hundreds of companies just like yours.

I have included new, step-by-step scenarios for you to work through both the response and planning process – individually or in teams – involving such crises as a shooter in the building, a pandemic, or a kidnapping. In the first half of the book I address immediate response – what to do if you are "blindsided" by a totally unexpected crisis.

In the second half of this book you will learn what you need to know about planning and training – learning from the lessons in the first half of the book, and then applying the best practices outlined here to design a full crisis response plan.

And if you already have a crisis response plan, you can fine-tune it based on the guidance in this book.

In this new 2ⁿᵈ edition, I include:

- How to apply the "reasonable person test" and the "Wall Street Journal test" to your crisis management decisions in advance – before your reputation and bottom line suffer in the courtroom or in the press.

- What it takes for you to become a "crisis whisperer" who is effective in the most challenging situations, and how to avoid falling into the "crisis red zone" which can cause your leadership effectiveness to evaporate.

- How to achieve the "new normal" for your workforce and other crisis survivors in the days following the most upsetting and disorienting crisis.

- The steps for developing crisis response teams – choosing the right team members, conducting training, designing and carrying out a range of crisis response exercises, and evaluating the outcome and lessons-learned.

- Practical steps for being organized in advance to handle the families of those who are injured or lost in a crisis event – including powerful, time-tested instructions for communicating the most tragic news in person with empathy and dignity.

Although I began the 1st edition of *Blindsided* before the attacks of September 11, 2001, I completed the book with recognition that the rules had changed. Today, those changing rules still prevail. A sense of safety and security once commonplace among employees and employers had been severely compromised. The possibilities for crisis in the workplace continue to be ominous and real. Regrettably, there is nothing that says the world is a less dangerous place.

Yesterday's crisis management plan does not accommodate the possibilities of tomorrow. For that reason, in this 2nd edition, I include a chapter on the crisis management risks and corresponding controls that are trending in our future. What's needed by businesses now is a proven method to ensure that not only your facilities and reputation are rebuilt, but that the spirit, cohesion, and productivity of your employees are, too.

It is my hope that the ideas and instruction contained in these pages will be thoroughly understood and practiced – and hopefully never put to the real test. "Hope for the best and prepare for the worst" certainly applies. But if you follow these guidelines and crisis does strike, you will be ready. You may feel concerned and unsure in some ways, but you will not be blindsided. It is my pleasure to assist you as you strive to achieve the calm assurance of preparedness.

Bruce T. Blythe, Chairman
Crisis Management International, Inc.
Atlanta, Georgia
Crisis Care Network, Inc.
Grand Rapids, Michigan
Behavioral Medical Interventions, LLC
Minneapolis, Minnesota
February, 2014

Foreword

Emerging elements of the modern world can threaten any organization. Yet with proper preparation and guidance from crisis management professionals, I know from personal experience that you can influence the effects that catastrophes have on your organization.

I can personally attest to the value of the crisis management system that Bruce Blythe outlines in *Blindsided*. With such a system in place, I have seen the people at a company work through a major crisis together to become a stronger, more compassionate organization.

No one can predict the site of the next catastrophe, but all of us can – and must – prepare for the possibility that it will hit our neighborhood. In its continually evolving forms, terrorism has become one more risk for all companies to face – along with workplace violence, industrial accidents, product tampering, and natural disasters.

Having served as CEO of a Fortune 500 company, I appreciate the importance of addressing the needs of the business and those of our valued shareholders. We can address those needs only by making a sincere effort to attend to our people, who are truly our most valuable asset.

Bruce Blythe has distilled his knowledge and experience into a book that is powerful, accessible, and complete. It will help you lead your organization through disaster – mostly by helping you prepare for it.

The goal of crisis management is for your organization to survive. You may never get back to exactly where you were before. But a well-managed crisis can actually leave your organization stronger, more resilient, and better tuned to the world than it was before.

The need to prepare your company for crisis has never been so clear. The guidance you need is in this book.

Luke R. Corbett
Former Chairman and Chief Executive
Officer, Kerr-McGee Holdings, Inc.
Member, Board of Directors,
OGE Energy Corp.

Foreword

Business, it seems, has entered the age of crisis. Almost every day, another venerable company or institution finds itself in the headlines, and usually not in a flattering context. In addition to a long list of global corporations, public sector institutions and non-profits are increasingly forced to deal with serious crises. Recent organizations on the list included, among others, retailer Target, financial giant JPMorgan Chase, and Italian pasta maker Barilla as well as Paula Deen and the NSA. The events that can trigger a crisis can come from anywhere: product quality or safety issues, attacks or boycott threats by radical activists, rogue employees, accidents, natural disasters, kidnappings, extortion attempts or cases of workplace violence. Often the specific incident mushrooms into a reputational crisis that can inflict lasting damage on companies and their leaders. There are various reasons for this development. The rise of social media accompanied by ever higher expectations about corporate conduct plus the complexities of operating in a global business environment have all contributed to the increasing crisis potential. And none of these mega-trends will reverse anytime soon. Business leaders are worried, and board members have started to take notice.

While leaders are increasingly aware of the importance of crisis management and preparedness, all too often they fail when the time comes. Executives have no shortage of advice. Crisis consulting is a thriving business, and crisis management books fill the book shelves. There is much useful advice available, but often executives struggle to follow that advice when it matters.

Bruce Blythe's book is different. It is packed with practically useful advice and covers virtually any type of crisis a company can encounter, from a workplace shooting to an industrial accident. The book is filled with useful checklists and concrete steps for how to set up effective crisis management processes, including crisis preparedness, assessment of foreseeable risks, review of current procedures, design of new processes and controls, and finally, ongoing review, learning, and improvement. In short, what we have is a step-by-step guide to process excellence.

The book really shines in its understanding of people. From the "reasonable person test" to steps for how to avoid falling into the "crisis red zone," Bruce puts the human side of crisis management front and center. Crisis management is not an abstract strategic exercise; it involves the whole person. It magnifies virtues and flaws and can bring out the best in people – and the worst. The book puts the reader right into the middle of a crisis, shows how even the best leaders can panic and why, and gives concrete and actionable advice to be mentally ready for the crucible of leadership. Crisis leadership is not only about knowing and doing; it is also about who we are as people.

But effective leaders connect deeply with their people, nowhere more than during a crisis. The essential need to take care of one's people during a crisis is one of the cornerstones of the book. This includes concrete steps from de-escalation meetings to crisis care. People, with their fears, concerns, and immediate needs, are always at the center of crisis leadership. Bruce calls it "management with a heart," and he takes the reader through some of the toughest moments in the life of a leader. But it is these moments that create legendary leaders or cut short a promising career.

In sum, Bruce Blythe's book is a veritable encyclopedia of crisis leadership, rich in strategic insights, invaluable for any leader who wants to improve his or her organization's crisis management capabilities.

Daniel Diermeier
IBM Distinguished Professor of
Regulation and Competitive Practice,
Director of the Ford Motor
Company Center for Global Citizenship,
Kellogg School of Management,
Northwestern University,
Evanston, Illinois, USA
March 14, 2014

Table of Contents

Chapter 5: Crisis Communications 119

Chapter 6: Reputation Management, Co-authored by Dr. Daniel Diermeier 151

Chapter 9: Analyzing Your Foreseeable Risks 225

Chapter 10: Re-evavaluating Your Existing Crisis Procedures 247

PART 1:

RESPONSE

Introduction

Now What Do You Do?

It is a normal Thursday morning – except that because it's raining, you had to drop the kids at school, so you got to your desk late. Of your 66 e-mails, 14 are flagged "priority," you have 12 voice mails – and you have to make a presentation to the top brass at 10:30 a.m. You are just settling in to go over your notes, when you hear a short burst of dull pops. So short and dull, that until the screaming begins, you don't actually register the sounds.

But you hear the second burst with heart-stopping clarity, and the third – and the shattering of plate glass, and the panicked screaming, and the commotion of chairs being kicked over and doors slammed, as people stumble for cover from the gunman who is terrorizing the place you work. Your instinct is to scream and hide, too. Except for one thing – you are the person who has been designated to manage crisis response.

This section will help you to:

➢ *Think about crisis scenarios as leadership moments.*

➢ *Understand and predict the four phases of a crisis.*

➢ *See what workers expect from management in the phases of a crisis.*

➢ *Be prepared for what you will need to know and do in the face of a crisis.*

Welcome to the world of crisis management. It involves a perpetual state of preparedness through repeated cycles of planning, training, and exercising. At an unexpected and inconvenient time, the grim reaper of crisis could come visiting. The Boy Scout motto of "be prepared" applies not only to your team and organization – it applies individually to you, as well.

0.1 Crisis Leadership Moments

Crisis Leadership Moment 1: Avian Flu. Imagine that it finally hits! An increasingly fatal strain of avian flu has just been confirmed to be highly contagious. One of your traveling employees has recently left the workplace and been diagnosed with this dreaded disease during an emergency room visit. Your workforce members are fearful that they might have been exposed and most are not personally prepared at home for an outbreak. But, you need most of them to carry out the company's business continuity plan (BCP) that has just been mobilized. Employees, en masse, want to take time off. What do you do?

> **If knowledge...were unveiled publicly, it would likely cause serious reputational and legal damage to your organization...But it would be worse if discovered later that you tried to cover it up.**

Crisis Leadership Moment 2: Toxic Substances. You learn that one of your facilities has been emitting low-level toxic substances for an undetermined amount of time. It is the fault of the company due to a prior decision to delay replacement of a faulty system in one of your facilities. However, it is now quickly remedied. Possibly, employees, visitors, and others have all been exposed to a small degree. Most likely, the exposure was minimal with no harm.

Unfortunately, a similar situation occurred at the same facility last year. You reported it to the authorities. The media, in learning about it, exaggerated the story, blaming the company for knowingly putting people at risk.

If knowledge of the present toxic emission were unveiled publicly, it would likely cause serious reputational and legal damage to your organization, now that it has happened again. But it would be worse if discovered later that you tried to cover it up. Only you and a couple of trusted subordinates know about the emission now. Do you go public proactively and risk the feared personal, reputational, and legal damage – or do you try to resolve the situation quietly with (hopefully) no public harm done?

Crisis Leadership Moment 3: Activist Bombs. Two bombs hit your facilities simultaneously in different locations. You receive a note from an activist group taking credit and promising additional attacks. Do you close all your facilities throughout the enterprise as a safety precaution?

If so, for how long?

If not, what are alternative responses?

Defining Decision: Each of these situations requires a defining decision.

▶ Initial information is at least partially wrong.

▶ Rumors are present.

▶ Action must be taken without time for sufficient consideration.

▶ The consequences are high.

▶ People are watching your every move.

▶ The velocity of incoming information is staggering.

▶ The stress is numbing.

Now, you make those decisions that may have life and death implications. You act in a manner that will be scrutinized later. You take that risk that may define your career as an excellent leader when the organization needed it most – or as an inept manager with poor judgment under pressure.

0.2 Imagining the Worst, and Picturing What to Do

The mental tool of focused imagery can help you be more effective as a crisis manager.

It's hard to imagine your company, let alone yourself, in the throes of a disaster or traumatic incident. Typically, when we confront the idea of crisis, especially of a traumatic incident, our minds dissociate or block it out. In many ways, that is a healthy response. It keeps us from being chronically anxiety ridden. But it can also prevent us from concentrating productively, as we should, on harmful possibilities. In the chapters which follow on preparedness, I will show you how to use focused imagery exercises to make sure that your crisis planning is thorough and relevant to the real risks you face.

Imagery can also help you make it through a "live" crisis. While consulting at crisis sites, I often imagine myself in the place of those involved. For example, to help management and public relations professionals craft the key messages that management should communicate to the media, I imagine myself as an aggressive reporter. As a reporter, what information would help me tell the most riveting story? What spin might I be tempted to put on the story as a result of past coverage or the company's image in the community? What evidence of controversy or negligence might I look for to attract attention? After doing this, you find yourself able, with surprising accuracy, to anticipate the questions the media will throw at management, and the spin the media might put on the incident.

This imagery technique will help you recognize what's needed, and will accelerate your response time – when there's no time to lose. **It's happening right here, and right now – to us.**

0.3 Crisis Phases

If a shooting occurred at your place of work, what would your employees need from you, the crisis manager? Put yourself in the place of any typical employee, and apply the focused imagery technique to our hypothetical situation of the rampaging gunman.

0.3.1 Impact Phase

Imagine that you are an employee working at your desk. Suddenly, you hear shots, breaking glass, and screaming. The first spray of gunfire was at a location you could not see, but now the shooter comes running up the hallway, toward and then past your office – stopping to blast into a few open doorways, terrifyingly, seemingly at random – as he heads for an exit.

While it may be uncomfortable, you should imagine as vividly as possible the shocking sounds, the sickening sights, the rush of adrenaline, and pounding of your heart, even the burnt metallic scent of the gunpowder.

What would be your immediate reaction? If you are like most of us, your reaction would be focused on survival. Your response would be to run, hide, play dead, or possibly attack the gunman if you were close enough and it appeared to be your best option for survival. Flee, freeze, or fight. Now what?

0.3.2 Immediately Afterward

Assume you and others have evacuated the building rapidly to a nearby sidewalk. Fellow employees are standing around, shell-shocked and stressed. Everybody feels physically bedraggled, too. Adrenaline is flowing. Some people are in tears.

Envision the reactions you would have at this point, five minutes to an hour following the incident. What might you imagine feeling? Your sense of safety, security, and control is shattered. There is fear that the shootings may not be over. You feel exposed. You are shocked, stunned, and dazed. The need for information is tremendous – questions abound, and answers are few in the immediate aftermath phase. It seems unreal, almost like a dream that you are observing. The incident is too shocking and big for your mind to grasp adequately. You have multiple feelings – yet you feel numb, too.

0.3.3 Hours Later

Continuing the imagery, you've returned home after giving a statement to the police and being released by your superiors. As you sink into a comfortable chair or huddle over tea at the kitchen table, the enormity of the events of the day starts to hit you with a vengeance.

Adrenaline courses through your body throughout the rest of the day and into the evening. There is a continuing need for information – some of which may come eerily to you over the media or through calls from family members, friends, or colleagues.

Before long, the phone intrusions will begin to feel overwhelming and you may withdraw from further contact. Stress and exhaustion struggle for supremacy, but you are wired, unable to rest. You refuse food, perhaps indulging in a stiff drink rather than anything more wholesome. Denial and the reality of the experience hit your mind in waves, alternately numbing and flooding.

By bedtime, you are strangely exhausted physically and emotionally, but not sleepy. As your head hits the pillow, flashbacks from the events of the day spill into your mind, colliding crazily. You want to rewind the experience as if it hadn't happened at all, or had been nothing more than a nasty nightmare. You start to second guess yourself in other ways and, although you know it's pointless, can't stop. The questions of "what if" and "if only" are dragging you mentally to places you don't want to be.

"What if I had been one of those he shot?" "If I had rushed him, could I have saved people?" "What would my family be experiencing now, if I had been killed?" "What are the families of those who were shot going through now?"

Sleep seems impossible. As the hours tick by, guilt begins to push through the cracks of your fragmented soul. Anger takes up residence as well. Anxiety reactions are as likely as the sunrise. Flashbacks, intrusive thoughts, and concentration difficulties abound.

> **You and your coworkers will want evidence that you are safe, with visibly increased physical security. Management needs to show overt signs of compassion and caring. You need accurate and timely information.**

0.3.4 The Aftermath Phase

Now you find yourself in the aftermath phase. After a sleepless, despondent night, you have been asked to return to the workplace. You comb the newspaper to gain needed information. Without breakfast (your stomach continues to revolt), you begin the physical and emotional journey back to the site of the shooting.

How do you feel as you arrive on the property? What might you experience as you walk into the building? Feelings of anxiety, maybe even panic, are likely, though you attempt to put on your best face. Some coworkers are busying themselves at their workstations; others seem dazed and barely able to function.

Nobody, it seems, looks as bad as you feel. You begin to ask yourself, "Have I lost it? Am I going crazy?" Despite the lack of sleep, you feel surprisingly awake. But the idea that you might have to apply yourself fully to work tasks seems almost a joke – there is absolutely no way you could do it.

As an **employee** in the aftermath, what do you really need? Now, ask yourself, "*What do I need from management,* as I arrive back at work for the first time following the horrible tragedy?"

You and your coworkers will want evidence that you are safe, with visibly increased physical security. Management needs to show overt signs of compassion and caring. You need accurate and timely information. You want some understanding regarding your inability to work at a 100% productivity level, no matter how pressing work demands may be.

Full concentration on work is simply beyond your mental, emotional, and physical capabilities right now. You may or may not want to see the scene where the incident occurred. You want answers as to why the incident occurred and what could have been done to prevent it. You want acceptable evidence that management is doing everything humanly possible to prevent this kind of thing from ever happening again.

If you are a leader in a time of crisis, once you go through this focused imagery exercise, the needs of your employees no longer seem vague. You can begin to see the concrete things you should do to protect and support them during the aftermath phases of a crisis.

Focused imagery can be used with any affected group or individual. What if you were a member of the board of directors of the company? What if you were an employee of your company in another city? What if you were the spouse of a casualty, a reporter, an emergency medical technician, a customer, or a stockholder? Your crisis management effectiveness will soar when you move from an arm's-length, detached perspective to an intimately imagined understanding of all these various experiences. And when you do this exercise, don't neglect to imagine your own experience so you will be prepared for your own reactions in the heat of a crisis.

Programming Your Brain for Effectiveness

As a crisis manager, you can program your brain through focused imagery, simulations, and training. It's the same mentality used in military training, simulation training for commercial airline pilots, and the teaching of martial arts. The learned, exercised response becomes routine, even in an emergency or other stressful crisis.

Preparation will leave you less bewildered and your employees more secure in your ability to safeguard them in time of need. It's like an insurance policy that you would never consider canceling. The process of step-by-step planning, training, exercising, and visualizing provides your brain pathways with a system that can be activated smoothly and efficiently when the time comes.

0.4 Managing Your Way Through a Crisis

Let's go through the exercise again, using the same workplace shooting incident. Only this time, the experience you imagine will be your own, as one of the crisis managers of the company.

0.4.1 Impact Phase

Like everyone else, you experience the natural human impulses of fear, flight, or fight as crisis manager. But you know your obligation is to spring into action. Through an act of sheer conscious will, you catch your breath, focus on the situation before you, and start working. You may find yourself running against the stream. As others are running out, you are running to the scene or to your predesignated crisis command center to take your initial response actions.

0.4.2 Immediately Afterward

What must you do first? The tasks seem too numerous, and overwhelming, but you discipline your mind to put them in a logical order.

- Verify that adequate police and emergency medical help have been summoned.

- See that everyone who was not injured is evacuated to a safe place.

- Try to determine where the shooter has gone, if he remains a threat, and who he might have been.

- Secure those areas where the shooting occurred.

0.4.3 Hours Later

The police and ambulances arrived, followed almost immediately by the television vans and throngs of reporters. The police cordoned off the building and determined that the gunman has left the vicinity. After taking statements from the uninjured employees, the police are ready to release them. It seems, from these statements, that the shooter was a former employee who was laid off in a recent downsizing. The police need someone from the human resources department to give them details that could help track him down.

Meanwhile, the employees are distraught at the idea of leaving on their own and confused about whether they should come to work tomorrow. You need to address their concerns and help get them off the premises. That's going to involve protecting them from the pack of reporters lining the driveway. You need to assure them it is best for them not to talk to any reporter and that a spokesperson from the company will handle the press.

The first breaking news and prolific social media alerts have brought family members of many employees to the site, desperate to know if their loved ones were among the injured or killed. You will need to delegate someone to receive these family members, take them someplace protected, tell them what happened, and connect them with their loved ones as soon as possible.

> ...observing and tracking your response, and noting the things you wish you'd had in place, will be invaluable for future crisis planning...

0.4.4 The Aftermath Phase

The suspected shooter, your former employee, has been arrested at his home. Presumably no more actual danger is present. But uncomfortable questions are already being asked about his tenure at the company, why and how he was let go, and whether you could have realized that he posed a danger. You need to develop a coherent message about this incident for dissemination both to the outside world and internally. Customers, suppliers, members of your board, and others are all clamoring to know what happened, what you expect to come of it, and how it is being handled.

If possible, your people will be coming back in the morning at your direction. How will you welcome them and help them work through the trauma? You need to plan meetings, professional psychological first aid, and onsite treatment for them. Perhaps the scene of the shooting should be preserved long enough for anyone who wants to revisit it, minus gruesome sights like blood on a carpet.

You're exhausted. And there's still so much to do. But things have begun to calm down, and two questions occur to you: How are you managing? How are those persons to whom you have delegated responsibilities functioning? As things begin to settle down, you realize that observing and tracking your response, and noting the things you wish you'd had in place, will be invaluable for future crisis planning, and you make some notes.

About this Book: How to Avoid Being Blindsided

To prepare adequately for crisis, you need to see what you are up against.

The book is divided into two sections – crisis response and crisis preparedness. I placed the section on crisis response before that on crisis preparedness to give you a full understanding of what you will encounter in a real disaster or other crisis – before you start to develop or enhance your plan. I keep it simple, offering concrete, take-and-use guidelines to help you improve your crisis IQ and skill base.

I have organized this information in this way because I have witnessed the devastation that can result when unprepared managers are left to respond through improvisation. Conversely, I have seen the overwhelmingly centered, positive results when employers reach out with appropriate communications and actions to manage not only the physical, but also the emotional after-effects of a crisis.

Part 1: *Response*

But what if the crisis is happening right now and preparedness is something you have not done adequately?

The first half of this book covers field-tested approaches for crisis leadership and responding to critical incidents during the heat of battle. I share experiences, tools, and techniques to help ensure that you and your employees avoid being blindsided by a crisis incident. They are the same field-tested strategies and tactics that I put into action with my clients, many of which are some of the best known companies and governmental organizations in the world. I'll provide leadership strategies and tactics for responding in the aftermath of a crisis. The concepts can be tailored to apply to "big bang" catastrophes and other crises such as misconduct and improprieties that can disrupt reputation and careers.

Each chapter is followed by a Quick Use Guide, a tool for instant reference during a time of crisis.

Part 2: *Preparedness*

Crisis preparedness is the second of the twin disciplines you must master to protect your company from danger. The material in the second half is designed to be used at a slower pace, as you plan and enhance your crisis preparedness over time. It will lead you through the defensible steps of analyzing foreseeable risks and creating a master plan for crisis response – before another crisis strikes your organization.

By being prepared and knowing how you would respond if a crisis or catastrophe hit your company today, you can lessen the human, reputational, and financial after-effects of the incident. Why do you need a written crisis response plan? Even if you were to be blindsided at this very minute, unaware of the disaster coming your way, an up-to-date plan allows you to know what to do to assist your management team, organization, and employees clearly in a productive and meaningful way. In the second half of the book, I provide an easy-to-follow outline to assist you in your planning.

1

Crisis Leadership: The Crisis Whisperer

You may not always make the right decisions in a fast-moving, high-consequence, unexpected, and highly visible crisis situation that presents unknown and incorrect information. However, by following the time-tested guiding principles in this book, your decisions can stay "within the guardrails" and keep you and your organization out of the ditch. In today's popular culture, a person who displays noteworthy calm and effective influence is often dubbed a "whisperer" – one who gains unexpected positive results – whether with horses, ghosts, dogs, or – toughest of all – people. In this book, we expand that definition to include a highly effective crisis leader as "crisis whisperer."

This chapter will help you to:

➢ *See what it takes to become a crisis whisperer.*

➢ *Apply the be-know-do principle.*

➢ *Stay out of the crisis red zone.*

➢ *Follow the five guiding principles of crisis leadership.*

➢ *Understand the crisis leadership mindset.*

1.1 Finding Crisis Leadership

Crisis leaders or whisperers can be found throughout the ranks of any organization. Certainly, the board, CEO, and top management are tasked with leading at high levels. But, anyone with leadership responsibilities within his or her silo of responsibility can, and should, be a crisis leader when his or her number is chosen to be on center stage of a crisis. Let's take a look at what we know from experience that differentiates an excellent crisis leader from a more tactical responder.

Significant differences between tactical crisis management and strategic crisis leadership can be identified. An effective crisis leader must consider and respond to both the tactical and strategic issues that emerge during a crisis. Some of the high-level differences are:

Tactical Responder	*Crisis Leader*
Reacts to issues as they arise	Anticipates what is ahead
Short-term focus	Long-term, consequence-related focus
Process oriented	Directed by guiding principles
Narrow focus	Wide focus
Implements tactical tasks	Uses judgment

> **Crisis leadership is more about who you are than what you know.**

Strategic crisis leadership involves high-leverage skills that are vital to corporate recovery in the midst of a crisis of any sort. To be a crisis leader, you will need skills that:

▶ Define the crisis beyond the obvious.

▶ Anticipate the effects of the crisis on impacted stakeholders.

▶ Assess the impact of the crisis on core assets.

▶ Forecast the intended and unintended consequences of decisions.

▶ Follow the values and guiding principles of the organization – and your own ethical standards that may be tested to the limit.

Crisis leadership is more about who you are than what you know. At the risk of being redundant, I'm going to say that one more time to assure clarity. *Crisis leadership is more about who you are than what you know.* No set of learned crisis leadership techniques will overcome a lack of character, ethics, or integrity – or will offset unlawful behavior. An effective crisis leader must act deliberately, quickly, effectively, and ethically with honesty and high moral values. Unfortunately, as human beings, we are only partially aware of our character flaws, incompetencies, and knowledge gaps that may emerge when we are in full-stress, high-consequence situations.

1.2 Becoming a Crisis Whisperer

Several years ago, I was called into the office of the CEO of a large oil and gas company, not sure why I was being summoned. This CEO told me that his company was obviously in a high-risk industry in which crises unfortunately tend to occur. He said his observation was that, as CEO, he was the only person in the company looking out for the enterprise as a whole during crisis response. Everyone else seemed to be looking down his or her own silo of responsibility without regard for the impacts of his or her individual actions on other silos and the enterprise as a whole. So, he asked me to develop a Strategic Crisis Leadership Checklist for all the managers in the company to follow during company crises. Without a doubt, they still needed to fulfill the tactical, silo-driven responsibilities assigned to them. However, this CEO wanted all the managers up and down the organization to be acutely aware of the impact their actions could have on the enterprise as a whole and upon other silos within the organization.

He gave me one last order related to the Strategic Crisis Leadership Checklist. It had to be on one sheet of paper or he wouldn't read it. I complied, but did cheat one little bit. I put it on one sheet of paper, but used both sides! Fortunately, he let me get by with it. The checklist that I developed has now been implemented with senior management teams throughout the world in several languages, and it is included at the end of this chapter for you and your senior management team to use for strategic crisis response.

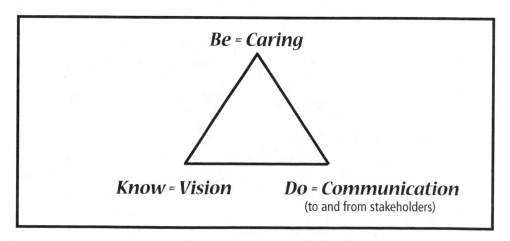

Figure 1-1. Be-Know-Do

1.3 Be-Know-Do

As I embarked on the development of the Strategic Crisis Leadership Checklist, I found no definitive books on crisis leadership at that time. Having served in the US Marine Corps, I decided to investigate the training provided for combat officers to see if I could transpose their combat leadership training into the corporate culture. Combat officers must lead in uncertain, high-consequence, fluid environments. That sounded like corporate crisis management to me. So, I embarked on a journey through the various US military combat officer training manuals.

As shown in Figure 1-1, the US Army defines the three basic components of leadership as *be-know-do* (US Army, 1999).

- ▶ "Be" is about who you are.
- ▶ "Know" is about the skills and knowledge you have acquired.
- ▶ "Do" is about the actions that you take on a timely basis.

Purposeful attention to all three components of strategic crisis leadership will increase the likelihood that you'll know what to ask, what to do, and how to do it. And more importantly, you'll learn to manage the unexpected.

What are the skills needed to meet these strategic crisis leadership responsibilities?

Imagine this situation: You don't know it now, but you are about to receive the initial notification that something dreadful has occurred. When that information arrives in this earliest phase of a crisis response, certain behaviors lead to success. Let's look at the characteristics of some of the most effective crisis leaders whom I have observed: the crisis whisperers.

> **Caring during crisis response is not a feeling. Caring is a set of corporate and personal behaviors that elicit the perception in impacted stakeholders that you and your company truly care.**

1.3.1 What Do You Need to *Be*?

You need to be caring. In my experience, I have observed that demonstration of caring is more important than all other leadership traits combined. If you come across as uncaring, people will become outraged, they won't trust you, and they will be less likely to cooperate. Caring during crisis response is not a feeling. Caring is a set of corporate and personal *behaviors* that elicit the perception in impacted stakeholders that you and your company truly care.

Crisis whisperers assume a demeanor of what I have labeled as "calm assertiveness." They respond to crisis situations in a composed manner, do what they need to do, and use a template of caring to filter decisions and actions.

Being calmly assertive. "Calm" means the leaders are free from agitation, excitement, and disturbance. They remain emotionally balanced. Like the duck on water, their feet (and minds) may be paddling frantically beneath the surface. Externally, they model a sense of calm control for others without the distractions of assigning blame and judgment. The "assertive" component means that the crisis whisperer is moving *toward* active crisis involvement while remaining calm and balanced. Assertiveness is in contrast to the aggressive behavior of some less effective crisis leaders who move *against* the crisis and people. Also, the calm assertive leader is in contrast to the avoidant leader, who tends to passively move away from the crisis by isolating or detaching from the behavioral, emotional, and cognitive challenges of the crisis. Aggression and immobilization are not good crisis leadership strategies.

Two mayors in crisis. We all have noticed that some leaders are excellent crisis managers when the unexpected occurs and others fail miserably. Compare the reputational outcome relating to the response of two mayors in crisis.

- Mayor Rudy Giuliani of New York City was named "person of the year" by *Time* news magazine following his widely applauded response to the 9/11 terrorist attacks. He recognized the extreme need of people to receive accurate and timely information. Giuliani bravely remained on the streets of New York City, potentially at his own peril, not knowing where a next attack might occur. Even though he couldn't see them, he recognized that people throughout all five boroughs of the city (and ultimately the US and world) needed information. He remained highly visible and conveyed accurate and timely information through the media in a caring and compassionate manner. It is important to note that Giuliani was absolutely committed to crisis management planning, training, and exercising prior to the terror attack of 2001. Crisis preparedness has its advantages.

- So, when Hurricane Katrina flooded New Orleans, we expected a similar response from Mayor Ray Nagin. We expected Nagin, like Giuliani, to demonstrate his ability to assist community members and other impacted stakeholders in a timely and compassionate manner. Instead, there was wide criticism of Nagin not following the city's evacuation plan, even though the school buses to be used were widely available. Additionally, he was perceived as self-serving when he evacuated himself, leaving thousands of people to fend for themselves. Then, instead of taking responsibility, he publicly blamed the federal government and Governor Kathleen Blanco for their inadequate responses. There apparently was some truth related to the poor response of FEMA and Governor Blanco, but it did not absolve Nagin of perceived incompetence in crisis leadership. He didn't demonstrate that he was commander in chief of New Orleans when the city needed crisis leadership the most. Even after Governor Blanco had called a state of emergency for Louisiana prior to landfall, Mayor Nagin did not decisively take charge. In his press conference just hours before Hurricane Katrina demolished New Orleans, casually dressed with an apparent lack of urgency and command, Nagin stated to the media, "Although the track could change, forecasters believe Hurricane Katrina will affect New Orleans. We may call for a voluntary evacuation later this afternoon or tomorrow morning."

Being in the red zone. Those crisis leaders like Nagin, who do not maintain this state of calm assertiveness, are prone to enter what I call the "crisis leadership red zone." When calmness is not maintained in the fast moving and chaotic pace of a crisis, a combination of frustration and a need to dominate or avoid tends to manifest. Additionally, if a calm assertive balance isn't maintained, crisis leaders can easily move toward a meltdown where they lose focus and effectiveness.

How can crisis leaders compensate for their unknown character flaws, incompetencies, and knowledge gaps that often emerge when "the heat is on"? The Strategic Crisis Leadership Checklist at the end of this chapter can help, especially the included five guiding principles. Later chapters will cover the common "stress styles" that can affect leaders while in crisis.

1.3.2 What Do You Need to *Know*?

As a crisis leader, you must have a vision and know the values (guiding principles) of your organization for crisis resolution. Without a clear and compelling vision and full knowledge of your personal and organizational values for response and recovery, you will not be able to lead your people adequately during times of crisis. In this early phase, it is very important to define for yourself and others what you want to happen. What would a good outcome look like? Once the desired outcome is identified, consider doing reverse sequence planning. In a guiding principle-oriented manner, plan backward to the present what you need to decide and do to move in that direction. The early phases of crisis response tend to bring the most action. The velocity in the early phases of a crisis is generally faster than after the crisis is contained and you're in the aftermath and recovery phases. So, what do you need to know? This is a time to know your guiding principles as a foundation for effective crisis decision-making.

What do you need to know to be an effective crisis leader? Clearly define and know your vision, values, and guiding principles that address the greater good of the organization and its stakeholders. Then use those principles as a beacon when making decisions and implementing actions.

1.3.3 What Do You Need to *Do*?

The single most important action is two-way communication. Simply put, you will never be any better at responding to crises than your communications. That process involves not only how well you listen in order to obtain the facts but also how well you speak openly and clearly with impacted stakeholders. Because crises are fluid and the fact pattern is ever changing, it's important to implement timely corrections and to communicate those changes on an ongoing basis. "Timely" is when stakeholders expect it. Period. As soon as practically possible, fill in the blanks in your actions and communications according to the developing story line. Because the initial information coming in will invariably include incorrect information, make decisions based on what you know and anticipate. While remaining within their established values and guiding principles, effective crisis whisperers are quick to change course and keep stakeholders informed, as appropriate, when new and verified information comes in.

> **What do you need to do as a crisis whisperer? First, do the right things according to industry knowledge, established higher purposes, and with moral values and ethics beyond reproach.**

With that said, you can't communicate your way out of inappropriate actions during a crisis. Even if mistakes are made, the old adage of "do the next right thing" is the mantra of crisis whisperers. For example, the CEO of a large organization developed serious reputational problems following a significant data breach from within his company. Sensitive information was exposed that involved hundreds of thousands of people. It was anticipated that the data breach, when announced, would cause a significant downward spiral in shareholder value. However, FBI agents had good leads on the perpetrators. They asked the CEO not to announce the data breach publicly until they could complete their investigation and hopefully make arrests. That was reasonable grounds for not communicating the data breach immediately.

In the few weeks during the FBI investigation, the CEO had a large volume of stock options that he could exercise. Knowing that the stock price would soon diminish, what would you do if you were in his situation?

This CEO decided to exercise his full options. Soon thereafter, the data breach was announced publicly and the media discovered the CEO's apparent self-serving exercise of his stock options prior to the drop in shareholder value. He communicated that he simply sold his stock at a pre-established time. While his communications were true, he was viewed publicly as self-serving. Outrage immediately flared. Ultimately, he lost his job.

What do you need to do as a crisis whisperer?

▶ First, do the right things according to industry knowledge, established higher purposes, and with moral values and ethics beyond reproach. Even if you make mistakes, involved stakeholders will recognize honest intent. And remember that no matter what communications spin you put on the story, self-serving and inappropriate actions don't work in crisis management.

▶ Second, keep the communication channels open. Highly visible communicators tend to be more effective than those who send out clandestine directives. Focus on giving factual and timely communications in addition to establishing channels to receive information from all involved stakeholders. Two-way communication is the life blood of effective crisis management. More about this in the chapter on crisis communications.

1.4 A Crisis Whisperer in Action

I have worked with many very competent CEOs and other senior executives, and one stands out as having demonstrated what I consider to be a best example of a crisis whisperer in action. I have had the opportunity to work in a crisis situation with Gary Garfield, then general counsel and later CEO and President of Bridgestone Americas, Inc. The approach he took to crisis response is one that I deem to be applicable to any crisis situation. I consider these seven steps he intuitively took to qualify as a model for being a crisis whisperer:

1. **Questioning:** He asked questions of those in the know to get an accurate fact pattern.

2. **Input:** He asked for input and suggestions from others in a brainstorming format.

3. **Options:** He laid out the field of options for crisis response.

4. **Decisions:** He made the decision-making process collaborative when possible, but made unilateral decisions when needed.

5. **Actions:** He demonstrated the moral courage to implement decisive actions on a timely basis, even though every fact was not yet available.

6. **Corrections:** After implementation, he asked for feedback and made corrections in a timely and nonjudgmental manner.

7. **Calm assertiveness:** He remained respectful, nonthreatening, and emotionally calm throughout the crisis response process until resolution was achieved.

1.5 The Five Guiding Principles of Crisis Leadership

1. Wellbeing of people first, with caring and compassion.

2. Assume appropriate responsibility for managing the crisis.

3. Address needs and concerns of all stakeholders in a timely manner.

4. All decisions and actions based on honesty, legal guidelines, and ethical principles.

5. Available, visible, and open communication with all impacted parties.

Your organization may want to add to this list. For example, if you are in an industry that can cause environmental damage, protection of the environment may also be one of your guiding principles during crisis response. In a pharmaceutical company that conducts testing on laboratory animals, a guiding principle may be to endorse animal rights laws.

In any case, guiding principles for crisis response that are established prior to your next critical incident can be a crisis leadership roadmap throughout the organization for strategic crisis decision-making. Following these five principles can help crisis managers overcome unrecognized character flaws that can emerge when blame, chaos, high-consequence threat, and other stress-inducing situations are involved.

Example – Johnson & Johnson. The late James Burke, former CEO of Johnson & Johnson (J&J) – who can be considered a pioneer of corporate crisis management – did not have a formal crisis plan in 1982 when the

Tylenol poisoning crisis hit. However, he did have the advantage of the timeless credo written in 1943 by Robert Wood Johnson (one of the three brothers who founded J&J) that served as his guiding principles and is summarized below:

J&J's responsibilities (in order of importance) are to the company's

▶ Customers.

▶ Employees.

▶ Communities.

▶ Shareholders.

Reportedly, Burke's senior management team, the FBI, and the US Food and Drug Administration all advised him against taking Tylenol off the shelves following the fatal Tylenol tampering in Chicago. The argument was for Burke to avoid any action that could reinforce the criminal who perpetrated the incident. His management team pleaded with him to consider the negative effects on market share and shareholder value. Ultimately, Burke referred to the credo that clearly stated the first priority (guiding principle) was to its customers. People were dying, and there was no assurance more would not soon follow. So, Burke ordered all $110 million of Tylenol nationwide to be taken off the store shelves. The full story has been shared many times, and I won't go into more detail here. But, the crisis leadership lesson learned is that guiding principles can be invaluable beacons during the chaos of crisis decision-making.

In the following example, we will explore the outcome of a crisis leadership challenge in which the guiding principles shared above were followed, but a wrong decision was made.

Example – Hurricane Rita. In 2005, Hurricane Rita was the fourth most powerful Atlantic hurricane in history. Right before this, gasoline prices had spiraled upward because of Hurricane Katrina. Prior to the landfall of Hurricane Rita, Governor Sonny Perdue of Georgia expected gasoline shortages, wildly higher prices, and long waiting lines for fuel due to anticipated damage to oil refineries in Texas and Louisiana. In an effort to get ahead of the crisis, stockpile fuel, and hedge against rising prices, Perdue ordered on a Friday afternoon that all schools in the state be closed on the following Monday and Tuesday. Parents were outraged as they scrambled to arrange for daycare and other accommodations for all the school children.

As it turned out, the refineries weathered the storm, and there was no gas shortage. So, what happened to Sonny Perdue's reputation due to this miscalculation that caused state-wide disruption for hundreds of thousands of families? According to the guiding principles listed about, he put the greater

Remembering Be-Know-Do Traits

I have used mnemonics – methods to help the memory – to assist in my public speaking throughout the years. One mnemonic technique is called "anchoring." For example, rather than making a list, I visually imagine items I want from the grocery store on various places of my body, from the top of my head to my feet. Imagined broccoli is on top of my head; carrots are sticking out of my ears; milk is on my shoulders. You get the idea. Each grocery item is anchored to a part of my body and I don't forget a thing, even without a list.

This same anchoring technique can be used for crisis leadership response. When your next unexpected crisis hits, you will likely not have this book readily available and people don't tend to read during a crisis. So, how can you remember what be-know-do stands for as you embark on your crisis response?

Think of your heart, eyes, and mouth as your anchors.

Heart. What do you need to "be"? Your anchor of the heart stands for caring. This will remind you to use caring as a template through which every decision you make in crisis response is filtered. Since caring is manifested in your actions, ask yourself if the actions you are about to take will be perceived as caring by impacted stakeholders. Self-serving, dishonest, and late crisis response behaviors are the opposite of caring. Caring actions include sufficient sacrifice and attention to address the needs and concerns of involved stakeholders. Timely, highly visible, and transparent communications can be perceived as caring, depending on the content of your crisis response actions and messaging.

Rudy Giuliani went to multiple funerals following the 9-11 terrorism in New York City. He said his only regret was that he couldn't go to all the funerals of the perished firefighters, police, and emergency medical personnel because so many were held at the same time. This was a great sacrifice of time by a busy mayor in the aftermath phase of a huge crisis. Through his funeral attendance, Rudy Giuliani demonstrated caring. Contrast his funeral attendance with those trite "I feel your pain" and "our hearts go out" statements often made by leaders without sufficient sacrifice and action to back them up. Crisis caring is behavioral.

We know from experience that your crisis will be less severe and will move faster toward resolution if you and your organization are perceived as caring. Conversely, if you are perceived as uncaring, people will not like you, the crisis impact will linger, and the desire for retribution will surface. Outrage is not your friend in a crisis. A caring response will cost you much less, even if it costs more up front. Respond with your heart and a template of caring.

> **Eyes.** What do you need to "know"? When your crisis hits, think of your eyes that represent vision. Without an effective vision, based on the company's values and guiding principles, it is hard to lead during a crisis. How can you establish a vision of the correct response during a crisis? Research has repeatedly demonstrated that writing helps to increase cognitive clarity, judgment, and timeliness of your defining decisions. For example, write down the facts (verified and unverified), anticipated and known problems, ways the crisis can escalate, involved stakeholders, and potential solutions. This process gets the fragmented thinking of a stressful situation into a cogent format for decisive crisis leadership action.
>
> **Mouth.** What do you need to "do"? Remember your need for communication through the anchor of your mouth. From whom do I need to receive information? What communication do I need to give out and to whom? Two-way communications (to and from) will be the life blood of your crisis response. What communications need to stop and start? Who are the involved stakeholders who need information and what communications do we need to obtain from them? Once again, you are never any better in crisis response than your communication. You cannot lead effectively during a crisis without timely and ongoing communications to and from all involved stakeholders.

needs of people first by hedging against rising prices and long lines for fuel. He took responsibility on a timely basis for responding to the anticipated crisis. His crisis leadership decision was based on an honest assessment of the anticipated crisis impact, as evidenced by the previous price increases from Hurricane Katrina. Finally, he communicated with his constituents in a visible and open manner. The fallout for Governor Perdue was only a mild blip on the radar screen with his reputation untarnished. This is one example of how the guiding principles listed above can protect your reputation, even if you make a wrong decision.

1.6 Crisis Leadership Mindset – CIA

The crisis has hit with a vengeance. Managers and executives who are used to feeling in control are trying to regain a semblance of rule and order in the midst of an escalating crisis. The scenario often goes like this as I meet with executives and managers in crisis. They look to me to tell them what to do.

One inappropriate response from me and the crisis consultation will come to an abrupt halt. But, if I identify the leverage points that will accelerate crisis resolution, my services will be credible, useful, and greatly appreciated. Much like the fable of the boy who pulls the thorn out of the lion's paw and gains the lion's lifelong loyalty, I am in a position to enhance the reputation of the organization and gain widespread favoritism among those who are impacted by a crisis.

What are the things I tend to focus on when I'm in the hot seat as a crisis consultant? Again, let's go back to our mnemonics to help you remember. This time we'll use the acronym of CIA to remember what to focus upon in the heat of the situation. The CIA is a secretive, intelligence getting department of the US federal government. So, let's focus on the invisible mindset that I use in responding to crises. In applying effective crisis leadership principles, I recommend that you look at these three rules of thumb to focus your response.

1.6.1 Core Assets

The "C" of the CIA acronym stands for the *core assets* that are at risk by a given crisis situation. I look for the crisis beyond the obvious by looking at the threatened core assets, e.g., people, reputation, and finances. Are people in harm's way? Is there possible damage to your company brand, reputation, or shareholder value? Will your ability to deliver goods or services be significantly disrupted? A full list of core assets is included in the Strategic Crisis Leadership Checklist at the end of this chapter.

Let's go back to CEO James Burke during the Tylenol poisoning crisis. With all due respect for the families, J&J's strategic crisis response was not about dead people in Chicago. Yes, the company absolutely needed to respond to these families with caring, but there was a corporate crisis that was outside the bull's eye of the Chicago area. The crisis beyond the obvious was about the core asset of trust. Customers simply would not buy Tylenol and other J&J products if they didn't trust they were safe. While others focused on the financial costs of product recall and not reinforcing the criminal, James Burke focused on the core asset of trust and took Tylenol off the shelves everywhere. He then introduced tamperproof packaging in order to maintain trust in the J&J brand.

> **Good crisis leaders look out the windshield of the crisis to identify what is on the horizon.**

1.6.2 Involved Stakeholders

The "I" of the CIA acronym stands for *involved stakeholders*. Identify all stakeholder individuals and groups who are harmed (real or perceived). Who is impacted, involved, and interested in your crisis? Media and social networks cannot be overlooked. Internally, your employees are a vital component of most crisis response initiatives. As a general rule, any stakeholder or constituent group that is overlooked in your crisis response will likely be a problem for you and your organization. Identify who they are and address their needs and concerns on a timely basis. A list of potential stakeholders is included in the Strategic Crisis Leadership Checklist at the end of this chapter.

1.6.3 Anticipation

The "A" stands for *anticipation*. Good crisis leaders look out the windshield of the crisis to identify what is on the horizon. Good crisis leaders balance their perspective on immediate and short-term responses with a focus on where the fact pattern may be headed. Controlling a crisis comes from anticipating what is potentially coming up, and being prepared to address it before it actually occurs. Otherwise, waiting until something occurs and rushing to respond leaves you and your organization out of control. Anticipate the potential progression of events and reactions by involved stakeholders. This can involve the anticipated reactions of people inside and outside your organization.

Quick Use Response Guide

Chapter 1: Crisis Leadership: The Crisis Whisperer

Strategic Crisis Leadership Checklist

Strategic Mapping

Define the crisis (beyond the obvious).

Issues/impact on core assets. What business issues are at risk?

- People.
- Key relationships.
- Reputation.
- Brand.
- Trust.
- Finances.

- Shareholder value.
- Business operations.
- Intellectual property.
- Physical property.
- Product/service delivery capabilities.
- Other.

How can this situation escalate in severity and longevity? (Anticipate progression of events and stakeholder reactions.)

What is unknown to stakeholders that could cause damage if exposed?

Stakeholders

What would successful resolution look like for each stakeholder?

What would you want if you were within their positions?

- Employees.
- Families.
- Contractors.
- Facility/site managers.
- Staff managers (HR, legal, IT, etc.).
- Senior managers.
- Board of directors.
- Business partners.
- Institutional investors/shareholders.
- Government regulators.
- Affected community members.
- Industry activist groups.
- Distributors.
- Customers.
- Visitors.
- Politicians.
- Government regulators
- Competitors.
- Media representatives.
- Internet (users/bloggers).
- Union/labor relations.
- Insurance representatives.
- Suppliers (vendors, bankers, etc.).
- First responders: law enforcement, emergency medical, firefighters.

Communications *to* and *from* each appropriate stakeholder.

- One time or ongoing?
- How often?

Impact

What could be the impact (intended/unintended) of our actions in the following areas?

- Employee relations/HR.
- Environmental/ health and safety.
- Security.
- Media/PR/communications.
- Operations/ business continuity.
- Partnerships.
- Legal.
- Investor relations.
- Financial.
- Union/labor relations.
- Government relations.
- Risk and insurance management.

Implementation

What needs to start? What needs to stop?

Who is going to do it? When? Report to whom?

Timing. Does it need to be done? If so, when?

- Immediately.
- Within minutes.
- Within hours.
- Within days.
- Beyond.
- Wait and see before implementing.

Guiding Principles

1. Wellbeing of people first, with caring and compassion.

2. Assume appropriate responsibility.

3. Address the needs of all stakeholders in a timely manner.

4. All decisions and actions are based on honesty, legal guidelines, and ethical principles.

5. Available, visible, and open communication with all stakeholders.

Crisis Leadership Model

Be: Good character demonstrated through corporate caring.

Know: Discern relevant fact pattern, corporate guiding principles and strategic vision for response.

Do: Implement priorities on a timely basis.

What Works?

- Speedy and timely response.
- Listening and gathering information.
- Clear overarching vision of a caring solution.
- Outward communications that demonstrate caring, capability, and assurance.
- Honesty and transparency.
- Addressing the needs and concerns of all impacted stakeholders.
- Being available and visible to stakeholders.

▶ Taking responsibility to resolve the crisis.

▶ Making a sacrifice.

▶ Ethical and lawful response.

▶ Unselfishness.

▶ Being calmly assertive and emotionally balanced.

CIA

When crises emerge, use a mental mindset of CIA to help you focus strategically on how best to handle the situation. The acronym of CIA stands for:

▶ **Core Assets:** What are the core assets that are threatened and how can they be protected?

▶ **Impacted Stakeholders:** Who is involved in the crisis and how should we respond to them?

▶ **Anticipation:** Where are the facts and perceptions headed regarding the crisis and how can we prepare before they occur as anticipated?

Chapter 1 – Questions for Further Thought and Discussion

1. Where in your experience have you dealt with a leader who could be called a crisis whisperer? While such leaders can be found in the corporate and business worlds, you may also have seen them in military, medical, government, neighborhood, law enforcement, and other situations. What were the traits and actions of this individual?

2. Have you ever worked with a leader who entered the red zone at a critical point in a crisis? What were the short-range and long-range outcomes for the situation, and for the people involved? If you had been in that leader's position, what might you have done differently?

3. Are there additional guiding principles for crisis management that you feel are applicable to specific industries or your present situation?

Exercise: Crisis Scenarios Revisited

So, how does this chapter apply to real life situations? Look again at the three scenarios in the introduction of this book: **avian flu,** employees exposed to a **toxic substance,** and simultaneous **bombing of your facilities** by an activist group.

Preparedness: With no prior notice, you must make on-the-spot decisions and implement rapid-fire responses when crises unexpectedly strike. Your people will be stressed out and deadlines time-compressed. Information will be inadequate and the high consequences of your responses could determine if people will be harmed, careers ruined, and your company seriously damaged.

Experience and empirical research all agree – it is best to prepare. Use these scenarios to help you in crisis leadership planning, training, tabletop exercises, and simulations – they all play an important part in helping you as a potential executive, managerial, or tactical crisis leader. Use the Strategic Crisis Leadership Checklist and guidelines in this book to help you with this exercise.

1. **Flu Scenario.** With the fatal avian flu scenario, consider first addressing the wellbeing of your most important asset, your people. For example, provide masks, gloves, hand sanitizer, and hygiene protocol within the workplace. Get your hands on cash, food, and water. If you don't already have these things, move fast. The early bird gets the worm during crisis management. Isolate and quarantine people in the workplace, as much as possible, and establish who can work from home. Once your people are addressed, focus on other stakeholders who might need priority attention such as your customers, suppliers, and distributors. Prioritize and do what you can to address the needs and concerns of all impacted stakeholders within your control and influence. What are other core assets of the organization at risk, or that could be utilized to bolster your company's reputation, trust, and loyalty? Is there a way your organization can assist with the greater good of the community? Those stakeholders that you don't adequately address will likely be your problem areas. Stakeholders that you assist at a time when they need it most will be loyal to the organization for a long time to come. Anticipate their needs by imagining what you would want or expect if you were in their position.

2. **Toxic Exposure Scenario.** The toxic exposure scenario involves information that is known to you, but not to those who may be at risk. It would be easy for uninvolved advisors to recommend that you come forward immediately and let the chips fall where they may. It's hard to hide damaging information and it's best to follow the guiding

principles of taking responsibility in an honest, legal, and ethical manner. In general, good crisis management will require protection of the greater good over personal concerns. While I don't generally recommend it, there are times in the real world of crisis management when the decision is made to conceal known information. Right or wrong, if the damage of being forthcoming is considered too much to bear, some people will decide not to come forward. If you are tempted to conceal, you must come up with a rationale that will pass the "reasonable person test." Consider confidentially getting a multidisciplinary group of advisors to discuss your best alternatives. Possibly, a specialist in toxic exposure should be consulted for guidance. Anticipate the reactions of people who perceive harm if they learn of your concealment. If you do not feel comfortable defending your rationale on the front page of the newspaper, you are taking a risk that could seriously damage your organization or even take it down. Lying and concealing information are two quick ways to escalate the severity of your crisis. Think Lance Armstrong, NFL quarterback Michael Vick, Arthur Andersen Company, Catholic Church, Bill Clinton, Penn State University, or Martha Stewart.

3. **Bombing Scenario.** Finally, the scenario of a simultaneous bombing in two work locations was presented. Your employees and customers (if they come on site) will have the natural fear of reoccurrence. One issue is to not reinforce the violent acts of a hostile activist group. Another issue is that your reputation will be seriously damaged if stores remain open and it is perceived your organization placed profits over the safety of people. Conflicting needs will likely arise. Employees will want to keep their jobs and paychecks without disruption. Shareholders may have fears that their investments are not secure. The media may sensationalize the story and even look for ways to blame your company. Your job of crisis leadership is to anticipate these and other reactions by impacted stakeholders and address their needs. A strong physical security response may be needed to help assure employees and customers. Can sales be increased online? Can deliveries be provided? Maybe, customers could call in orders with pickup to minimize their time at your stores. Possibly, an aggressive approach to help apprehend

the offenders would be effective, like offering a generous reward for information and arrest. Methods for efficiently giving and receiving communications would be a vital component for dealing with this crisis.

References

US Army Field Manual 22-100 (August 1999) *Army Leadership*.

2

Taking Decisive Action

It's one of those things you never forget – the precise moment in time when you learned some dreadful piece of news – like the death of a loved one, the assassination of a political figure, or a fatal accident where you live or work. You probably remember the period during that incident quite vividly. Time may have slowed eerily. Thoughts and movements thickened. You felt dread and fear – a nauseating feeling that grips you and won't let go. Even when the context is professional, the reaction is personal. As a manager confronted with a fire that's consumed your workplace and threatened your staff, the sickening sensations are the same as those experienced by someone who learns a personal tragedy has occurred. As a leader, you have two options. Your leadership can make you the crisis whisperer, helping turn chaos into ultimate order. Or you can find yourself in the crisis red zone, and the chaos can compound, spinning irretrievably out of control.

This chapter will help you to:

> ➤ *Ask the four fact finding questions.*

> ➤ *Use the SIP-DE crisis decision-making model.*

> ➤ *Follow the general guidelines for taking immediate actions.*

> ➤ *Orchestrate a rapid response.*

> ➤ *Compile a checklist of immediate action items.*

2.1 Three Ways You Could Get the News

Notification of a crisis at your place of business can take one of three forms. None of these scenarios is easier or more ideal than the others. Each has advantages and challenges. In each case, you are likely dealing with partial information that carries emotional weight for people involved, including yourself. We all have varying abilities to cope with such stress – and, of course, some do it better than others.

2.1.1 Personally Involved

You may be personally involved in the incident, and a firsthand observer. In this case, your initial perceptions and responses will be altered inevitably by the fact that your reactions will range from deep concern to being shocked, stunned, and dazed. But you'll need to take steps to overcome those sensations more quickly than others because you must manage this unfolding crisis situation.

> **When an event occurs that pushes us beyond our normal coping mechanisms, we enter an emotional and cognitive zone that is out of the ordinary.**

2.1.2 Near But Not Involved

The second way to receive initial notification is when you are near the incident scene, but not directly involved – perhaps in another part of the building.

In both the first and second scenarios, despite your proximity to the events, accurate information may be difficult to obtain. Rumors bubble up quickly. A true and accurate fact pattern may not have yet emerged. One company that I work with has a sign in the crisis command center that states, "The initial facts coming in are mostly false."

2.1.3 Remote From the Incident

The third possibility is that you will be remote from the incident. Here, the most difficult challenge is to obtain accurate information and to get a feel for the situation from people who may or may not have been directly involved. Even if the person reporting to you was directly involved, the perceived fact pattern may be skewed or incorrect – consider the different stories police receive from eyewitnesses following a motor vehicle accident or crime. Be ready for timely corrections as refined information is given during the timeline of a crisis.

2.2 Breaking It Down

When an event occurs that pushes us beyond our normal coping mechanisms, we enter an emotional and cognitive zone that is out of the ordinary. An automatic reaction is to dissociate or push back the information, symbolized by the "Oh no!" reaction common among those who take in bad news. It's that feeling that the mind and body have become temporarily disconnected – a psychic and physical numbness.

Think about the experience of eating an apple. The only way it can be ingested is in bite-size pieces. Learning of a tragic event that affects people we know well is like asking the mind to gulp in an entire apple. The shock and sense of unreality are the mind's way of letting you know it can't cope with this giant intrusion.

This is a place where you, as crisis whisperer, should follow the series of steps we discussed in the last chapter:

- Questioning to get an accurate fact pattern.

- Input and suggestions obtained from others in a brainstorming format.

- Options socialized and formulated for crisis response.

- Decisions collaboratively made when possible, but unilaterally when needed.

- Actions implemented with moral courage on a timely basis, though all facts aren't available.

- Corrections made in a timely and nonjudgmental manner as feedback is received.

- A calm, assertive manner prevailing throughout the process.

You can process and respond best to incoming information by breaking it into bite-size pieces. Those pieces come in many forms and over time. They will coexist with the flashbacks, concentration difficulties, intrusive thoughts, and sleeplessness that you and many survivors of a traumatic incident may experience. But as a crisis response manager in the aftermath of a critical situation, you will have to concentrate all your mental energy on examining and ingesting all the fragments of pertinent information that come your way. Processing your personal responses will be put on hold until your managerial duties have some breathing room.

2.3 You'll Need to Act Fast

Picture yourself as a corporate manager in an office where a shooting has taken place. Without warning, gunfire and screams shatter the morning calm. Windows shatter, doors slam, furniture is knocked around, people rush by in the hallway. You hear the shouts: "Nancy's been shot! Oh, God, Jorge is dead!" Shots and screams are heard from several locations in the building, and someone yells, "There are people with guns!" You see one man, with a gun, run past your office, and down an exit stairway that leads to the back. The head of building security orders an evacuation, out the front doors.

Your initial notification was the sound of gunshots and screams, which informed you that something awful was happening. You saw one shooter run toward the exit. But you distinctly heard someone yelling about "people with guns." Meanwhile, the employees are now congregating in the front courtyard. Should that decision be reconsidered? If a second gunman is still in the building, aren't employees vulnerable there to further attack? What about the known gunman who ran toward the back? Could he return like Seung-Hui Cho did in the shooting at Virginia Polytechnic Institute and State University, Blacksburg, Virginia (Virginia Tech), in April 2007, where even more people were shot? You locate the head of building security, explain your worry, and together decide to move the group into a remote area of the parking deck away from cars and the trash bins with potential bombs. Within an hour, police and security staff have searched the entire campus and, fortunately, found no additional persons or threats.

> **Typically, the initial information includes erroneous assumptions and an inadequate fact pattern. You may need to revise your first response at a moment's notice.**

The erroneous impression that there was more than one perpetrator – part of your initial notification – caused you to move an already traumatized group of people a second time, having them wait in the less than comforting environment of the parking deck. Additionally, the lone gunman is now verified to be somewhere outside the building. Now, after police have cleared the building, you need to rescind the order to evacuate, bringing people back inside to a place where they and their immediate emotional needs can be addressed more comfortably, away from the crime scene. This is not to suggest the order to move them to the parking deck was incorrect, based on the information at hand. It's just that the initial information of multiple gunmen was wrong and the location of the shooter was not yet verified. The point is, typically the initial information includes erroneous assumptions and an inadequate fact pattern. You may need to revise your first response at a moment's notice.

2.4 The Hunt for Information: Four Questions

The search for credible information is the first action step that a crisis whisperer takes after notification of a critical incident. These four primary questions, if asked and answered efficiently, will yield the essence of the information you need to strategize and implement your response.

1. What happened?

2. How bad is it?

3. What is being done?

4. What is the potential for escalation?

These questions appear straightforward, but on closer reflection each is surprisingly multifaceted. It is essential to know what questions to ask. The information source may be frantic, injured, or downright confused. As a crisis whisperer, it's your job to extract the most important information as quickly and accurately as possible.

Let's examine them individually in some detail.

2.4.1 What Happened?

If you're getting firsthand information, determine if the source has actually witnessed the events. That is the difference between verified and unsubstantiated firsthand accounting. Even with a firsthand accounting, there can be misperceptions and misinformation. A second accounting from another person might be in order, as time will allow.

If you're getting secondhand information, find out who told your source. How did he or she know it is accurate? Did that person who told your informant actually see what happened, or has the information been passed down the line? Ask for the exact words that were used to describe the situation when your secondhand source was told.

If the information has not been verified, what steps need to be taken while verification is taking place? This could include dispatching of emergency vehicles, making internal notification, planning a statement to the media, referring to your crisis manual, mobilizing your crisis management team, and strategizing the details of your immediate response, should the incident and pertinent facts be verified. In each case, this is a point for fast action and strategically anticipating what may be coming. Respond to the immediate situation and begin preparations for anticipated outcomes, should they materialize.

Make every minute count. Have your prepared crisis manual and checklists ready so that you can act immediately upon verification. Electronic copies of your crisis responsibilities are critical and the Strategic Crisis Leadership Checklist in Chapter 1 can be beneficial. However, a hard copy of your checklists and manual is often easier to navigate for some people during crisis response. It is best if you have sufficient copies of your crisis manual stored at various locations, including at the office, at home, and in the car. I recommend that you keep copies both on your electronic handheld organizers (possibly a proprietary app) and in your computer system. Be certain you can put your hands on it within minutes no matter where you are – even while traveling.

> **The more vivid the word picture presented to you, the better sense you can gain of the situation's severity and the steps that must be taken to create order out of chaos.**

2.4.2 How Bad Is It?

As you take in information, your goal is to envision the scene as clearly as possible. Here again, visualization is an effective technique. Ask your informant at the scene, "Describe what you see or know in as much detail as possible." Have the informant describe the location and disposition of the various stakeholders, the status of damaged buildings or equipment, etc. The more vivid the word picture presented to you, the better sense you can gain of the situation's severity and the steps that must be taken to create order out of chaos.

Be careful not to spend too much time gathering initial information. You want to balance getting adequate information with taking necessary immediate response actions. Use a subset of questions to assess severity.

People:

- ▶ What is the impact on stakeholders? Any initial outrage toward the organization?
- ▶ Is there ongoing danger or harm to people? Of what?
- ▶ How many serious injuries or deaths? Are these confirmed?
- ▶ How many people are directly involved?
- ▶ Did some of those who were present feel life-threatened?
- ▶ How many appear to be indirectly involved?
- ▶ Are people in the wider community impacted? How?

Property:

- ▶ Has company property been damaged? How? Severity?
- ▶ Is the damage ongoing or contained?

Business Disruption:

- ▶ Are operations continuing at full/normal levels, partial levels, or stopped altogether?

Surroundings:

- ▶ How widespread is the damage?

▶ How have physical assets in the surrounding area been affected?

▶ Are there continuing threats to the surrounding area?

Liability and Reputation: Sometimes the cause of an incident can be more damaging than the incident itself. Various media outlets, regulators, competitors, your own employees, and others may be eager to affix blame following a critical incident. Obtain information about the following:

▶ Are there issues that could put the reputation of the organization at risk?

▶ Is the organization at fault, or perceived to be at fault?

▶ In what ways might the organization be blamed?

▶ Is there any apparent outrage directed toward the organization, individual employees, or management?

▶ To what extent is media involved?

▶ What spin is the media (traditional or social outlets) putting on the story, if any, at this point?

2.4.3 What Is Being Done?

The idea here is to get as accurate a picture as possible of the actions already being taken by onsite personnel and others. Again, think – and ask – in terms of people, property, business disruption, and surroundings.

People:

▶ Has the situation been contained so that people are safe from continuing harm?

▶ Is first aid being administered effectively? If necessary, provide coaching or summon assistance.

▶ Is everyone accounted for?

▶ Have a sufficient number of emergency vehicles been dispatched? Can this information be verified?

▶ Are driveways accessible to emergency vehicles?

▶ What is being done for the injured?

▶ What is being done with the bodies of fatalities?

▶ Which hospitals are utilized?

▶ Are employees being protected from distressing sights and media encroachment?

▶ Have accommodations been made for family members who may call or arrive at the site?

▶ Are members of the media being accommodated, yet restrained from excessive intrusion?

▶ What communications need to be given and received? To whom?

Property:

▶ What is being done to contain any continuing damage?

▶ Is the incident site being protected for investigation?

▶ How are the perimeters around the incident site and the entire facility being secured?

Business Disruption:

▶ Should production be reduced or halted?

▶ Can employees remain at the worksite safely?

▶ Should any areas of the facility be shut down? If not, do people need special attention to assure them that they are safe?

▶ What needs to be done to continue operations during this situation?

Surroundings:

▶ Are neighboring businesses and residents aware of the incident?

▶ Is there a need to notify them?

> The difference between a well-managed crisis and a situation spun out of control is often a crisis manager's ability to understand the potential for escalation and mitigate against it before it occurs.

2.4.4 What Is the Potential for Escalation?

This last of the four key questions can be one of the most important. You need to know how the situation might escalate in severity and what can be done to avoid a worsening of conditions. Does the crisis response need to escalate to higher management levels? The difference between a well-managed crisis and a situation spun out of control is often a crisis manager's ability to understand the potential for escalation and mitigate against it before it escalates.

Be sure to ask:

- How could this situation or the after effects spin out of control?
- What controls need to be put in place to avoid escalation?
- What is being done to contain the causes and effects of the incident?
- Are there early rumors that are fueling the severity of this crisis?

2.5 Keep the Big Picture in Mind

This is a time to ask yourself and others about the strategic crisis management issues, in addition to the immediate tactical responses. Take periodic time-outs to reflect quickly but effectively on your vision, values, guiding principles, and goals. Refer to the Strategic Crisis Leadership Checklist provided in Chapter 1. Write down answers to the following strategic issues to gain clarity and focus about the big-picture issues:

- What are the priorities that need to be considered this hour and this day? What most urgently needs to be addressed in order to contain the crisis and, for example, ensure the safety of survivors, prevent any ongoing danger or physical damages, begin crisis communications, and the like?
- What are the biggest problems we face? Are they primarily, for example, business disruption, or traumatized people, or blame toward the company, or mounting financial losses, or a compromised reputation?
- What strategic activities should be going on at the same time initial notification and actions are taking place?
- Where is this incident headed and what should we do about it?

Remember to focus on the CIA of strategic crisis leadership, as discussed in Chapter 1. What are your *core assets* at risk? Who are *involved stakeholders* that need attention? And, what do you *anticipate* will occur as this crisis unfolds?

2.6 Crisis Decision-Making

Time-sensitive, risky decisions cause conflict between analysis and intuition. On one hand, you will want to make careful, calculated decisions during these critical situations. Conversely, you'll need to make timely decisions when there is only partial information and the clock is quickly running. According to neuroscientists, reasoning requires emotion and intuition in addition to sequential analysis and technical rationality. Chapter 4 of this book provides more detail on crisis decision-making. For now, remember that writing down information on the fact pattern, problems, potential solutions, and other issues you deem important will help clarify your decision-making.

2.7 Use a Model to Optimize Decision-Making

What is a mental model you can use to optimize your decision-making within a fluid crisis environment? As the late Dr. Louis Pasteur said, "Chance favors the prepared mind." Again, we'll go back to mnemonics to help establish a mental model to prepare you for making good decisions in a crisis setting.

This time, we'll use the acronym **SIP-DE** (Scan, Identify, Predict, Decide, Execute). One day, when I was meeting with Doug Scovanner (prior to his recent retirement as CFO of Target Corporation), we were talking about strategic crisis leadership, and Doug showed me a method called SIP-DE he learned while taking a driver's education class for his motorcycle license. While this method and later derivatives are widely used in many states in driver's education, I adapted it to apply to crisis decision-making in a corporate setting. The SIP-DE model incorporates a common process we all use when driving, and this familiar process can be applied during crises by remembering each letter.

If you are interested in practicing your crisis management skills during daily living, I suggest practicing the SIP-DE model while driving. Your working knowledge of this decision-making model will be fine-tuned for organizational crises through this mental practice. And, you'll become a better driver in the process.

2.7.1 Scan

It starts with *situational awareness*. When driving, it is critical that you scan the environment around you and remain vigilant. Likewise, when a crisis hits, scan the crisis fact pattern to obtain sufficient information for addressing the unfolding crisis. Much like completing a jigsaw puzzle, you will have pieces that are correctly in place and others that haven't yet been found. The incomplete jigsaw puzzle yields a picture that is beginning to take shape, but it isn't completely clear. In order to make timely decisions, you will need to get as many facts as possible, within the insufficient timeframe allowed, and prepare to implement decisions with partial knowledge.

2.7.2 Identify

As you drive, you will *identify* potential problems within your scope of vision. Possibly, it's another driver who is looking the other way and about to pull out in front of you. It might be a texting driver who is sitting through a green light as you rapidly approach. Embedded within each crisis fact pattern are immediate problems and potential problems if decisive action isn't taken on a timely basis. The first step in solving any problem is to identify the problem.

2.7.3 Predict

What if that person does pull out in front of you or the texting driver doesn't hurry up and go through the green light? It is not best to rely on luck and hope these problems take care of themselves. Instead, you intuitively *predict* what might soon be going wrong and take corrective action as soon as possible. In crisis response, tactical leaders will address the obvious by putting "water on the fire" that is already raging. Additionally, as an excellent crisis leader, you will look out the windshield of your crisis to scan the fact pattern, identify potential upcoming problems, and predict what might be coming against you. This process of "looking around the corner" and anticipating what is about to occur is a key trait of excellent crisis managers and strategic crisis leaders.

2.7.4 Decide

With the potential of a traffic accident before you, preemptive action is taken to avoid a motor vehicle accident. We have all intuitively engaged in this process hundreds of times without giving it a second thought. In crisis management, this familiar process will need to be a bit more purposeful. When driving, you expect the unexpected. In crisis management, this situation was not on your to-do list. The anticipated events about to unfold are less visual and the crisis damage that has already occurred distracts your anticipation of what may be around the corner. But, as a prudent crisis leader, pay attention to the unfolding fact pattern and *decide* what needs to be preemptively implemented.

> **You may execute the wrong action in a crisis situation, but if your intentions are beyond reproach, stakeholders will most often accept your rationale even though it didn't work out as anticipated.**

2.7.5 Execute

Once your traffic hazard is identified and you have decided what to do about it, you skillfully execute preventive action. It might be to engage the brake and slow down, flash your lights, honk the horn, or move to another lane to give space. In executing a crisis response, the tools in your toolkit might be less tactical and not as immediately available. In any case, you want to execute according to priority. It might be to issue a warning or strategically place resources in a position for ready response, should the anticipated problem manifest. Ultimately, effective crisis management is about what you do on a timely basis. With partial information and high consequence, it may take courage to take risky preemptive actions. Crisis management is, after all, risky business. But, those who are afraid to take calculated risks in order to address the crisis are those who most often go down in history as inept crisis managers. As a general rule, execute those actions that serve the greater good of the organization and avoid self-serving, fear-based behaviors.

Sometimes, the actions you execute may be counter-intuitive. Assume you are unexpectedly approaching that vehicle sitting through a green light on a one-way street. You could easily pull into another lane, but there is a vehicle next to you. If there is not enough time to stop, you may choose to accelerate in order to move past the vehicle next to you, and then dart around the oblivious driver in your lane. This is a risky solution, but one you may choose rather than braking into the backend of the vehicle sitting through the green light. You may execute the wrong action in a crisis situation, but if your intentions are beyond reproach, stakeholders will most often accept your rationale even though it didn't work out as anticipated.

2.8 A Manager in Crisis

Let's put you back in the immediate crisis aftermath, but this time through another perspective. Earlier, you visualized a workplace shooting from the viewpoint of an employee who was in the room at the time the gunman entered. Later, you visualized yourself, a crisis manager working at your desk when the shootings took place. Let's pick up on that same situation, and examine what your initial responses as a manager might be.

You're at your desk when you hear shots and commotion. You hear screams, including someone yelling, "There are people with guns!" A lone Caucasian man in a red shirt runs by your door. You see him duck down an exit stairway that leads to the back.

You run spontaneously to the conference area on your floor where the shootings occurred without any sense of potential exposure to personal danger. As you arrive, you see shell-shocked employees frantically attempting to administer first aid to victims lying in pools of blood. Tables and chairs are overturned and the smell of gun smoke is pungent in the air. Adrenaline is flowing.

You observe through the windows that employees are pouring out of the building into the forecourt. Back in the conference room, one manager lies gravely wounded, and she appears dead. You are stunned. Others are down and appear seriously injured as well. Now you hear sirens outside the building. As you look out, you see the first police car arrive. Also, a television van and crew are pulling up to the front entrance. As the crisis manager, what are your immediate steps?

Let's take a look at issues that need management attention, based on what we already know.

We know there is a gunman on the loose, but we don't know where he is – or whether he is alone. Employees are outside the building, potentially exposed to the gunman – and now to the police, who don't yet know whom they are looking for. Several of your people are gravely injured, in need of prompt treatment. Media representatives have arrived, and you are about to become the lead story.

2.8.1 Damage Control

A number of immediate steps must be taken. Among the most critical are the following:

- **Minimize ongoing danger.** Employees are at risk since we don't know where the gunman is located, or if there is more than one. Quickly delegate some employees to direct others into a secured area, like a cafeteria. Assign another employee to ensure the cafeteria is safe. Have the employee establish monitors at the doors to ensure that only company personnel get in.

- **Help locate the gunman.** The police need a description of the perpetrator. Your sighting of a Caucasian man in a red shirt who has allegedly run out of the building is corroborated by other witnesses – and nobody claims to have seen a second shooter. Have someone inform the police now, even though the information may not be complete. What you know can help.

- **Begin to address emergency medical needs.** If there are known personnel who are trained in first aid, send scouts to find them immediately. Experienced attention is needed to save the lives of those who are injured, since Emergency Medical Technicians (EMTs) have not yet arrived. Assure to the best of your ability that the first aid being provided in the interim is appropriate.

- **Help obtain building access.** The media truck has stopped in the front entrance of your building. Assign someone to clear the driveway and to direct emergency medical vehicles to the incident area.

> **As a leader, you see that there are too many competing critical needs for you to handle alone. Your job is not to play every instrument in the orchestra. Rather, you are the conductor.**

Obviously, this is not the end of the list. These are examples to remind you of your several competing critical priorities; for example, the ongoing danger to employees, providing assistance to police, getting effective first aid to victims, and facilitating access to emergency medical squads.

2.8.2 Orchestrating Your Response

As a leader, you see that there are too many competing critical needs for you to handle alone. Your job is not to play every instrument in the orchestra. Rather, you are the conductor. Quickly assess priority issues and enlist available persons to take action. Notice in the above list of immediate actions that you delegated every task. Doing so puts you in a position to continue managing the crisis.

Delegating doesn't mean that you never get your hands dirty, but it is hard to manage the whirlwind of a crisis while you are giving CPR to a victim. Only if you are the solitary one qualified for CPR would it be best for you to consider direct treatment. Even then, you may want to instruct others in exactly what to do, monitor their techniques for effectiveness, and move on.

Now let's take a look at five personal traits of the crisis whisperer that you want to incorporate into your crisis management skills.

1. **A state of "deliberate calm."** Requires clear thinking, emotional control, and balance. Mentally visualize yourself being calm and assertive during this crisis response. The mind is a powerful tool. You have the ability to control your feelings even when the circumstances seem impossible or overwhelming. You can make it through the trials of crisis response if you prepare yourself mentally for the demands that will be placed upon you.

2. **Open-mindedness** as you take in vast amounts of information without developing tunnel vision. Requires keen listening skills and a focus on what issues need immediate attention and which are high-leverage responses that will best contain the crisis. Collaborate in your decision-making if possible.

3. **Decisiveness,** balanced with a willingness to consider ideas and input from others. Requires a willingness to prioritize and make decisions with only partial knowledge.

4. **Flexibility** to adapt to rapid change and modify your actions. Requires understanding that some (or most) of the early information about critical incidents is wrong.

5. **Persuasiveness.** Requires being able to convince others to follow your directions.

Identify foreseeable risks, develop plans to address these risks, and exercise your plans and teams through an ongoing crisis exercise program. This is the process of well-prepared crisis managers and organizations.

2.8.3 The Imperative for Rapid Response

The period immediately following serious traumatic injury is known as the "golden hour." It's been proven that patients have a far greater chance of successful recovery from their injuries if medical care is delivered within one hour.

Similarly, a well-planned, frequently reviewed crisis response plan can enable you to respond at top speed, and possibly save people's lives – and the viability of your organization, too.

Delegate. The only way to manage rapidly emerging consequences following crisis events is to utilize the resources that are available to you. Your job will be to gather information, assess the situation, and establish priorities quickly – and delegate. Be ready to give directives to remote individuals making the notification, onsite managers, available employees, and outside resources. As a crisis leader, your job is to look out the windshield and steer, not to fix the motor with your head under the hood.

Keep track. Maintain the ability to document your thoughts at all times during crisis response. Make a habit of writing down or entering information, as it becomes available, handwritten or into your personal electronic device (PED). Track the times of each entry. Log the names of people you talk with, and the content of the discussions. Highlight priority decisions and actions with the approximate time they are to be completed. Keep track of pending items that require additional information or will be implemented at a later time. Note the ideas and recommendations that come to mind, for later discussions with appropriate others, or as a reminder to yourself for execution. Of course, it will not be possible to note every action or thought you have in the chaos of an immediate response to a real-life experience like our imagined shooting incident. But as soon as you can, organize yourself through this invaluable record of the emerging fact pattern, decisions and actions, and responsibilities personally assumed or assigned to others.

Continue the recordkeeping from initial notification throughout the entire event up until the disengagement period. Documenting information you receive can help you keep track of all the needed things to do and help protect you or your company if you should be legally challenged about actions you took or your timeliness in responding.

For example, imagine that the family of a victim accuses your company of delaying notification that their loved one had been injured or killed. Your notes can identify the specific times you and they were notified, which could be of critical importance in resolving the dispute. It could also provide the rationale why the notification was reasonably delayed. Without documentation of the fact pattern, it can be difficult to defend your actions later.

Consult with your attorney regarding how and where to maintain this documentation. Note also the preferences of your legal team. Some attorneys prefer no notes be maintained. Research clearly demonstrates that writing helps managers make more effective decisions on a timely basis. If your legal team doesn't want documentation maintained, is it possible to organize yourself through notes that will be destroyed as a matter of policy as soon as they are no longer needed for crisis response?

Three Key Questions

One way to prioritize action items in the immediate aftermath is to ask yourself these three questions:

1. What needs to stop that is presently occurring?

2. What needs to start that is not presently happening?

3. In what ways can this situation escalate in severity?

In our shooting scenario, we needed to stop employees from roaming outside the building with a gunman on the loose and emergency services dispatched. We needed to start effective first aid and professional life support for the victims as soon as possible. And the situation could escalate if the gunman continued to shoot.

2.9 Four Categories of Concern

There are four basic areas of concern for senior management and all the people who support them whether in a crisis or during normal business. These topics – people, business disruption, reputation, and finances – can also help you identify your action priorities in the early aftermath of a disaster.

> **Beware, however, of outrage if you are perceived as putting productivity above the needs and safety of people. As a general rule, you must address the people needs before the back-to-business needs.**

2.9.1 People

No organization is better than its people. Human issues come first, especially when people are injured and deeply impacted. What should be done to address the needs and concerns of people? How wide a circle of people is impacted? Who are they? Are they in continuing danger? What information do we need to give and receive from these individuals?

2.9.2 Business Disruption

The ability of the organization to continue normal productivity can be seriously affected by a crisis. For example, business interruption may come about from loss of facilities and equipment, or a critical supply chain may become unavailable, or if the ability of employees to work normally may become disrupted. Determine the damage that is irreversible and determine what remains functional. Assess what areas of the organization are inoperable or need to be shut down. Also, determine what work is appropriate to continue. In some cases, as in nuclear plants and other power generating facilities, work must go on. Beware, however, of outrage if you are perceived as putting productivity above the needs and safety of people. As a general rule, people needs come before back-to-business needs. Prepared companies have comprehensive continuity plans in place for business and people, tested to ensure continuity of operations during crises.

2.9.3 Reputation

In the wake of workplace crises, there is typically a tendency for fault-finding. Reporters, journalists, plaintiff attorneys, government regulators, employees, family members, financial analysts, and community members may line up to assign blame for negligence. This is a time for honesty and integrity, and also a time to ensure you get the best message out to involved publics. In our shooting scenario, the media beat the emergency medical vehicles to the facility. An early action might be to contact your public relations firm or in-house PR counsel. Priority number one to protect reputation is to do the "next right things" while demonstrating empathy and caring.

2.9.4 Finances

Catastrophes and unexpected crises are not typical budget items. In establishing priorities, you may attempt to consider the financial impact of a crisis not readily contained. Possibly, your risk manager or insurance broker could be helpful in strategies to limit their exposures and yours, as well.

2.10 Other Priority-Setting Strategies

In prioritizing your initial crisis management actions, ask yourself what verified information or assessment is needed before proper action can be taken. There could be value in waiting for accurate information. I have been involved with two situations in which fatal corporate air crashes were reported, only to find out later that the tail number on the aircraft was not consistent with that of the plane reported down. Had families of those on the manifest been notified, the fallout could have been devastating.

Multiple timeframes. Yet another means to help you establish priorities is to actually anticipate future developments along a timeline. The idea is to look at what you anticipate will occur immediately, within minutes, within hours, within the day, and longer term. Decisions can be made to respond to and to prevent anticipated occurrences.

A balanced approach. Take a balanced approach to decision-making, and examine the situation from various vantage points. In our shooting scenario, our responses went only as far as addressing the critical items immediately before us. A balanced approach would require not only looking at the details before us, but also consciously taking a big-picture overview of the situation. If the shooter happened to be an employee with a history of making threats that we knew about, a big picture issue might be the collective outrage of those media representatives in our driveway and employees who now believe this foreseeable risk was not adequately prevented or managed.

Outside experts. Calling legal and public relations professionals may be imperative to address the anticipated reputational and financial issues. Beware that these professionals are often at odds in these situations. Preplanning and agreements on external communications need to be agreed upon during the crisis planning stage. Consider including external crisis consultants and others, like attorneys and PR professionals, in your crisis exercising. Beware that even though often called upon, most attorneys and PR consultants may be neither trained nor truly skilled at crisis management. Identify who has the needed skills and experience before a crisis hits.

Crisis teams. If you have established and trained the various crisis teams at the executive, managerial, and tactical levels, they will be available to assist you in prioritizing vital decisions and actions. However, in the early moments following a critical incident, before they can assemble, ask yourself what needs to be decided immediately. What needs input from other disciplines? For example, if a crime is involved you would *not* want to make decisions to begin immediate cleanup of the crime scene. You would first need to get legal, security, and law enforcement input.

As a general rule, if you are notified first, your job is to act on critical items that can't wait for the team to assemble and discuss. But remember – the best decisions are typically made by small, multidisciplinary teams trained and experienced in crisis management.

2.11 Checklist of Immediate Action Items

Your checklist of immediate action items can vary widely according to the incident. A kidnap and ransom situation will involve an immediate call to your insurer or an organization that specializes in hostage negotiations. A toxic chemical plume over a neighboring community would require an immediate call to the mayor or city administrator.

Add to the generic immediate considerations list below according to your culture, anticipated critical incidents, geographic location(s), and other applicable variables.

▶ **Continuing danger.** Take action to protect anyone in harm's way.

▶ **Emergency vehicles.** Verify dispatch in sufficient quantities. Ensure access to incident areas.

▶ **Assessment and verification.** What information needs to be verified? What immediate information do you need to better assess the situation?

▶ **Security.** Secure the incident area and perimeter; control ingress and egress. Determine how many security personnel are needed, where they are to be placed and for how long, and if they should be from internal or external resources. Establish who can be put in place until additional security arrives. Determine if security personnel should be armed or unarmed, and if arrest capability is needed.

▶ **Families.** Do families of victims need to be notified? By whom? How? Convey to employees what to say and not say to families and others calling in. Determine where calls from family members of casualties should be forwarded. Anticipate the needs of family members arriving on site.

▶ **Escalation.** How can this situation get worse? What can be done to prevent escalation? Does the response need to go to higher levels of management?

▶ **Notification and mobilization.** Who needs to be immediately notified for assistance?

▶ **Communications.** What communications are necessary? To whom? What communications need to be received? From whom? Which outlets need to be monitored? What methods should be used? What are your main messages for various audiences? To facilitate that people in high-concern situations hear, understand, and retain your messaging, keep your communications clear, brief, and to the point.

▶ **Legal and regulatory.** What immediate legal issues need to be addressed? What regulatory compliance issues need attention? Does initial investigation need to be conducted under attorney-client privilege? Remember that crisis response is more than legal liability mitigation. Balance legal response with reputational, humanitarian response, and communications. Crisis decision-making is a management process, and should not be driven solely by legal.

▶ **Specialists.** What internal and external specialists should be contacted immediately for assistance? Technical experts? Crisis mental health professionals? Trusted crisis consultant? Toxic exposure? Environmental? Medical? Communications? Safety? Strategic crisis leadership consultant for executives and key managers? Security and law enforcement? Risk management and insurance? HR, benefits, and labor relations? Others? In establishing your own checklists, establish an "all hazards" notification, activation, and response protocol that will be followed, regardless of the crisis content. We will cover additional information about this protocol in the next chapter. Then create separate lists with immediate actions and unique considerations for each type of crisis incident. (For guidance, refer to the checklists in the last chapter of this book.)

> In establishing your own checklists, establish an "all hazards" notification, activation, and response protocol that will be followed, regardless of the crisis content.

Even with years of experience in crisis management consulting, I still refer to my lists. I want pilots on flights I take to refer to their lists no matter how many times they have flown the jet! If I were CEO of your organization, I would want my crisis managers to do the same. And, as chief executive, I would reference my own strategic crisis leadership checklist, like the one provided in the last chapter.

There's no question that taking the right immediate action steps is a heady responsibility. But by breaking it down as we have in this chapter, you should be in a much better position to know what you face and to respond appropriately.

In Chapter 3, we'll move on to managing each phase of a crisis, the role of your crisis team leaders, and we'll look into a high-functioning crisis command center.

Quick Use Response Guide

Chapter 2: Taking Decisive Action

Receiving Initial Notification

What Happened?

- ❏ Incident described: Verify accuracy of information.

- ❏ Firsthand: Has the notifier seen it with his/her own eyes?

- ❏ Secondhand: Who told the notifier? How do you know the information is accurate?

- ❏ Not verified: What needs to be done while verification is being confirmed?

How Bad Is It?

People:

- ❏ What is the impact on stakeholders?

- ❏ Is there ongoing danger or harm to people? Of what?

- ❏ How many serious injuries or deaths? Are these confirmed?

- ❏ How many people are directly involved?

- ❏ How many appear to be indirectly involved?

- ❏ Are people in the wider community impacted? How?

Property:

- ❏ What are damages to company property? Severity?

- ❏ Is the damage ongoing or contained?

Business disruption:

- ❏ Operation continuing at full/normal levels, partial levels, or stopped?

Surroundings:

- ❏ How widespread is the damage?

- ❏ How have physical assets in the surrounding area been affected?

- ❏ Are there continuing threats to the surrounding area?

Liability/reputation:

- ❏ Are there issues that could put the reputation of the organization at risk?
- ❏ Is the organization at fault or perceived to be at fault?
- ❏ In what ways might the organization be blamed?
- ❏ Any apparent outrage toward the organization, individual employees or management?
- ❏ To what extent is media involved?
- ❏ What spin could media outlets put on the story?

What Is Being Done?

People:

- ❏ Has the situation been contained so that people are safe from continuing harm?
- ❏ Is first aid being administered effectively?
- ❏ Is everyone accounted for?
- ❏ Have sufficient emergency vehicles been dispatched?
- ❏ Are driveways accessible to permit emergency vehicles to enter?
- ❏ What is being done for the injured?
- ❏ What is being done with the bodies of fatalities?
- ❏ Which hospitals are utilized?
- ❏ What is being done to protect onlookers from distressing sights?
- ❏ Accommodations for family members who may arrive at the site?
- ❏ What is being done to accommodate and restrict media representatives?
- ❏ What communications need to be given and received? To whom?

Property:

- ❏ What is being done to contain continuing property damage?
- ❏ Is the incident site secured to protect investigation?
- ❏ What is the plan to secure the perimeter around the incident site and company site?

Business Disruption:

❑ Should production be reduced or halted?

❑ Can employees remain at the work site safely?

❑ Should any area of the facility be shut down, or require special attention to ensure security?

❑ What needs to be done to continue operations during this situation?

Surroundings:

❑ Are others in the surrounding area aware of the incident?

❑ Is there a need to notify others?

Escalation Potential?

❑ How could the effects of this situation escalate in severity?

❑ What controls need to be put in place to avoid escalation?

❑ What is being done to contain the causes and effects of the incident?

❑ Are there rumors that are fueling the severity of this crisis?

❑ Should the response escalate to a higher management level?

❑ What strategic activities should be going on at the same time initial notification and actions are taking place?

❑ Where is this incident headed and what should we do about it?

Crisis Decision-Making

Use the SIP-DE model

❑ Scan the fact pattern to obtain facts germane to your situation.

❑ Identify problem areas.

❑ Predict where the various problem areas may be headed.

❑ Decide what needs to be addressed.

❑ Execute decisively according to priority on a timely basis.

Implementation

❑ Waiting for all information to be amassed will cause a late response. Implement on a timely basis based on available information and intuition.

Continuing Danger and Harm

❑ Take action to protect anyone in danger.

❑ Mitigate stakeholders' real and perceived harm.

Emergency Vehicles

❑ Verify dispatch and sufficient quantities.

❑ Dispatch those trained in first aid in the interim.

❑ Provide direction and assistance for arriving emergency vehicles.

Assessment and Verification

❑ What information needs to be verified to take appropriate action?

❑ What communications do you need to receive?

Security

❑ Do you need security to protect the incident area?

❑ Secure the perimeter of the work site?

❑ What areas of ingress and egress need to be secured?

❑ How much security is needed? Where? How long?

❑ Armed or unarmed?

❑ Arrest capability or professional guard service?

❑ Who can you put in place until security arrives?

Families

❑ Do families of victims need to be notified? By whom? How?

❑ Response to telephone inquires? Content? By whom?

❑ To whom should inquiries from family members and other stakeholders be directed?

❑ Assign personnel to immediately meet and direct family members and other stakeholders who may arrive on site.

❑ Anticipate the needs of family members arriving on site.

Escalation

❑ How can this situation escalate in severity?

❑ What needs to be done to respond to or prevent escalation?

Notification and Mobilization

- ❏ Who needs to be immediately notified for assistance?
- ❏ Who needs to be mobilized?
- ❏ Establish a protocol for notification and mobilization.
- ❏ Who has the authority to mobilize internal and external resources?

Communications

- ❏ What communications are necessary? To whom?
- ❏ What communications need to be received? By whom?
- ❏ What are the main messages you want to convey to various audiences?

Legal and Regulatory

- ❏ What immediate legal and compliance issues need to be addressed?
- ❏ What regulatory and compliance issues need attention?
- ❏ Does initial investigation need to be conducted under attorney-client privilege?
- ❏ Remember that crisis response is more than legal liability mitigation. Balance legal response with reputational, humanitarian response, and communications. Crisis decision-making is a management process, and should not be driven solely by legal.

Specialists

- ❏ What additional internal and external specialists should you contact?
- ❏ Strategic crisis leadership consultant for executives and key managers?
- ❏ Trusted crisis management consultant?
- ❏ Technical experts?
- ❏ Crisis mental health professionals?
- ❏ Toxic exposure?
- ❏ Environmental?
- ❏ Medical?

❑ Safety?

❑ Security and law enforcement?

❑ Communications?

❑ Risk management and insurance?

❑ HR, benefits, and labor relations?

❑ Others?

Chapter 2 - Questions for Further Thought and Discussion

In order to assimilate the information from the Introduction, Chapter 1, and Chapter 2, let's continue to apply lessons-learned to the three scenarios, i.e., **avian flu**, employees exposed to a **toxic substance**, and simultaneous **bombing of your facilities** by an activist group.

1. For each of the three scenarios, what immediate actions can you identify that should be addressed related to the provided fact pattern and additional issues that would likely be occurring? What should stop and start? How can each situation escalate in severity?

2. For each of the three scenarios, apply the SIP-DE model as it relates to crisis management. What would you consider for each related to the provided fact pattern and additional issues that would likely be occurring?

3. In considering the strategic (big picture) issues of these three scenarios, what are the CIA issues that you can identify, i.e., *core assets*, *involved stakeholders*, and *anticipated progression*?

3

Crisis Containment

In a rapidly escalating crisis, you, as a crisis leader within your area of responsibility, will need your internal team at the top of their game. But, equally important, you'll want to have trusted and vetted external resources readily available. Lives and wellbeing of people, organizational damage or even survival, and careers are often on the line when crises hit. It's best to be prepared with a bench of internal and external resources to handle any foreseeable contingency.

The right place and the right people – plus the right preparedness process – will enable your orderly, effective response to crises of any type. A deliberate approach to crisis containment can make all the difference.

This chapter will help you to:

- ➤ *Know the six phases of containing and managing a crisis.*
- ➤ *Understand the role of the crisis management team (CMT) and leader.*
- ➤ *Create a high-functioning crisis command center (CCC).*
- ➤ *Conduct the initial crisis action team (CAT) meeting and identify action steps.*

3.1 We're Now Entering the Crisis Containment Phase

It's easy to know what you would do if a small kitchen fire breaks out in your home while your dinner is being prepared. If it's small and inconsequential, you would take immediate action to put the fire out before it spreads. Hopefully, you are prepared to contain small fires with needed tools, such as an appropriate fire extinguisher that is in a known location nearby and it is not outdated to the point of being nonfunctional.

We all handle small crises on a daily basis and keep them from escalating in severity, from driving a motor vehicle in heavy traffic to unexpected deadlines at work. For the most part, these small, emerging situations can be handled alone. But even in small situations, it is helpful to have people around who could come to your aid readily, if needed.

Back when agrarian cultures predominated, farmers and ranchers would enlist internal resources (i.e., family) to help contain crises such as a house fire. Outside resources were not readily available, and the family members needed to use their own resources to put out the fire – hopefully before the damage became unmanageable.

> Organizations are more interdependent and connected worldwide than ever before...
> The possibilities of harm to people, business operations, and reputation have never been higher.

At a corporate level, smaller and manageable crises can be handled by your internal crisis teams, possibly without the assistance of outsiders. Like having a fire extinguisher readily available in the kitchen, the more prepared your team members have become through planning, training, and exercising, the more they will be able to manage crises through internal resources effectively.

However, the damage of a corporate crisis can escalate at lightning speed. People and buildings are closer together. These proximities can intensify the severity of crises. News spreads with immediacy by tuned-in media and multitudes of social networks. Increasingly, cameras, phones, and video recording capabilities are in the hands of most everyone. Organizations are more interdependent and connected worldwide than ever before.

Arguably, global warming is causing increased severity and probabilities of natural disasters. The national grid and critical infrastructure of countries worldwide are vulnerable to determined hackers. The list goes on. The possibilities of harm to people, business operations, and reputation have never been higher. Board members, senior managers, institutional investors, and others are focused on anticipating, preparing for, and responding to the critical risks that threaten the viability of their organizations of interest. You should, as well. There is no reputable business management system out there that says, "Don't be prepared for foreseeable risks."

3.2 The Six Phases of Managing a Crisis

Earlier, we discussed how you can be individually effective during crisis response. But, serious crises are not handled alone. Crisis response is a team effort. However, many teams are not purposeful in how they conduct their business of crisis response in a sequential manner that can be replicated, no matter who is on the team or what crisis hits.

Remember that it is the primary responsibility of the entire crisis management organization within your company to protect core assets that may be threatened by a crisis. Whether threatened core assets are people, reputation, financial wellbeing or anything else, the team(s) should focus collectively on these overarching issues as a beacon for crisis management response decisions and actions.

Let's take a look at the six sequential phases of crisis response and discuss some best practice considerations for each. The six phases are:

1. Notification and activation.
2. Fact finding.
3. Decision-making.
4. Prioritizing.
5. Implementation.
6. Purposeful de-escalation.

3.2.1 Phase 1: Notification and Activation

The initial action will be to notify the appropriate internal and external team members on a timely basis. In order to do this, a systematic protocol should be firmly in place for notification and activation of the organization's various crisis-related teams. Large companies that are well organized for crises tend to have a three-tiered approach for crisis management. Small businesses may have the personnel for only one team. In either case, someone will need to have the clear responsibility and authority to notify and activate the various levels of crisis-related teams within the organization.

As shown in Figure 3-1, well prepared organizations have three levels of crisis response teams, each with unique responsibilities and duties. In addition, these three teams should be thoroughly coordinated and integrated for a seamless crisis management response system. These teams are discussed further in Chapter 11. Silos within the crisis management organization should be coordinated, with each area of responsibility aware of the interdependent impacts its specific actions have on the other functions within the company.

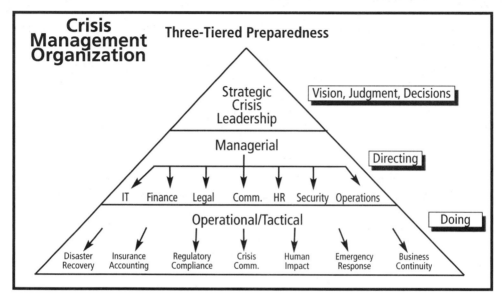

Figure 3-1. Three-tiered Crisis Management Organization: Executive, Managerial, and Operational Teams

Operational/Tactical Team(s): Starting at the bottom of the diagram, some crises will be managed only by the operational/tactical team(s). For example, if a data center goes down, a properly designed and tested IT disaster recovery plan would be executed with little or no disruption to the business. If continuity of operations is maintained, there may be little need to involve the crisis response up the corporate ladder. Possibly, only a notification to executive management would suffice that the outage occurred and effective response actions were implemented. Crisis response at the operational and tactical levels tends to take place at the site and field levels. This may include emergency response, tactical implementation of the business continuity plan, bringing in crisis counselors, or submitting an insurance claim for an isolated or non-catastrophic incident.

Managerial Team: One level up, the managerial team is charged with directing the crisis response on behalf of the organization. While the operational/tactical responses are "doing" oriented, the managerial team is charged with "directing" the crisis response. A primary function of the managerial team is to serve as an intermediary between the operational/tactical responders and executive management. Typically, this is the team that populates the crisis command center (CCC) if the team members are not functioning virtually. Every function of the organization should be represented on the managerial team. For example, initially mobilize all team members; then, if the nature of the crisis does not involve a corporate security response or an IT issue, these team members may be excused, as appropriate. However, the core managerial team should include managers who have oversight over every function of the organization. This managerial team is often named the crisis action team (CAT), but various names prevail.

Executive/Crisis Management Team: The executive team typically consists of executives and senior managers who are charged with strategic crisis leadership for the organization. As a general rule, if core assets of the organization become threatened at an organizationally defined threshold level, the executive team will be notified and activated. The role of the team will be to focus on issues that threaten the viability of the organization. Key relationships may be threatened. Institutional investors could consider selling huge shareholder stakes. Politicians may consider regulations, new laws, or other controls that would reduce the free enterprise of the organization. Reputation or public trust may be at risk. As with these and other macro-level repercussions, the executive team will be activated to address higher-level organizational threats.

> As in the emergency medical field, if treatment is provided within one hour or less of the critical incident, the likelihood of survival is significantly improved. This same approach has been applied to crisis management...

Sometimes, the executive team could be activated without the involvement of the other response teams. Issues of financial improprieties, ethical misconduct, unlawful corporate behavior, and others may contain little or no role at the operational and managerial levels. In any case, someone within the organization should be charged with the responsibility and authority to ensure the proper team resources are applied to the crisis at hand.

The objectives of the notification and activation phase are to ensure that the appropriate internal and external people:

- Receive notice of the threat or crisis.
- Assess and implement the correct activation level.
- Assemble and be uniformly briefed within a defined time period.

In the last chapter we introduced the "golden hour" rule as it applies to crisis response. As in the emergency medical field, if treatment is provided within one hour or less of the critical incident, the likelihood of survival is significantly improved. This same approach applies to crisis management. If it takes longer than one hour for the appropriate crisis-related teams to be notified and effectively activated, the crisis may be out of control before the crisis response begins.

However, one hour before the organization begins its response could seem like an eternity. In addition to impacted people, places, and operations, the reputational damage that can occur in the immediate aftermath of a crisis must be monitored, identified, and addressed – now! Social media enthusiasts will be active. Shareholders may start selling their financial stake in the company immediately if a decisive response by the organization is not apparent. Customers may stop buying immediately. For example, Wendy's Old Fashioned Hamburgers restaurants reportedly had an immediate 50% drop in sales as soon as a conniving patron, Anna Ayala, falsely claimed she bit into a human finger in her Wendy's chili in March 2005.

In preparation for immediate notification and activation needs, many organizations have implemented emergency notification systems. For example, following the shooting massacre of 33 people by Seung-Hui Cho in 2007, Virginia Tech established the capability to notify the entire student body, staff, and faculty with a single "push" message. Organizations are now able to bridge their crisis teams into an immediate conference call, collapsing the notification and activation process into one seamless procedure. Software applications have emerged that assist organizations in organizing their crisis response in an immediate and organized manner. Many multinational companies have remote cameras at company sites that allow corporate managers to see what is happening worldwide in real time. Well-prepared companies have these vital systems in place in response to the ubiquitous public challenges that are now commonplace through a connected world that is watching. Why? Delayed or ill-informed response increases the likelihood of escalating severity and longevity of your crisis.

Early Notification Culture: No matter what system you use, consider establishing a culture of early notification for your internal and external crisis responders. There are three levels of notification that can be installed within the organizational crisis management culture:

▶ Information only.

▶ Alert.

▶ Respond/activate.

For example, if incidents are reported in the news or industry publications that could also happen to your organization, consider an *information only* notification to team members within your crisis management organization. The object is to maintain a culture of notification. In this case, it would be for team members' information only. No action would be required, but it breeds familiarity with the notification process.

Alert notifications are used when a potential crisis situation is looming that could involve the organization. Examples could include a wind storm or flooding that could impact your facilities. Possible extended power outage, potential product recall, looming employee strike, activist groups that are targeting your industry, and other harbingers of threat to the organization could elicit an alert notification. Crisis team members at appropriate levels would be instructed to stay on call and to ensure their immediate availability until further notification. This is a good time for team members to anticipate what might happen and to consider preparedness and response issues proactively.

The *respond/activate* notification is used when there is an assessed need by the individual(s) in authority to mobilize the appropriate teams. Depending on the nature of the crisis, the response may be immediate or at a defined time. If the situation is urgent, it is best to give minimal to no details when activating the managerial or executive team(s). This saves time when spreading the word to activate and ensures everyone gets the same initial information once the team is mustered. The exception may be the operational/tactical teams that would need to know the nature of the incident immediately in order to mobilize the proper emergency-related resources at the scene or if everyone is on a bridge line at the same time when an emergency notification system is used.

> **The most frequent failure point in crisis response is not getting the appropriate crisis teams assembled and briefed on a timely basis.**

No matter what the crisis, the process of notification and mobilization should remain relatively the same. The object is to get the correct team members and resources notified, assembled, and briefed as soon as possible. This initial notification and activation process positions the organization for effective crisis response. The most frequent failure point in crisis response is not getting the appropriate crisis teams assembled and briefed on a timely basis.

These are key activation questions to keep in mind:

▶ For what reasons would we activate the team(s)?

▶ Who has the authority to activate?

▶ Which respective team(s) will be activated under which circumstances?

▶ Where will we assemble? What are our alternatives to the primary site?

Whom to Activate: As mentioned previously, when activating your team(s), it is best to initially activate all the core team members. For example, in a given crisis, HR may appear not to have a role initially. But, until it is clear which resources will be needed, it is best to include all core team members and appropriate specialists.

Another best practice for the activation process is to enlist both the primary and alternate (backup) crisis teams initially. The rationale for having everyone involved in the initial briefing is that it is important for all crisis responders to know the initial fact pattern and strategic approach the organization will take to address the crisis. Additionally, the most work tends to be in the first two hours in the immediate aftermath and crisis containment phases. The additional "boots on the ground" will help the organization gain control of the situation.

Extended Response Time: As soon as it becomes apparent that the crisis response will be protracted beyond 8-12 hours, arrangements should be taken to establish a second shift (and possibly third shift) to take over from the initial response team. This means that a multidisciplinary team with collective responsibility over all involved areas of the organization will be asked to go home to rest in order to be ready to replace the exhausted first shift of crisis responders. Undoubtedly, you will meet with resistance from the replacement team members, who naturally want to stay involved in the high-consequence actions. However, it is critical that they be rested and ready to take over at the appropriate time.

Let's assume all team members have worked during the first two hours of the crisis response. It becomes apparent that the crisis will run on possibly for days, requiring close management attention around the clock. The 2010 BP oil spill in the Gulf of Mexico is one example of the type of crisis that would need an extended response. After the first two hours, the replacement team(s) will be assigned the task of getting sleep and to remove themselves from the action. In approximately eight hours, appropriate team members are to come back to the crisis command center (physically or virtually). The initial and replacement teams will work together for approximately an hour to transition from one team to the next. The initial response team will then be relieved of their duties in order to rest. The replacement team will take over until the next shift change. In crises that are truly 24/7 operations, you will typically need three teams to take eight hour shifts (plus one transition hour) apiece. Exhausted, overworked managers increasingly lose effectiveness. Make certain your managers on each shift comply with an appropriate work/rest schedule.

A common mistake in the team transition process is that senior managers with authority to make critical decisions tend to remain on the initial team. Subordinate managers are then sent home to cover the subsequent shift(s). It is far more effective to place a mix of senior and subordinate managers on each team so that you will have decision-makers with authority on each team. Otherwise a subordinate-level team with limited authority to make critical decisions could become immobilized or defer to senior managers who are resting at home. It is best to mix the teams strategically with the authority, responsibilities, and diverse talents to maintain a seamless response capability.

> **Think of the initial information like a tabletop jigsaw puzzle with hundreds of pieces that need to be assembled.**

3.2.2 Phase 2: Fact Finding

Once the appropriate teams have been notified, activated, and uniformly briefed with initial information, the next crisis team process is to gather critical information beyond the initial crisis notification report. While you will have to make immediate decisions and take actions, the crisis fact pattern will most likely be incomplete and will contain wrong information.

The initial fact pattern available to your crisis teams will likely be a mix of accurate, inaccurate, and missing information. Think of the initial information like a tabletop jigsaw puzzle with hundreds of pieces that need to be assembled. The initial fact pattern is like an incomplete puzzle that has some correct pieces in place. However, there are many pieces that are not yet in place. Other puzzle pieces may be incorrectly placed. At this point, the response team members are trying to get a visual picture of the situation. But, much like the incomplete puzzle, the picture is not clear. Your best judgment will be needed to determine which timely actions to take with partial information and which will be delayed to gather additional information.

Firsthand information is always best. However, even people who witnessed the situation can have distorted perceptions of what has happened. We know stories can be conflicting, as demonstrated by contradictory versions by eyewitnesses to motor vehicle accidents. So, be careful not to lock into one version of the fact pattern that may later turn out to be inaccurate. Go with what you have, but be ready to alter your understanding of the fact pattern at any time.

The term *fact pattern* is used because effective crisis management involves interconnected issues that must be managed. Focus on how the various bits of information are connected. Consider the impact your actions can have on other areas of your response. For example, transparent communications may position the company as trustworthy and caring, but could increase legal liabilities. Much like a balloon, if you squeeze on one side the other side bulges out. The fact pattern is inclusive of what has occurred to create the crisis and also the intended and unintended consequences of your ongoing crisis response actions.

Crisis responders must address both the actual fact pattern and also the perceptions of involved stakeholders effectively. Just because a misunderstanding or rumor isn't true doesn't mean it shouldn't be managed or that the consequences aren't real. Thus, it is important to gather information from every source possible. Eyewitnesses, your own employees, outside friends of the company, social media, traditional media outlets, law enforcement, and other multidisciplinary sources of potentially accurate and inaccurate information should be monitored and communicated to your team members on an ongoing basis.

Fact finding is an ongoing process. Information channels and feedback loops should remain open during your entire crisis response.

3.2.3 Phase 3: Decision-Making

We will discuss crisis decision-making in depth in later chapters. For now, it is important to understand that decisions will need to be made with partial information throughout the crisis response process. Timeliness is equally important as doing the right things in crisis response. The right response, but too late, will be ineffective. As the fact pattern continues to surface, there will be issues that need immediate action, even with many unknowns. Other action items can be delayed as deemed appropriate. Effective decision-making comes from information received, prudent judgment, calculated risk-taking, courage to take action in uncertain times, and anticipation of stakeholder reactions. From a strategic standpoint, your decision-making should be consistently in accord with the team's overarching vision of how best to handle the crisis. While this may all seem like too much for any individual or team to handle, I will simplify the process in the next chapter.

3.2.4 Phase 4: Prioritizing

With so much information coming in fast, it is imperative to prioritize during crisis response. Whether you use a software application, mobile application, spreadsheet, notebook, or low-tech easel, your team will need a functional process for compiling information, and then prioritizing decisions and actions.

One of the best methods for prioritizing is to establish a visible place to receive, post, and respond to information about the events as they transpire. At a minimum, the following three primary types of information should be displayed conspicuously:

- The evolving fact pattern.
- Priority actions.
- Pending items.

> ...a fact pattern can turn on a dime. What were thought to be solid tips become misinformation, and facts that appeared fully corroborated can vaporize as new input is gathered.

Prioritized information is the raw material of which your crisis response is crafted. The quality, accuracy, and timeliness of how that information is used will greatly affect your response. Let's examine each of these three categories individually.

Evolving Fact Pattern: At first blush, "evolving fact pattern" might appear a contradiction in terms. But when the subject is a flash flood, terrorism, a plane crash, or an industrial accident, a fact pattern can turn on a dime. What were thought to be solid tips become misinformation, and facts that appeared fully corroborated can vaporize as new input is gathered.

Posting of the evolving fact pattern is essential. It should be highly visible and easily accessible. The methodology your team uses will depend on your infrastructure, back office system, command center layout, and other culturally specific issues. In any case, consider using a grid that spells out the facts, date, and time of entry, verified or not, by whom (see Table 3-1).

Table 3-1. Posted Emerging Fact Pattern

Date: _____

Emerging Facts	Time Entered	Verified	By Whom
Ten fatalities	13:01		Hans Strauss
Media onsite	13:05	✔	Ellen Cohen

Such documents record when information was received in sequential order. While some attorneys don't want any documentation during crisis response, crisis team effectiveness will be diminished if the incoming information is not compiled, organized, verified, and posted during the crisis. Posting of information will also help to update anyone with a need to know about what has been learned and when. This keeps the team from having to stop their crisis response in order to brief the executive who may be late to the game. It also has helped with defensibility. For example, you may be falsely accused of a delay in notifying the family of someone who was fatally injured. Your structured compilation of incoming information will increase the likelihood that you have the exact time the information was received and notification was given to the family.

Some companies prefer not to visibly display any emerging facts until they have been verified. The rationale is that the team is not having to respond to issues that turn out not to be true. This can be a mistake. A key component of staying ahead of a crisis is to anticipate what may be coming and prepare before it occurs. For this reason, it is best to post all incoming information and indicate visually whether it is verified.

I was involved in a kidnap and ransom situation where senior management of the company learned that, after several days in captivity, their employee had been killed. This information was not verified, and the individual who notified corporate heard this report from another person who was allegedly at the scene. I received a call from the CEO who wanted to know if there was anything they should do at present about the unverified death notification. I suggested that selected senior managers take the corporate jet and fly to the airport nearest to the wife of the captive employee who was alleged to be fatally injured. As soon as the information was verified, they were to take prearranged ground transportation immediately to the home of the deceased employee to notify the wife in person. However, if the unverified report turned out to be wrong, then they would quietly fly home. As it turned out, the employee was in fact killed, and the CEO and another senior manager were positioned to make the death notification immediately before she heard it from the media or outside source. This is an example of how it is important to consider the "what ifs" related to unverified information and how it can help your team stay ahead of the crisis response curve. (See Appendix A of this book for more about delivering bad news to families.)

Priority Actions: Crises have myriad information coming in of varying importance and urgency. The team is looking for the high-leverage actions that will help to contain and resolve the crisis as quickly and efficiently as possible. From the posted fact pattern, various action items will be established that are of high importance and urgency. These become the priority items that should be posted in accord with the following grid.

This grid is relatively simple – you want to chart each priority action, the person responsible for implementation, and the time by which the action will be taken. A "completed" check-off box for each item will indicate completed tasks (see Table 3-2).

Table 3-2. Posted Priorities

Date: _____

Priority Actions	Responsible Person	Deadline	Completed
Secure incident site	Frank Schultz (site security)	13:30	✔
Shut down operations	Jurgen Stein (site manager)	13:30	

Like the fact pattern, the priority actions evolve and change. After you've gotten your employees and guests out of a burning building, other priorities move to the top of the list, such as notifying family members of casualties, and drafting a press statement. Unfortunately, one priority doesn't always wait for the next. In reality, all three of these actions – evacuation, family notifications, and press statement – probably need to be executed very soon, ensuring that any press statement with names happens only after families of seriously injured individuals are notified.

However, items will manifest that are important, but not before other higher-priority issues are addressed. These pending issues need a place where they will be brought forward when the time and circumstances are right.

> As the crisis unfolds, most pending items will become priorities at the appropriate time. Move pending items to the priority list or check them off as completed...

Pending Items: During a crisis (or a crisis simulation), you can expect a steady flow of entries to pass from the pending items list to the priority actions list. For example, your CEO may want to make a visit to a distraught family who has lost a loved one in a workplace incident. But it goes on the pending items list because other issues need immediate attention. Possibly, the priority is to send a trained member of your family representative team to the family immediately.

The CEO visit will become a priority later. The immediate aftermath of a crisis is not the time for your CEO to show up on the doorstep, especially not while the media and the board of directors are demanding attention and information. The family is in deep shock and, following proper notification and sufficient information, needs to retreat as the news sinks in.

As the crisis unfolds, most pending items will become priorities at the appropriate time. Move pending items to the priority list or check them off as completed at the appropriate times. Other pending items may make their way off the list at a later time (see Table 3-3).

Table 3-3. Posted Pending Items

Pending Items	Responsible Person	Time Frame
Meet with families re: benefits	Christine Koehler (HR)	Day 2
Works council briefing (union)	Klaus Balon	Day 3

3.2.5 Phase 5: Implementation

With multifaceted tasks occurring simultaneously within and between each active team, it is easy to lose control of the implementation process during crisis management. People don't hear, understand, and retain information during stressful, high-concern times as well as they do during normal, daily living situations. So, once decisions are made, it is important to be very purposeful to assure things get done during the implementation stage.

At the most rudimentary level, implementation involves who, when, how, and where decisions will be effectively executed. Additionally, it can only take a moment, but a SWOT (strengths, weakness, opportunities, and threats) analysis of your implementation strategy can avoid major mistakes. To omit this fundamental process is a major cause of implementation failure during crisis response. I have seen it happen often. Because of urgency, implementation strategies are not fully considered. The process may be flawed. Opportunities may be overlooked and unintended consequences arise.

The delegation process is also a primary failure point during high-consequence situations. Orders are barked out and it's assumed everything will run smoothly from there. The individuals receiving the delegated tasks may misperceive the orders. Persons who are assigned responsibility may not have the knowledge or skills to effectively implement the plan. Also, others who will implement your plan may not agree with your delegated orders. For this reason, it is important to provide a quick rationale that will pass the "reasonable person test" as to why the delegated task is important. A quick question about any questions or concerns is important as a part of the delegation process, especially in fast-paced, chaotic situations. This is an important point in time where those in crisis leadership positions remain calm and centered when assigning tasks. Make sure delegated assignments are sufficiently explained, considered, and understood before the implementation process begins.

Finally, expectations are high among involved stakeholders, especially those who may feel harmed by your crisis. Meanwhile, it is easy for any team or individual to become overwhelmed with too many responsibilities during crisis response. With so many people watching, it's vitally important that your plans be implemented on a timely basis. Even the best strategy and plans can create outrage if not executed on a timely basis. Thus, the implementation process must include methods for tracking progress and accountability. That's why the tables earlier in the chapter include timeframes, deadlines, and tracking of successful completion.

3.2.6 Phase 6: Purposeful De-escalation

With the heavy scrutiny that crises bring, even the terms you use can have an impact. When the time comes to phase down the crisis response, avoid using the terms *disengagement* or *deactivation*. De-escalation implies that the team is phasing down to "watchful waiting." This means that the team will remain vigilant for any developments that might rekindle the crisis response. To disengage or deactivate implies that the team is no longer monitoring the aftermath of the crisis. You don't want to appear negligent due to premature disengagement when a monitored de-escalation of the crisis aftermath would be more defensible and sensible.

When to De-escalate: The rationale for purposeful de-escalation must pass the reasonable person test. Tony Hayward (BP's gaffe-prone CEO during the 2010 Gulf of Mexico oil spill crisis) appeared to be personally de-escalating his involvement when he took time off for sailing his yacht, instead of dealing with the ongoing oil spill. This created widespread criticism and outrage toward him and his company.

It is best to use benchmarks to help determine when it is time for teams and individuals to diminish or stop managing the crisis. Examples might include:

- Demand for team attention ends.
- Traditional media, social media, stakeholder attention sufficiently diminishes.
- Operations come back to (new) normal.
- Shareholder value stabilizes.
- A positive (or at least a neutral) outcome is realized.
- Multidisciplinary judgment of the team justifies de-escalation.

Phased De-escalation Process: De-escalation does not imply uniform 100% termination of duties for all crisis responding personnel. Typically, de-escalation is not a process where "all the lights are on" one day and the next day the lights are all turned off like a light switch. The de-escalation process has a jagged edge, meaning that there typically is a phasing process back to a new normal. Team members begin to work on daily duties that have been deferred while the crisis response was in full gear. However, unfinished business and smoldering issues may still need part-time attention during the phasing back to more normal and stable times at work.

The de-escalation process is best ratcheted down to the alert or information level that we discussed in the previous notification and activation section. Meanwhile, the executive team could disband before managerial team involvement ends. It is likely that the emergency response will de-escalate well before the managerial and executive teams. However the process unfolds, it is important to be purposeful about each component of the de-escalation process.

De-escalation Checklist: When teams disband, there are a few items to address during the process. A de-escalation checklist will help to assure no stakeholders feel neglected and methods are in place to address rekindled issues. A sample checklist might include:

- Appropriate stakeholders are notified of the de-escalation with feedback about the company's intent to de-escalate the crisis response.

- Warning signs of potential re-escalation are identified and communicated appropriately to stakeholders and how they should notify the company if they feel an issue rekindles.

- An internal monitoring system remains in place. For example, ongoing social media references would be monitored and responded to, as appropriate.

- Debriefing of lessons-learned is completed and improvements implemented.

- A "process guardian" is assigned the responsibility to ensure that elements such as the crisis plan, notification lists, team training, and exercise schedule remain up-to-date. The process guardian would also ensure that lessons-learned are sculpted into the crisis management organization within the company.

- **Defensible documentation** is compiled (possibly with extraneous notes destroyed) in a manner that meets the culture and policies of the organization.

Debriefing Lessons-Learned: It is human nature to want any crisis to be behind you. Daily responsibilities of work and home can remain unattended while the all-consuming task of crisis management is orchestrated. Team members are emotionally and physically spent. Finally, the time comes to phase back into a normal work/life routine and there is much to do to catch up on time lost.

So, it makes sense that team members may resist meeting again after the crisis is contained, recovery is in full swing, and de-escalation has occurred. But that's exactly what needs to happen very soon after the crisis response is de-escalated. There are invariably lessons to be learned from the experience. But, those lessons can soon be forgotten or not captured for future crisis management improvement if a lessons-learned debriefing is not conducted.

In order to ensure this debriefing meeting takes place and is attended by all, it will involve a couple of important components. First, debriefing should be a *required* component of the crisis response process. A senior manager with full authority should sign off on this process as a part of the crisis management policy and protocol within the company. Second, the process guardian should be empowered to require every team member to attend the debriefing, unless one or more senior managers want to assume that responsibility themselves.

Each level of response team (operational/tactical, managerial, and executive/strategic) should conduct a debriefing. A scribe should compile all observations and suggestions. A method should be defined for deciding which improvements and new controls need to be implemented. Responsibility and accountability for implementation are also a part of this crisis response improvement process.

Typically, many lessons-learned and areas of improvement will be observed by team members during the crisis response. However, because of the whirlwind of issues and responsibilities, the ability to remember all these improvements becomes a blur after the crisis de-escalates. For that reason, another important component of crisis planning, training, and exercising is to have each team member develop the habit and system for compiling future improvement ideas while the crisis is unfolding in real time. Some may say they are too busy to take the time and effort to compile improvement ideas. I disagree. During every one of the hundreds of crises I've handled over two and a half decades, I have carried a notebook where I jot down ideas for improvement – during the crisis. My preference is to use a traditional notebook and a pen rather than an electronic medium like a tablet or laptop because, for me, writing is faster and more convenient than reopening and saving a list electronically. This is just my preference, but the issue is to establish a method that works for each team member to ensure lessons-learned are captured.

Defensible Documentation: Documentation of the crisis response strategies and activities of the company will be based on your legal counsel's preference. Some attorneys prefer no documentation at all, fearing evidence that can be used against the company following crises when the perennial litigation hits. On the other hand, if constructed properly, documentation is preferred by other attorneys for defensibility. This is especially true with all the electronic communications coming in and out of the company related to the crisis. Many attorneys are quick to prohibit e-mails by employees following a crisis, but invariably there will be discoverable documents that could help or hurt any case against the company.

Legal liability concerns notwithstanding, lack of documentation during crisis response creates other problems. Documentation helps to keep organized the voluminous amounts of crisis-related information coming in and out of the organization. I've worked with organizations where no documentation is allowed by attorneys during crises and the response rapidly becomes disheveled. Ironically, the crisis response is clearly not as organized, timely, and on the mark, which leads to outrage and an increase in litigiousness. One attorney would allow documentation only on erasable white boards during crisis response, which was cumbersome and ineffective. But there is merit to both sides of the documentation debate.

> **The object is to have only one set of compiled documentation and the rest of the notes are to be destroyed as standard operational procedure... Legal counsel for the organization should review, approve, and house this documentation.**

If crisis response documentation will be generated, some established guidelines and protocol can help. Ask each team member to funnel all their documentation into one location, such as a personal notebook or word processing document. No notes should be generated outside this single location. In this manner, all notes can be collected at the end of the crisis response and compiled into one official set of documentation. Consider assigning a scribe to compile, condense, and memorialize the crisis response into one official set of documentation. The object is to have only one set of compiled documentation and the rest of the notes are to be destroyed as standard operational procedure (assuming there is no legal reason to keep the original team members notes). Legal counsel for the organization should review, approve, and house this documentation.

A simple documentation format could include known facts/situational analysis, decisions made, and actions taken. For major or potentially controversial decisions, document the rationale for those decisions and actions (or inactions) in a manner that would pass the reasonable person test. One rationale that you do not want to document is that any given action is too expensive. Plaintiff attorneys will be most pleased to show your company what expensive looks like if someone is harmed because preventive or remedial action was considered too expensive.

Finally, ask yourselves if your documentation is thorough enough to withstand scrutiny from others who may question or challenge crisis response team decisions and actions. Verify that all supporting documents are filed in the case file and approved by appropriate persons in authority within your company.

3.3 Crisis Command Center (CCC)

The nerve center of your crisis response is the crisis command center (CCC). Such a center may also be called an emergency operations center (EOC) or emergency response room (ERR), but CCC is the term we will use in this book. Increasingly, crisis teams assemble virtually through conference bridge phone lines, video conferencing, and crisis software applications. However, multitasking and sidebar conversations among team members are more difficult through a common IT or teleconference connection. One additional contingency to consider is if electricity, mobile connectivity, or phone lines are down – as happened with Hurricanes Katrina and Sandy in the northeast US. If possible, consider getting as many team members together in one physical location to maximize communication and team cohesion. If your team meets virtually, consider alternate communication plans for contingencies such as an electromagnetic pulse attack or a power grid shutdown.

3.3.1 Location

Identifying the location for your CCC is an essential first step. You may find that the space you ultimately choose was not your first choice, or is less than ideal. For example, the CCC for New York City was located in the World Trade Center and was obviously not available during the 9/11 terrorist attacks. But I've seen highly effective responses even from small, cramped quarters. And I've witnessed astoundingly marginal responses from spacious, well-equipped spaces. The goal is to identify and retain an excellent location that's sizable, accommodates the needed technology, and is strategically located.

High-risk operations such as chemical companies, nuclear facilities, and oil and gas companies tend to have sophisticated CCCs. Quite simply, such operations are more likely to need them than a real estate or financial services company. What do these facilities look like? Just envision a smaller version of the television images you've seen of NASA's control center: a sleek, high-tech operation including computer workstations, video conferencing capabilities, generators to ensure electrical power, sophisticated methods for visually displaying information, breakout meeting rooms, and phone banks staffed by alert teams.

More common are less elaborate centers, such as a room with tables arranged in a horseshoe configuration to permit everyone to share the same view of the front or a typical conference room with a large table. The room is equipped with printable white boards or perhaps mounted easel pads.

3.3.2 The Ideal Room

The ideal CCC is well-equipped technologically, with capability for sending and receiving electronic messages of all sorts; multiple phone lines that are separate from the company's switchboard to circumvent jammed phone lines; projectors and monitors with cable or satellite capabilities and recording capabilities; two-way and satellite radios; and video conferencing. Even a decidedly low-tech communication device – a bullhorn – might be found!

Adjacent rooms might have some cots for catnaps by team members or other key players who are on extended service. It is good to be near restrooms, a kitchen, or other food service. There should be controlled access. An open, bullpen-style space, for example, may be a challenge because of the inherent difficulty of controlling traffic in and out.

Many companies opt for a space that offers one or more breakout rooms – smaller nearby rooms in which senior management or other individuals can gather and work comfortably. Media and communications personnel typically have a separate adjacent room to monitor news and create written communications.

For a list of suggested equipment for the CCC, see the Quick Use Response Guide at the end of this chapter.

3.3.3 Other Possibilities

Alternative CCCs may include a computer-connected training room or other convertible space, a board or conference room, or even a plant manager's office. These can be adequate.

Several years ago, Coca-Cola Enterprises was faced with a catastrophic incident near McAllen, Texas. Tragically, a school bus carrying 81 students collided with a Coca-Cola delivery truck. The bus veered into an excavation pit partially filled with water, and 21 students drowned in the accident. Although the event captured international media attention and inspired a book, criminal charges against the driver, and years of legal wrangling over benefits paid to the families, the company was able to manage this event effectively from a small CCC in the local manager's office, maintaining effective communications with the community and other stakeholders. On behalf of Coca-Cola, I was personally involved in communications with multiple stakeholders, including company management (corporate and local), victims' families, the local and international media, school administrators and teachers, overwhelmed Catholic priests, city mayor and business manager, local mental health providers, and more. Within days, Coca-Cola Enterprises was recognized in the community for its caring crisis response, and sales of Coca-Cola in the area actually increased following the tragic incident. Clearly, excellent crisis management is possible even from makeshift facilities.

3.3.4 Special Roles

Gatekeeper: Whatever space you designate, you should call for a trusted gatekeeper who is not a member of the crisis team, whose sole purpose is to manage traffic in and out of the room. This person should be armed with a list of team members, backups, and invited experts. If sensitive information is posted on the walls, it makes sense that only authorized personnel should be allowed into the room. There's no question that things can get a little crazy in your command center. The importance of controlling traffic and communications cannot be overstated.

It is vital that during an actual incident, crisis team members receive important information from arriving personnel and are able to delegate actions to selected outsiders who need direction. The gatekeeper should balance that need for people and information coming into and going out of the CCC with the potential for distractions, communication leaks, and the opportunity for chaos.

Runners: You'll also want to appoint several runners to deliver messages or items between the CCC and others on the outside. Runners also tackle tasks assigned by the crisis team. This is an important function that keeps the crisis teams cohesive and "at the table." Without runners, there is a tendency for the team to disperse as members race to cover needed tasks.

3.3.5 Additional Command Center Tips

Consider these additional tips for a high-functioning CCC:

▶ Have everyone maintain phone logs of calls that come into the CCC. These logs can be an invaluable reference when captured in a consistent format. The log would be compiled as long as your CCC is operational. It is best to capture:

❑ Who called and when.

❑ To whom.

❑ The nature of the call.

❑ The phone number.

▶ If activated, your humanitarian response team (a team that addresses only people-related issues that I will discuss in detail later) should have an established site of operation. This can be in a separate room, adjacent or quite close to the CCC or elsewhere. This team needs mental and physical space for the very tough job of managing the people issues. Use available means – cell phones, runners, instant messaging – to exchange messages and update information between the two locations. The purpose of this separation is to keep the humanitarian response team members away from the distractions of the physical response side of the crisis. Their job is exclusively the people side.

▶ Keep your managerial team members focused and cohesive. I've observed a tendency for team members to jump up to accomplish tasks, such as running down needed information, or seeking personnel files. If Harry's errand keeps him away from the CCC for 15 minutes, you've lost a quarter hour of input. Then, Sue is off on a 30-minute task, and Steve, your team leader, is making inquiries back in his office. Before you know it, your team has disappeared and its ability to manage the crisis has been compromised. Keep team members in place and ensure that there are sufficient runners.

During a crisis exercise at a private middle school, the headmaster, a member of the crisis management team, decided to meet the family of an injured child immediately at a local hospital. He then left the command center. Since it was only an exercise, when he returned a couple of minutes later, I put him in the corner – something I had always wanted to do as a student. He was not allowed to give input because he was now "gone" to the hospital. Why? In a real life crisis, he could never have made his way to the hospital, met with the family, and returned in two minutes. His absence was keenly felt and valuable input was lost while he was out. Someone else could easily have accomplished that early contact with the family, as important as it was. There was time later, when the crisis was successfully contained, for the headmaster to visit the hospital.

3.4 Crisis Action Team (CAT) Leader

Your managerial-level leader of the CAT needs to be empowered – by policy and by practice – to take action. Of course, the ability to collaborate and delegate is also essential, but your leader needs authority that is broad enough to permit him or her to function effectively.

> **Making order out of chaos is a fairly unusual job description, but it describes the job of the CAT leader precisely.**

Some companies follow the incident command system (ICS) protocol that was originally established in the early 1970s to establish common communications and coordination among firefighters, hazardous materials teams, rescuers, and emergency medical teams. As some corporations have adopted the ICS model, the incident commander (IC) has been assigned authority over the entire crisis response. However, that individual might be junior to managers he or she is commanding during a crisis. This can work, but it must be absolutely clear that the IC's decisions prevail, no matter what the hierarchy may be during normal times.

Making order out of chaos is a fairly unusual job description, but it describes the job of the CAT leader precisely. This is someone who can manage noise, uncertainty, stress, fear, and grief, in the midst of crisis – while simultaneously conveying calm and stability.

Those who are old enough – or who watch reruns – are familiar with the plate spinner, a frequent guest on TV variety shows like Ed Sullivan of the 1950s and '60s. This individual gets multiple plates spinning on wooden dowels and, magically, manages to run among them, giving each just enough tweak to keep it in the air, while looking out for the next wobbling plate and rushing to its rescue. Miraculously, none comes crashing down. This type of person – armed with planning, training, and a supportive and capable team – is your ideal leader.

Follow the Leader: A common scenario to be avoided involves the tension between the team leader and the CEO. Typically, when companies are in a crisis, there is someone like a risk manager or corporate counsel leading the response. But then the CEO instinctively decides to do what he or she always does – lead. Suddenly, this individual is there with sleeves rolled up, making unilateral decisions. Ideally, your CEO will choose to be involved and all enlightened senior executives will go to the assigned crisis team leader at the managerial level and ask how they can help. Make no mistake – the senior officers are the ultimate leaders of your company at all times in all situations.

But effective crisis leadership is achieved through orderly and clear desig-nation of roles and responsibilities – and that includes permitting the managerial CAT leader to lead with authority and the various crisis response teams to work as integrated units. They would have planned, trained, and exercised with the managerial CAT leader in charge and empowered. That's the way it should function during a real crisis, as well. Each level within the crisis management organization should be allowed to do what they know to do best within their silos of responsibility.

> **Remember the basic questions that should seem familiar by now – what happened, how bad is it, what is being done, and what is the escalation potential?**

3.5 Initial CAT Meeting

The immediate goal of the initial CAT meeting is to communicate the needed facts to team members and their alternates. Alternates might also gather in the CCC, but perhaps not at the team table. Executives may attend to obtain the latest fact pattern, as well, but typically the executive leadership team will meet in a separate location to consider strategic issues, should the crisis rise to their level.

Remember the basic questions that should seem familiar by now – what happened, how bad is it, what is being done, and what is the escalation potential?

The team leader should facilitate the discussion and keep it moving and on track. Take the opportunity during this session to briefly discuss the issues and to assign priority items. Refer back to Chapter 1 for the process of a model crisis whisperer. Crisis management is active. It is what the team actively does – communicating, delegating, empowering, and dispatching resources – that contains a crisis.

This is also the time to set the tone for the management of the crisis. This is best done by ensuring that key decisions have been made and will be respected. Among these are:

- ▶ Means of communication to and from the teams. None of your crisis response teams can function any better than the communica-tions they give and receive. The various team leaders need to be front and center for all incoming and outgoing communications.

- ▶ A series of checks and balances. Keep track of activities, who will take responsibility for each, and by when. Have someone keep track of responsibilities that aren't completed by the designated time and make contact with the appropriate people to facilitate appropriate action.

▶ Established priorities for the team leader's involvement that delineate which decisions must be made with his or her involvement, and which can be made by others.

▶ Tasks that will be delegated to others outside the team.

▶ Decisions that will require senior management approval.

Valuable Lessons: Recommendations for a CAT

Here are some recommendations I made for members of one crisis action team after its first crisis response exercise. Your team can benefit from them, too.

1. Refer to your manual and checklists from the outset to ensure that key points are sequentially covered in a timely way.

2. Encourage team members to use the focused imagery technique to imagine the needs and concerns of outraged and other impacted stakeholders, especially when planning interactions with deeply affected family members.

3. Prioritize actions, not just information, to speed up handling of initial crisis management needs. This applies to humanitarian as well as other crisis content actions.

4. The initial team meeting (and subsequent ones) took too long. Make priorities and dispense with extraneous details.

5. Avoid too much monologue by the team leader along with not enough team decision-making. Quickly brainstorm decisions and actions among team members.

6. Focus your communications on action items; if no action is needed, move on to the next item.

7. Use periodic time-outs! This is a means of taking control of the process (and managing the chaos) and making sure the left hand knows what the right hand is doing.

8. Team members should stay in control of phone calls by keeping them short, getting others to take and receive calls, and insisting that callers get to the point and then let you go.

9. Delegate as much as appropriate so that the team can continue to "look out the windshield" at where you are headed. Avoid getting bogged down in the details that others can handle.

Interestingly, this CAT handled every one of these issues in their second exercise adequately. Practice and the debriefing of lessons-learned pay off.

Quick Use Response Guide

Chapter 3: Crisis Containment

Establish Protocol for the Six Phases of Crisis Team Management

▶ Notification and activation.

▶ Fact finding.

▶ Decision-making.

▶ Prioritizing.

▶ Implementation.

▶ Purposeful de-escalation.

Crisis Command Center (CCC)

▶ Have you identified and prepared a room(s) for the crisis action team (CAT)and other teams to meet during crisis response?

▶ Extended hours capabilities.

▶ Alternative offsite location, if needed.

▶ Posted security guard/gatekeeper.

Is the room configured for maximum efficiency?

▶ Information posted visibly.

▶ Proper ventilation.

▶ Is it technologically connected?

❑ Presently equipped.

❑ Ready to be retrofitted.

Possible equipment in the CCC

▶ Generator for sufficient backup power.

▶ Multiple phone lines (with some unpublished numbers separate from the normal phone system).

▶ Phone headsets.

▶ Speaker phones.

▶ Chargers for cell phones.

▶ Computers with e-mail, fax, and Internet capabilities.

▶ Printers.

▶ Televisions for monitoring media, with recording capability.

▶ Satellite or cable television connections.

▶ Two-way radios.

▶ Video conferencing capabilities.

▶ Sufficient office supplies.

▶ Defibrillator and first aid supplies.

▶ Flashlight and other emergency equipment.

▶ Bullhorn.

▶ Method established for visually posting pertinent information on easels, white boards, and projectors.

▶ Digital photographs, maps, real-time video surveillance of remote worksites.

▶ Other pertinent information, equipment, and resources.

Crisis Action Team (CAT) Leader

▶ Is the team leader empowered with the authority and access to senior management to fulfill the duties of crisis response?

▶ Have a sufficient number of runners and assistants been designated for delegation so the leader can keep the CAT together?

Initial Crisis Management Team (CMT) Meeting

▶ Have a method established for documentation (per legal counsel's direction).

▶ Establish a phone log system.

▶ Generate a sufficient number of methods for communications to and from the team.

▶ Utilize checklists for team member immediate considerations (according to the incident at hand).

▶ Assign one person to serve as the liaison between the CAT and the executive leadership team. Tactical/operational teams typically report to the manager on the managerial CAT who has authority over them.

Humanitarian Response Team (HRT) (discussed in detail in Chapter 5)

▶ Utilize this team to exclusively address the myriad people-related issues of a traumatic or distressing incident, when there is outrage, or other times when there is significant impact on people.

▶ The CAT leader will delegate any people-related issues to the HRT for implementation and follow up.

▶ Position the HRT near the CAT to facilitate coordination between the two teams.

▶ Assign one person on the team to serve as the liaison between the HRT and the CAT.

Chapter 3 - Questions for Further Thought and Discussion

1. Since the CCC is the nerve center of a crisis response, what are several things that could go wrong, e.g., power outage? What contingency plans can you identify for each?

2. If a policy is established that only those persons with a contributing purpose (regardless of rank) are allowed in the CCC, what are the several reasons this policy should remain an enforced rule?

3. If communications are so important, why shouldn't the executive CMT and the CAT be located in the same room?

4. What information, equipment, and resources should be in the CCC that are not listed in this chapter?

5. What are the traits and capabilities that should be considered when choosing a CAT leader? What should be the process of choosing a CAT leader? Should the leader be rotated, and if so, why and how often?

4

Order Out of Chaos

A t this point, your crisis teams have positioned themselves onto the front lines and are prepared to do battle. Each team is ensconced in its appropriate bunker (the crisis command center, remotely, etc.). They have established methods of communication (runners, phones, videoconferencing, e-mail, etc.) internally and with the outside. Everyone knows who is in command – and plenty of healthy food, coffee, and supplies are available.

And that's good, because you could be in for a long siege.

We now turn to the orderly process of relieving chaos. I use the word *orderly* with caution because, when push comes to shove, crisis management can become pretty frenzied.

This chapter will help you to:

> ➢ *Identify the real crisis.*

> ➢ *Understand the elements of crisis decision-making.*

> ➢ *Anticipate common crisis management problems.*

> ➢ *Address the human side of a traumatic incident.*

> ➢ *Ask ten questions to assess your decisions and actions.*

4.1 Understanding the Crisis

To start, you must identify accurately the true crisis you are about to manage. At first blush, that would appear obvious. It's the sexual harassment, flood, fire, or insider trading, right? Not necessarily. Apparently, defining the crisis beyond the obvious is a lesson that needs to be relearned with each generation of corporate leaders.

Johnson & Johnson (J&J) has basked in the positive reputation earned in 1982 as a result of its handling of the tampering situation where seven people in Chicago were killed after ingesting cyanide-laced Tylenol. CEO James Burke realized that the corporate crisis was not about people who died in Chicago. That situation needed to be handled with care and sensitivity, but the real crisis that he defined and managed was one of reputation and customer trust in J&J products. Despite the opposition of the FBI, Food and Drug Administration, and his own senior staff, Burke had the "chutzpah" to take all Tylenol capsules off the shelves until triple tamper-proof packaging was developed. Only then was the product reintroduced to store shelves.

So, one would think that subsequent J&J leadership would continue in the same manner when crisis situations occurred. Fast forward to 2009. John R. Kroger, the attorney general of Oregon, criticized and sued J&J for using outside contractors to purchase Motrin from store shelves, claiming it was an effort to avoid the negative publicity of a formal recall. Since then, J&J has recalled millions of items, including Motrin, Rolaids, Adult and Children's Tylenol, Liquid Tylenol, Sudafed, Sinutab, Benadryl, Mylanta, Pepcid AC, and more. Unfortunately, the recalls came only after a manufacturing flaw and other quality problems were discovered by the FDA. Additionally, a children's advocacy group boycotted Johnson's Baby Shampoo, claiming cancer-causing chemicals were in a number of baby products. Public sentiment appears to indicate that William Weldon (J&J's now replaced CEO) was more focused on the financial savings of avoided recalls than on engendering public trust. In one example regarding the outcome of poor crisis management, J&J's sales of Children's Liquid Tylenol and Motrin decreased more than 60% while drugstore brands gained 93% during the same time period.

> **Whether your crisis involves multiple deaths and injuries, or "only" involves a perceived injustice or negligence, the steps you take to manage the crisis will involve addressing the reactions of people.**

The way that I identify the "crisis beyond the obvious" is to focus on the core assets of the organization that appear to be threatened. The question is this: What impact will the content of this crisis (e.g., quality problems, fire, product recall, boycott, or lawsuit) have on the core assets of the organization? Is the impact diminished reputation? Possibly, the ability of the company to operate will be affected if regulators prohibit production. Maybe your crisis could threaten the financial wellbeing of the company. The core assets listed at the end of Chapter 1 are provided again for your reference.

▶ People.

▶ Key relationships.

▶ Reputation.

▶ Brand.

▶ Trust.

▶ Finances.

▶ Shareholder value.

▶ Business operations.

▶ Intellectual property.

▶ Physical property.

▶ Product/service delivery capabilities.

▶ Other.

Ultimately, strategic crisis management (where the focus is on protecting core assets) is about managing the reactions of people. Possibly, the reaction is outrage about perceived injustice. Maybe it's traumatic stress or grief over a loss that was caused by the company. Demands may surface to right a perceived wrong. Whether your crisis involves multiple deaths and injuries, or "only" involves a perceived injustice or negligence, the steps you take to manage the crisis will involve addressing the reactions of people. In any case, people tend to be deeply affected and are looking for a timely, responsible, and caring response.

4.2 Crisis Decision-Making Revisited

Crisis decision-making is not only about lofty core asset issues. Tactical details must also be addressed. In order to make good decisions during crisis response, you need to apply both art and science to the process.

Typically, crises make their initial appearance during unexpected times. Crisis management was not on your morning "to do" list. Now the situation has hit a threshold where you must drop everything else and focus fully on crisis issues. The situation unfolds with great velocity, and others are watching in judgment of your decisions and actions.

The objective is to execute high quality and timely decisions during unexpected situations where the following issues are typically involved:

▶ Personal stress.

▶ High consequence.

▶ Inadequate information.

▶ Insufficient time.

▶ Close scrutiny by stakeholders.

▶ Blame and outrage directed toward the company and managers.

It's interesting to note that some managers are excellent at crisis management. Conversely, other managers become inept during unexpected, high consequence times. Let's look at what works during crisis response.

It starts with making good decisions under stress. Practicing good judgment when engaged in crisis response is both an art and a science. In the heat of the battle, you must rely on emotion and intuition, not just sequential analysis and technological rationality.

Crisis decision-making is located somewhere between intuition and analysis. It's a balancing act where extremes are to be avoided. Rely solely on "gut level feeling" and impulsive mistakes will be made. On the other end of the continuum, taking too much time to analyze the situation causes decisions to be late. Hasty decisions and analysis paralysis are to be avoided. It will seem like the 50-50-10 rule will be in effect, i.e., with a 50-50 chance you'll be right 10% of the time. However, crisis managers who are highly effective use the right mix of analysis and intuition. Let's look at what experience and research can tell us about effective crisis decision-making.

> **The right decision made too late will likely be ineffective.**

It is a false assumption that the quality of a crisis response decision is correlated directly with the *time* and *effort* invested. We have all heard these adages: weigh all the alternatives; list the pros and cons; haste makes waste; look before you leap; and, don't judge a book by its cover. Especially in situations of high importance, we want to slow it all down to ensure quality decisions are made. However, of equal importance is the timeliness of crisis response. The right decision made too late will likely be ineffective.

If crisis decision-making is to involve an intuitive component in order to balance the criteria for timeliness, then let's look at the science of intuitive decision-making. The Max Planck Institute for Human Development in Berlin, Germany, has conducted high quality studies related to decision-making.

Less is more: The findings at Max Planck Institute are counter-intuitive and apply to crisis decision-making. For example, in uncertain situations "less is more." Too many choices confuse decision-making. Shoppers will buy more when faced with fewer choices (Katsikopoubs, 2010) and novice financial investors will outperform professional stockbrokers simply by choosing companies with recognizable names (Gigerenzer, 2007). The findings demonstrated repeatedly that simple rules for judgment were less prone to calculation errors.

Conversely, complex analytical decision-making in uncertain situations lead to poorer outcomes. In sports, increased analysis tends to decrease performance. A basketball player will hit more free throws when he or she gives less thought to the nuances of shooting the ball. Instead, the best way to increase accuracy is to minimize time looking at the basket and shorten the "thinking process" while preparing to shoot (Kelbick, 2013).

When analysis is minimized (to a point) during crisis decision-making, partial knowledge will increase the quality of the decision more than considering additional information. This doesn't mean to completely omit analysis. Colin Powell (former Army General, Chairman of the Joint Chiefs of Staff, and US Secretary of State) espoused his "40-70 rule" that applies to crisis decision-making (Anderson, n.d.). He said not to take action until you have enough information to give you at least a 40% chance of being right. But, he adds, don't wait until you are 100% sure, because you will almost always be late. Once you have 40-70% of the information in a high-velocity situation, it's best to implement with your gut level decision at that point.

Crisis decision-making is a balancing act of (1) gathering just enough salient information to get a general mental picture of the crisis situation, (2) analyzing the fact pattern to identify problems, opportunities, priorities, and leverage points, and (3) acting intuitively with your best judgment. Then, as additional information comes in, you repeat it all again for as long as needed.

Effective crisis decision-makers often tend to focus on only one strategic leverage point. A well-known example is Rudy Giuliani's response as mayor of New York City following the 9/11 terrorism. He easily could have focused on the emergency response and myriad other issues that needed to be addressed. Instead, Giuliani chose one role that leveraged his leadership and influence. He chose the single task of informing people through the media about what was happening. James Burke did the same at J&J in 1982, when he chose the single leveraged task of taking all Tylenol off the shelves in order to contain the tampering crisis.

> ...effective leaders use a balance of analysis of the fact pattern with their unconscious intelligence to guide their intuitive decision-making and action plans.

Unconscious intelligence: Research at the University of Iowa (Bechara, Damasio, Tranel & Damasio, 2005) further demonstrates how the brain will help crisis decision-makers intuitively know the right answer, even before they are consciously aware of it. In this study, the subjects were provided with decks of red and blue cards. Each subject would draw from any pile and accumulate or lose money according to what each drawn card indicated. Unknown to the subjects, the red cards would provide large payouts, but even larger losses. The blue cards were more conservative and would yield a small gain over time. Each subject was wired to a machine that measured stress-induced sweat on their palms from galvanic skin response. While it took approximately 80 cards on average for subjects to get a conscious understanding that the red cards were stacked against them, the machines measured stress activation related to the red cards after only 10 cards drawn.

This study indicates that an unconscious intelligence or your "intuitive sense" contains an early indication of the correct answer long before you are consciously aware of it. Once partial knowledge is obtained in a crisis situation, effective leaders use a balance of analysis of the fact pattern with their unconscious intelligence to guide their intuitive decision-making and action plans.

4.3 Common Crisis Management Problems – ACE

In my many years of assisting organizations, large and small, I have noticed three common weaknesses that inhibit effective crisis containment and recovery. I share these three areas of crisis management difficulty through the acronym ACE (authority, communications, and expectations) to help you remember areas that could complicate effective crisis response.

4.3.1 Authority

During a crisis is not the best time to determine who has authority for important decision-making. A common failure point occurs when individuals do not assume authority and responsibility when it is expected. If not fully empowered with clear boundaries and guidelines, people have a tendency to back away – especially for important decisions accompanied by vague guidelines about what is the best action to take. The default action is avoidance or delay in order to obtain guidance from a superior who may not be as close to the "action" and could make wrong decisions. Precious time is lost and the effectiveness of the crisis response is compromised.

The converse is also problematic. In this case, individuals assume positions of authority without prior approval. The result can easily turn into a situation where more than one person is making related decisions during crisis response. Without clear guidelines about the strategic direction of the response, communication channels, and limits of authority, the crisis response can quickly lose focus.

It is critically important that appropriate individuals know they are to assume authority at defined levels. It should be clear to whom they are to report, especially if an incident command system (ICS) process is utilized in which the crisis commander may be someone other than an individual's normal boss, or if a crisis specific hierarchy differs from normal times. Thresholds should be established clearly so individuals know the limits of their authority and at what point they need to garner approvals from superiors.

4.3.2 Communications

A second crisis management failure point is communications. No crisis team is any better than its communications. Timely and accurate two-way information should flow between crisis managers and appropriate internal and external stakeholders. Depending on the incident, communications can be compromised with power outages, attorneys with liability concerns who may attempt to prohibit transparency and information flow, inoperative mobile phone towers, overloaded phone systems, rumors, misinformation, misunderstandings, fear of disclosure, employees and others who may speak without authority, or other impediments. Good planning should include contingencies for these occurrences. We will discuss this further in Chapter 5.

> **Establish what can be expected from each department and key individual... These expectations should reach out beyond the silos of the organization.**

4.3.3 Expectations

The third common failure point relates to your people not knowing exactly what is expected of them. One way to integrate your crisis response organizationally is simply to identify what is expected of each staff function during various crises. Establish what can be expected from each department and key individual and what they expect from others in return. These expectations should reach out beyond the silos of the organization. In this manner, an awareness of impacts on other areas of the response will be better known. For example, a facilities manager should know to protect the scene of an incident where a crime is suspected. Corporate security, legal, and law enforcement will all want the scene undisturbed. If this expectation is not known, an eager facilities manager might restore the incident site quickly in an attempt to reestablish a sense of normalcy and continuity of operations.

Considerations that will help in the planning process for establishing purposeful expectations during crisis response:

- ❯ Who will assume which responsibilities?
- ❯ What are the expectations of the various stakeholders?

▶ List foreseeable risks and staff expectations for each.

▶ Are interviews compiled on a relational database system for ease of keeping up to date?

▶ Information and directives wanted from others.

▶ Information and directives given to others.

4.4 Psychological First Aid

The term *psychological first aid* refers to the initial response associated with addressing the people side of a traumatic crisis. It is not about providing immediate professional or amateur counseling, psychological assessment, or asking people about their innermost feelings. Instead, it's about practical, caring assistance you can bring to people who are distressed over an unexpected traumatic incident. Psychological first aid can include a number of actions, such as:

▶ Accounting for everyone and assessing immediate needs.

▶ Establishing calm and order, and minimizing confusion.

▶ Protecting employees and others from exposure to traumatic sights and experiences.

▶ Making contact with victims, witnesses, and others experiencing traumatic stress reactions and listening or providing assistance for their concerns.

▶ Helping to meet needs during the early aftermath (from contacting loved ones or finding lost keys, to physical comforting and providing transportation home).

▶ Giving those affected good and timely information about what has happened.

▶ Organizing a "buddy system" for support in coping during the early aftermath.

4.5 Rallying the Troops

A first step following a traumatic incident is to rally your troops. It is best to set up a location for everyone to gather so that you can determine who is accounted for and who is not. When assigning an emergency meeting place, make sure to have a backup location in case the primary spot has become inaccessible or inappropriate.

Unfortunately, accounting for everyone may be a difficult task. After a hurricane during which I helped orchestrate the response, one building at

BellSouth Corporation in south Florida where approximately 450 persons worked was uninhabitable, without electricity or air conditioning. And 80% of the employees working in that building had either lost their homes or sustained severe damage. Imagine the difficulty of getting this workforce back on the job. But, we did it and according to news reports, we did it faster than any other large employer in the area.

Transportation was difficult, with downed trees, stoplights out, landmarks blown away, and street signs gone. Phones were dead, leaving few options for finding people other than physically going to their homes. We set up a networking system to establish the known status of missing employees – many unwilling to leave their homes for fear of looting. Managers and selected employees were dispatched to look for those on whom we had no information.

> **Keep in mind, crises are a time that can significantly enhance your personal and organizational reputation.**

Employees were taken supplies and offered housing. We knew no employees would come to work until they had a stable (even if temporary) place to live. Thus, steps were taken to immediately secure housing for employees, even before everyone was accounted for. Also, with schools and daycare facilities inoperable, we secured alternatives in the nearest undamaged town and provided roundtrip shuttle service for employees' children. Additionally, the company made food, childcare, supplies, and even cash available to employees at their building. The word spread, and many previously unaccounted for employees came in for assistance. This helped us account for everyone in record time.

Depending on the size and scope of the crisis, you may recognize that you need help in making order out of chaos. Whoever is in charge on the ground needs the latitude to enlist reinforcements. Ideally, such reinforcements would include employees and external providers – like crisis counselors and contractors – who are willing and able to respond to your instructions. At this time, you need to enlist all resources available to you, with discretion. Some companies have provided assistance to other companies through an organized employee effort, providing an opportunity to raise the profile and reputation of the company during crisis times. Keep in mind, crises are a time that can significantly enhance your personal and organizational reputation, much like Wal-Mart did by widely providing supplies following Hurricane Katrina.

Beyond the obvious benefit of additional hands in a time of need, putting others to work when they are themselves reeling from what they've experienced can help many people gain a sense of composure and productiveness.

4.5.1 Who Is Hurting?

Once you have attempted to account for your people following a traumatic incident and have enlisted some assistance, it's time to make an initial assessment of those who may be physically injured (some without realizing it), traumatized emotionally, or otherwise deeply impacted. This informal process involves the step of simply asking those you see if they are aware of others who are having difficulty.

Obviously, a person dissolved in tears is suffering some degree of emotional distress. But often, it's not that simple. Look as well for people who seem to be scattered, shocked, stunned, dazed, or confused. Especially, look out for those who are withdrawn. Many people suffer quietly. The intent is not to single out people who are reacting normally to a traumatic incident. Rather, you want to make contact for assessment and potential assistance (informally or possibly professionally) with those people who are in obvious need of assistance. Just because someone is crying doesn't mean he or she should be herded into a manager's office for assessment. Crying and stunned, fearful, and confused behaviors are normal reactions following traumatic incidents.

Ask employees and managers to be on the lookout for those who are in obvious need of help and to bring them to your attention. Professional crisis mental health intervention may be provided at some point, but just your caring and understanding response may be enough. In any case, the immediate response will likely be by the company during the immediate aftermath phase. Compile a list of individuals who ask for or need assistance and what they may need. A timely and appropriate response can make a difference that is greatly appreciated.

For groups of traumatized people in the immediate aftermath, gently encourage everyone to gather in a predetermined, comfortable space. Try not to use a large, open space like the company cafeteria, which can contribute to a feeling of vulnerability. Avoiding a space with many windows will enhance a feeling of safety and keep out inappropriately inquisitive reporters or onlookers. As you escort them to the space, take care to shelter them from grisly images, if needed – like corpses being carried off, or bloodstained areas.

A common reaction among those who have been traumatized is to obsess over a single lost object or issue, like a shoe or set of keys. The "small stuff" looms so large in their minds because that may be all they can process mentally at the moment. Meet their needs. Find coffee, a tissue, a cell phone – whatever it takes to bring comfort and address their immediate needs.

Meanwhile, the arriving media will do everything possible to speak with your impacted employees. Warn your employees that they will likely be approached and the rationale for not speaking with the media (See Section 4.5.3).

4.5.2 Prepare for Family Members

While some members of your team are helping to keep people comfortable, others should prepare for the arrival of family members. Bad news travels fast and family members may make their way to your site more quickly than you can imagine. Establish a gathering place for arriving family members. (For more about dealing with the families of the injured, see Appendix A of this book.) One strategy I recommend is to position sentries at the end of the driveway or entranceway to your facility. These are probably employees. If you have suffered fatalities, these official "greeters" should know the names of the dead. The strategy is simple – as cars or pedestrians come up, one of the sentries asks their affiliation with the company and the name of their loved one. If they are family members of someone who has died, a sentry will escort them to a private room where an appropriate manager will make the death notification, as appropriate, or provide transportation to the location where their loved one has been taken.

Whether the employee is injured or not, family members will want to see their loved ones immediately. Employees who are not injured should be connected with their loved ones as soon as possible in a family gathering area. Families of hospitalized employees would be escorted to another area of the building, where transportation to hospitals would be provided quickly, since people under duress are at risk of having auto accidents.

> **Don't speculate....Remember that misinformation can lead to outrage.**

Do everything you can to connect family members with loved ones. Ideally, you will know who has been injured seriously and where they have been hospitalized. Common protocol for shooting victims in hospitals is to register them under an alias name. As emergency responders are transporting injured people, ask to which hospitals so that you can communicate this to the families. In incidents with mass casualties, it is likely that more than one hospital will be used. The last thing you want is to send frantic families on a chase from one emergency room to another.

You will be barraged with questions. What happened? Who or what was responsible? Who was nearby when the crisis hit? Was anyone killed? How many were injured?

Your duty is to be as informative as you can, delivering straight, truthful information. Don't beat around the bush, but don't speculate either. It's not up to you or other team members to offer a medical prognosis. Remember that misinformation can lead to outrage. Dispel rumors if you can, and be forthcoming, but be careful not to give speculative or unverified information.

Typically, death is not "official" until a coroner pronounces the fatality. However, to avoid being perceived as deceptive, you will need to make a judgment in very obvious cases on whether to tell family members that the person "appeared to have been killed, but the coroner's report has not yet been released."

4.5.3 Tell What They Know

If a crime was suspected or committed, the law enforcement will arrive to take statements. You will benefit the investigation by discouraging those affected from conversing among themselves about the events. This might mean separating eyewitnesses so they won't discuss what they saw. The desire to commiserate and swap accounts is strong, but law enforcement (and your own corporate investigators) will want to get the cleanest possible story from each witness – an account untainted by the recollections of others.

You could provide pads and pens for those who wish to make notes about what they saw before they talk with law enforcement. This can aid the investigation, but sometimes traumatized people are simply too shaken to concentrate on writing.

Rationale for Employees Not Talking to the Media

While citizens have the right to exercise freedom of speech by talking to the media, consider conveying to employees:

▶ The wrong statement to the media can potentially harm you, your coworkers, the company, and others involved.

▶ The media are looking for the most emotional and controversial thing any employee will say or do. It's best to ignore their advances and not respond in any manner. They will take what employees say out of context, many times misquote it, and replay it repeatedly.

▶ Employees are typically shocked and stunned following traumatic incidents and not prepared to make public statements.

▶ Employees cannot predict what will be asked and will lack well-thought-out responses.

▶ If any employee insists on talking to the media, they should understand that they may not make any statement regarding company policy, or speak in any way on behalf of the company.

▶ It is best to allow people who are trained and prepared to speak to the media.

▶ Employees do not even need to tell media whom to contact. Tell your people, "If you are approached by the media, simply wave them off and don't let them engage you."

4.6 Employee De-escalation Meetings

Following statements to law enforcement, your people will probably be eager to get away from the site, but don't let them go just yet, if possible and appropriate. Consider holding "de-escalation meetings" where you take stock of what has happened, convey key information, and assess their wellbeing.

Ideally, these meetings are short and take place soon after the incident, before employees are sent home. Local management typically leads them. They can be conducted in large or small assemblies. If police are taking statements, wait until perhaps five or ten people have been interviewed before holding each session, or fewer people if the wait is too long. If your facility operates more than one shift, or if people finish giving police statements at different times, you will want to conduct enough de-escalation meetings to adequately meet the needs of all impacted and help them get home sooner.

The de-escalation meeting is a discussion session that gives management an opportunity to:

▶ Give and receive current, appropriate information to and from employees following a traumatic incident.

▶ Stabilize and calm employees from the emotions of the traumatic incident.

▶ Acknowledge potential stress reactions and symptoms.

▶ Collect information.

▶ Dispel rumors.

▶ Inform employees about what will happen the next day back at work.

4.6.1 De-escalation Meeting Content

The essential topics to cover during a short de-escalation session include the following:

▶ **Acknowledge the significance of the crisis** with words like, "We are all deeply saddened and shocked ..."

▶ **Reconstruct the facts** to the degree that is possible, knowing that in the early aftermath, the story line will not be fully developed. Elicit input from those with different perspectives or accurate information. Make note of rumors or unsubstantiated reports, and promise to investigate and report back at a later time.

▶ **Advise everyone not to talk to the media.** Explain that members of the press may be waiting with cameras and microphones in hand outside the building or even outside their homes. Those who have never experienced the onslaught of the press may feel compelled or required to answer questions asked (or shouted!) to them. But employees need to be told how easily their words can be twisted out of context since few of them will have an understanding of potential liability and reputational issues for your organization. So they should be encouraged not to talk. Make sure they understand that company representatives will make official statements and that individuals have no need to talk to the press.

▶ **Discuss expected reactions.** Tell people to expect some level of anxiety and adrenaline-like reactions, loss of appetite, sleep disturbance, intrusive thoughts, and concentration difficulties. Let employees know these reactions are normal.

> Promising up-to-date information is the best way to get everyone to return to work at the earliest possible opportunity.

▶ **Instruct everyone to come to work** on the next workday if it is at all possible to bring them back. Explain that the first day back will not be a normal workday and that a management led meeting will take place soon after they arrive. They will be briefed on the latest information about the situation. If your facility has been damaged and you don't yet know where the meeting will be held, let everyone know how they will be notified. Tell them, "It will be best for everyone if we can all work through our reactions together, instead of isolated at home." Promising up-to-date information is the best way to get everyone to return to work at the earliest possible opportunity.

▶ **Ask for questions from the group.** Even if the initial silence is slightly awkward, be patient – employees almost always have important questions, concerns, or comments.

▶ **Establish a buddy system.** Following severe situations, especially if surviving employees witnessed deaths or felt their lives threatened, consider assigning each person a coworker buddy and ask that they make "meaningful contact" with each other by phone for the next few days. Instruct them not to ask, "How are you doing?" during buddy contacts, but to ask instead, "What reactions have you had regarding this incident?" Concerns about buddies should be reported to a designated person so assistance can be offered.

▶ **Arrange transportation** for anyone who requests it or appears too distraught to drive safely. Don't underestimate the power of distraction; even those who believe they are fine may find themselves shaking, confused, or simply too upset to drive safely.

▶ **Remain afterward** to speak with anyone who still has questions more comfortably asked one-on-one.

▶ **Supervisors and local managers should be advised** to come early the first day employees will return to work to be briefed prior to employee arrivals.

Considerations for Achieving "Order"

▶ Your first task is to contain the crisis, protecting people, property, and other core assets from additional harm.

▶ Following emergency response, define the core assets at risk as you start taking action.

▶ Be prepared to make timely decisions with only partial information, utilizing a balance of analytic and intuitive components.

▶ Beware of the three common crisis response failure points, i.e., authority, communications, and expectations (ACE).

▶ Communication to and from affected stakeholders is the foundation of crisis response.

▶ Management needs to be visible and timely in their response.

▶ When there are limited resources, the early bird gets the worm. Identify and lock down resources as soon as possible.

▶ Secure the incident site and establish a sense of safety.

▶ Protect impacted individuals from unwanted outsiders and influences.

▶ Give direction regarding what people should expect and do in the near term.

▶ Anticipate what could escalate in severity and take actions to prevent it.

▶ Tell the truth and take appropriate responsibility to resolve the crisis.

▶ Establish a recovery system that involves all impacted stakeholders.

The focus is on day-one crisis response activity and assuring that you are doing all you can to keep those plates spinning simultaneously in the air.

4.7 Taking Stock

Creating order out of chaos is not a definitive process – as if one moment there's chaos and the next moment resolution. Rather, it's an evolutionary process that includes both the reactions of people and the content side of the crisis, e.g., containing the fire.

Crisis response is not linear. Sequential events do not follow neatly and chronologically. The opposite is true. Many things are happening at once. The image of overlapping concentric circles may be a useful way to visualize the distinct, yet intersecting events and responses typical of day one and beyond.

At this point, we'll take a time out, just as your crisis teams should be taking periodic time outs to coordinate efforts and gain perspective. We'll review a generic checklist of issues to be considered. This is a "go to" chapter, meaning that it is an annotated list you can return to as needed to help ensure that you are, in fact, covering your bases.

Crisis management is a circular process. And it doesn't always make intuitive sense to people who operate in a patterned, linear way. The steps look like this:

▶ Information gathering.

▶ Situation assessment.

▶ Decision-making.

▶ Remedial action.

Let's take a walk through this checklist of considerations. We'll start with anticipated business impact.

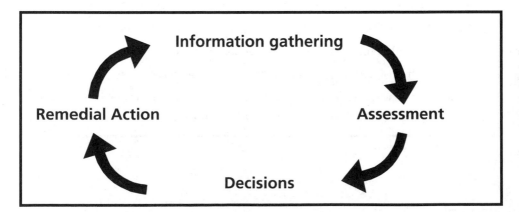

Figure 4-1. The Circular Nature of Crisis Management

4.8 A Tale of Two Traders

Consider what happened in the aftermath of the shootings by the day trader Mark Barton in Atlanta, Georgia in our corporate headquarters building of Crisis Management International, and the lessons to be learned.

4.8.1 Background

After killing his wife and two children the night before, Barton terrorized two day-trading offices where he had been a losing trader, namely, the Atlanta office of All-Tech Investment Group, and Momentum Securities, a day trading company, across the street. Barton first shot eight, killing four at Momentum, then ran across the street and shot fourteen at All-Tech, where he killed five. Twenty-two people total were shot within a matter of a few workplace violence minutes. Essentially the same event at the same time, but the companies responded very differently. Corporate management from All-Tech reached out for crisis consultation with Crisis Management International (conveniently located two floors up) just hours after the shooting, to assist with the aftermath of the traumatic events.

4.8.2 All-Tech Response

I urged All-Tech decision-makers to manage their response to impacted stakeholders, carefully. In this case, that included day one discussions and planning with top management in how to first address the surviving victims, all impacted families, plus all other stakeholders with care and compassion. Primary stakeholders included surviving employees and day trading customers (injured and uninjured) and families. Representatives met family members at hospitals and at the homes of the fatally injured. Media representatives were provided with timely communications. Insurers were notified to verify coverage for a timely return to work, as soon as appropriate. Cleanup crews were quickly dispatched once law enforcement released the site.

In order to orchestrate an organized and caring response, employees, families and customers were contacted that evening and told that the company would be open the next day in order to provide information and services for all impacted persons. They were told that the most accurate, transparent and up-to-date information would be provided to those who came in or who called with inquiries. Any needs, concerns, or questions would be addressed as people mustered back at the office where the shooting had occurred. All details of this briefing meeting were planned during the evening of the first day and orchestrated in an orderly fashion the next day following the shooting. Those who preferred not to return the next day had contact information and live resources to address their needs and concerns.

On the next workday a room full of day traders (All-Tech customers) and surviving employees arrived. Family members also showed up. Ongoing informational briefing meetings – conducted by our crisis management consultants, along with corporate and local management – were held throughout the day to assist those who came in at various times.

Quickly, management had replaced the blood-soaked carpeting, shattered computers, and other obvious signs of terror. By the next workday, the physical space was essentially ready to receive any employee, customer, and family member who chose to attend the informational briefing.

In the early hours before the first scheduled 10:00 a.m. briefing meeting, many day traders came to the shooting site obviously dazed. Few people had a restful night of sleep. But, they came in wanting to know the latest emerging facts, seeking answers to their many questions about the incident. Prior to the meeting, police conducted their interviews with all those who had yet to be contacted. One issue that was not considered was the stock market. Many day traders had abandoned their trading when the shooting occurred, and some had lost money due to the disruption. Management was so concerned (rightfully) about the emotional impact of the traumatic incident that they overlooked the trading issues as a matter of concern. Even so, the briefing process allowed for these issues to be addressed.

In the first briefing meeting, management expressed their concern for the wellbeing of survivors and all families. Facts were given relating to the latest findings about Mark Barton (the perpetrator), his deceased family, and the other shooting across the street at Momentum Securities. Incorrect issues reported in the media were corrected for all to know. Company leaders explained the decision to remain open. People could come back on their own time schedule and as a focal point for obtaining ongoing information. All were apprised of the actions management had taken to reestablish order as much as possible during those early hours following the shooting the day before. Everyone was allowed to ask questions, and answers were provided – except there was no good answer for *why*, as is the case in these senseless crimes.

Once the formal management briefing was complete, I seamlessly continued the meeting by asking anyone who preferred to discuss the situation further to remain in the large circle of chairs around the trading room floor. The standing-room-only crowd began to pull up additional chairs. Many had been through mind numbing fear the day before as they crouched under furniture or ran to avoid Barton's wrath. Family members had been through their own nightmares as they had learned of the shooting.

Simply and clearly, we discussed common reactions of people who have experienced seriously traumatic experiences. Without rehashing the gruesome sights, sounds, and personal experiences, we discussed known methods to manage unwanted and intrusive reactions in healthy ways. People within the group shared how they were beginning to manage their physical, mental, and emotional reactions during that early aftermath phase. Tears were shed. Anxieties were normalized, and heartfelt support emerged within the group. Plans were made for meeting the needs of others not in attendance.

After about an hour of collective support and shared learning, one of the traders turned away from the circle and quietly rolled his chair over to his computer terminal. He began intermittently gazing at the screen and then turning back into what was being said in the group discussion. An individual who had witnessed horrific events only hours before responded by doing the most normal thing in the world for a day trader – checking the progress of the market! But only after he was able to identify his difficult reactions as normal was he able to refocus his attentions on finances. Soon, the cloud of gloom was lifted enough that others began checking their computer screens. Were they over it? Not a chance. There would be very difficult adjustments over the next several days. But, All-Tech management provided the crisis leadership and overt caring that allowed their customers and employees to accelerate their personal recovery. Generous accommodations were made for those day traders who had lost money when they left their accounts open without monitoring following the shooting. People experienced and appreciated the overt "caring" that All-Tech management had provided.

> **People and businesses recover much faster when a caring, structured, and timely response is implemented.**

4.8.3 Momentum Response

The posture adopted by All-Tech Investment Group differed considerably from choices made across the street by the leaders of Momentum Securities, the first of Mark Barton's stops on that fateful day.

The firm accepted ill-equipped, yet free, crisis counseling offered by the mayor of Atlanta. Intuitively, management decided to remain closed for some time to allow people and the company to cope. "Some time" morphed into about six weeks, an eternity to a business as entrenched in the moment as day trading.

Momentum reopened, but, as you may already have guessed, the doors closed before long. For lack of a better term, the firm had lost its "momentum" among customers and surviving employees. The closing precipitated by day one decisions gave the business the aura of an unprepared, injured enterprise that would never regain its formerly robust character.

No reputable expert would counsel a business to act as if a life-changing crisis had not happened. But it can be unnecessarily detrimental to individuals and to a business to lie dormant too long in the wake of traumatic events. People and businesses recover much faster when a caring, structured, and timely response is implemented. Conversely, responding in a disorganized and untimely manner that appears uncaring can (and often will) take an organization to its knees or, at best, increase the longevity and severity of the crisis impact.

Experience has repeatedly shown that it is best to spend appropriately with effort and money in the aftermath of a crisis. Those organizations that invest the most in doing the right things tend to spend less overall. As Momentum soon found out, taking the cheap way out with a non-visible, non-caring response can lead to crisis response failure.

4.9 Day One CMT Checklist

Feel free to supplement this generic list with concerns specific to your situation. (A supplemental listing of immediate actions and unique considerations for specific crises is provided in the last chapter of this book.)

▶ **Work continuation.** Whether to close what parts of the business and for how long are complex questions with big implications. Sometimes, certain work must go on. Employees understand that some areas of the organization must remain operative. Business continuity plans most often focus on business operations. Remember also that the most often ill-prepared aspect related to continuity of operations is the "people side" of crisis recovery. Few business continuity plans will work if employees are not first stabilized with their primary needs first addressed.

For example, Georgia Power Company had an employee shooting in the payroll department right before payroll was due. While the supervisor and the manager of the department suffered gunshot wounds and the perpetrator killed herself, 15,000 others still needed their checks. Here the job was to balance getting payroll out while compassionately assisting those who witnessed the shootings. As a general rule, you must meet "people needs" before back-to-work needs. Otherwise you risk creating an atmosphere of resentment. A rule to live by in crisis management is "people first with demonstrated caring and compassion."

Experience has repeatedly demonstrated that organizations recover with less cost when they spend more at the beginning to contain and mitigate the crisis by doing the "next right things."

▌ **Financial considerations.** These can be staggering. Many times in the chaos of crisis response, there is little or no tracking of expenditures incurred. The surprise and second guessing then comes at the end. Software programs are available that provide real-time tracking of expenditures during crisis management, logistical tracking, documentation of decisions, and more. Some programs comply with the incident command system (ICS) that is mandated by the Coast Guard following incidents at sea, while others do not. No matter how sophisticated or rudimentary your system, keeping track of expenses during crisis management should be a high priority. Obviously, an early call to your insurer will help determine your financial exposures. In any case, crisis response is a time to be forthcoming with supportive resources. Experience has repeatedly demonstrated that organizations recover with less cost when they spend more at the beginning to contain and mitigate the crisis by doing the "next right things." This adage certainly applies to crisis management: "Pay now, or pay later, but it will cost more later."

▌ **Legal concerns.** Crises create liability and law suits. Liability will be one issue that will remain an overlay to your crisis response. But, it should not be the primary, overriding concern. Many other issues will emerge – arguably more important than liability exposure – such as reputation, brand protection, and key relationships. Do you need local or specialized legal help to ensure that you're minimizing legal risk? It may also be necessary to hire any consultants through your legal counsel, rather than directly. This can provide a layer of legal protection by safeguarding information under attorney-client privilege.

In my crisis management experience, I have observed two types of attorneys – the "can do" and the "can't do" variety. The "can't do" lawyers have an easy answer for almost every request: "No." That response is usually based on an overly conservative concern for the kind of fallout a particular action might have on the attorney's ability to defend it. It also reflects a strong self-preservation instinct. Look for attorneys who will recognize legal concerns, but work with you in taking the crisis management actions that are needed by saying, "Yes, some legal hurdles need to be considered, but let's address them the best we can while addressing other important issues." Management, not attorneys, should drive crisis response. Your legal representatives are key partners in your effort to recover from a crisis; they shouldn't make your job more difficult. Crisis decision-making is a strategic management function that takes all core assets of the organization into consideration and should not be overrun by zealous attorneys who don't consider the bigger picture beyond the legal silo.

While it may seem that I'm being overly tough on attorneys, experience has demonstrated that a focus on any one silo of responsibility at the expense of others can cause serious harm to an enterprise. Often, attorneys seize an over-abundance of influence over naïve and inexperienced executives during times of crisis. Whether it is too much focus on media response, shareholder value, or legal liabilities, crisis management should not be managed in dispro-portionately influential silos. It should be a balanced and integrated response for maximum effectiveness and accelerated recovery. The best antidote for dispro-portionate crisis response is a multidisciplinary leadership team that is prepared and recognizes that crisis management should focus on all core assets of the organization, even when there may be competing concerns and priorities.

> ▶ **Employee access.** In the case of disasters and traumatic incidents, some employees will shy away from the site, while others will want – and may even need – to return to the scene to help them mentally grasp the incident. If employees will be allowed back in soon, the environment should be clean and safe, but not necessarily overly sanitized. A company that had experienced a workplace shooting in Miami knew that some employees were interested in seeing the incident site. But when I arrived prior to employees' return to work, I saw a picture hung on the wall about eight feet high, up in a corner in order to cover a bullet hole from the previous day's shooting. I recommended it be taken down so employees who wanted to see the scene could get a "feel" for what had happened. Furniture remained overturned during the first day back. Only the blood-soaked carpet and wallpaper were ripped out.

You will have other decisions to make about the workspace, desk, or office of each deceased worker. One possibility is to remove any sensitive business materials and files. Leave personal items, like pictures of the family. Then announce that any employee can informally visit the deceased person's workspace to say last goodbyes. This typically remains in place until the funeral.

In any case, the employee reentry to work process should be carefully orches-trated. Employees and other involved stakeholders will need transparent communications, a show of caring, and signs of reestablished order.

Anticipate reactions of persons who will reenter the workplace after a disruption. Consider it from their perspective. What will be their concerns and emotional reactions? For example, if there is a large layoff, those who survive the cut may feel guilty that others lost their jobs and they did not. Anticipated stress of having to do more with less and the insecurity of not knowing if more layoffs are coming may be issues. How will this affect productivity, morale, and loyalty to the organization? Communications and actions of management should preemptively address these anticipated concerns.

If a traumatic situation occurred at the workplace, especially if there was loss of life, we can anticipate that the facility may be anxiety provoking and seem eerily strange when employees or customers reenter. This was an issue for the Century movie theatre in Aurora, Colorado where James Holmes opened fire in July 2012 with multiple firearms at a midnight movie, killing 12 and injuring 58 people. After closure of several months, the theatre had to anticipate the reactions of customers and employees when the theatre first reopened. The public outcry by some was to tear down the entire building. Instead, Century decided to completely redecorate and redesign the theatre to give it a new feel and appearance. But, that still may not have been enough. So, they decided to provide free tickets for movie-goers in order to facilitate the reentry process.

▶ **Management outreach.** Clarify what support the company will and will not offer. Will the company fly in relatives of dead or seriously injured employees? The balancing act with families is to accommodate, while determining what is reasonable. One commercial airline decided to do the right thing and provide hotel expenses for families of hospitalized passengers following a crash. Unfortunately, they received a bill for a Rolex watch that a relative of a hospitalized passenger charged to his hotel room. In this instance, the airline decided to pay the bill and be taken advantage of, rather than fight the issue. Although there may be some abuses, it is best to be forthcoming regarding reasonable (and sometimes unreasonable) requests. This is not a time to be penny wise and pound foolish.

> **Assign a team to monitor social media. This function could be outsourced to a public relations firm if internal resources are not available.**

▶ **Outgoing messages.** The messages you wish to convey (internally and externally) should be thoughtfully crafted – and recrafted as needed – by your PR/communications department, the crisis team, and other company leaders, as appropriate. At a minimum, you should agree on the main messages to each stakeholder group that you want to get out through your communicators. Realize that the needs of stakeholders could be conflicting. For example, employees may not want to return to work immediately, while shareholders demand rapid recovery and continuity of operations.

If the media is involved, determine the deadlines reporters must meet, in order to get timely coverage of your side of the story. Stay in the driver's seat by regularly updating reporters, giving the media meaningful information, and monitoring coverage.

Assign a team to monitor social media. This function could be outsourced to a PR firm if internal resources are not available or sufficiently experienced. Responses should be provided on a timely basis. This should involve clear policies about who has authority to approve outgoing messages or quickly respond, when appropriate. The protocol should also include what social media information is communicated to management and how it will be compiled. (Media relations are discussed in more detail in Chapter 5 of this book.)

If you bring on outside PR assistance, choose carefully. The profession has many subspecialties. Expertise at investor relations does not necessarily translate to the area of crisis management. You want someone who knows your industry, your media market, and how to lead your communications efforts through chaotic times. Your PR professional should lend valuable counsel about matching and integrating your messages to the various target audiences.

▶ **Role of labor organizations.** The quality of your relationship with labor before the crisis will likely define the quality of your post-event interaction. Many companies have found that union stewards and other leaders can contribute significantly to crisis management, serving as team members, family representatives, and in other ways appropriate to your organizational culture. They can also be quick to attack. Keep the needs and concerns of union leadership in mind during crisis response.

> Good crisis management is about anticipating the upcoming sequence of events and preparing ahead of time to address those eventualities. Waiting until something happens and rushing to respond keeps an organization "behind the curve"...

▶ **Controlling blame and outrage.** A forthright approach to communicating about your crisis can help defuse outrage. Usually, outrage emanates from rumors or beliefs that the cause for the incident was intentional, foreseeable, avoidable, or unjust. Possibilities for addressing outrage include giving accurate information about the incident, educating the public about the hazard, taking appropriate responsibility for the occurrence and response, showing heartfelt caring and compassion, and taking resolute actions to help ensure it will never happen again.

▶ **Mitigating further escalation.** Every action causes a reaction. It is important to consider the chain of events that could play out in the aftermath of your crisis. Play the "if...then" and "what if..." games to anticipate what could happen in the foreseeable future. Only when you accurately anticipate the various repercussions of your situation can you adequately prepare for, rather than react to, potential escalations. Take intermittent time outs to ponder where this situation may be headed. Think also about the long-term consequences of the actions you are taking today. Good crisis management is about anticipating the upcoming sequence of events and preparing ahead of time to address those eventualities. Waiting until something happens and rushing to respond keeps an organization "behind the curve" and allows external developments to control the response. Instead, adroit management can contain the immediate issues and anticipate what likely will need to be addressed in the future to mitigate further escalation.

▶ **Time off policy.** It may appear counterintuitive, but it's often better for workers to get back to work soon after traumatic incidents. Balanced approaches of remaining productive and pampering oneself will usually accelerate personal and corporate recovery. Management should understand employees will initially not be 100% productive for awhile. Acknowledge this and show compassion as you evolve back into full productivity over time. Supervisors should be instructed from the top of the organization to be flexible and reasonably accommodating with their stressed, post-incident employees. Employees with reactions of concern should be referred to the employee assistance program (EAP) or other resource for appropriate support. Ultimately, being sensitive to employee needs during the return-to-work process will increase short- and long-term productivity.

▶ **Funeral/memorial service attendance policy.** Will employees be given time off to attend funeral services of coworkers killed on the job? Will it be paid or unpaid leave? Is there a need for a company sponsored memorial service? This may be especially important if a deceased coworker's funeral is in a distant state. Consider providing a bus for transportation of employees and family members from the worksite to local funerals. This helps with maintaining cohesion of the group, provides an opportunity for natural support of each other, and offers them the convenience of not having to find their own ways to the location.

▶ **Shrines and memorials.** Beware of employees' and families' desires to establish shrines and memorials on your property. These can transform your lobby into something resembling a cemetery over time. Families of employees killed in the past or in the future will also want the same commemorative accommodation once the precedent is established. Many companies are willing to place a memorial wreath of flowers in the lobby until the time of the funeral. I also like the idea of planting a tree on company grounds with a small plaque "in memory of" on or near the tree trunk. It is important to assure the tree doesn't die in the foreseeable future once planted.

▶ **Investigation.** As a part of your response actions, a team of individuals should be assigned the task of investigating the incident. Make sure incident sites are quickly secured in the most undisturbed manner possible if a crime is suspected or a causal investigation is to be conducted. Do not investigate with employees or provide operational debriefings before law enforcement has had an opportunity to get sworn statements from witnesses, especially if a crime is suspected. Consider working with legal counsel to orchestrate how investigations can be conducted best while protecting legal liability concerns.

Review of Day One Checklist

This list is by no means comprehensive. It is provided as a beginning list of issues that your team may need to address beyond the initial emergency response.

▶ Protection from ongoing harm to people.

▶ Contain the crisis from further escalation.

▶ Incoming and outgoing communications.

▶ Immediate family notification of victims after verification.

▶ Family assistance representatives assigned to support families.

▶ Management outreach to victims and impacted stakeholders.

▶ Investigation plan.

▶ Incident site cleanup and repairs.

▶ Controlling blame and outrage.

▶ Rumor control.

▶ Media messages.

▶ Security access controls.

▶ Phone log. (Who called, for whom, when, and for what reason? Was contact made among appropriate parties and is there any follow-up needed?)

> ▶ Arrange for crisis mental health specialists to meet with traumatized people.

> ▶ Enlist professional external crisis management consultation.

> ▶ Secure, clean up, and repair the site of the incident.

> ▶ Work continuation, and re-entry/return-to-work issues. Plan first day back to work.

> ▶ Policy for employees taking time off.

> ▶ Funeral/memorial service attendance policy.

> ▶ Financial considerations.

> ▶ Legal concerns.

> ▶ Role of union/labor.

> ▶ Shrines and memorials.

> ▶ Perform other day one action items as you deem appropriate.

4.10 Ten Questions to Assess Your Decisions and Actions

Many of my client companies have found useful a ten-question checklist that helps them gauge the appropriateness of crisis decisions and actions. Consider these – and feel free to alter them to suit your organization. You may wish to keep these questions posted in the CCC. For every crisis response action, ask:

1. Does it protect core assets of the company, e.g., the wellbeing of those affected, reputation, shareholder value, etc?

2. Will it accelerate the recovery process?

3. Does it consider broad, long-term implications?

4. Have contingencies been carefully appraised, and are reasonable contingency plans in place?

5. Have alternative courses of action been considered?

6. Are concerns of all involved stakeholders adequately covered?

7. Are our decisions and actions based on substantiated facts, or informed judgment in time sensitive circumstances?

8. Are our decisions and actions based on sound business practice?

9. Are adequate monitoring and quality assurance measures in place to ensure our response is working?

10. Would we feel comfortable defending this decision or action if it ended up on the front page of the newspaper?

Quick Use Response Guide

Chapter 4: Order Out of Chaos

Identify the crisis beyond the obvious:

▶ Identify the crisis beyond the obvious. Start by looking at the core assets of the organization that may be at risk, e.g.,

- ❑ People.
- ❑ Key relationships.
- ❑ Reputation.
- ❑ Brand.
- ❑ Trust.
- ❑ Finances.

- ❑ Shareholder value.
- ❑ Business operations.
- ❑ Intellectual property.
- ❑ Physical property.
- ❑ Product/service delivery capabilities.
- ❑ Other.

▶ Be prepared for crisis decision-making that will require timely decisions, appropriately balancing analysis (fact finding and situational awareness) and intuitive (gut level) response.

▶ Have you provided for the administering of psychological first aid that includes the tasks listed below?

- ❑ Accounting for everyone and assessing immediate needs.
- ❑ Establishing calm and order, and minimizing confusion.
- ❑ Protecting employees and others from exposure to traumatic sights and experiences.
- ❑ Making contact with victims, witnesses, and others experiencing traumatic stress reactions and listening or providing assistance for their concerns.
- ❑ Helping to meet needs during the early aftermath (from contacting loved ones or finding lost keys, to physical comforting and providing transportation home).
- ❑ Giving those affected good and timely information about what has happened.
- ❑ Organizing a "buddy system" for support in coping during the early aftermath.

▶ Have you planned for employee de-escalation meetings in the immediate aftermath that will accomplish the goals listed below?

- ❑ Stabilize those traumatized or highly concerned.

❑ Establish accurate information.

❑ Encourage employees not to talk to the media.

❑ Inform people about plans for tomorrow and the near future.

▶ Have you referred to the considerations for achieving order listed in this chapter?

▶ Have you addressed the common failure points of crisis response?

❑ Authority levels defined and assigned.

❑ Communications to and from impacted stakeholders.

❑ Expectations known between internal silos and externally for each foreseeable risk and contingency.

"Day One" Guidelines and Considerations

This list is by no means comprehensive. It is provided as a beginning list of issues that your team may need to address beyond the initial emergency response.

▶ Protection from ongoing harm to people.

▶ Contain the crisis from further escalation.

▶ Incoming and outgoing communications.

▶ Immediate family notification of victims after verification.

▶ Family assistance representatives assigned to support families.

▶ Management outreach to victims and impacted stakeholders.

▶ Incident site cleanup and repairs.

▶ Controlling blame and outrage.

▶ Rumor control.

▶ Media messages.

▶ Security access controls.

▶ Phone log. (Who called, for whom, when, and for what reason? Was contact made among appropriate parties and is there any follow-up needed?)

▶ Arrange for crisis mental health specialists to meet with traumatized people.

▶ Enlist professional external crisis management consultation.

▶ Secure, clean up, and repair the site of the incident.

▶ Work continuation, and re-entry/return-to-work issues. Plan first day back to work.

▶ Policy for employees taking time off.

▶ Financial considerations.

▶ Legal concerns.

▶ Investigation plan.

▶ Role of union/labor.

▶ Funeral/memorial service attendance policy.

▶ Shrines and memorials.

▶ Perform other day one action items as you deem appropriate.

Considerations that will help in the planning process for establishing purposeful expectations during crisis response:

▶ Who will assume which responsibilities?

▶ What are the expectations, needs, and concerns of the various stakeholders?

▶ List foreseeable risks and staff expectations for each.

▶ Interviews with involved staff members should be compiled on relational database software for flexibility with changes over time, and include:

❑ Information and directives each staff position wants from others.

❑ Information and directives each staff position will give to others.

Has your team considered these ten questions to assess your decisions and actions?

1. Does it protect core assets of the company, e.g., the wellbeing of those affected, reputation, and shareholder value?

2. Will it accelerate the recovery process?

3. Does it consider broad, long-term implications?

4. Have contingencies been carefully appraised, and are reasonable contingency plans in place?

5. Have alternative courses of action been considered?

6. Are concerns of all involved stakeholders adequately covered?

7. Are our decisions and actions based on substantiated facts, or informed judgment in time sensitive circumstances?

8. Are our decisions and actions based on sound business practice?

9. Are adequate monitoring and quality assurance measures in place to ensure our response is working?

10. Would we feel comfortable defending this decision or action if it ended up on the front page of the newspaper?

Chapter 4 – Questions for Further Thought and Discussion

1. Why is it important to identify the crisis beyond the obvious and how can that be achieved best in the midst of crisis chaos?

2. What do you feel is the right balance of analysis and intuitive response for you personally when making high-consequence crisis decisions? How can a crisis manager overcome natural tendencies toward one extreme (of over-analysis or impulsive decision-making)?

3. What are examples of crises from your personal experience (or are publicly known) where one of more of the common crisis management problems (with authority, communications, or expectations) caused a crisis malfunction? How can each of these problems be adequately addressed during the preparedness process?

4. If you had an onsite traumatic incident, like an explosion with injuries, what would you say, in the short de-escalation meeting, to traumatized employees before sending them home?

5. In addition to the ten questions to assess your decisions and actions, what other issues do you feel should be considered to ensure quality crisis response?

References

Anderson, S. L. (n.d.). *The 40 – 70 rule*. Retrieved from:
http://integratedleader.com/articles/40-70rule.pdf

Bechara, A., Damasio, H., Tranel, D. & Damasio, A.R. (2005, April). The Iowa gambling
task and the somatic marker hypothesis: some questions & answers. *Trends in Cognitive
Sciences*, 9 (4). Retrieved from:
http://citeseerx.ist.psu.edu/viewdoc/download?doi=10.1.1.137.6124&rep=rep1&type=pdf

Gigerenzer, G. (2007). *Gut feelings: the intelligence of the unconscious*. New York: Penguin
Group, p. 237.

Katsikopoubs, K. V. (2010, July). The less-is-more effect: predictions & tests. *Judgment &
Decision Making*, 5 (4), pp. 244-257.

Kelbick, D. (2013). *How to improve free throw shooting*. Retrieved from:
http://breakthroughbasketball.com/

5

Crisis Communications

From your experience in the business world, you surely know the crucial importance of effective communication. No doubt you have worked hard to develop your communication skills – learning to express yourself with precision and economy and to listen well.

During a crisis, you will need to rely on all those same skills. But just as a moment of disaster is different from any routine time, crisis communications are far different from normal, day-to-day communications. In a crisis, everything is more emotionally charged, and moving at top velocity. You and your actions are unusually – perhaps uncomfortably – visible. Everything is said and heard within the context of rumors, potential misunderstandings, and high scrutiny.

This chapter will help you to:

> ➤ *Set ground rules for internal and external communication.*
> ➤ *Control and monitor relations with the media.*
> ➤ *Create an integrated notification plan.*
> ➤ *Give and get critical information.*
> ➤ *Establish a humanitarian response team (HRT).*
> ➤ *Make death or serious injury notifications to family members.*

5.1 Setting the Ground Rules for Effective Crisis Communications

Crisis communications are more than just speaking clearly, on a timely basis, to the right audience. Crisis communications should be a system that follows pre-established guidelines.

As the situation unfolds, a crisis is filled with incorrect information and rumors, especially in the early aftermath. People are desperate to know what is going on and will do whatever they can to get that information. Meanwhile, it is extremely important that the crisis team work to compile incoming information, verify facts, and determine what to do with that information. Incoming and outgoing communications must be managed adeptly.

> ...responses to the many forms of public communication should be constructed through a multidisciplinary team with expertise and authority to respond on behalf of the organization.

Communication containment: In the event of suspected criminal activity or regulatory investigations, early communications from the company can have a conflicting effect on these activities. So, it is important that the incoming fact pattern is contained, coordinated, and well managed by the crisis team.

Managing crisis communications includes a gatekeeper function to receive, compile, and verify incoming information into one central location, as appropriate and possible. As many channels of communication should be monitored as possible, with confidential information closely guarded. With the wide proliferation of social media, corporate attorneys may quickly require employees not to engage in e-mails, social networking, and other forms of communication regarding the incident. This is easier said than done in the midst of a fluid situation where everyone wants detailed information. It is important for the company to monitor social media, e-mails, and other communications about the situation. As appropriate, responses to the many forms of public communication should be constructed through a multidisciplinary team with expertise and authority to respond on behalf of the organization. In this manner, information can be obtained and verified, rumors addressed, and outgoing messaging contained.

Case Study: A Case of Uncontained Communications

It was a holiday. Most miners were enjoying the New Year with a day off on Monday, January 2, 2006. It's not unheard of, but uncommon, that a winter lightning storm on this day would descend upon West Virginia. As an early morning lightning bolt hit the ground above the Sago Mine, 13 miners were preparing for a long shift, two miles below ground. The wet earth served as a conduit and the lightning traveled down to a sealed off area of the mine that was filled with explosive methane.

The blast immediately killed one miner who was in the main shaft. His body was recovered quickly during the early rescue attempts, while 12 others were in the far left section of the mine and not directly hit. However, they were trapped with debris and toxic air between them and the exit, which was approximately one mile away. They built a curtain to seal off the toxic air and pulled out their oxygen masks that would last for a short while.

Unfortunately, the Mine Safety and Health Administration (MSHA) officials prohibited further search and rescue efforts due to toxic air and fear of a secondary explosion. For 42 long hours, the crisis team set up their command center in the superintendent's office above ground, waiting for an opportunity to begin the rescue efforts. State officials, international media, law enforcement, rescue teams, the governor, corporate management, and others descended upon the command center. Some had roles to play; others were just interested. Speaker phones were connected to the landline near the mine entrance, just in case the trapped miners made it to the entrance of the mine.

As the many long hours passed, the families, who were gathered at the nearby Sago Baptist Church, became increasingly pessimistic that their loved ones could be alive. It would take a real miracle for them to survive for so long in these toxic conditions. One executive from corporate assigned himself as the lone spokesperson between the command center and the families. Families were not to trust any messages except from this one executive. Intermittent updates were provided as they all waited.

Finally, after 42 hours of waiting, MSHA cleared the rescue team to enter the mine. One person was stationed near the entrance of the mine at the landline phone with the responsibility of receiving walkie-talkie communications from the rescuers who would trek approximately one mile straight back into the mine, take a left turn, and then move into the far left shaft. There was water and debris throughout. The rescuers were wearing oxygen masks since the air was still barely breathable.

As the rescuers passed the curtain that had been established by the trapped miners, they found an ominous sight. All the miners were evenly spaced throughout the cavernous room, lying down. As they checked each miner, they found one after another dead, most with notes written to loved ones. But, furthest away from the curtain there was a miracle.

Randal McCloy was barely breathing, but he was alive. Immediately, they started giving him oxygen and sent a walkie-talkie request for medical backup with one person alive. After two relayed walkie-talkie messages through gas masks, the person at the mine entrance got the garbled message that all 12 were alive and needed medical assistance immediately.

As the unconfirmed message was relayed to the command center, exhausted managers who had worked 42 hours non-stop were waiting along with various other people. The communications came over all the speaker phones simultaneously. All 12 miners were miraculously alive! Immediately, people in and near the command center called the church to notify families. Church bells began to ring. The news traveled worldwide through the media. People everywhere couldn't have been more excited that, against all odds, all 12 miners had survived.

Within minutes, back at the command center, the errant message was clarified. In fact, only one person had survived and at that time no one knew the identity of the lone survivor. The exhausted management team was frozen. What to do? There was fear of confronting families with the horrible miscommunications that their trapped loved ones, whom they had presumed dead, were found alive. Now the families had to be told that these workers were actually not alive at all – except for one. The management team decided to delay further communications to families until management could confirm the accurate information (for sure this time). Meanwhile, families continued to celebrate.

Ultimately, management reportedly asked a state trooper to relay the unfortunate news to the families, instructing him to tell the clergy at the church and let them handle it from there. Meanwhile, management stayed back at the mine. Unfortunately, in the commotion, the message was not delivered by the state trooper. Families remained jubilant for hours, waiting for the loved ones to meet them at the church after exiting the mine. Finally, in the early hours of the morning, Sago management (heavily accompanied by law enforcement) went to the church to give the families the belated news that the report of their loved ones being alive was, in fact, wrong – except for one miner, yet to be identified, who was rushed to the hospital. As expected, the disbelief and outrage were enormous. Management left the hostile scene quickly under protection of law enforcement.

Lessons-learned: Many lessons can be learned from this crisis communications debacle.

▶ First, Sago had a crisis plan that had been hanging untouched on a bulletin board for years. A mining company with obvious foreseeable risks of explosions and trapped miners, Sago had not taken the time to prepare. Let's call this one **negligent planning and preparedness**. From here, bad things will invariably happen.

> ▶ Through their lack of preparedness, the **command center structure was established on an impromptu basis.**
>
> ▶ **Untrained crisis teams were not staged in shifts** to provide relief to exhausted managers in the command center who had worked 42 straight hours.
>
> ▶ **No security had been established** to keep extraneous people out of the command center. Communications were not contained to prevent eavesdroppers from listening in, even at the point when managers realized that media representatives were intercepting their messaging.
>
> ▶ **Reports from within the mine were not verified** before being leaked to the families and media. Once the error was discovered, the one "trusted" spokesperson for the families decided that he would no longer communicate. Allegedly, a state trooper had been assigned the communication role, but no follow-up was conducted to ensure that accurate information reached the families. Finally, even when new information was known and verified, management delayed telling families.
>
> This disaster offers a tragic lesson in making sure communications are contained and properly managed during crisis response.

Crisis messaging: It's hard enough to get people to understand communications during normal times. Add the ingredients of distress, fast-paced events, and chaos of a crisis situation and communications become even more difficult.

Research has been conducted by Dr. Vincent Covello, Columbia University Center for Risk Communications (n.d.) to determine how best to communicate during high concern situations. It is well established that people in high concern situations tend not to hear, understand, or retain incoming communications. Anyone who has received unexpected, distressing news like "You're fired," knows that anything said thereafter is a blur. So, how can one best communicate with important stakeholders during crises so they will hear, understand, and retain?

By means of empirical evidence, Dr. Covello established that crisis messaging can contain only three primary points in order for people to understand and retain information. People quickly lose retention if a fourth point, or more, is provided. This is not unexpected. While we have learned for years to provide three key messages when addressing the media and other important audiences, now empirical evidence backs up that method. But, effective communications during times of high concern involves more than simply limiting the number of messages.

Dr. Covello's research results identified a maximum number of words that could be used for each of the three messages. This is where most communicators make mistakes. People will best understand and retain messages that contain no more than 12 words. Provide additional verbosity and you will lose your audience. Limiting messages in this way is extremely hard to do without adequate preparation. It is my experience that the best way to keep verbiage down to 12 words or less is to write down each one before delivery to chosen audiences. Once succinctly established, repeat your three messages as needed to convey the information you want to impart.

> **People in chaotic situations often misunderstand verbal directives...it is imperative that they have no questions about what has been assigned and what is expected as an outcome.**

The late Johnny Cochran employed clear, succinct, and dramatic messaging as defense attorney during the 2005 murder trial of former NFL football star, O.J. Simpson. The prosecution had an incriminating glove that had been found at O.J. Simpson's estate by Detective Mark Fuhrman. O.J. Simpson tried on the glove in the courtroom to see if it fit – it turned out to be small for his hand. Johnny Cochran then established his seven-word messaging that arguably won the case for the defense, "If it doesn't fit, you must acquit."

Bottom line is this: Make your crisis messaging clear, short, and to the point. This brevity will significantly increase the likelihood that audiences will hear, understand, and retain during high concern situations.

5.1.1 Delegating During a Crisis Response

Delegating tasks during a crisis is a critical juncture during which your response can become derailed. People in chaotic situations often misunderstand verbal directives. Also, those who are delegated tasks may not agree with the assignment. That the crisis team or crisis leadership makes a decision doesn't ensure that others will agree and carry out their assignments effectively. For these reasons, it is imperative that they have no questions about what has been assigned and what is expected as an outcome.

> ▶ Employ the communications technique of the military and the airline industry: Repeat back what you hear. If someone repeats information incorrectly, it will be recognized immediately, and the dangers of inaccuracy and misunderstandings avoided.

▶ You face the chance that persons who are to carry out delegated tasks lack trust in your intentions or motives, may have misunderstandings as to why certain actions are needed, or may not agree with your decisions. These cases increase the likelihood that delegated tasks will not be executed in an effective manner. To address these smoldering issues preemptively, consider developing the habit of quickly conveying during the delegation process "why" tasks are needed and important. If your explanation passes the reasonable person test and the listeners understand the importance of the delegated task, individuals and teams will be much more effective in carrying out the tasks at hand with excellence. You may think that you don't have time, but the small investment of time is insignificant compared to important tasks not being executed effectively on a timely basis.

▶ Orient all communications toward action. Effective crisis response is not passive. It is what you *do* that is most important. Actions need to be well thought out, but all communications and discussions should be focused. Ask, "What do we do with this information?" When information comes to you that does not call for action, move on. Let the pontificators sound off on their own time. Crisis teams don't have that luxury.

▶ Ask for any questions or concerns as a final step in the delegation process.

5.1.2 Giving Information Out: Keeping Control of the Message

Staying in control of your outgoing message means being clear about both how it is delivered and what it contains.

> All outgoing public communications should be funneled through a gatekeeper for accuracy and consistency, as well as conformity to your response strategy, before being released.

Who should do the talking? While others may provide information, depending on the intended audiences, it is best to have a primary spokesperson. Decide who will be your spokesperson(s), brief them on the agreed upon messages and prepare them for each appearance they will make. The intended audience will determine who should address them and what will be told. Spokespersons can be individuals from the communications or legal departments, senior management, site management, those with applicable technical knowledge, outside specialists and experts, or others. Beware of divergent or contradictory statements being made from within your organization. Also, pay attention to the implicit message your chosen communicator may convey. For example, having an attorney as the spokesperson may suggest to audiences that protecting legal liability is more important than responding to harmed stakeholders in a caring manner.

All outgoing public communications should be funneled through a gatekeeper for accuracy and consistency, as well as conformity to your response strategy, before being released. If your organization is international, you may require special coordination of the timing and information that reaches the investment communities in affected countries. In general, it is usually best to minimize the number of communicators and strive to provide "one voice" for message consistency.

To whom are you speaking? Identify each audience that needs communication from you. Establish and maintain a schedule for both initial and ongoing communications to each of them. The possible audiences include the following:

- Employees, including staff management.
- Employees' families.
- Senior management.
- Board of directors.
- Business partners.
- Investment community.
- Insurance representatives.
- Suppliers, distributors, and franchisees.
- Customers and other key relationships.
- Government and law enforcement officials.
- Industry activist groups.
- Media representatives.
- Unions.
- Affected community members.
- Retained technical experts.

And don't neglect your own family, who will want to know how you are.

How should the parameters of the crisis be defined? It is up to you to identify the breadth, severity, and expected longevity of what has happened. Doing so quickly and decisively can go a long way toward preventing counterproductive speculation and sensationalism. Quarantine what is affected from what is not affected. This is called "isolating the crisis."

For example, if you determine that fire has destroyed your northwestern distribution center, you will be able to make that statement while adding, "All our other distribution centers are fully functional and will pick up the slack for timely deliveries to our customers by executing our existing business continuity plan."

> **Remember to provide only three key messages, each of 12 words or less, in order to communicate clearly in a manner people will understand and retain.**

What needs to be communicated immediately? Most likely, you will make an initial statement, or series of them, even before solutions to the problem have been set in motion. Usually these statements report what is known and verified, and make clear that further investigations are underway and responses set to go. As a general rule, come up with solutions to realistic and perceived problems and communicate those solutions to affected audiences as soon as possible. Remember to provide only three key messages, each of 12 words or less, in order to communicate clearly in a manner people will understand and retain.

What are the main things to say? Determine your main messages for both external and internal audiences and then prepare consistent answers to the questions you can anticipate from each group.

If people have been traumatized physically or emotionally, always begin your statements with a heartfelt concern for the wellbeing of everyone impacted. This also applies if they feel harmed in any manner or are afraid they may have been harmed. In this, be careful not to leave out any affected groups, even those indirectly affected, such as distressed but uninjured employees, families of casualties, or members of your local community who may have felt threatened.

Sometimes managers are reluctant to say "I'm sorry" or express regret for damage or injuries that have occurred, fearing that to do so might encourage people to consider the company liable. But it is certainly possible to express contrition and regret without taking blame or responsibility inappropriately. Indeed, expressions of contrition might have the ultimate outcome of diminishing your exposure to lawsuits by defusing the sense of outrage that helps to generate them.

In your communications, strive to isolate the crisis to the smallest scope that can contain it, to keep it from escalating into or being perceived as a company-wide issue. If you don't know the answer to "why the incident happened," inform concerned audiences that investigations are underway. However, crisis containment might need to be much bigger in scope than the specific bull's eye of the incident. Remember Johnson & Johnson recalled Tylenol nationwide, even though the deaths from tainted pills were only in Chicago. Conversely, Charles Steger of Virginia Tech tried to contain an initial murder of two by not notifying all students and exposed an additional 31 people to the mass murderer approximately two hours later. So, first do the right things. "Spinning" communications will almost never overcome poor crisis decision-making.

Typically, it's best not to admit negligence or liability. Make no promises concerning financial compensation or repair of damages unless fully agreed upon as a solution by your management team. When appropriate, put the situation into perspective by noting, for example, the outstanding safety record of your company or its leadership in community affairs; the one-in-a-million chance that this incident could happen; how it is isolated to only a small portion of the company; or how the company itself may have been victimized. In 2005 for example, Anna Ayala publicly reported (ultimately falsely) that she "chomped" down on a human finger in chili at a Wendy's restaurant. Among other messaging, the communications from the company needed to remind the public that the restaurant chain sells thousands of delicious bowls of chili to satisfied customers every day. Strive to "paint word pictures" in the minds of audience members that convey your desired messages and replace unwanted mental images.

> **Any evidence, or even hint, that you are being dishonest or withholding important information can be expected to elicit immediate and uncomfortable scrutiny from them all.**

5.1.3 Honesty – the Best Policy – Does Not Mean Saying Everything

Dishonesty can cause a crisis to escalate faster than any other single mistake. When you or your organization are in the crisis spotlight, the media, attorneys, government officials, and the public are naturally looking for scandal, negligence, and scapegoats. Any evidence, or even hint, that you are being dishonest or withholding important information can be expected to elicit immediate and uncomfortable scrutiny from them all.

However, you don't have to say everything you know in your outgoing communications. Sometimes you may have information that you, quite appropriately, choose not to divulge publicly. It is rarely a good idea, for example, in the immediate aftermath of the crisis to discuss issues of responsibility and cause. You will rarely know the entire story yourself at this point, and you will have plenty of time once things settle down for investigations both by yourselves and by any interested outside parties. You also want to avoid any statement that could be construed as the basis of a liability action.

However, beware of giving an appearance of deception by omission, if it should be learned that you are holding back important information. Discuss both the pros and cons of how much to tell. Consider, for example, what impact there could be if the information is disclosed willingly by you – or, alternatively, is uncovered by a reporter.

5.1.4 Communication Is a Human Art

In this book, I emphasize the too often ignored human impacts of crisis. At a time of crisis, your employees and other key relationships of your company can be allies – or your enemies. They have inside information. And what they hear from you, and how they hear it, can make a difference. Make sure the people in and close to your organization are given accurate and timely information. Outrage has been the observed result time and again on crises I've handled when employees obtained information from sources outside the company, instead of from management.

Your employees spend one third of each workday with you. The company provides their livelihoods and a considerable part of their sense of self-identification. They will identify closely with any crisis that hits the company, and feel affected, whether they are injured or not. Unfortunately, the unenlightened company pays attention only to external constituencies at a time of crisis, addressing only the immediate needs of those who might be injured. However, wise management takes a more holistic view, supporting – and in turn being supported by – its workforce and other key stakeholders.

5.2 Media Relations During a Crisis

If your crisis gets their attention, the media will put out a story, whether you participate or not. While you do not have control over reporters and editors, you can manage the information you give them, and have a great deal of influence on how you are presented.

When a crisis starts. At the most rudimentary level, use prepared holding statements if the media contacts you before you are prepared to provide incident specific statements. Holding statements can be prepared ahead of time and preapproved by management for use in the early aftermath of any crisis. This will buy time until you can organize your response and draft messages specific to the event. Convey who within the organization has authority to provide these holding statements and to which audiences.

As information comes in, all involved persons should know the exact process for developing statements to various audiences, the authorization process, and who is to serve as spokesperson(s).

Advertising concerns. Consider whether you want to stop paid advertising for the time being. Could yesterday's ads be putting out a message that, in light of today's crisis, is suddenly inappropriate?

Tune in. Stay abreast of the evolving stories about your incident in the news and social media by monitoring broadcasts, websites, blogs, Twitter, and other forms of mass communications. This can be a big job, and you might delegate outsiders to handle it, freeing your team for other necessary tasks. Keep your management team informed about the coverage on a timely basis. Invariably, the media will publish misinformation.

> **Develop your message. Anticipate reporters' questions so that you will be prepared with answers you can control.**

Remember that the media can serve as a source of information for you, too. Many times, reporters have provided vital, up-to-date information to the company during phone calls while they are in pursuit of additional information.

Timeliness is vitally important, but be cautious about what you say. Outgoing communications should be prepared in conjunction with legal counsel, your communications department, your management team, and law enforcement, as appropriate. Just as you do not want to say anything that could increase your liability or reputational damage, you do not want to jeopardize any possible criminal investigations.

Develop your message. Anticipate reporters' questions so that you will be prepared with answers you can control. Prior to press conferences, it is to your advantage to ask what they will want to know. Here are some typical questions you can expect to be asked.

- ▶ What happened? How bad is it? What is the extent of property damage or injuries? What is the intensity and scope? Is there continuing danger?

- ▶ Why did it happen? How did it happen? Who is responsible? Do you feel responsible? Has this happened before? Are there any signs of impropriety?

- ▶ Were there warning signs? What did the company know prior to the incident and when? What did the company do to prevent this from happening?

- What is the company doing in response? How soon will the situation be under control?

- What is being done to keep it from happening again? How are you preparing to respond to future incidents? What are you doing for those who may have been harmed?

5.2.1 Before a Press Conference or Interview

In planning for a press conference or media interview, decide on the three key points you want to get across. Script and rehearse these messages. Even in an interview where your spokesperson may have to answer questions that are unexpected or that come in a surprising order, he or she should get those points into the response.

If people have been traumatized, begin by expressing compassion and genuine concern for all those affected. Say, "First, let me express on behalf of our entire organization, my heartfelt sorrow for...." Then keep your statements concise and factual. You don't want to appear wooden, but that does not mean you should let yourself speculate or be drawn. Be truthful, but don't overly elaborate. Everything conveyed should demonstrate that the company is a caring and concerned organization. Demonstrate through your statements that the company is responding with expertise and is committed to doing the "next right thing." Remember, you don't have to tell everything you know, but people want a transparent and candid response. If questioning starts to get out of hand, you can conclude the conference by announcing that you will take just one more question, reiterate your key points, and then leave.

5.2.2 Working With the Press Corps

My experience is that reporters can be an excellent source of information in the aftermath of crises. You will benefit if you establish good relations and two-way communication with them.

Respect the professional needs of media people like the deadlines they face. Inform them how often you will provide updated information and stick to that schedule. Assure them that you will let them know as soon as possible if significant news breaks – and then do so. Do your best to accommodate their requests and always treat them with respect. If the media is to be camped out at your location for the long haul, provide accommodations for the reporters, such as access to food, water, toilets, and shelter.

However, do not cede control of your message to them. Do not, for example, allow them to film your spokesperson with the company logo – or worse yet, your burning building – in the background. You hardly want this to be the main image people retain of the incident. Do not respond to media requests haphazardly or in an unprepared manner. When appropriate, take the initiative by organizing press conferences and providing press statements or social media updates.

5.2.3 Beyond the News Media

Keep in mind that monitoring and responding to the news media and social networks are not the only information conduits you can utilize to give and receive vital information. In many crisis situations, you can make valuable use of communication methods such as:

▶ Supervisor meetings with their employees.

▶ Town hall meetings (beware of group outrage if the company is the target of blame).

▶ Phone trees.

▶ Toll-free hotlines.

▶ Surveys and questionnaires.

▶ Paid advertising.

▶ Lessons-learned debriefings.

▶ Union meetings.

▶ Bulletin boards and other forms of electronic communications.

▶ Websites (consider dark sites with background information and other predeveloped messaging that would be activated only during times of crisis).

5.2.4 Protect Your People From Media Intrusions

When a crisis hits, inform all employees quickly regarding where calls from frantic family members, media, and others should be directed. Inform them that only appointed company spokespersons are authorized to speak to the media, regulators, and other authorities. Advise them as appropriate not to engage in social media communications, e-mails, or other forms of external messaging.

Remember that sometimes the media can serve as a resource in communicating with your employees, for example, by broadcasting announcements regarding the temporary closing of a facility.

Refer to Chapter 4 for an in-depth discussion of the reasons employees, other than designated spokespeople, should not talk to the media.

> **Remember to give communications to and from your various crisis teams the highest priority. They are the lifeblood of your effective crisis response.**

5.2.5 Ongoing and Long-term Communications

Sometimes a crisis extends over a considerable time. Here are some tips for managing media relations in such a situation:

▶ Utilize a single person to communicate with the media over the long haul.

▶ It is critical that this spokesperson be readily available to the media.

▶ Monitor the statements and reports of the media and take steps to correct any misinformation or misperceptions.

▶ Instruct all managers and other employees to remain courteous toward media people, but not to make unauthorized statements.

▶ While some reporters may be more favorable toward the company, be careful not to show obvious favoritism toward them. You certainly don't want to irritate any reporters through perceived favoritism.

Remember to give communications to and from your various crisis teams the highest priority. They are the lifeblood of your effective crisis response.

5.3 Notifying Others of the Situation

You will face the all-important task of informing others of the situation. You need to take your list of contact names and numbers (hopefully current) and transform it into a comprehensive checklist that will guide you through the process of notifying individuals and mobilizing those who will help your company through this crisis. At this point, you must mobilize the team and needed resources without needless delays, share essential information, and elicit additional knowledge from those who matter most.

5.3.1 Notification vs. Mobilization

Determine whether you are calling people simply to notify them or to mobilize them into action. If you don't have the authority to mobilize the team and needed resources, then your first contact will be with the person who does have that authority. Even if information is not verified or causes investigated, it's best to notify those in authority immediately so they can enlist organizational resources as early as appropriately possible.

For example, assume that you work for a global energy company at the home office. Over a thousand miles from the headquarters, one of your oil rig employees in Ecuador has gone missing. Coworkers reported that he did not show up for third shift with the others in his group and he can't be found in the compound.

Understanding the foreseeable risk of kidnapping that stems from the political environment in which these workers operate, you determined that your CEO should be notified. According to your notification policy, the call is made to his home, just after midnight. He is clearly concerned and appreciative to have been informed. He asks you to monitor the situation personally and confidentially over the next two hours before any further steps are taken.

No one is mobilized in this case due to the fact pattern. If the employee was known for going into the nearby town of Lago Agrio for extended periods and having a few beers, or if he had been missing before, the mobilization of the CMT and others may be delayed. If this is out of character for the employee, or if you have some evidence of foul play, then immediate mobilization of company resources would be indicated.

Other scenarios may be less clear cut and require you to make more subtle distinctions between notification and mobilization. The checklists I provide in this book will help you cut through the confusion of the moment; use them as tools to keep yourself focused and effective. You will find a fairly comprehensive list of possible notification contacts below.

5.3.2 Key Contacts

The list of potential key notification contacts includes the following:

- Crisis team leader and members.
- Other senior managers.
- Board of directors.
- Administrative staff, including:
  - ❑ Legal/compliance.
  - ❑ Security/assets protection.
  - ❑ PR/communications.
  - ❑ Human resources.
  - ❑ Employee/labor relations.

- ❏ Risk and insurance management.
- ❏ Facilities management.
- ❏ Finance.
- ❏ Benefits.
- ❏ Medical.
- ❏ Other.
- ❯ Employees and their families.
- ❯ Law enforcement.
- ❯ Customers.
- ❯ Distributors.
- ❯ Franchisees.
- ❯ Financial and stock analysts.
- ❯ Government regulators.
- ❯ Industry activist groups.
- ❯ Industry associations.
- ❯ Business partners.
- ❯ Media representatives and spokespersons.
- ❯ Union representatives.
- ❯ Suppliers.
- ❯ Consultants (crisis management professionals, legal, security, employee assistance program, crisis mental health specialists, technical specialists, medical spokespersons, PR, industry specialists).
- ❯ Insurance companies (according to various types of coverage that are involved).
- ❯ Third-party administrator.
- ❯ Insurance broker.
- ❯ Hospitals.
- ❯ Community contacts.
- ❯ Local and national elected officials.
- ❯ Embassies or consulates.
- ❯ Retained technical experts.

> Retained medical or public health professionals.

> Repair services.

> Cleanup crews.

> Your own family.

5.3.3 Beyond Phone Numbers

An essential component of a notification plan is the list of phone numbers and other contact methods. Agree on exactly how everyone on the "needs to know" list will be alerted. If your organization has an emergency notification system, then everyone on your list can be notified with one simultaneous contact. Know who should immediately be bridged into a conference call. Have backup people, with numbers, for each individual on the list. A manager who is assigned the task of "process guardian" or an outside vendor should keep your list of contacts always pristine and up to date.

For key individuals, such as members of senior management, the list should indicate how and when the person prefers to be notified, for example: first by cell phone; in the middle of the night, only in certain circumstances; or only when certain thresholds have been met.

For example, if you face a hurricane with multiple businesses and residences demolished, the immediate needs of your public relations person may not be as paramount as it would be if yours were the only company affected by a crisis. Ideally, you would have a notification list that included the core people to be informed, plus a specialty list according to the needs of each foreseeable incident.

Immediately, you may need to work internally to notify your emergency response team, crisis management team (CMT) senior management, various key staff positions, and possibly even the board of directors. Let's look at essential notification information for several of these.

> **Define to the best of your ability which situations would include automatic emergency response team involvement and scope, and which would require a judgment call by someone in authority.**

5.3.4 Emergency Response Team (ERT)

If your crisis involves life safety or ongoing threat to physical property, you will want to bring all the appropriate internal and external resources into your crisis response. However, many crises will clearly not elicit an emergency response. Product recall, financial impropriety allegations, demonstrations by activist groups, management or employee wrongdoing, whistleblower, and other situations nonthreatening to life or property will not involve the emergency response team. In some situations, such as a hostage standoff within your workplace, the emergency response team's presence might create unwanted consequences. Define to the best of your ability which situations would include automatic emergency response team involvement and scope, and which would require a judgment call by someone in authority.

5.3.5 Crisis Management Team (CMT)

If leadership notification is deemed appropriate, an immediate decision to make is whether to put your executive team on notice, or fully mobilize them. If the decision is to mobilize, this should be a relatively straightforward process. If CMT members are at their homes during off hours and are asked to physically meet together, contact those who live the furthest away before members who live nearby to give them extra time to reach the assembly point. You and they should be in agreement about their roles, their ability to work together, and their aptitude for taking action when confronted by critical incidents. With remote access becoming increasingly sophisticated, remote connectivity should be considered. However, realize that in situations of widespread power outage or electromagnetic pulse attack, remote connectivity will likely be more difficult. Limited resources like satellite phones may be an only source for CMT connectivity.

Depending on the size of your organization, you will have core crisis teams. But for every foreseeable risk, there will likely be auxiliary team members you can call in as needed.

Auxiliary team members might include a health care specialist, law enforcement officer, external attorney, crisis management professional, public relations, industrial hygienist, hazardous materials (hazmat) expert, structural engineer, or specialized investigators.

As you develop your notification plan, ask questions like, "If we have a chemical plume hanging overhead, what special expertise might we need?" The answer might be, for example, a specialty physician to make determinations about health risks to workers and members of the community. An expert on the chemical itself (perhaps from the Centers for Disease Control (CDC) or local health department) might be most appropriate or perhaps key individuals from the municipality with whom you will coordinate any evacuations, joint communications, or the like.

During the notification/mobilization process, your duty vis-à-vis these auxiliary experts is to apprise them of the situation, clearly delineate the information or action steps you expect of them, and come to an understanding about when and how these requirements will be carried out.

> **Waiting too long to notify top leaders about a crisis can dangerously delay the application of essential corporate resources to the problem.**

5.4 Notifying Throughout the Organization

As you make notifications, you may run into a fairly common scenario – a tendency for the individual charged with notifying senior management (possibly you) to delay notification of top brass in order to learn more about what's really happened and to investigate why the incident occurred. It's only natural that your CEO will have immediate questions, and you will want to be prepared to answer them. But sometimes you just can't. It is usually more important to notify early and answer, "I don't know," than to wait to cover all the bases before notification.

Waiting too long to notify top leaders about a crisis can dangerously delay the application of essential corporate resources to the problem.

5.4.1 Board of Directors

Although board members do not typically play an active role in the day-to-day operations of most companies, they do have fiduciary responsibility for the organization and its wellbeing. Notifying board members can help your organization manage the crisis and minimize exposure, depending on your board's areas of influence and expertise.

Most often, the CEO is the one who notifies the board. In any case, senior management should determine the threshold for contacting board members in the immediate aftermath of the crisis. The threshold for contacting the board of directors can be defined ahead of time, or when management feels that their input would be beneficial. In the event of significant financial, reputational, or business resumption threat to the company, the board probably will want to be notified sooner rather than later. Information that you provide about the crisis might be the catalyst for notification to the board of directors. Stay vigilant for core assets that may be at risk as the crisis unfolds and know whom to notify within your organizational culture.

What information might you need from board members? It depends, again, on the imminent risk and the type of crisis. Are there high-level contacts in the industry or in government who could help the company manage a response to a serious crisis situation? Board members are chosen for their many contacts, industry-related expertise, or other valuable experience they have. Their input and assistance could be invaluable.

5.4.2 Corporate Counsel

In nearly every imaginable scenario, your corporate counsel would figure high on the call list. Crises are high probability times for litigation. Containment of liability exposures will be essential as you move through the post-crisis period.

Depending on your culture, the lawyer may become the designated spokesperson. However, this can give the impression that the company is primarily interested in minimizing legal exposures. It is typically better to have a non-attorney spokesperson, one who is perceived as authoritative and well briefed about the legal boundaries in outgoing communications. Whether or not your attorney is your spokesperson, you may face an inherent conflict between legal and PR concerns. Attorneys are concerned about minimizing communications that could increase liability. PR personnel are communicators whose role is to get clear, transparent, and timely messages out to reduce misunderstandings and to tell the company's side of the story.

Another reason to notify your attorney early on is to safeguard evidence while establishing attorney-client privilege, when appropriate. Should a member of the legal staff be on hand to ensure that there were no improprieties or any kind of tampering? Coordinating early defense decisions with your insurer and appointed defense attorneys is yet another action that your legal staff may need to address. This is the time to find out what your attorney would want according to each foreseeable risk.

If the headquarters of your company is at a considerable distance from the site of the crisis or if outside legal expertise is needed, it may be of immediate importance to retain a local law firm to represent your interests there.

5.4.3 Corporate Security

Your security/assets protection manager may have a significant role to play in the immediate post crisis response. Determine in advance what this person will need to know. Anticipate questions such as, *"Is a crime suspected?"* and *"Is the perimeter of the facility secure?"* In turn, what do you need to know from him or her? Your immediate security actions can make a huge difference in your defensibility. If you allow evidence to be contaminated, there may be a lingering perception that you are culpable. Timely notification and coordination with your security department will help your organization take critical defensive action.

5.4.4 The Rest of the List

The list also includes other staff positions, customers, vendors, franchisees, trade groups, unions, financial analysts, silent partners, insurers, government agencies, remediation services, other external contacts, and even your own family. Don't underestimate the impact crisis response may have on you, as a crisis manager! It can be more exhausting, stressful, and demanding than you may have imagined if you overlook anybody on this list.

> **In a rapidly evolving situation, it is hard to ensure everyone has the latest information unless they are told at the same time.**

5.5 Delivering Initial Notification

Whomever you're addressing – whether it's the CEO, your benefits manager, HR vice president, or a representative of the media – think back to the four essential information-seeking questions. These cover the basic facts and are what most people, those assisting you and those reporting on you, will want to know. They are:

▶ What happened?

▶ How bad is it?

▶ What is being done?

▶ What is the potential for escalation?

You asked these questions when you received the initial notification. Now you will likely be asked to convey what you learned as you are informing those on your immediate call list. However, it is best not to get into detailed discussions about what happened with individuals who are being contacted for mobilization and crisis response. Instead, best practices typically include an initial call for the team to muster and then everyone is given the most up-to-date information available all at the same time. In a rapidly evolving situation, it is hard to ensure everyone has the latest information unless they are told at the same time.

5.6 Notifying Family of Fatalities and Serious Injury

Intervention with families is a delicate job, and you get only one chance to get it right.

Few duties are more difficult than meeting with family members whose loved one has been killed while at work. Even so, the role of the company in these situations could not be more important.

You might assume that law enforcement, medical personnel, or a coroner's office would take care of notifying relatives of persons fatally injured in a workplace tragedy. This is especially true in the UK. But even there, law enforcement has readily welcomed the willingness of corporate managers to accompany them during death notifications. Whatever the culture, it's a mistake to assume that you can simply pass the duty of death notification on to law enforcement or medical personnel.

It is imperative that contact be made with families soon after any serious injury incidents or deaths related to your workplace. Expect significant outrage if communications are not established with surviving family members in a proper manner by company representatives who are right for the job.

Whether you meet grieving families in makeshift morgues, at four-star hotels, or in remote fields strewn with airplane fragments, the same principles apply.

> **Try to remember how it felt when others used the right (or wrong) approach during your own times of need following traumatic incidents.**

Although the techniques outlined can make a significant difference in your interactions with impacted family members, much of your success will be the direct outcome of your initial approach. Try to remember how it felt when others used the right (or wrong) approach during your own times of need following traumatic incidents.

Before you go on such a visit, spend a few minutes visualizing what these individuals are facing. What mix of emotions are they most likely to be experiencing? What information do you anticipate they will need?

Unfortunately, I have been called in following many horror stories about family notifications "gone bad." One manager was faced with the task of notifying the spouses of three workers involved in a gas company explosion – one had died and the other two were hospitalized with severe burns. The facility was located in a small town and, as is common in such communities, the manager knew all three spouses. He chose to notify the wife of the fatality first at her home. Upon hearing the news, she was understandably overcome. She pleaded with the manager to stay with her and threw her arms around his neck, wailing in shock and grief. To her great outrage, the manager promptly tore himself away – his sense of duty compelled him to reach the other two spouses, knowing they would want to rush to the hospital to see their loved ones, perhaps for the last time.

In order to avoid such a costly emotional blunder, the manager should have acted quickly to select other employees or managers to accompany him to the house as he shared the horrific news. Or, better yet, appropriate managers could have been chosen to independently notify the three families. This would not have been hard to do in a small community, and it would have ensured that the devastated widow not be left alone.

It should also be noted that in the event of life-threatening injuries, family members should be prioritized as "first in line" for notification. This priority will allow family members an immediate opportunity to visit with their loved one before potential demise. The manager in the explosion example above should have arranged for the spouses of the severely burned employees to be notified immediately and transported to the hospital without delay.

Family Notification Guidelines

▶ Remind all managers and employees not to release the names of the deceased or seriously injured to the media or others until it is verified that immediate family members have been notified.

▶ If an individual is critically injured and death is imminent, make the notification as soon as possible, even by phone, to allow the family members an opportunity to spend final moments with their loved one.

▶ Make death notifications in person, preferably accompanied by someone else (best if a team of one man and one woman). Another person can help share the emotional burden and help manage emotional reactions, including possible hostility. Two notifiers can also substantiate the details of the visit, if necessary.

▶ Ask to enter the home. Unless safety is a concern, don't make a death notification on the doorstep.

▶ Ask those present to sit down. Do not sit in Dad's recliner, especially if he is the one who was killed. Pull up a dining room chair if possible and place it in a strategic position for visibility of each person. You may prefer to sit nearest the door, just in case you experience a hostile reaction.

▶ Be factual, honest, direct, and caring. Get to the point quickly. Do not communicate a false sense of hope. Use words like "dead," or "died" rather than "lost" or "passed on."

▶ Be supportive if family members react with hysteria, weeping, anger, or shock. If you believe hostility or physical violence might ensue, arrange to be accompanied by a law enforcement officer.

▶ If family members wish to go to the hospital, encourage them not to drive themselves. Drive them or arrange for transportation.

▶ Be prepared to make appropriate arrangements if you discover young children in the home who might be left alone. One of the notifiers could stay with the children until other family, friends, or neighbors arrive to care for them.

▶ If the family members are away from home or living out of town, you are still responsible for notifying them. However you reach them, the same rules apply. You might find someone who has experience in family notification in remote locations by contacting the local fire department, law enforcement, or military personnel.

▶ Arrange for a high-ranking company official to contact the family personally as soon as crisis management demands allow. Such contact can be quite reassuring and serves to demonstrate sensitivity and caring by the company. Far too many times, I have seen families outraged because no one from the company reached out to them following a tragedy.

▶ If your company has a family representative program that trains and designates employees to assist family members with their needs and communications to and from the company following an incident, it's best to have other individuals do a death notification. You don't want the family representatives who are assigned the role of assisting family members to be thought of as the messengers who brought the bad news.

5.7 A Team With Heart

One means to assist you or others responsible for family notification is to establish a team separate from the crisis team that is charged with managing this and other humanitarian aspects of a crisis.

Even the best crisis teams can easily become overwhelmed by the business needs, communications, and other demands of a crisis. The tendency, thus, is to overlook people who may have averted physical injury and others outside the direct circle of impact. As we all learned following terrorist attacks, natural disasters, workplace violence, and other traumatic events, one does not have to be injured physically to be traumatized or outraged. Even close identification with the incident can cause deep emotional reactions.

A humanitarian response team (HRT) is a multidisciplinary internal group of managers specially trained to address the emotional, communication, logistical, and adjustment needs of those affected by the crisis. Such a team should be considered as an adjunct to your various crisis teams. External providers that have expertise related to the human side of crisis may also be included on the team, such as disaster and crisis psychologists, or national crisis response companies like Crisis Care Network. Those who witnessed the event, people injured, surviving family members, non-injured employees, bystanders, community members, and anyone else associated with the crisis who feels overwhelmed or needs communication and support in the wake of the events would be under the caring assistance of this HRT.

Depending on the desires of management, tasks the HRT could orchestrate include:

▶ Family notifications of death or serious injury.

▶ Identification of "at risk" individuals who need appropriate attention.

▶ Psychological first aid services.

▶ Meetings with employees and other stakeholders that need communications.

▶ Initial psychological and communications support for those severely impacted.

▶ Family representatives dispatched to seriously impacted individuals and families.

▶ Communications between impacted stakeholders and the company.

▶ Identification of needs for stakeholders and provision of appropriate assistance.

▶ Psychological support (group and individual briefings/intervention, individual assessment and counseling, EAP services, etc.), as appropriate.

▶ Assistance for families and other stakeholders with funerals and memorial services.

▶ Emergency travel arrangements and assistance, as needed.

▶ Support with benefits issues and social services.

▶ Financial assistance for impacted workers and their families, as appropriate.

▶ Communications and support during medivac transport services.

▶ "New normal" return-to-work and reentry to the workplace assistance.

▶ Stakeholder focus groups and ongoing communications to ensure normalization over time.

▶ Orchestration of crisis-related outreach, volunteer, and giving programs.

It is easy to overlook the myriad people-related needs during a crisis response. That is why an increasing number of companies are creating HRTs. Your organization may be well served to follow suit. Four months after the 2001 terrorism upon the US, the Reputation Institute observed:

The more impressed people were with the corporate response to September 11th in general, the more positively they rated companies' reputations across each of the six areas of reputation – emotional appeal, financial performance, products and services, vision and leadership, social responsibility, and workplace environment. Not only was the public impressed by the corporate response, but also most felt that companies' actions made them more "human" and more "sensitive" (2002).

5.8 Management With a Heart

5.8.1 Senior Management Visits

Typically, between 12 and 48 hours after a serious injury or death, a senior manager should visit the families of serious and fatal casualties. Beforehand, a family representative who has already made personal contact with the family should prepare a short "backgrounder" sheet with information needed to greet the family appropriately. This may include the names and pertinent facts about individual family members, their requests and needs, and personal information about the victim. (For details about speaking with families and finding the right thing to say, see Appendix A of this book.)

The senior manager may wish to have as many as two people accompany him or her – perhaps a crisis mental health specialist and an HR manager who is knowledgeable about benefits. If the family representative has established a good rapport with the family, it may be good to have them there too, but do not overwhelm the family with too many visitors. Everyone who goes should have a designated role, or else they should not attend during the senior management visit. The same guidelines presented above, such as making a proper introduction and expressing heartfelt condolences, apply to senior managers.

The ability to respond to the situation with such an authentic and healing expression of concern is characteristic of the "crisis whisperer" we described at the beginning of the book.

5.8.2 Saying the Right Thing When it Matters

But then what? After those initial sentiments are conveyed, an uncomfortable silence often descends upon the room. The key is to keep conversation flowing. For example, the executive might ask a spouse or parent, "Where were you when you first heard about the incident?" Keep things going with questions like, "So what happened between the time you got the phone call and when you arrived at the hospital?" Without prying, the executive is giving the distinct impression of caring about the people involved. Another strategy is to say, "Tell me a little about Charlie. What was he like at home?" It would also be good if the senior manager or other company person in attendance could relate some interesting facts about the victim at work or messages from coworkers.

I've seen this approach work time and again. Families usually want and need to talk about what they have been through and about their loved ones. It happened when I accompanied the president and founder of a national pizza chain to a hospital. He had the unenviable task of meeting with the parents of a young man, a delivery driver, who had been seriously injured as he attempted to help a stranded motorist. I could actually see the parents' comfort level rise as they spoke lovingly about their son, answering the company president's polite, gentle questions. The meeting ended with hugs. And the grateful parents wrote the executive a letter, thanking him warmly for his expression of concern. The ability to respond to the situation with such an authentic and healing expression of concern is characteristic of the crisis whisperer we described at the beginning of the book.

Quick Use Response Guide
Chapter 5: Crisis Communications
Corporate Communications in Crisis

- ▶ Have you employed the military's technique, repeating back what you hear?
- ▶ Have you oriented all communications toward action?
- ▶ Right at the start, have you asked the right questions?
  - ❏ What happened?
  - ❏ How bad is it?
  - ❏ Who can tell us more?
  - ❏ What else might happen?
  - ❏ Who or what is responsible for the incident?
  - ❏ What is being done so far in response?
  - ❏ How is the media involved?
  - ❏ What is the potential for escalation?
- ▶ Have you decided who should do the talking, and channeled all communications through a gatekeeper?
- ▶ So people can understand and retain, have you identified your three (no more) key messages and limited each to no more than 12 words?

▶ Have you considered all your potential stakeholders?

- ❑ Employees, including staff and management.
- ❑ Employees' families.
- ❑ Senior management.
- ❑ Board of directors.
- ❑ Business partners.
- ❑ Investment community.
- ❑ Insurance representatives.
- ❑ Suppliers, distributors, and franchisees.
- ❑ Customers and other key relationships.
- ❑ Government and law enforcement officials.
- ❑ Industry activist groups.
- ❑ Media representatives.
- ❑ Unions.
- ❑ The general community.
- ❑ Retained technical experts.

▶ Have you defined the parameters of, or isolated, the crisis?

▶ Have you developed your succinct and clear messages for both external and internal stakeholders, and prepared consistent answers to the questions you can anticipate from each group?

- ❑ Have you discussed the pros and cons of how much to tell?
- ❑ Have you considered the emotional impact of the incident on your employees, and secured their support through quick communication?

▶ Have you prepared to manage your relations with reporters and social media?

- ❑ Have you prepared and approved initial holding statements?
- ❑ Have you considered whether to suspend paid advertising?
- ❑ Are you monitoring news coverage of your incident and participating in social media?
- ❑ Have you prepared outgoing communications in conjunction with legal counsel, your communications department, your management team, and possibly law enforcement?

❏ Have you anticipated, and asked for, reporters' questions in advance of any news conferences or interviews?

❏ Have you decided on specific points to get across in any statements to the media?

❏ Has your spokesperson rehearsed your message?

❏ Are you respecting the professional and personal needs of media people who are covering the story?

❏ Have you taken steps to protect your people from media intrusions?

▶ Have you considered other forums you can use for giving and receiving vital information?

Your Notification Plan

▶ Have you implemented a notification plan that:

❏ Considers who should be notified?

❏ Identifies who has the authority to mobilize needed internal and external resources?

❏ Identifies what information is needed to and from each source?

▶ Have you determined the thresholds that indicate notification vs. mobilization, especially regarding members of your crisis management team?

▶ Have you reviewed the key contacts list (internal and external) to determine which are most relevant to your given crisis, and established protocol for enlisting each?

▶ Have you established procedures for notifying the families in the event of death or serious injury, such as:

❏ Who will make such notification?

❏ Key steps to follow during the notification?

❏ Training and guidance for those who would serve in this notification capacity?

Addressing the Families of Casualties

▶ Are you prepared for family interactions including:

❏ Assisting arriving family members?

❏ Protecting families from the media and interfering attorneys?

❏ Techniques for meeting families at home, at the hospital, other public places, or over the phone?

▶ Has a group of employee volunteers been selected, trained, and prepared for dispatch as family representatives to serve the needs of families of casualties and other impacted stakeholders?

▶ Have you established a humanitarian response team (HRT) that is an adjunct to your crisis team(s) to assist with the human-side-of-crisis needs of affected people?

▶ Has a manual of guidelines been provided to family representatives?

▶ Have you prepared senior managers for visits with family members?

▶ Has personal and crisis leadership assistance been offered or arranged for senior managers?

▶ Have you established disengagement policies and procedures for family representatives? (For more details about addressing families of casualties, see Appendix A in this book.)

Chapter 5 – Questions for Further Thought and Discussion

1. Questions are provided to be asked during the initial notification phase of an incident. What are additional questions that you believe should be included?

2. Once initial information has been obtained, what are immediate actions for consideration that fit the culture and expectations of your organization?

3. Which stakeholders do you consider to be appropriate for the HRT to assist and which should remain the responsibility of the crisis action team and CMT?

4. What are additional questions and actions that can be prepared for family representatives to use when making contact with families?

5. What statements and actions should not be used with impacted families? What is outside the scope of family assistance services?

6. Why is it important for family representatives to meet in pairs (one male and one female) and what would be the unique roles of each?

References

Covello, V. (n.d.). Dr. Vincent Covello of the Institute for Risk Communication granted permission to provide information about his studies on "caring" in crisis leadership and crisis messaging.

Reputation Institute (2002). Results of private study provided with permission of the Reputation Institute. www.reputation institute.com

6

Reputation Management

Dr. Daniel Diermeier,[1] author of Reputation Rules, joins with me in co-authoring this chapter to discuss the impact of crisis management on organizational and personal reputation.

Like many managers, you may be confident that the internal communication or public affairs department of your organization – or external public relations (PR) consultants – will be all that you need to preserve your company's reputation in a crisis. You may believe that all you have to do in a crisis is to use your pre-written media statements, make a timely response, put the right spin on your messages – and reputation risk will be handled adequately. In reality, while communications and PR are important components of crisis management and protecting reputation, you cannot rely on them alone.

This chapter will help you to:

➢ *Go beyond PR to preserve reputation in a crisis.*

➢ *Identify the components in building and maintaining trust.*

➢ *Understand the psychology of leading under pressure.*

➢ *See the crisis leadership role in reputation management.*

---

[1] Daniel Diermeier (d-diermeier@kellogg.northwestern.edu) is the IBM Distinguished Professor of Regulation and Competitive Practice and Director of the Ford Motor Company Center for Global Citizenship, Kellogg School of Management, Northwestern University. He is the author of the book *Reputation Rules: Strategies for Building your Company's Most Valuable Asset* (McGraw-Hill, April 2011), which serves as the basis for some of the content of this chapter.

6.1 The Age of Crises

Headlines during the last few years have highlighted industry leaders battling major crises – Toyota, Goldman Sachs, HP, News Corporation (News Corp), and BP, to name just a few. JPMorgan Chase's trading losses, the hacking scandal at News Corp, the bribing allegations at Wal-Mart, or Apple's issues over working conditions at supplier Foxconn's Chinese factories are additional examples. Similarly nonprofits have faced challenges, such as the controversy over the Susan G. Komen Foundation's funding issues regarding Planned Parenthood or Penn State's pedophile scandals.

While the sources of the crisis may vary from case to case and from industry to industry, in all cases, loss of public trust led to a severe and often sustained erosion of market values. Financial setbacks are only the beginning of the troubles for such companies. Lawsuits, public hearings, and investigations soon follow. In some cases, public officials may pursue policy agendas or play the role of heroes taking on corporate villains. In other cases, regulators and politicians respond to public pressure to take decisive action that changes competitive environments.

> **Organizational crisis management should never be delegated to functional specialists such as the legal or PR departments.**

In every case, analysts have pointed to specific mistakes by senior management, offering advice on how to avoid similar disasters. Even when the gaffe is created by an individual within the rank and file of the organization, the focus of blame tends to be directed toward the leadership of the organization.

From tactical to strategic. It would be erroneous to focus on the specific *tactical* mistakes in any given case and miss the broader trends revealed in ever more frequent and severe corporate crises, trends that have pointed to the need for effective crisis management. Unfortunately, many leaders fail routinely at this task, even as they excel in other dimensions of leadership. These are problems that you can overcome through a *strategic* approach to crisis management.

▶ First, the nature of corporate crises is frequently misunderstood. Often the initial reaction of management is to interpret an emerging crisis solely as a threat. This view has two negative consequences:

❑ It triggers a damage control mindset, where the best you can hope for is zero damage.

❑ It leads to an exclusive focus on the specific operational, ethical, or legal trigger of the crisis.

▶ Secondly, a "threat limited" mindset ignores the ever present, but frequently hidden, opportunities for companies facing a crisis. Recognizing such opportunities is the task of leadership – it requires conceptualizing crises as business issues connected closely to the strategy and core value proposition of your company.

Core assets. Rather than focusing on assigning fault or identifying legal liabilities, you must be cognizant of how the ensuing crisis connects to the sources of value of the company. Examples include damage to the relationship of your company with customers as well as other key relationships, e.g., suppliers, distributors, investors, employees, communities, media, and regulators. Through expanded vision, you can balance these effects and integrate them into your crisis response strategy. Because the crisis will impact core assets of the organization, it is important that your crisis teams be led by the most senior manager with business responsibility for the affected operating unit. Organizational crisis management should never be delegated to functional specialists such as the legal or PR departments. Rather, you should integrate their functional expertise with members of the business leadership and other disciplines to form a diverse, cross-functional team. Such a team will focus not only on the threat, but also on opportunity and reputation enhancement opportunities.

Trust. Very often the main business issue involves the reputation of your company with its customers, people, business partners, and other key stakeholders. Crisis management is about people, and trust is now an essential part of business success. However, public trust in business leaders is perennially low, along with journalists, financial advisors, and politicians. For example, the Edelman Trust Barometer annually surveys more than 30,000 respondents in 26 markets around the world to measure trust in institutions, industries, and leaders. According to survey results, less than 20% of the general public believes business leaders and government officials will tell the truth when confronted with a difficult issue (Edelman, R., 2013).

To maintain trust during a crisis, your company almost always faces two crises at once.

▶ On the one hand there is the specific operational crisis.

▶ On the other hand the company is being evaluated regarding how it handles the operational crisis.

During a major crisis your company is on stage, often illuminated by the traditional media – and increasingly by social media. While you are on stage, others (customers, employees, competitors, business partners, regulators, etc.) are paying close attention. Because of their keen interest, they remember, sometimes for a very long time. For example, we still remember the Tylenol crisis and the Exxon Valdez oil spill decades after they occurred. Thus, how your company conducts itself in a moment of crisis will have a significant and lasting effect.

Case Study: Martha Stewart

Many real-life examples demonstrate the lasting effect of reputation and trust on organizations and their managers. Martha Stewart (television personality, author, magazine publisher, and founder of Martha Stewart Living Omnimedia in 1996) is a good example (Wallace, B., 2011).

In December 2001, Martha Stewart allegedly received insider information from her stock broker at Merrill Lynch. Stewart quickly sold her entire $45,673 stock position in ImClone, and the stock dropped 16% in value the next day. Confronted with allegations of insider trading, she made false statements to federal investigators, which resulted in a felony conviction for lying under oath, a five-month federal prison sentence, two-year supervision following her release, $225,000 in settlement costs, and the significant downturn of her company.

Upon her release, Stewart began her comeback through relationships with Kmart, Sears, Macy's, Sirius satellite radio, daytime television shows, and others. Even as she worked to rebuild her image, the media published frequent reports of her autocratic, controlling, and difficult management style and of executives leaving her organization soon after starting. The shareholder value of Martha Stewart Living Omnimedia consistently drifted down, and huge losses mounted in the years following her release from federal prison. Subsequently, Macy's sued Stewart for breach of contract (D'innocenzio, A., 2013) because she had allegedly signed a deal to sell her products through J.C. Penney, in conflict with her exclusive rights agreement with Macy's. Stewart and Macy's reached a settlement, but the legal friction between Macy's and J.C. Penney continues (Cheng, A., 2014).

Sacrifice: Chronic and acute behavioral patterns can either enhance or damage a reputation. Arguably, Stewart's business decisions had the potential to cause deep-seated, unfavorable opinions about her reputation among the public. However, in the eyes of the public, Stewart was viewed as having more than paid the price for the insider trading scandal and lying under oath. The public compares her situation to that of President Bill Clinton and his lying about the Monica Lewinsky sexual affair. In public perception, Clinton was given no punishment for lying under oath. In contrast, Martha Stewart's actions caused little harm to the general public, yet she spent five months in federal prison and endured two years of supervised monitoring after release.

Lessons-learned: When people and companies engage in transgressions, the public can be forgiving under the right circumstances. If the individual or company is seen as having paid a price that is at least commensurate with the harm caused, then people tend to forgive.

An example of an organization that was seen as not paying sufficiently for the harm it caused is BP with its enormous 2010 Gulf oil spill. When the company was perceived as minimizing the amount of oil released into the Gulf, the public felt deceived. They viewed Tony Hayward, BP's gaffe-prone CEO, as non-remorseful and uncaring. They considered the billions of dollars that BP expended in restoration to be insufficient. People perceived widespread harm and could easily identify with the businesses, property owners, and natural habitats that were deeply impacted. In an attempt to restore reputation and trust, BP provided ongoing advertising about the recovery of the Gulf Coast for years following the spill. BP took steps to rejuvenate tourism, took actions to prevent future incidents, and made a commitment to the quality of living throughout the affected areas. Even so, in spite of voluntary payments and heavy fines, BP was initially perceived as not sufficiently sacrificing. Thus, BP had to resort to costly reputation restoration through long-term advertising in an attempt to convince the public that the harm was not as severe as once believed and that the company is continuing to take responsibility.

The good news is that, even in the most difficult situations, the reputation of your company can be improved by doing the right things for as long as it takes to influence a shift in public perception.

Time will tell how long and severe BP's crisis response-induced reputational damage lasts. Through BP's consistent reputation reparation efforts, it appears it has made progress. The *New York Times* Op-Ed columnist, Joe Nocera, usually not a friend of BP, praised BP's efforts and defended it against trial lawyers (Nocera, J., 2012).

> **The good news is that, even in the most difficult situations, the reputation of your company can be improved by doing the right things for as long as it takes to influence a shift in public perception.**

6.2 The Good Samaritan Principle

Natural disasters, terrorist attacks, or workplace shootings, while usually beyond the control of the management of an organization, can put your company on stage where the leadership team is being evaluated in how it is responding. That means:

- Acting authentically (rather than appearing motivated by profits).
- Acting competently (sending the right kinds of relief in a timely manner).
- Communicating in a non-self-serving way.

We call this approach the Good Samaritan principle: caring combined with competence. A relief effort that meets these criteria can be much more valuable than financial donations of any size. Failing to meet them, no matter how genuine the intention, can do the business reputational harm. It is not just the thought that counts. Corporate caring is not a feeling. It is behavioral. Stakeholders must see and believe that your organization cares about the welfare of others by observing "caring behaviors," not just empty public relations statements of concern.

6.2.1 Response of Wal-Mart and Sears to Hurricanes Katrina and Sandy

An example of the Good Samaritan principle is Wal-Mart's swift and comprehensive relief efforts in the wake of Hurricane Katrina in 2005 and the response of Sears to Hurricane Sandy in 2012.

Because Wal-Mart understood the problem and delivered what victims needed (e.g., water and nonperishable food) even faster than the government, Wal-Mart scored major goodwill with the public while serving an important cause. In the case of Hurricane Sandy, Sears launched a similar, albeit smaller scale, effort to help by partnering with a housing organization to rebuild New Jersey's Little Ferry Hook & Ladder Company No. 1 firehouse, which had taken in three feet of water and had to be gutted.

> In the context of natural disasters like hurricanes, the public views the company more as a community member than profit-seeker, and expects the business to behave out of altruism rather than self-interest.

Effective crisis response strategies like those of Sears and Wal-Mart tend to resonate more deeply with the public and generate goodwill because they follow several unwritten rules of corporate citizenship. In the context of natural disasters like hurricanes, the public views the company more as a community member than profit-seeker, and expects the business to behave out of altruism rather than self-interest.

In the specific context of natural disasters, a well-intended response may even be viewed negatively. For example, if a beauty products company were to send cosmetics or skin moisturizer to victims needing clean water, the public would likely pan that company for it, seeing the move as self-serving. Beyond natural disasters, in any type of crisis where stakeholder needs are high, the corporate response must be appropriate with no perception of self-serving. In 2000, when Philip Morris widely publicized the $115 million it had contributed to battered women's shelters and other causes, the company was extensively attacked. Blowing your own horn too loudly leads the public to suspect ulterior motives.

In contrast, Wal-Mart's strategic communications around its efforts to help victims of Hurricane Katrina in 2005 highlighted the competence and warmth of the corporation, yielding large reputational benefits. It started with Wal-Mart's CEO, Lee Scott. He reported to his corporate management team, *"These are extraordinary times and I expect an extraordinary response."* He then empowered his store managers throughout the storm-impacted areas by saying, *"A lot of you are going to have to make decisions above your level. Make the best decision that you can with the information that's available to you at the time, and, above all, do the right thing."* As a result, the company supplied water and other supplies well before the relief efforts by the federal government. Store managers and truck drivers talked directly to the media. The emotional impact of their personal stories of neighbors helping neighbors played an important role in boosting positive perceptions of Wal-Mart and energizing the company's employees (Diermeier, D., 2011).

Capturing decisive moments, as Wal-Mart did in the aftermath of Hurricane Katrina, can be turning points that will positively shape how your company is being perceived by the public.

6.3 Trust-Building Components

Even though the advantages are obvious, leaders continue to struggle with building and maintaining trust, especially during high-consequence crises. Research has identified four major factors that influence the level of trust among stakeholders involved in a crisis. You would do well to consider them as shown in Figure 6-1 (adapted from Diermeier, 2011).

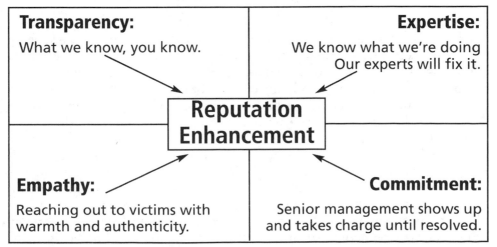

Figure 6-1. Trust Factors in Reputation

6.3.1 Transparency

To see the importance of *transparency*, you will find it useful to keep in mind what undermines trust. One example is if the audience believes that your company is withholding relevant information willfully. Or, to say it positively, full transparency is reached when, in the mind of your audience, all relevant questions have been answered. What is considered relevant will depend on your audience, not on your company. It will also vary for different audiences. What is transparent to an investor may not be transparent to a customer.

Transparency is not the same as full disclosure and it is possible to reach transparency without full disclosure. This will be the case if the company conveys a rationale for limiting disclosure shared by the relevant audience. For example, in many cases privacy concerns or investigations may limit what can be disclosed. Connecting such limits with a concern for the privacy of the audience provides a clear and understandable reason for limiting disclosure. As a general rule, the rationale for limiting disclosure must pass the reasonable person test, meaning that it will seem justifiable to most people.

It's hard to feign transparency when one is not being truthful.

It is also possible to fail to reach transparency despite full disclosure. That will be the case when the company, in its attempt to fully disclose an issue, fails to be understood. Technical mumbo-jumbo, a complex explanation, or legalese, even if it involves disclosing relevant information, will not be considered transparent by the general public. Rather, an audience will assume that a company is hiding behind incomprehensible jargon rather than speaking plainly and in a straightforward manner.

Further, trying to give the impression of full transparency while hiding salient facts can lead audiences to doubt the veracity of what they are being told. For example, President Bill Clinton's first statement to the media following the accusations of sexual misconduct with Monica Lewinsky was doubted by many, even though most were not quite sure why. Clinton was asked in a press conference if he had been having a sexual affair with Lewinsky. His now famous response, "There is no sexual relationship," caused people not to trust his denial. Why? Clinton was asked about his behavior in the past tense, but he answered in the present tense. Technically, he was not having a sexual relationship in the present while he was conducting a press conference. But, any capable linguistic analyst could quickly point out that he answered deceptively by answering a question about his past behavior in the present tense. It's hard to feign transparency when one is not being truthful. Ask convicted felon Martha Stewart, baseball's Barry Bonds, cyclist Lance Armstrong, and so many more.

There may be times when your management does not want to release known information. If this is the case, you can anticipate the reaction of stakeholders if it is found out through other means than direct communication from the company. Will the rationale for not disclosing the information pass the reasonable person test? Most often, it is better to get bad information all released at one time, than to withhold information that continues to trickle out over time.

6.3.2 Expertise

Perceived lack of *expertise* can undermine trust quickly. This is often a problem for nonprofits or government entities. The reputational catastrophe suffered by the Federal Emergency Management Agency (FEMA) due to their bungling response during Hurricane Katrina was not driven by the belief that FEMA had bad intentions, but that it was incompetent.

In contrast, companies are usually viewed as competent. The public usually does not doubt their ability, but they often doubt their willingness to do the right thing. That said, for companies the expectation of competence often has a threshold structure. Companies get little credit for exceeding expectations, but are heavily criticized if they fail to meet them.

If there is a perceived lack of expertise, bringing in third-party experts with high credibility is a simple way to address this concern. However, the motives of external third-party experts may be questioned if they are hired by the company. This is often not an easy decision for a CEO who may fear looking incompetent if an outside expert is brought to the table. In this context, a board member or other trusted advisor may want to point out to the CEO that what matters most is that the perceived lack of expertise needs to be addressed, whether this perception is accurate or not. However, experts with knowledge well outside the expected expertise of management will likely cause no perception of management incompetence. For example, a well-respected public health physician from the Center for Disease Control (CDC), prestigious university, or local health department will have medical knowledge about diseases or toxic exposures that management would typically not be expected to know.

> **People expect leaders and their organizations to have the expertise to take full preventive action and to be prepared to respond quickly, decisively, and effectively when crises occur.**

Questions of expertise. Two universal expectations related to expertise arise among your impacted and involved stakeholders when a crisis occurs. These expectations typically lie dormant during normal times. Then when stakeholder harm is feared or realized, people immediately ask questions about the expertise and preparedness of the organization and its leaders.

▶ First, stakeholders will ask, "What did the organization do to prevent this crisis situation?" When it is humanly possible to prevent or significantly decrease the likelihood of occurrence or harm, the widely held belief is that preventive action should have been implemented. If the company appears negligent, dismissive, or incompetent, then outrage will occur.

▶ Second, stakeholders expect your company to remain prepared and "ever ready" to manage a crisis effectively when it occurs, especially when the crisis was considered foreseeable. The excuse that "we didn't think it would happen to us" holds no defensibility in these times where almost any harmful event is considered foreseeable.

Reputation and trust in your company and its leaders will diminish significantly when the expertise to prevent and respond to the crisis is perceived as inadequate. The Penn State university pedophilia crisis is an example of a preventable crisis. Most people believe the university leadership could have prevented untold numbers of sexual abuses had they taken appropriate preventive and response actions immediately when they learned of the horrible child sexual abuse situation. Similarly, on the post-crisis response side, Virginia Tech was widely seen as unprepared to handle its crisis when its slow response allowed an initial double homicide to become a mass murder of 30 additional students and injury of 23 others.

Lack of crisis management expertise will cause outrage and diminished reputation for unprepared organizations. Lesson learned? There is no credible business practice that says, "Don't take action to prevent harmful crises and don't prepare to respond effectively if a crisis occurs." People expect leaders and their organizations to have the expertise to take full preventive action and to be prepared to respond quickly, decisively, and effectively when crises occur.

> The most powerful and direct way to signal commitment is for leaders to show up in a highly visible manner and take charge.

6.3.3 Commitment

At the end of the day, your stakeholders want to make sure that the problem is addressed and, to the extent possible, they are made whole. One problem with this expectation is that in the short window when stakeholders are actually paying attention to a crisis, it is frequently impossible to establish even the most basic facts, let alone find a solution. Companies, however, can ill afford not to "get to the bottom" on an issue, as the window of opportunity for leaving a positive impression will rapidly close. So what is a leader who serves as a crisis whisperer to do? The third factor is *commitment*.

The most powerful and direct way to signal commitment is for leaders to show up in a highly visible manner and take charge. It demonstrates accountability and sends the message that nothing is more important than resolving this particular crisis.

- When a Virgin train from London bound for Glasgow crashed after derailing due to a line defect, CEO, Sir Richard Branson, not only cut short a family vacation to help handle the situation personally, but he also visited crash victims in the hospital and praised the train driver's courage and actions that potentially saved more lives.

- On the other hand, Exxon's CEO, Lawrence Rawls, resisted speaking with the media after the Valdez oil spill and took three weeks before visiting the disaster area in Alaska's Prince William Sound. This delay undermined trust in the company by giving the appearance that Rawls was not committed to mitigating and resolving the crisis.

- Rudy Giuliani, mayor of New York City, provided high-visibility crisis response in the immediate aftermath of the 9/11 terrorism. He demonstrated commitment by staying in the streets of NYC during frightening times and putting his own safety at risk in order to address the information needs of people.

- Conversely, during Hurricane Katrina, Ray Nagin, mayor of New Orleans, and Mike Brown, FEMA director, were perceived as uncommitted with what appeared to be a lack of high-visibility personal involvement and concern.

To an efficiency-minded CEO, a crisis response ritual may look like a waste of time, a precious resource during any crisis. Ironically, it is exactly this "inefficiency" that creates the strong symbolic value. In fact, it is by showing up with the full resources of the company that a CEO signals that nothing is more important that taking care of this crisis. That creates a sense of commitment.

Does it always have to be your CEO? No, the right level of commitment depends on the perceived magnitude of the crisis. To use a fire fighting analogy, when the burning house is a small building on a neighborhood block without victims, the local fire lieutenant will do just fine, but if the Clock

Tower housing Big Ben in London (recently renamed Elizabeth Tower) is on fire, nothing less than the fire commissioner will do, even if operational control is located at a lower level in the hierarchy. If in doubt, use someone a little higher in your management hierarchy, even if the executive is not directing the operations. The importance of perceived commitment also casts doubt on the extensive use of PR professionals as spokespeople. The problem with PR people is that they do not have operational responsibilities. They are not in charge, and stakeholders know it. In a crisis, people want to hear from their leaders. Depending on the crisis, it's best to use skilled media spokespersons for ongoing briefings in conjunction with the highly visible presence of the leader of the organization.

> ...a leader reaching out to perceived victims with warmth and authenticity can be very effective, whether there is an apology or not.

6.3.4 Empathy

The final component, *empathy*, is often the most important factor of the four and the easiest to miss. Showing empathy is not the same thing as apologizing. We show empathy with colleagues at work, neighbors, and family members even if we do not feel responsible. As we saw in the example of natural disasters during a crisis, stakeholder attention may shift to a community mindset. Stakeholders do not see the company as an anonymous provider of goods and services, but a member of the community. And a member of the community is expected to care and show empathy. That said, in many crises, customers and other stakeholders expect a sincere apology, but the apology needs to be authentic. An apology that appears formulaic, insincere, or calculated is worse than useless.

On the other hand, a leader reaching out to perceived victims with warmth and authenticity can be very effective, whether there is an apology or not. In response to Virgin's train accident, Sir Richard Branson expressed both sorrow for the loss of life while also supporting the driver who helped the vast majority survive the crash. Likewise, when asked about the loss of life in the early aftermath of the 9/11 terrorism, Rudy Giuliani replied with empathy, "The number of casualties will be more than any of us can bear." People want to know leaders and their organizations "care" when there is real or perceived harm. Remember that caring is behavioral, not just a passive feeling. An effective crisis whisperer engages in behaviors that lead people to believe the organization truly cares.

Case Study: "Domino Effect" –
Turning Crisis Into Opportunity

It was 2009 on a slow Easter Sunday in the small town of Conover, North Carolina. Kristy Hammonds and Michael Setzer were working together at Domino's Pizza. They decided it would be fun to make a video to pass the time. Kristy used her smart phone to record Michael placing cheese up his nose and sneezing into the food as it was being prepared. Unfortunately, the video found itself on the Internet the next day.

A loyal customer and blogger first notified corporate headquarters. Most executives were out of town for the holidays, but the company immediately began to verify and monitor the situation. The store in question was yet unknown and efforts to identify the two aberrant employees began within two hours. Once the store location was identified, that same evening, local law enforcement and the health department were notified immediately. Patrick Doyle, USA President of Domino's, cut his Florida vacation short and joined the crisis management team. The company communicated the incident to its entire franchise system. The offending employees were fired immediately and turned over to the police with felony charges.

In the first 48 hours, even though management was quietly taking the incident seriously, they neglected the escalating volume of social media. They hoped naively that it would just go away. In two days, over one million persons viewed the video on YouTube. Then the traditional media picked it up through all the major networks and news organizations. The reputational damage was raging out of control. Shareholder value of Domino's dropped 10% that week.

Within hours after the video hit the Internet, people on social networks asked, "What is Domino's doing about this situation?" Any response taking more than 24 hours was considered late. Finally, 48 hours after the video's release, the company responded to the mounting reputational damage.

Their public crisis response, turned into an opportunity (Agnes, M., 2012), can be examined through the trust components listed above, i.e., transparency, expertise, commitment, and empathy.

Transparency: Patrick Doyle appeared in a video on YouTube, the same medium that had been used to send the story into a viral stratosphere. He admitted the incident openly and positioned the company as victims by relating the fact pattern of two aberrant employees.

Expertise: Doyle told YouTube audiences about the decisive actions management had taken in identifying the perpetrators, pressing for felony charges against them, working with the local health department to destroy all open food items in the offending store, and the proficiency of the company in making one million pizza deliveries in 60 countries every day.

Commitment: Doyle appeared personally on the initial YouTube video response by the company and then within multiple media outlets. Additionally, Domino's established a strong social media presence during and after the crisis. The company opened a dialogue of feedback to and from customers in a manner that changed the ingredients for all its pizzas. This invigorated the brand to be improved and stronger than ever.

Empathy: Domino's, while initially late, set up a Twitter account and apologized immediately. They enjoined with customers by positioning themselves "also as victims" to this disgusting hoax and requested that readers spread the message by retweeting to others. Along with the sincere and transparent video of Patrick Doyle, the Twitter messages assured customers they could continue to trust the Domino's brand. They humanized themselves by positioning the incident as something that Domino's didn't do. Then, they opened a dialogue of listening to customers through social media, which established them as a caring and stronger organization.

Lessons-learned: While Domino's was new to social networking when the crisis hit, one month prior to the incident the company had established a social media team which was preparing to launch the organization into the social media realm. Even that rudimentary preparedness helped Domino's respond effectively (Jacques, A., 2009). Companies that are best at protecting reputation prepare before a crisis occurs. Domino's portrayed itself as the victim of a felony. Such an approach can be useful in a clear-cut case, such as the pizza incident. However, it is of limited use in many circumstances, since there is little public sympathy towards corporations.

6.4 Anticipation and Preparation

Well-prepared managers and their organizations develop both prevention and preparation strategies. Prevention strategies consist of the identification, reduction, and mitigation of risks. Examples include quality control and also the anticipation of possible concerns about services and products, as in the case of genetically modified food and outsourcing critical functions to foreign countries.

But you cannot anticipate or prevent all crises. This requires that you develop comprehensive all-hazards preparation strategies, which involve the implementation of protocol and processes that are the same every time a critical incident occurs. No matter what the crisis, your response team(s) will be notified, mobilized, and structured in the same manner. Even if the crisis situation was not anticipated, you have a "well-oiled" system in placed to address the response.

Contingency plans should be in place if the prevention strategies fail or if your organization is blindsided. This includes not only the development of crisis plans, response teams, and sufficient exercising, but also the creation of organizational capabilities to deal with the novel and surprising aspects that crises present. We advise you to establish a "crisis anticipation committee" to consider the unconsidered. What are incidents and situations that could cause serious damage to your enterprise that have not been previously considered?

In addition to internal personnel, include external consultants on your committee in order to gain outside perspectives. An example of "previously unconsidered," was that a crisis would cause all air traffic in the US to be grounded indefinitely. At the time of 9/11, many companies had emergency plans which assumed that they could move people, backup tapes, equipment, etc. to backup sites via plane. (One company we talked to at the time had an 18-hour interruption in international transactions while it rented buses to transport workers from New York to a branch office in Chicago.)

> ...most reputational challenges do not happen because of some external event or misfortune, but instead arise as the direct consequence of your company's actions before and after crises occur.

In many cases, your effective crisis management will involve finding new and unusual solutions to rapidly changing environments. Crisis decision-making is an ever changing process as the fact pattern unfolds. The success of your decisions frequently does not result from the flawless execution of a previously defined set of steps, but from "innovation under pressure." This capability comes from comprehensive crisis preparedness measures. However, while your crisis plans are important, especially for typical business risks such as a product recall, corporate plane crash, or environmental contamination, they also may give companies a false sense of security. What is equally important is for you to have the ability to create an environment where innovative thinking can occur. An important component of being a crisis team leader is that you orchestrate a participative team response rather than barking out autocratic orders.

Crises often arise from any area of day-to-day decision-making, but executives too often make decisions without consideration for the reputational impact. Assessing reputational risk requires that you anticipate what a reputational crisis would look like and then take proactive steps to prevent and prepare. Consider including "blame" directed toward the company by stakeholders in your crisis exercising. Too often, exercises position the company in the victim role only. Companies need to understand that their decisions are creating a record today that will serve as the basis of how they are judged tomorrow, as Martha Stewart learned.

Underneath these topics lurks a hard truth: most reputational challenges do not happen because of some external event or misfortune, but instead arise as the direct consequence of your company's actions before and after crises occur. In other words, companies usually bear at least some responsibility for finding themselves in trouble. Why? Companies often make decisions without considering the short- and long-term reputational impact of those decisions and fail to act as the stewards of their reputation.

The spotlight will focus not only on the current actions of your company, such as how (and if) the CEO answers questions and what the company will do to fix the problem, but also on its past actions. Reporters will ask you when the company first knew about the problem, or why management didn't do more to prevent it. For example, in the Domino's Pizza case, audiences may question whether the company's hiring processes were adequate to screen out irresponsible employees in the first place. The thought process behind each past decision can be brought into the public arena and questioned. Past actions and decisions are a part of the record and cannot be changed. Even those actions that looked reasonable at the time may wither under scrutiny from hostile stakeholders in a crisis context after their negative consequences come to light. After the Gulf of Mexico oil spill, every minute decision that BP made concerning its safety processes took on disproportionate significance, leading to severe criticism of the company. When Toyota had to recall its cars, commentators quickly alleged that its aggressive growth strategy had sacrificed quality and safety. Similar dynamics occurred in the context of the Fukushima nuclear power plant following the Japan earthquake and tsunami.

The "Wall Street Journal Test"

Reputational risk goes beyond understanding the trade-offs between reputation and business opportunity. A decision may look very different once it comes under public scrutiny. One way to evaluate a decision is to apply what Gartner calls the "Wall Street Journal Test." In this test, you evaluate whether you would be comfortable to see an accurate report of your decision featured on the front page of the *The Wall Street Journal*. One way to see if your decision passes the test is to consider the ten questions listed below.

Ten Test Questions for Crisis Decision-Making

1. Is this decision based on substantiated facts and desired outcomes?

2. Has appropriate communication to and from all parties been conducted?

3. Have contingencies been carefully appraised and are reasonable contingency plans in place?

4. Have alternative courses of action been considered for comparison?

5. Have appropriate legal, compliance, and ethical issues been considered?

6. Does this decision consider issues and concerns of involved or impacted stakeholders?"

7. Does this decision demonstrate corporate caring?

8. Is this decision based on sound business practice, i.e., passes the reasonable person test?

9. Does this decision include continued contact or monitoring, for as long as appropriate?

10. If decisions and actions/inactions end up on the front page of *The Wall Street Journal* or other media does management feel comfortable in defending this decision?

Answering these questions should put to rest any misconception you have that reputation management can be left only to enterprise risk managers or specialists from the communications, legal, or compliance function. The key to successful reputation management is that all decision-makers in your organization view themselves as stewards of the company's reputation. Through your multidisciplinary business decisions today, you are, in fact, increasing or decreasing reputational risk tomorrow.

6.5 Leading Under Pressure

6.5.1 The Psychology of Reputation

Prepared companies conduct exercises of varying content and complexity on a regular basis. However, one common manifestation of the crisis situation is often excluded from crisis exercises. As mentioned briefly above, most crisis exercises are designed to address critical incidents where the company is the victim. A horrible earthquake, hurricane, or other natural disaster harms the business. Or, possibly a terrorist or a pandemic disrupts operations. Infrastructure issues, like power outages, are contemplated. Or new crises, such as electromagnetic pulse attacks or data breaches that compromise the critical infrastructure of the country, are addressed. In all these cases, the company is viewed as not at fault or blamed for the cause of the crisis.

> **Blame, no matter how deserving or unreasonable, can cause reputational damage.**

In the real world of crisis management, people who feel or perceive harm have the natural tendency to assign blame. They may blame God or even themselves to some degree. However, the most likely villain will be your organization. No matter how innocent, your organization can quickly be placed in the spotlight of blame. For example, it was interesting that following Hurricane Katrina, Shell Oil Company in New Orleans did all the right things from a caring and responsibility standpoint. Their building in New Orleans was inoperable and almost all of their 600 New Orleans employees were without homes. Shell provided temporary housing and work facilities outside New Orleans at an area they called Camp Robert. Other employees were moved temporarily to Texas to reestablish a sense of order and to maintain their employment. After deliberation, senior management decided to continue supporting New Orleans and not move out of the area. A purposeful "reentry process" was planned and implemented that reestablished Shell into the New Orleans community. Yet, Shell was blamed by some for Hurricane Katrina.

People who were anxious to place their anger externally complained that the oil and gas industry, including Shell in New Orleans, was responsible for global warming that created Hurricane Katrina in the first place.

Blame, no matter how deserving or unreasonable, can cause reputational damage. So it is important to understand the anatomy of blame that people will affix to companies, including yours. This psychology of blame is universal, crossing international boundaries and cultures.

6.5.2 The Anatomy of Blame

People who are impacted by crises have common perceptions and beliefs that constitute blame. These attitudes are red flags that serve as omens of potential reputational damage that you can anticipate and address through effective corporate crisis-related actions and communications.

- **Intentional:** People will become outraged if they believe that your organization or an individual empowered by your company did something that was perpetrated intentionally. For example, the widespread disgust directed toward the US Congress and other politicians worldwide comes from the belief that these supposedly trusted servants have intentionally engaged in favoritism or self-serving activities. The same holds true for those who are implicated in financial fraud that harms investors. If you are perceived as having engaged in nefarious behavior on purpose, you will be blamed.

- **Unfair:** We, as human beings, all have a strong sense of right and wrong. Even very young children react negatively when they sense unfair treatment. When a person's subjective beliefs are violated regarding how others "should" behave, blame and a desire for vengeance tend to emerge.

- **Foreseeable:** If the offending person or company "should have" recognized that the harmful event could have happened, they will be held accountable in the minds of stakeholders. Foreseeability is a common component of litigation, even when the individual or organization is not directly at fault. If foreseeable, actions to prevent and prepare for the potential occurrence will be expected.

- **Unprepared:** Responsible organizations are prepared through all-hazards planning. Even if the incident is unanticipated or unforeseen, the process of crisis response is well rehearsed, no matter what the incident. Crises magnify weaknesses. Even issues that you would hope the authorities could handle, like death notification, can create huge reputation issues and outrage if not correctly prepared and executed by organizations.

▶ **Negligent:** Failing to exercise the care expected of a reasonably prudent person in like circumstances will create a perception of blame. Society has preexisting standards and expectations regarding proper behavior. Failing to provide a "reasonable" level of care – such as crisis prevention, preparedness, and response – will create a perception of organizational negligence. Claims of negligence will arise if you or your organization are perceived as careless, inattentive, or remiss in a manner that caused harm to others. From a legal standpoint, Caremark and Stone v. Ritter (Court of Appeals, sixth Circuit, 2001) demonstrates the need for leaders to exercise appropriate attention to risks of the organization. In this case, "unconsidered inaction" emerged as a failure of corporate leaders to act in circumstances in which due attention could have prevented the loss.

Blame toward organizations and individuals in crisis situations will cause outrage and a desire for vengeance. When blame and outrage are not properly mitigated, your corporate crisis will tend to increase in intensity and longevity. People will more likely dislike and even express hate toward your organization and individuals targeted for blame. As a part of protecting the reputation of your organization and individuals within your company, blame should be anticipated and addressed as an important component of crisis containment and recovery.

> **The CEO's role is particularly important in the first 24 hours, both with respect to identification and containment of the crisis.**

6.5.3 Crisis Leadership Roles

Crises are the crucible for corporate leaders. Crises create corporate heroes or villains, winners or losers. For prepared organizations, the roles of all leaders (senior executives, middle managers, and tactical responders) are clearly delineated through a comprehensive strategic crisis planning process. This three-tiered plan identifies the roles, authorities, and expectations of the executive team, managerial team, and tactical teams into a seamless crisis response.

The CEO's role is particularly important in the first 24 hours, both with respect to identification and containment of the crisis. First, if there is harm to human beings or significant environmental damage, the CEO must consider personally addressing the public. The main purpose is to demonstrate the company's commitment to resolve the issue and to show empathy for the victims, their families, and communities. The key reputation-saving message should be one of care and concern, and then backed up with decisive "caring" actions. However, after the first 24 hours, the CEO is not always the right spokesperson. This is particularly true for localized or operational crises that do not reach enterprise-critical levels.

Choosing the right spokesperson can be an effective containment strategy. When appropriate to the crisis, an engineer with good communication skills can be far more credible and reassuring to the public than a polished PR expert with little engineering expertise. Consider the example of an environmental disaster at a power plant. Having a safety engineer with local knowledge as a spokesperson gives credibility to the crisis management approach of the company.

Using spokespersons as a containment strategy is effective only if you have identified the crisis issue correctly. For example, following the collapse of a factory building in India where multiple employees were killed, the focus on the structural integrity of the building was far less important than why the organization was utilizing a foreign manufacturer where safety and quality were in question.

When the crisis hits an enterprise level or threatens core assets of the organization, the CEO must take charge of the internal decision-making process immediately. One of the key tasks in managing reputation during crises is to communicate directly with the company's employees, board, and immediate stakeholders, such as suppliers, dealers, or customers. Company employees may face their own personal crises in their communities, and among their families, friends, and neighbors. Employees need to be kept informed with up-to-date facts and continuously assured that management is on top of the issue. The use of company e-mail, intranet, and face-to-face meetings can prove invaluable for this purpose. Otherwise, employees may quickly lose trust in their leadership and be less effective team members at a critical time for the company. In extreme cases, this lack of trust may lead to leaks or unauthorized media contacts. A crucial component of any internal communication strategy is a reminder of the company's values. They create an emphasis on the interconnectedness and commonalities among all company employees, and they focus on the possible opportunities in a crisis situation and how they can be seized, without appearing to forget the harm created for impacted parties.

Finally, when the crisis hits a strategic level where core assets of the organization may be at risk, the CEO needs to assemble the crisis management team (CMT), the cross-functional team that has authority over every function of the organization. If not led by the CEO, your team should be led by a senior manager with operating responsibility, such as the head of an operating company or division. In many cases, it is worthy of consideration that your CEO maintain close connection to the CMT without actually chairing it. This allows your team to prepare and recommend strategic options for the CEO without having him or her already vested in one of them. (For details about creating your CMT, see Chapter 3 in this book.)

One last word of consideration: your crisis leaders and crisis teams have a common concern. After investing significant energy and time planning, training, and exercising for crisis response, there is a concern that the CEO or other ranking executive (who has ignored the preparedness process previously) will take over the crisis response, potentially creating an untested, impromptu response. As is the practice in the often used incident command system (ICS), the assigned crisis leader is charged with the authority to manage the crisis and should not be usurped of power, authority, or responsibility.

> **Most importantly, companies...need to avoid delegating the design and execution of their crisis management strategy to outside specialists.**

6.5.4 Outside Advisors and Consultants

Ultimately, your crisis decision-making is the responsibility of management. However, a frequent question is whether to use outside advisers and crisis management consultants. There is no universal answer. Most importantly, companies (even small ones with little or no internal expertise in crisis management) need to avoid delegating the design and execution of their crisis management strategy to outside specialists. Even if the external experts exhibit an appreciation of the business issues (and good crisis advisors do), it is unlikely that in the available time they alone would be able to gain a sufficiently deep understanding of your organization's market environment, strategy, culture, customers, and suppliers.

Nevertheless, outside advisers can be very helpful if they work in conjunction or as part of your company's internal team. This is especially true if they have been oriented to your business and a trust relationship has already been established with management. Crises are (hopefully) rare events in the life of an organization. Thus, management usually has little experience or institutional knowledge in how to handle the details of crisis management. Experienced external crisis management consultants can be very helpful in these circumstances as long as they have the discernment to keep their influence within the realm of their knowledge and expertise.

Outside specialists can help overcome the interdisciplinary tensions by adding credibility and case examples from other organizations that faced similar issues. Also, external specialists can provide an independent evaluation of the company's strategic plan and actions, making them particularly useful in the post-crisis evaluation stage or when the board is in need of a neutral, objective perspective.

Finally, it is often easier to handle someone else's crisis than your own. The stress and other personal complexities that arise when you are inside the "crisis bubble" make it hard to gain proper perspective. Significant stress gives rise to personal and organizational weaknesses. Research conducted at Syracuse University (Schoenberg, A.L., 2004) identified four critical components of crisis leadership, i.e., information, preparedness, experience, and external conscience. The external conscience component of effective crisis leadership could come from a trusted peer, like a senior manager or board member from another company, or from a highly experienced external consultant. In practice, a seasoned crisis consultant can supplement all four areas. Information can be supplemented from knowledge of other organizations in crisis and how they handled the situation effectively. Preparedness comes from the study of crisis management and handling a vast cross section of crises in the past. Experience of external crisis consultants comes from involvement in actual crises over years of practice. And the external conscience can be the essence of bringing this know-how to your organization in any given crisis response.

> **The real values of an organization are defined by practice and set by example. Shaping these values in the right way is perhaps your biggest challenge in crisis leadership.**

Crises are pivotal moments in the life of your organization. Properly understood, they are not external events that are unrelated to the company, but test cases, decisive episodes that reveal the strengths and weaknesses of your organization. Good crisis management focuses on the business challenges. All other aspects (stakeholder management, litigation strategy, public relations, etc.) need to be integrated with your specific business strategy. On the one hand, crisis leaders need to think what the company is about and act strategically. On the other hand, they need to understand and appreciate the need for timely and effective tactical response issues. In this context, a strong set of values to guide your company is a key management tool in protecting reputation and other core assets when crises hit.

As a crisis leader, you should be aware that values of your company are its guide in a crisis. Many of the most successful examples of reputation-saving crisis management involved a company with strong values that served as a beacon for crisis response. To be useful, however, these values must be lived inside the organization and well entrenched within the minds of every corporate leader. Enron famously had one of the most elaborate lists of corporate values and a comprehensive code of ethics – but these values were not lived, and they did not shape the company's decisions or its culture. This is an especially important foundation for crisis decision-making. The real values of an organization are defined by practice and set by example. Shaping these values in the right way is perhaps your biggest challenge in crisis leadership and reputation management.

6.6 Towards a Reputation Management Capability

Today, your company is in an environment of increasing expectations that, in turn, lead to higher reputational risk. You are under more scrutiny than ever. Amateur public "paparazzi" are equipped with cameras, video and audio recorders, and internet access – ready to spread the word on a whim. While reputational risks have risen significantly, reputation management capabilities have not kept up. An increase in risk without a matching improvement in prevention, preparedness, and response capabilities will lead to more frequent and severe crises.

Your company's reputation is shaped not just by its direct business partners, customers, and suppliers, but also by a myriad of external constituencies. Frequently, stakeholders that have lain dormant for many years can suddenly spring into action, particularly in the case of reputational crises. They include not only the media, but also advocacy groups, influencers, whistleblowers, regulators, politicians, and now an emboldened public – as Domino's found out in the earlier example.

Successful reputation management requires that you have the ability to assume the perspectives and viewpoints of each stakeholder group that is involved in an organizational crisis. This "outside-in" vantage is achieved by imagining the needs and concerns of various stakeholders who are looking in at your organization. Many of these stakeholders (although certainly not all) are motivated by moral or ideological concerns that your company or its managers do not share, and indeed may be openly hostile to your company's business practices once a crisis puts your organization in the spotlight. When this spotlight leads to a defensive, reactive posture on the part of business leaders, the result may be overly emotional reactions.

A strategic approach requires you to demonstrate the emotional fortitude to treat reputational difficulties as understandable and even predictable challenges to be expected in today's business environment. As a result, your company should handle reputational crises like any other major business challenge: based on principled, prepared leadership, and supported by sophisticated processes and capabilities that are integrated with the business strategy and culture of the company.

The adage that "crises don't build character, they expose it" certainly applies in the arena of reputation management during crisis response. Effective reputation management will always be challenging. Like any business skill, reputation management will call upon you to provide innovation, adaptation, and excellent character traits. However, appropriate capabilities achieved through preparedness can dramatically help you to reduce the complexity of reputational challenges, spot problems early, and develop effective strategies that are deeply integrated with your business as a whole.

Quick Use Response Guide

Chapter 6: Reputation Management

▶ Reputation management is a multidisciplinary process.

❑ Who and what should be incorporated into the crisis response that goes beyond the traditional public affairs and communications department, external public relations firms, or attorneys?

▶ Good Samaritan principle.

❑ Have we utilized the template of caring combined with competence as a filter for all crisis decision-making and actions?

▶ Corporate caring is not a feeling, it's behavioral.

❑ In what ways are we overtly showing involved stakeholders that we are a concerned and caring organization?

▶ Ten Test Questions for Crisis Decision-Making.

❑ Are these guidelines known to all appropriate managers and applied appropriately during crisis response?

▶ Trust building components.

❑ Has the company balanced appropriate levels of transparency, expertise, commitment, and empathy in its crisis planning and response?

▶ Prevention and preparedness to respond.

❑ Is your organization ready to address stakeholder expectations related to the following questions?

❑ What did the organization do to prevent this situation from occurring in the first place?

❑ What preparedness actions were implemented in order to be ready to effectively mitigate the crisis once it occurred (foreseeable risk preparedness and all-hazards preparedness)?

▶ Anticipate that the "crisis spotlight" will focus on how the CEO or other appropriate spokespersons answer questions and what the company will do to fix the problem in a caring manner.

▶ Is blame toward the company included in crisis exercises and anticipated in crisis response, rather than only scenarios where the organization and management are victims?

   ❑ Blame should be anticipated and addressed as an important component of crisis containment and recovery.

▶ If the organization or management is blamed, understand that stakeholder beliefs will include a subset of the following:

   ❑ The company *intentionally* did something harmful.

   ❑ The company acted in a manner that was *unfair*.

   ❑ Management should have *foreseen* the crisis and averted it or been more adequately prepared.

   ❑ Management was *unprepared* to effectively handle the crisis.

   ❑ Reasonably prudent care was not exercised, thus the company was *negligent*.

▶ Have we anticipated these five (5) components that make up the anatomy of blame and addressed them appropriately?

▶ Remember that outrage will increase the intensity and longevity of the crisis.

   ❑ Where do we anticipate stakeholder outrage and what should we do proactively to mitigate it?

▶ Are the roles and responsibilities of senior executives, middle managers, and tactical/site responders clearly defined and delineated?

▶ If there is significant harm to people or the environment, the CEO should address the public to demonstrate the company's commitment and to show empathy.

   ❑ If the CEO is not the right spokesperson, choose the appropriate person(s) with reasonable expertise and authority relating to the crisis.

▶ When the crisis causes core assets of the organization to be at risk, including reputation, the executive-level crisis management team (CMT) should assemble and provide strategic oversight and direction for the organizational crisis response.

   ❑ Remember that the CMT should integrate and support the other teams and their leaders, rather than usurp the planning, training, exercising, and experience that has been previously prepared.

▶ External specialists can provide valuable experience and expertise to the team.

    ❏ However, all decision-making is the responsibility of management and should not be delegated to external specialists. Experienced external consultants can help to orchestrate and facilitate effective decision-making during crises.

    ❏ Who are the external specialists that should be retained and oriented to the organization prior to various foreseeable crises?

    ❏ Consider including external specialists in crisis exercises.

▶ Establish and thoroughly socialize the values of the organization that should be maintained and followed during crisis response.

▶ Successful reputation management requires the ability to assume perspectives and "outside-in" viewpoints of each stakeholder group that is involved in an organizational crisis.

Chapter 6 – Questions for Further Thought and Discussion

1. How can your organization build reputational equity with each anticipated key stakeholder group prior to a crisis?

2. What are enhancements or additions to the Ten Test Questions for Crisis Decision-Making?

3. Compile statements and actions that would demonstrate a lack of transparency, expertise, commitment, and empathy.

4. Generically, what are the roles and responsibilities of senior executives, middle managers, and tactical/site responders for protecting organizational reputation?

5. What are the qualifications and roles of an external specialist who would be appropriate to consult with a senior management team or the CEO during a crisis?

6. What external specialists should the organization integrate into their crisis response capabilities before the next crisis hits?

References

Agnes, M. (2012, March 22). *Domino's Pizza: a look at the timelessness of a social media crisis plan*. Retrieved from: http://www.melissaagnescrisismanagement.com/dominos-pizza-a-look-at-the-timelessness-of-a-social-media-crisis-plan/

Cheng, A. (2004, January 2). Macy's settles lawsuit with Martha Stewart. *Wall Street Journal*. http://www.marketwatch.com/story/macys-settles-lawsuit-with-martha-stewart-2014-01-02

Diermeier, D. (2011). *Reputation rules: strategies for building your company's most valuable asset*. New York: McGraw-Hill, especially Chapter 5. For empirical evidence see: Jordan, J., Diermeier, D., & Galinsky, A. (2012). The strategic Samaritan: how effectiveness and proximity affect corporate responses to external crises. *Business Ethics Quarterly*, 22(4): 621–649.

D'innocenzio, A. (2013, February 25). Martha Stewart battle leads Macy's CEO, J.C. Penney CEO to testify. *Huffington Post*. Retrieved from: http://www.huffingtonpost.com/2013/02/25/martha-stewart-jc-penney-macys_n_2758490.html

Edelman, R. (2013). *Executive summary: 2013 Edelman trust barometer*. Retrieved from: http://www.edelman.com/trust-downloads/executive-summary/

Jacques, A. (2009, August 17). Domino's delivers during crisis: the company's step-by-step response after a vulgar video goes viral. *Public Relations Strategist*. Retrieved from: http://www.prsa.org/Intelligence/TheStrategist/Articles/view/8226/102/Domino_s_deliver_during_crisis_The_company_s_step

Nocera, J. (2012, January 10). BP has performed admirably after the spill. *New York Times*. Retrieved from: http://www1.realclearmarkets.com/2012/01/10/bp_has_performed_admirably_after_the_spill_122256.html

Schoenberg, A.L. (2004). *What it means to lead during a crisis: an exploratory examination of crisis leadership*. Syracuse, NY: Syracuse University.

Wallace, B. (2011, July 31). The comeback that wasn't. *New York Magazine*. Retrieved from: http://nymag.com/news/features/martha-stewart-2011-8/

7

Establishing the New Normal

After a major traumatic incident, everything can seem different. The world suddenly seems unsafe and unpredictable – and can continue to feel that way for some time to come. Your trust in people, relationships, God, government, institutions, environment, and the world can become a concern.

Your people are likely to feel this way in the aftermath of a disaster or situation that rocks their established senses of normalcy. The common sentiment is, "We can never go back to normal around here. Things will never be the same." This is natural enough. After all, they have been emotionally traumatized, they may be mourning, and they may be frightened. As a result, it's a good idea to avoid framing the task ahead as "getting back to normal." Instead, introduce the concept of establishing a "new normal," which builds in the recognition and acknowledgment of what has occurred while phasing back into productive work.

This chapter will help you to:

> ➢ *Prepare to lead your organization through a period of adjustment.*

> ➢ *Handle the first day back with sensitivity.*

> ➢ *Provide the psychological first aid for recovery.*

> ➢ *Support employees in returning to full productivity.*

> ➢ *Help your team to recognize and act upon the lessons-learned.*

7.1 It's Back to Work We Go

The good news is that people tend to be resilient. Just as we naturally overcome a common cold, people have coping mechanisms that allow them to return to a state of balance that is much the same as prior to the crisis situation. This is not to say that those who experience permanent losses will not experience difficult adjustments, such as surviving family members following the death of a loved one. They will. But, we know from experience that human beings in crisis are adaptable. Most people will recover, and the recovery process can be accelerated when management does the right things for impacted stakeholders.

The concept of a new normal is something people can understand and grasp emotionally. It can help them move forward. It removes the implication that they are being asked to act as if nothing has happened – as if Helen and Jack are still at their desks, or that irreplaceable historic building still stands, or those persons who lost limbs in the Boston Marathon bombing will be good as new. The new normal sets up the expectation that there may be some personal and organizational adjustments, but we will reestablish a sense of normalcy.

> The longer people stay out, isolated and brooding over what has happened, the more abnormal things will feel.

It's usually best to get people back to work as soon as possible after a traumatic workplace incident. There is nothing normal about staying home in recovery mode. People are more likely to become depressed, anxious, angry, and fixated on perceived harm when they "drop out." The longer people stay out, isolated and brooding over what has happened, the more abnormal things will feel. Getting people back to a work routine with organizational support, on the other hand, gives them an opportunity to process the experience together, in an organized way, which you can facilitate. It allows them to have accurate and timely information, too, which is essential to recovery.

This is not to say that you should ask people to conduct a regular workday immediately after a distressing experience. Instead, the first day back at work should be a day for "slaying the dragon" – confronting what happened by, for example, returning to the building where the incident occurred. Management should be highly visible on this day. Up-to-date information should be flowing in a caring and concerned manner. There should be clear acknowledgment of what has occurred, and structured opportunities for asking questions and venting the very difficult reactions that people will naturally be experiencing.

7.2 Your Window of Opportunity

As a general rule, the sooner that management makes contact with concerned, outraged, and impacted people following an unexpected crisis incident, the better. If possible, personal contacts may be preferable, via phone or face-to-face. Whatever the medium, leaders should be visible, with a show of control, caring, and commitment to resolving the crisis.

In the workplace, if it is impossible for employees to go back to the workplace within 72 hours, you should still strive to bring everyone together. Consider having them (with their families, if appropriate to the situation) meet at an offsite location like an appropriately-sized hotel conference room, school, or church.

Avoid leaving your employees out of touch for a long period. If the incident occurred on a Friday, when employees would normally have been off until Monday, consider contacting them during the weekend with a standardized, prepared statement of up-to-date information. This could be done on the first evening of an incident, even if people are to come back to work the next day. In severely traumatizing situations, set up a buddy system, in which employees can check in with each other and special needs or concerns can be conveyed to managers who can help within the company. Possibly, supervisors could set up a buddy system for their direct reports.

An emergency communications system for mass notifications – where one outgoing message goes to everyone simultaneously – is increasingly common in businesses throughout the world. For those who don't have these capabilities, a low-tech phone tree system in which managers and supervisors call all their direct reports is one way to accomplish this outgoing communication and obtain an assessment of people's states of mind at the same time. When appropriate and in addition to delivering prepared information, questions could be asked about how each person was involved in the incident, about their wellbeing, and their needs, reactions, and concerns. Those making the calls, such as supervisors, should be cautioned not to get into "counseling sessions." Callers should establish early in the conversations that calls must be short, since several contacts are to be made. Anyone who appears to be having significant difficulty could be identified and then contacted separately by a crisis-experienced behavioral health (formerly called mental health) professional or appropriate person within the company.

7.3 The First Day Back

As a general rule, management should be present, visible, and accessible when employees are arriving back at work for the first time. If bulletins have been prepared regarding the incident facts and the day's schedule, managers could be the ones to hand them out as employees arrive. You want to make the simple gestures of contact that let people know you are aware of what they are experiencing. Some companies have mounted large banners to welcome employees back. That's what Transamerica Insurance Group did in Los Angeles, California, in 1994, following the Northridge earthquake. The high-touch message the company wants to convey is that we are glad to see people back, things are stabilized (to the best extent possible), and we care about the wellbeing of our employees and their families.

7.3.1 The Management Briefing

The first thing that should occur on the first day back is a briefing for employees by the senior-most managers available, at which attendance by all is mandatory. The company will want to get all messaging delivered with consistency, so this should be just like any other important meeting where people are expected to participate.

The briefing is intended to help employees feel informed, cared for, listened to, and understood. It is an opportunity to provide them with up-to-date information, and to discuss management's response actions following the incident. It is the place to squelch rumors and establish a consistent core message about what specifically has occurred. It is the time to tell employees what to expect in the near future, and for them to ask questions. Its purpose is to provide information and show management's understanding of what employees have experienced. The need for accurate and timely information is typically of highest importance to employees following a distressing situation. This forum is designed to address that need.

During the briefing, management should establish how ongoing communications about the crisis will take place. You may be planning additional face-to-face briefings, an information telephone hot line, intranet or private website, e-mail or text updates, or phone tree notification system. Increasingly, social media networks are utilized to communicate to and from internal and external groups. Now is the time to explain the methods you plan to use.

People will want to know that they will be kept in the information loop as the situation unfolds. Let people know when updated information will be provided and stick to that schedule on a timely basis. If possible, inform your employees with updates before you provide that same information to the media. Your people want to hear from you, not feel neglected by hearing from management through a local evening news reporter. If your outgoing communications are through fast-moving, real-time social networking channels, inform employees to monitor these same networks for information. So management can stay in control of their messaging, ask employees not to participate with their own information in these social networks about the company's crisis.

> **Receiving accurate and timely information from every part of your organization is vital to your ongoing management of a situation. Do not leave this function to chance.**

7.3.2 Ways of Listening

For most companies I have observed during crises, methods for receiving information tend to be less well organized than methods for giving information. Receiving accurate and timely information from every part of your organization is vital to your ongoing management of a situation. Do not leave this function to chance. Set up a purposeful system for getting information. It might include an open door policy for top managers; communications conveyed up the ranks through supervisors; a hot line or reporting line (with guaranteed anonymity, if warranted); an old-fashioned or electronic suggestion box for written ideas; designated managers who will accept and deal with e-mailed comments; focus groups; feedback surveys; or other mechanisms for inbound communication. These should all be explained and encouraged for use at the initial management briefing.

One method for obtaining grassroots input from employees is to set up a "new normal" committee of employee representatives. Its job will be to gather feedback from employees, discuss ideas for effectively establishing a new normal, and providing input to management with their ideas. The committee needs to understand that its suggestions must be reasonable and in the best interest of both the organization and employees.

Case Study:
When the First Day Back Was Six Months Later

The Century movie theater in Aurora, Colorado experienced an unexpected mass shooting by James Holmes (killing 12 and injuring 70) on July 20, 2012, during the midnight screening of a new Batman movie. It immediately became a worldwide news event. Due to the shock and profound grief related to the tragedy within the Aurora community, the theater remained closed indefinitely. A community-based online questionnaire was developed for citizens to share their ideas about what Cinemark (the theater owner) should do with the theater where the horrible mass murder occurred. Responses varied widely, from demolishing the building and constructing a memorial to rebuilding the entire multiplex center. Some suggested that the multiplex should reopen, while others recommended the theater remain permanently closed. This is the point where a multi-disciplinary "new normal" committee can help to ensure all stakeholder issues are adequately considered, knowing there will ultimately be disagreements by some.

After deliberation, Cinemark decided to provide a significant refurbishment of the existing theater and reopen six months following the shooting. Clearly, this new normal was not acceptable to all, especially many families of victims. But, everyone won't be happy in these situations. Apparently, not adequately anticipating the reactions of victims' families, Cinemark decided that it would be appropriate to send special invitations to these family members to attend the reopening of the theater. This was two days after Christmas with many families already having a difficult time with intensified grief during the holidays. The reaction of families was public outrage and the news media focused their attention on the perceived insensitivity of Cinemark.

A large number of people in Aurora reportedly felt that Cinemark took the cheapest route to maintain their business at that location at the expense of those who continued to suffer from the tragedy. Unfortunately, the new normal that Cinemark established was divergent from the opinions and feelings of many victims' families and thus the media.

On the first anniversary of the shootings, July 19, 2013, the city sponsored a "Day of Remembrance." Cinemark announced that it would have no midnight film showing that night. In the months since the tragedy, the community has provided activities for citizens' healing. This has included music, yoga, meditation, counseling, art projects, and community service projects. An organization like Cinemark is well advised to consider the appropriateness of helping to support such activities in a low-key manner that does not look like self-aggrandizement.

To Cinemark's credit, the action of continuing to use the facilities where tragic shootings occurred was not unprecedented. Virginia Tech (not known for its post-crisis prowess) reopened Norris Hall where Seung Cho killed 30 students in 2007. However, Columbine High School opted to demolish the library where 10 students were shot to death in 1999 and rebuilt it as an atrium. Likewise, Ft. Hood Army Military Base in Texas totally rebuilt the Soldier Readiness Processing Center following the 2009 mass shooting by Army Major Nidal Hasan. And in May 2013, in Newtown, Connecticut, 5 months after the shootings of 20 students and 6 adults at Sandy Hook Elementary School, a task force of elected town officials recommended that the school be demolished and rebuilt on the same site with the same name.

Lessons-learned: As this situation demonstrates, establishing a new normal isn't always easy. Many times, even the best intentions can be misconstrued by stakeholders who hold a grudge. As guiding principles, listen and stay close to impacted constituents; use a template of caring over every decision and action; and do nothing that appears self-serving, especially above the wellbeing of those who feel harmed.

7.4 A Program for Recovery: Psychological First Aid

You owe it to impacted stakeholders, and to the continued health of your organization, to institute a structured program that facilitates recovery and the establishment of a new normal. In many cases, this may include crisis-experienced behavioral health assistance, an intentional "phasing" back into productive work and operations, ongoing monitoring, and a strategy for purposeful "disengagement" at the right time from the crisis intervention and response activities.

It is important for management to provide effective social support for traumatized stakeholders. People respond well to a psychological first aid (PFA) process that is widely used by organizations – corporate, public sector, and civic – in the early aftermath of an incident. Management's role in PFA can include providing impacted stakeholders with appropriate levels of practical assistance, physical comfort, and accurate information in the early aftermath of a distressing crisis. As appropriate, consider providing food as a gesture of corporate caring. A free lunch can be a simple way to demonstrate that the organization cares.

> No one should be coerced to "talk about" his or her experiences. Instead, positive coping strategies should be discussed individually or in groups

7.4.1 Traditional Psychological Debriefings Not Recommended

One common post-crisis practice has come into controversy. For years, employee assistance program (EAP) providers and other behavioral health professionals have provided psychological group debriefing sessions for employees and other impacted stakeholder groups. I use the term "psychological debriefing" to differentiate from the "operational debriefings" that we will discuss later. Commonly referred to as critical incident stress debriefings (CISD), these group sessions historically have included discussions regarding traumatized employees' experiences during the incident, reactions since the event, and traumatic stress symptoms that could emerge.

Unfortunately, the outcomes of these CISD group debriefings were not tested adequately prior to implementation. Recent research (Rose, Bisson, & Wessely, 2003) has concluded repeatedly that debriefing sessions (and their many workplace variations) can create a measurable increase in traumatic stress for some participants, whether delivered in individual, couples, or group sessions. One year following CISD sessions, a select few participants were found to have higher rates of post-traumatic stress disorder (PTSD) than nonparticipants. Yet, many behavioral health professionals continue the practice of CISD at the risk of harm to impacted people and liability exposures for companies they serve.

7.4.2 Positive Coping Strategies Needed

PFA techniques, cognitive behavioral therapy (CBT) strategies, and resiliency-based methods for assisting emotionally traumatized people are showing promise for assisting people following exposure to distressing events. Management should insist that behavioral health professionals avoid CISD rehashing of traumatic experiences and predictions of potential traumatic stress symptoms for employees. No one should be coerced to "talk about" his or her experiences. Instead, positive coping strategies should be discussed individually or in groups along with the provision of practical assistance in regaining a sense of normalcy.

Just because the CISD model ran into problems does not mean that the "baby should be thrown out with the bathwater." Individual and group meetings with employees tend to be overwhelmingly well received when provided in the proper manner. There is a social expectation among employees that management will demonstrate a caring and concerned response. These individual and group contacts can meet that expectation when provided by behavioral health professionals with training and experience in proper methods of crisis response.

7.4.3 Individual Assessment and Counseling

Following traumatic incidents, some individuals will be identified as needing professional crisis counseling. Remember, though, that most people will establish a successful recovery without professional counseling services, especially if management provides the caring services discussed in this chapter and appropriate early intervention services are provided to support resiliency. Make it safe for people to request help for themselves and for affected family members. Provide confidential professional assistance at onsite and offsite locations so it is easy for people to use.

Treatment providers should be skilled in CBT methods, including exposure therapy for traumatic stress. Exposure therapy involves a participant's repeated recall of the traumatic incident in a structured manner with a qualified therapist to reduce distressing mental images of the incident and overwhelming emotions. This technique can rapidly get people on their feet and back to work at an appropriate time, especially when provided in a context of caring management actions. As with any treatment modality, there are exceptions, and some people will need additional or alternative assistance.

As mentioned previously, most trauma-exposed people are resilient and will make adequate self-adjustments in their personal, social, and work lives. It is not possible to determine who will need treatment in the early aftermath of a traumatic incident. Those who openly cry may be much improved in a few days, while those who show no reaction could end up needing professional assistance to bounce back. Evidence of those who have true coping difficulties (as opposed to transient adjustment reactions) will typically begin to emerge within the first four weeks following the incident. Consider utilizing an empirically validated survey to identify those employees who are at risk of PTSD or chronic coping difficulties.

7.4.4 Early Intervention

Insurers and large corporations are increasingly using psychological consulting firms, like Behavioral Medical Interventions, to assist with return-to-work issues. These firms use case review methods, professional peer-to-peer consultations, and other methods to determine if optimal treatment is being utilized by treating professionals. Often, they are not. The result from incorporating these additional methods is accelerated return-to-work.

Self-insured corporations are also establishing early intervention programs to get people back to work. Family Dollar is a national discount retailer in the US. It established an early intervention program through Crisis Care Network, Inc. for employees involved in traumatic incidents, like armed robberies or natural disasters (Oller, 2013). Family Dollar has drastically reduced workers' compensation costs and the number of employees quitting their jobs (post-incident) with reported huge savings to their bottom line.

> If there have been flower wreaths or banners up, establish a time to put them away. The point is to provide a moment when everyone, symbolically, resumes regular activities.

7.5 Phasing Back Into Productive Work

Just as it is crucial to acknowledge and memorialize the crisis and its impact, it is essential to bring the period of post-crisis processing toward a close, and get back to work. Depending on the crisis severity and circumstances, you might phase into normal work on the second or third day or following any funerals. In other instances, it could take considerably longer; for example, it took three weeks before employees could return to work following the 1993 World Trade Center bombing, and many employees were without homes for months following Hurricane Katrina.

You can use all kinds of symbolic but potent markers to pinpoint the transition back to work and a new normal. For instance, if you normally observe a business attire dress code, you might relax it for the immediate period following the incident, then resume the dress code on an announced day to symbolize a return to normal work. If there have been flower wreaths or banners up, establish a time to put them away. The point is to provide a timeline when everyone, symbolically, resumes regular activities. Meanwhile, management can continue to assess the wellbeing of the workforce and demonstrate corporate caring as the regular work routine resumes.

7.5.1 Supervisory Monitoring

Managers and supervisors have an extra role to play with their employees in the aftermath of a disaster, as the eyes and ears of your recovery and human support efforts. Since they know your employees best, they are in the position to recognize those who are having continued difficulty and evidencing distress. Let supervisors know that they should be alert for unusual behavior, and where to report their concerns about non-recovering employees. This is one way to identify employees who may need referral for further treatment, especially during the first month following a traumatic incident.

You should be aware that persons who continue to experience traumatic stress reactions for a month or more may meet the legally accepted diagnostic criteria for PTSD. By monitoring and treating employees who experience continuing stress reactions, you will be better able to avoid significant medical costs, formerly productive employees quitting, and lost productivity down the line.

Case Study:
Establishing a New Normal
Following a Mass Workplace Shooting

In 1989, Joseph Wesbecker worked for Standard Gravure, a newspaper printing company in Louisville, Kentucky, but had been on a one-year leave of absence for a stress-related illness. After 12 months, his disability payments stopped. Unannounced, he returned to the workplace and shot 21 people, killing 8. Because the company printed time-sensitive advertising for daily newspapers, there was a great need to reestablish a new normal as soon as possible. I was called into Standard Gravure that evening by senior management to expedite the recovery process. A crisis management team (CMT) was quickly established.

Paradoxically, the first step in reestablishing productivity was to shut down production. However, at my suggestion, management asked all employees to come to the worksite the day following the mass shooting for a full management briefing on the incident. Supervisors came in two hours prior to employees' arrival in order to plan out their role for the upcoming day. Management was to provide communications for all employees,

---

to be delivered through the supervisors since no place was available within the factory that was suitable for an all-employee meeting. Two-way communications were to be established through structured company-wide employee briefing meetings, provided by the supervisors. Additionally, supervisors were to identify employee needs and concerns, then relay that information back to the CMT.

Management greeted arriving employees. Supervisors provided up-to-date information. Employees were paid for unworked time the day of the shooting. Production for the day was minimized and customers were notified of the disruption. Media surrounded the building and employees were encouraged not to speak to any reporters, as the CEO had agreed to be the spokesperson for the company. Lunch was provided for employees as a gesture of caring. Security was established to stop media encroachment and provide a sense of safety. Crisis counseling groups and individual sessions were provided throughout the day. To facilitate the two-way communication process, anonymous questionnaires were distributed for employees to give direct feedback to senior management about their reactions, needs, and concerns.

The first day back, an employee crisis recovery committee was established to allow designated employees to gather information from coworkers and brainstorm solutions to problems and concerns. The committee had direct access to the CEO and executive VP of the company. Issues that were obtained and addressed included a company-sponsored memorial service at a local hotel ballroom for all employees and their families. Additionally, provisions were made for employees to attend funerals and to be paid if they attended during work hours.

Lessons-learned: Ultimately, the generosity of management, flexibility in meeting employee needs, and demonstrations of caring allowed the company to rapidly return to a full work schedule. Supervisors were briefed and instructed to monitor their employees for adjustment problems and deteriorating work performance. Those employees who needed additional assistance were provided confidential supportive assistance.

While the incident was devastating, a new normal was established and productivity resumed. The employee crisis recovery committee remained in place for months following, which served as an ongoing conduit of connectivity between management and the employees to ensure emerging problems didn't go unaddressed.

7.5.2 Purposeful Disengagement

The point will come at which you can disengage your crisis intervention and response activities. "Purposeful disengagement" means that the process used to de-escalate the crisis management process passes the reasonable person test and takes into consideration the disposition of all involved stakeholders. There are a variety of indicators, both internal and external, that purposeful disengagement is appropriate. Disengagement considerations might include answers to the following questions:

- Is the crisis resolved to the satisfaction of your multidisciplinary crisis team?

- Has traditional and social media coverage of the event subsided, or taken a positive turn?

- Have involved stakeholders and the organization found a "new normal" equilibrium that is demonstrated through return to normal productivity, satisfactory morale, or other key indicators of normalcy?

- Have rumors stopped or diminished dramatically?

- Has evidence of lingering outrage diminished significantly or stopped?

- Have sales returned to pre-crisis levels or stabilized?

- Have your stock price and financial expenditures stabilized?

- Has continuity of operations been restored?

- Are threats to core assets (e.g., people, reputation, brand, trust, finances, shareholder value, or key relationships) sufficiently mitigated?

- Have issues that caused or escalated the crisis been identified and rectified?

- Have positive outcomes been realized from your crisis response?

- Have sufficient operational debriefings been completed and lessons-learned implemented?

7.5.3 Anniversary Effect

Part of disengaging is acknowledging what happened, and you may want to consider some ways to memorialize it in the future. But beware of "anniversary overkill." Many companies over prepare for the one-year anniversary of a crisis event. But don't ignore the anniversary, either. These dates may indeed occasion some noticeable reaction in your work force. Consider doing something symbolic but restrained, like publishing an acknowledgment in an internal newsletter, placing a wreath in the lobby, or inviting interested individuals to participate in a task force to talk over the lasting effects and lessons learned from the incident. In some situations, it is appropriate to have crisis counselors available on the first anniversary of a traumatic incident. If such counseling is provided, it is best to work with a knowledgeable crisis consultant to plan the availability and role of counselors in a manner that is appropriate.

> **Even after disengagement, with the new normal in place, consider a continuing program of monitoring your organization for lingering effects of the crisis.**

7.6 Operational Debriefing for Lessons-Learned

Once the crisis response is completed, there is typically little emotional energy or interest in taking time out to analyze the crisis response of the team(s) and company. But it is important that as a committed policy an operational debriefing be conducted at the conclusion of each crisis response. A senior manager with sufficient authority needs to ensure lessons are learned from how the organization managed the situation. Identify and capture the strengths, opportunities, and positive outcomes in your response and the areas that will need improvement for more effectively managing future incidents. Then make sure the positive outcomes are capitalized upon and needed changes are implemented. Look for ways to prevent similar occurrences and how to be better prepared to respond during the next crisis. Make note also of those individuals who excelled during the crisis response. Some people are simply better at handling unexpected crisis situations than others no matter how much training is provided. These will be your "go to" folks for crisis preparedness and your next response.

Even after disengagement, with the new normal in place, consider a continuing program of monitoring your organization for lingering effects of the crisis. You will want to know, and develop a response, if you find that any of the following are occurring in a significant way:

▶ New and related issues arise.

▶ Rumors concerning the crisis.

▶ Indication of lowered employee productivity, morale, or loyalty to the organization.

▶ Negatively affected key relationships internally or externally.

▶ Diminished customer sales, loyalty, and trust.

▶ Speculations or resurfacing coverage about the company in the media.

▶ Discernible negative effects on company reputation and diminished goodwill in the eyes of the public.

▶ Continuing financial implications.

▶ Negative impact on any core assets.

▶ Triggering events, such as litigation and criminal trial that could rekindle a focus on the crisis.

But the most valuable outcome of operational debriefing and monitoring the aftermath of each crisis will be the information it furnishes that you can use right now to prepare yourself for future crises.

In the next section of the book, I will lead you through the steps of creating a comprehensive preparedness plan for your organization. With it in place, you need not be blindsided again.

Quick Use Response Guide

Chapter 7: Establishing the New Normal

▶ Did you get people back to work as soon as appropriately possible after the crisis?

▶ On employees' first day back at work:

❑ Was management highly visible?

❑ Was there clear information flow regarding what occurred, what management has done, and what employees can expect in the near future?

❑ Were there opportunities for employees to report rumors, ask questions, and discuss concerns?

❑ Did every appropriate person attend a briefing by senior management?

❑ Did you set up a system for giving *and receiving* ongoing information?

▶ Are return-to-work enhancement methodologies implemented through appropriate psychological consulting firms to diminish treatment, workers' compensation, disability, and turnover costs?

▶ Were impacted stakeholders provided PFA and practical post-incident assistance?

❑ Did you ensure that any behavioral health services such as psychological first aid (PFA), crisis counseling, group and individual educational meetings, etc. for impacted stakeholders utilize research-supported and resiliency-based methods?

▶ Did management's response support the wellbeing of employees first, before focusing on a return to productive work?

▶ Did you frame the period of crisis aftermath processing, so that everyone knew when to phase back into a new normal work routine?

▶ Were managers and supervisors briefed on their role to recognize employees who need additional support in readjusting?

▶ Were those individuals who appeared to need additional help provided with professional assessment and intervention, especially within the first month?

▶ Did a multidisciplinary team make a purposeful decision that passed the reasonable person test regarding when to disengage from crisis response?

▶ Did you debrief your crisis response performance for lessons-learned to capitalize on any positive outcomes, opportunities, and weaknesses?

Chapter 7 – Questions for Further Thought and Discussion

1. What are ten things that should be considered and organized by management prior to employees' first day back at work after a traumatic workplace incident?

2. What would you want from management if you were an employee who was returning to the workplace where people had been injured or killed?

3. Stakeholders need to feel heard and understood following crises where there is perceived harm. What are various channels of communication that would be effective in giving *and* receiving information from both internal and external stakeholders?

4. What is "purposeful disengagement"? Why is it important to creating the "new normal"? What are additional considerations for purposeful disengagement that are not listed in this chapter or that would better fit your corporate culture?

5. What are questions that should be asked during an operational debriefing following a crisis response?

References

Oller, S. (July 2013). Prepare and protect: retailers learn importance of being ready for the unexpected. *CSP Magazine*. Retrieved from: http://www.cspnet.com/sites/default/files/magazine-files/1307-F3_Crisis.pdf

Rose, S., Bisson, J., & Wessely, S. (2003). A systematic review of single-session psychological interventions ('debriefing') following trauma. *Psychother Psychosom*, 72:171-5.

PART 2:

PREPAREDNESS

8

The First Step to Preparedness

Unprepared organizations have much more costly crises and go out of business at disproportionately higher rates than prepared organizations. Even so, many executives and managers put preparedness for foreseeable risks on the back burner. It is human nature to focus first on growing the value of the organization at the expense of a strong defense. While some management teams rely on the strategy of "it's better to be lucky than good," well-managed companies focus on creating their own luck by being fully crisis prepared. As Gary Player, the South African golfer, once said, "The harder you work, the luckier you get."

In effective crisis management, the twin disciplines of effective responsiveness and preparedness go hand-in-hand. These are the disciplines you must master to protect your company from crisis-related harm to core assets. In the first half of this book, we have just looked at responsiveness to a crisis. In the remaining chapters, we will focus on preparedness.

This chapter will help you to:

- ➤ *Value the financial impact of preparedness.*
- ➤ *See what it takes to be a prepared manager.*
- ➤ *Recognize the human side of crisis impact.*
- ➤ *Understand and apply the five-step preparedness process.*
- ➤ *Organize an effective crisis planning committee (CPC).*

Case Study: Miracle on the Hudson

It was a clear and cold morning on January 15, 2009, with excellent flying conditions. US Airways flight 1549 had an uneventful initial takeoff. However, approximately three minutes after takeoff from New York's LaGuardia Airport, the Airbus A320 plane flew into a flock of Canadian geese. Simultaneously, both engines failed with no thrust capabilities.

Over one of the most populous areas in North America, Capt. Chesley "Sully" Sullenberger notified the control tower that an emergency landing was needed immediately. While alternative airports were discussed and prepared, Capt. Sullenberger realized that the plane's rapid descent made landing at nearby Teterboro Airport too risky. He had only seconds to decide. Without hesitation, he turned the jet southbound, gliding parallel with the Hudson River. The jet was ditched into the river with all 155 passengers safely evacuated by nearby ferries.

Sullenberger and his flight crew were awarded the Master's Medal of the Guild of Air Pilots and Air Navigators. He has been identified repeatedly as a hero for his "unique aviation achievement" with no loss of lives.

Lessons-learned: In one of his first nationally televised interviews (Couric, K., 2009) following the critical incident, Sullenberger said, "One way of looking at this might be that for 42 years I've been making small, regular deposits in this bank of experience, education, and training. And on January 15th, the balance was sufficient so that I could make a very large withdrawal." He ascribes his achievement to one simple concept – preparedness. Team and individual preparedness was the singular key component for his successful life-saving crisis response.

8.1 The Financial Impact of Preparedness

The financial importance of preparedness was underscored by a seminal study, *The Impact of Catastrophes on Shareholder Value*, published by Templeton College, University of Oxford (1996).

> ... companies whose management responded well to the crisis experienced recovery... companies whose management did not respond effectively experienced further decline.

"Firms affected by catastrophes fall into two relatively distinct groups – recoverers and non-recoverers," the study found. And the recoverers tend to increase their shareholder value over time when compared to unprepared companies, or non-recoverers. "Although all catastrophes have an initial negative impact on value, paradoxically they offer an opportunity to management to demonstrate their talent in dealing with difficult circumstances." Among the essential differences between the recoverers and non-recoverers, the study concluded that "the issue of management's responsibility for accident or safety lapses appears to explain the shareholder value response."

As illustrated in Figure 8-1, the Templeton study found that after a catastrophe, a sharp initial negative impact on the value of a company's stock occurs. Those companies whose management responded well to the crisis experienced recovery; on the other hand, those companies whose management did not respond effectively experienced further decline.

I urge you to have the following in place:

▶ Tiered plans (executive, management, and tactical).

▶ Established trained teams.

▶ Regular exercise/practice schedule.

When you prepare yourselves for the crises you can reasonably anticipate, you will also help your management team respond to incidents that are totally unexpected. By taking an "all hazards" approach to your preparedness, you will allow for a carryover effect that will help you, no matter what occurs.

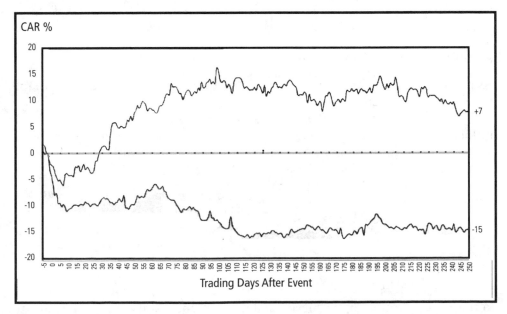

Figure 8-1. Templeton Study Graph of Shareholder Value.

8.2 The Prepared Manager

What does it take to manage with "strategic vision"? You need to balance your efforts in two areas: growing the value of your organization, and understanding and addressing the risks it may face.

For example, keenly aware of the need and competitive advantage of unparalleled safety for employees and customers, one vice president at the national retailer Target Corporation had the foresight to initiate a corporate-wide "safeness program."

Target instituted a comprehensive campaign for training and security (what it calls "assets protection"), making sure that both managers and employees were acutely aware of how to respond to issues of safety. After implementation, the program was monitored to guarantee that it was effective and working well. Next, Target set up a system to gauge any foreseeable threats to the organization. One person instigated that entire program and implemented it with the support of the senior management team.

Following Hurricane Katrina, Minneapolis-based Target crisis management team took notice of needed supplies that were in short supply during the Katrina response in New Orleans. Once the need was identified, Target filled a semi-trailer truck with pallets of food, water, and emergency supplies and staged it near the Minneapolis headquarters, just in case a catastrophe occurred near the local area. Soon after, on August 1, 2007, Minnesota's fifth busiest bridge carrying over 140,000 vehicles each workday collapsed during rush hour. In the incident, 145 people were injured and 13 killed. Due to Target's foresight and preparedness, the company moved a semi-truck of necessary supplies to the scene within 40 minutes of the collapse – a prime example of how anticipation and crisis preparedness pay off.

As a manager, you might have responsibility for a small work unit, or perhaps for thousands of employees. No matter the scale, you have an enormous responsibility to protect the core assets that correlate to your areas of influence and the organization as a whole. It begins with simple precautions and information to recognize and reduce the inherent hazards of your operations. The initial step in solving any problem is, first, to identify it.

> You and your management team can work effectively and look very good when you're in the crisis spotlight. Your crisis could even turn into unforeseen opportunities.

8.2.1 How Prepared Are You?

Perhaps your company has developed crisis plans, established teams at the executive, managerial, and tactical levels, or had a few training sessions and put crisis response checklists together. These efforts are laudable, but it is very easy to gain a false sense of security, especially if you don't allow yourself to visualize in detail the aftermath and fallout of your foreseeable incidents.

For example, an employee assistance program (EAP) is an effective way to address personal problems of employees and their families during normal, non-crisis times. Often, though, HR professionals rely on EAP counseling as a sole remedy for a traumatized workforce. But management must also "do the right things" for employees following critical incidents. Turning over responsibility for employee recovery to the EAP or other specialists is only half of the equation. Management must also work in tandem with EAP, communications, benefits, legal, corporate security, and other departments for an integrated and cohesive response on behalf of the workforce.

Risk managers and their insurance brokers analyze your company's needs on a regular basis. Your company insures against foreseeable losses with carefully analyzed policy limits for various types of coverage. Shouldn't your management make the effort to prepare their response for foreseeable crisis incidents with the same care?

You and your management team can work effectively and look very good when you're in the crisis spotlight. Your crisis could even turn into unforeseen opportunities. As demonstrated in the example above, Target enhanced the company's reputation in Minneapolis following the bridge collapse. The key is developing and implementing a preparedness strategy.

8.3 Crisis Management Is About People

When an emergency occurs, the visible seems to demand our attention. We rush in to assist and evacuate the wounded, put out the fires, address security issues, and take control of the TV crews and social media aficionados that are suddenly turning up. And it's true that all those tasks are urgent.

But in the chaos, often crisis managers neglect the less visible involved and impacted stakeholders. Since they're not bleeding or overtly visible, they may seem not to have been affected significantly.

Maybe this is because the more visible needs seem more urgent. People's invisible, internal reactions may seem too nebulous for managers to get their arms around. But they are real. Involved stakeholders are watching. They have needs and concerns. Expectations form beliefs about what the company should have done to prevent the situation and respond effectively once it happened. Attitudes and biases are formed that can destroy or bolster reputation about you and your company.

Whether the crisis is about a fatal incident, information technology (IT) outage, data breach, ethical misconduct, workplace violence, business disruption, product recall, or other occurrence, the crisis is really about the impact the incident has on people. If a tree falls in the woods, there is no concern. If a tree falls on your house or car, you immediately have a problem. For this reason, the primary focus of crisis management should be on how the crisis affects people and what can be provided to mitigate their negative reactions. Meanwhile, keep an eye out for potential positive outcomes.

8.3.1 Impacted Employees

Perhaps managers think that when it comes to the employee impact of a disaster, medical benefits, workers' compensation, and EAPs will adequately cover their crisis needs. Let's look at why this is only partially true.

Medical benefits are commonly either underutilized or abused by employees following traumatic incidents. A symptom of traumatic stress is to avoid anything that reminds the affected individual of the incident. People try to block out the experience mentally. Some may become immobilized and deny their physical and emotional symptoms. Others will overuse alcohol or drugs and medical services in an attempt to cope. These maladaptive solutions can cause costly long-term problems for employers, employees, and their families.

Workers' compensation benefits are typically the sole medical remedy provided to employees who are physically or mentally injured while working. In many states, uninjured employees affected by traumatic incidents in the workplace do not qualify for benefits. And some workers prefer to remain on the job without seeking benefits, perhaps out of embarrassment at admitting to psychological problems, or hassles related to the workers' compensation system.

In many states, psychological injuries are not considered compensable under workers' compensation law; thus, medical treatment is covered for physical injuries only. In other states, an employee must first be physically injured before psychological injury treatment will be considered. Some states allow workers to claim compensation coverage for psychological injury even when no physical injury has occurred.

In any case, workers' compensation coverage is insufficient.

Management action is needed to respond with decisive and caring action in addition to any benefits and workers' compensation-related services provided. Caring and decisive management action has repeatedly demonstrated that post-crisis awards of workers' compensation are reduced significantly when management "does the right thing" for employees.

In addition to workers' compensation for employees, management should assume appropriate responsibility for:

- Facilitating emergency assistance to all injured stakeholders.
- Providing psychological first aid to affected people.
- Notifying families of casualties. (See Appendix A of this book for how to handle conversations with families.)
- Accounting for people, and arranging security to those who were on the scene.
- Establishing communications with all stakeholder groups on a timely basis.
- Implementing a family representative program to deal with relatives of casualties.
- Visiting hospitals and homes of those injured or killed.
- Maintaining ongoing communications to and from affected stakeholders.
- Securing the crisis site and containing the crisis to minimize exposures that could cause additional harm.
- Addressing and monitoring the needs of employees on their first day back to work.
- Orchestrating skilled professional crisis intervention services at appropriate levels for all involved and impacted stakeholders.
- Providing needed benefits to employees beyond normal limits of coverage, as needed.
- Identifying at-risk employees and other stakeholders who are in need of follow-up assistance.
- Developing a crisis recovery committee that focuses on the human side of crisis response.
- Orchestrating appropriate memorials and funeral attendance, when needed.
- Balancing the post-incident need for corporate caring with productive return-to-work.

You can see from this partial listing for employees that the human side of a crisis is complex, and that managing it effectively demands planning and a commitment of effort. Preparedness is the key, and the same considerations should be established for the "human reactions" of other key stakeholders. These stakeholders can include customers, suppliers, distributors, business partners, contractors, traditional and social media, regulators and politicians, environmental protection constituencies, and nongovernmental organizations, as well as others that may be interested in or impacted by your crisis response.

> **Management needs to be prepared to address both the content side of the crisis...and the people side, regardless of the crisis at hand.**

8.3.2 Your Organization Is a Human System

Just like parents in a family, your management team is a member of the corporate "family system" and should be an active participant in addressing the human needs, concerns, and attitudes of all the system's participants during crises. Employees, customers, the media, attorneys, government regulators, the investment community, and boards of directors look to management to take responsible actions following critical incidents. Management needs to be prepared to address both the content side of the crisis (e.g., execute a product recall effectively or rescue documents from a soon-to-be-flooded building) and the people side, regardless of the crisis at hand.

8.3.3 Good vs. Poor Crisis Response

An organization's reputation – and their image in the marketplace – can be altered significantly for better or worse by how they prepare for and respond to a crisis.

Good Response

Let's consider components that indicate the aftermath of the crisis is being well managed:

- The problems at hand and the potential for escalation (in severity and longevity) are promptly addressed.
- The true nature of the crisis is appropriately identified and defined by focusing on threatened core assets of the organization.
- Timely and decisive actions address the urgent content of the crisis by regaining control of the situation and mitigating progressive damage (crisis containment).
- Responsibility is taken for solving crisis-related problems no matter who is at fault.
- Crisis communications are established and maintained to and from all involved stakeholders for as long as needed.
- Compassion and caring are demonstrated in words and observable actions.

▶ Management is accessible and visible to affected stakeholders.

▶ Ongoing steps are taken to make appropriate short- and long-term changes.

▶ Duration, breadth, and severity of the crisis are minimized.

▶ Lingering outrage, damaged reputation, business disruption, negative financial impact, and harm to all impacted stakeholders are mitigated to the best humanly-possible level.

▶ Sales, stock prices, and other financial indicators are stable at pre-crisis levels.

▶ Root causes are identified, investigated, and addressed.

Poor Response

Indicators that a crisis has not been handled well include:

▶ Management responds slowly or without coordination.

▶ Immediate and emerging problems, including escalation potential, are not identified.

▶ Actions address surface symptoms and consequences only, rather than including strategic components of the crisis that affect core assets.

▶ Management is reluctant to assume responsibility for appropriate response.

▶ Anticipation and assessment of ongoing response needs are not identified and addressed properly.

▶ Communications to and from all involved stakeholders are ineffective.

▶ Management strategy for response is nonexistent, inadequately communicated, unknown, or misunderstood.

▶ Caring and compassion are not communicated and not observable by stakeholders.

▶ Leadership is not visible or accessible to stakeholders.

▶ The crisis is prolonged by inaction or missteps.

▶ Crisis-related costs and reputational damage escalate beyond expectations.

▶ Stakeholders express lingering outrage and blame toward the organization.

The Five-Step Preparedness Process

This preparedness process applies across the board, to any crisis situation. This process gives you a way to address the risks inherent to your organization sequentially, no matter what they may be. It also allows you flexibility to address these hazards in a manner that fits your culture, budgetary constraints, and availability of time. Here's how it works.

Step 1. Analyzing foreseeable risks. First, analyze the risks that are unique to your organization and industry. This could include new and emerging risks. Chapter 9 will take you through this process.

Step 2. Evaluating existing and new procedures. Next, you evaluate new procedures, policies, and other controls, along with those that are already in place. Evaluate how you can enhance these existing controls with a minimum investment of new resources. Assessing new, existing, and enhanced controls will help you develop a template for your foreseeable risks preparedness. Chapter 10 will show you how.

Step 3. Organizing new controls and drafting the new plan. You will organize and integrate the new policies, procedures, and other management controls that will fill in any gaps in your existing crisis management capabilities. This way, you make sure you have considered a comprehensive defense for each of your identified risks. Here you organize the planning process. You establish your priorities. You set timelines. You integrate the various plans and responsibilities vertically and horizontally across the enterprise. You break your goals down into doable tasks. We'll discuss this in Chapter 11.

Step 4. Putting plans and teams in action. Chapter 12 looks at the process of executing your plan according to your corporate culture, budgetary constraints, and timeframe.

Step 5. Evaluating your results. Only ongoing monitoring and testing will ensure that your procedures are, in fact, working. Regularly scheduled reviews and scrutiny are an essential part of the preparedness process. This is the subject of Chapter 13.

8.4 The Process of Preparedness

As with any management system, effective preparedness is based on a series of components that are followed and practiced diligently. I have organized these components into a clear, logical five-step preparedness process, which I have found to be applicable to all the crises we deal with in this book – and any other challenging scenario you might find yourself confronting.

> **In the case of crisis preparedness, we just don't want to think about ourselves as being vulnerable.**

The late psychotherapist Dr. Albert Ellis suggested that certain irrational and self-defeating beliefs and behaviors are common to most people. From his extensive work on the topic of human thinking and behavior, he identified the common irrational belief that "it is easier to avoid life's problems than to face them." Some people in your company may believe it's easier to avoid preparing for crises, just as some find it easier to keep smoking than to quit. With characteristic bluntness, Ellis referred to this phenomenon as "stupid behavior by nonstupid people" (Ellis, A. & Harper, R.,1979).

The problem is not lack of intelligence, but rather that common beliefs, biases, and emotional discomforts get in the way of rational behavior. In the case of crisis preparedness, we just don't want to think about ourselves as being vulnerable. Mistaken beliefs that may keep us from implementing the preparedness process include: "It won't happen here," "I have other more important things to do," and "I'll handle it when it happens."

Much like purchasing insurance to cover risks, you can invest affordably now or rely on the hope and luck that nothing will happen in the future to cause serious damage. Crisis preparedness is another form of insurance. It's the "pay now or pay more later" syndrome.

Enlightened people are those who analyze their risks carefully and prepare in both their personal and professional lives. If you prepare, you will experience the calm assurance that comes from knowing that you and your teams (or family on the personal side) are prepared for critical situations.

We can compare preparedness to an ongoing effort like exercising regularly. You can't just try it a time or two and expect beneficial results. Optimally, it is an ongoing process. Doing a little bit of exercise is better than not doing any at all, but we all know that regularity is the key to staying in shape and enjoying the rewards of improved health. It's a simple equation: The more consistently you perform an appropriate exercise program of physical activity, the better off you'll be. Those who do might even save their own lives with a renewed sense of wellbeing.

The same is true of corporate crisis preparedness. When it comes to your company and employees, we're talking about a regimen of preparedness and exercises that just might save lives, jobs, and the vitality of your organization or work unit.

Cognitive-Emotive Dissonance

The equation of getting started in the preparedness process in earnest has one more piece. Even though people understand what is best, they still have something that keeps them from following through. The process that holds them back is called cognitive-emotive dissonance, a psychological term for a simple process. Mainly, it means that sometimes we must follow through even though we don't feel like it.

Think of the analogy of driving your car on the opposite side of the road. If you grew up in the US, for example, your thinking (cognition) and your feelings (emotion) both tell you to drive on the right-hand side of the road. But, if you were to travel to England and drive a vehicle, you would quickly experience the process of cognitive-emotive dissonance. Your rational thinking would say "drive on the left" because you are aware that you're driving in England where they drive on the left. But, your gut level feeling would tell you to drive on the right-hand side of the road, which you have been doing all your life. Even though driving on the right-hand side of the road in England is obviously a behavior that could quickly get you and others killed, your ingrained feelings tell you to keep doing what you've always been doing – drive on the right.

Overcoming thoroughly ingrained habits that are unproductive or harmful is a process of doing what your rational thinking tells you is best, rather than what "feels comfortable in the moment." I go through this process every morning when the alarm goes off in the early hours of the morning. My gut level feeling says, "Stay in bed and get a little more sleep." But, my rational thinking tells me that I will feel much better if I get up and maintain a regular exercise routine. Here is the decision point of cognitive-emotive dissonance. Do I stay in bed, which feels better in the moment? Or, do I do what I know in my rational thinking is best, namely, get out of bed and exercise, which helps me feel better later on that day and, generally throughout life, as the routine is regularly followed?

> **All it takes is to do what your rational thinking says is the correct and beneficial thing to do...This concept also applies to crisis preparedness. Even though it may not feel like the best thing to do right now, when crisis time hits you will praise the day you prepared.**

You can apply the same process to overeating, stopping smoking, and other self-defeating habits that need changing. All it takes is to do what your rational thinking says is the correct and beneficial thing to do, even though you may not feel comfortable doing it at the time. This concept also applies to crisis preparedness. Even though it may not feel like the best thing to do right now, when crisis time hits you will praise the day you prepared. Once you decide to get yourself crisis prepared, the next step is to pursue a methodical process, outlined below in the five-step process.

8.4.1 Applying the Five Steps: Two Examples

8.4.1.1 Workplace Violence

Let's take a look at a hypothetical example of how you can apply the above preparedness process to the possibility of workplace violence within your organization.

Step 1: Analyze your foreseeable risks. In this case, you will want to analyze the possible motives for workplace violence. Do you have a polarized workforce, perhaps as the result of union-management conflicts, where tensions could lead to violence? Do you have cash registers where robbery could be a motive for violence? Do you have a large number of women in the workplace whose presence might increase the possibility of domestic violence creeping into your facilities when abusive spouses show up? Are there signs in the workplace of drug abuse, gang membership, hostile supervisors, or violent crime in the neighborhood? Analyze the prerequisites that could lead to workplace violence.

Step 2: Evaluate new and existing procedures. Next, you will evaluate the existing controls you have in place that address identified motives for violence. Can existing controls be enhanced? Is there a need for new controls? To deal with union-management conflicts, you may have an arbitration process for disputes, but this could be enhanced to include other forms of alternative dispute resolution. For robberies, you might have a strong corporate security department and bright lighting. New controls could include surveillance cameras and strict procedures for depositing money. For domestic violence, you may have an EAP from which employees can receive confidential counseling regarding domestic concerns. Would a corporate domestic violence program be a good addition?

For expediency and cost effectiveness, look first for ways to enhance existing controls. Possibly, in addition to arbitration, a supplemental mediation process could be established. For robberies, signs could be publicly displayed announcing that cameras are in use. And for domestic violence in the workplace, a review of the internal policies and procedures for how your EAP handles potentially violent situations could be implemented.

Step 3: Organize new controls and draft your (new or enhanced) plan. The organizing and planning process is designed to address weaknesses in your existing preparedness efforts. The object will be to utilize existing controls that are adequate, enhance present controls that can be improved, and establish new controls that need to be implemented. Let's assume you already have an established, trained, and experienced multidisciplinary threat response team. It doesn't need enhancement presently. So, the team will be plugged in as it presently exists. However, there is a need for setting up a threat notification system and a workplace violence policy that is publicized throughout the workplace. Special emphasis will be placed on employee and supervisory hostilities that have been a recurring problem. For robberies, a safe with timed access will help prohibit robberies and minimize financial losses. Implementing awareness and response training throughout your organization can curtail domestic violence in the workplace.

> Stay on top of your planned implementation schedule. You don't want to appear negligent when a crisis occurs because you didn't follow your own prevention and preparedness implementation schedule.

Your next step in the planning process is to prioritize and organize your prevention and post-incident responses for each identified risk. You may need to establish an implementation schedule over time if all your identified enhancements and new controls cannot be put into operation immediately. But, stay on top of your planned implementation schedule. You don't want to appear negligent when a crisis occurs because you didn't follow your own prevention and preparedness implementation schedule. If running behind, review the schedule regularly and adjust it as needed, but don't just forget it in a manner that could appear negligent later.

Step 4: Put your plans and teams in action. Implementation of your plan is the next step. Here, you will utilize the methods that were identified and prioritized to address your identified risks. This might entail a pilot program, a phased implementation process, or an exercise program to evaluate the effectiveness of your crisis plans and teams. For some, it will be utilizing your planning and teams in a real crisis situation.

Step 5: Evaluate your results. The last step is to establish a management information system that allows you to track the success of your crisis preparedness program on an ongoing basis. Annual or periodic reporting about the effectiveness and success of your prevention and post-incident programs would be reported to senior management to determine if changes are needed. A key ingredient for adequate scrutiny would be an operational debriefing by all involved crisis team members following all exercises and actual crisis responses. It could also involve a benchmarking program against other organizations. Training and attending conferences could also identify issues to rectify. Like a good quality assurance process, crisis preparedness scrutiny is an ongoing process.

8.4.1.2 Executive Air Travel

There is a realistic possibility (albeit unlikely, but high consequence if it does occur) that one or more of your company's executive leadership team could be seriously injured, or killed, while flying on business. A careful application of the five-step process would prepare you ahead of time should an air tragedy occur involving one or more members of your executive leadership team. Consider how a crisis preparedness plan might affect this situation proactively.

Step 1: Analyze your foreseeable risks. You identify the foreseeable risk that executives in your organization could be killed or seriously injured in an air crash, especially given your awareness of terrorism directed toward aircraft, and also in-flight near misses within the air traffic control world.

Step 2: Evaluate new and existing procedures. You determine that you already have a policy that senior managers are not to fly together on the same flights. However, this policy has sometimes been breached in the past as noted by the internal auditor. An enhancement might involve the internal auditor meeting with the board of directors to reassert and monitor that no two senior-level executives will fly on the same flight together. Additionally, a decision is made to conduct random audits and inspections of the company that provides maintenance services on your corporate jet. Another new control might be to conduct random drug testing on the corporate pilots.

Step 3: Organize new controls and draft the new plan. The new and enhanced procedures will be implemented as discussed above. In this process of thinking about what would happen if a senior executive were to be killed in a plane crash and examining controls, the board realizes the need for an enhanced succession plan.

The board of directors and CEO might meet to develop a succession plan by identifying internal and external candidates who could be groomed to take over for the unexpected loss of a key executive(s). Additionally, a recruiter could be retained to keep a listing of qualified candidates who would be appropriate for senior management positions of your organization.

Step 4: Put plans and teams in action. Depending on the culture of the company, the board might oversee a coaching or mentoring process to groom the identified internal candidates for senior-level assignments. Hiring of upper-level managers might take into consideration the ability of candidates to replace selected senior executive team members.

Step 5: Evaluate your results. Last, the board of directors might schedule six-month and annual reviews of the executive travel practices, aircraft maintenance audits, pilot drug testing, and succession plan to ensure they protect the needs of the organization in case senior managers were victims of air crashes or other causes for loss of a key executive.

8.5 Set up the Crisis Planning Committee (CPC)

The word "committee" tends to induce a groan. But corralling the right multi-disciplinary group of people to execute the five-step preparedness process is imperative to your success. Before you can effectively take the first step, you will want to create your crisis planning committee (CPC).

Selecting a CPC is a lot like building your dream house. That's a big challenge, and one you can't possibly take on alone. The ultimate decisions may be up to you, but you need to rely on your architect, contractor, landscape architect, and interior designer for the best advice.

It may be tempting to go it alone, especially if your boss assigns the task to you. But that would be a mistake. You will find great strength in numbers.

> **Nobody knows all the answers, but input from multiple sources will raise considerations you would otherwise overlook. Diverse people forge a thorough solution.**

8.5.1 Multidisciplinary Perspectives

When you build your CPC, you will want to draw from the appropriate disciplines or departments in your company, as well as from appropriate resources outside your company. Within reason, the more perspectives you have, and the more varied the expertise, the more comprehensive your outlook will be.

For example, if exposure to a toxic substance from a neighboring factory is a foreseeable risk, your HR department may be concerned about what kind of benefits or psychological trauma assistance your employees will require. The onsite nursing staff will have suggestions for immediate medical care and emergency responders. Your facility management, meanwhile, will need to establish an evacuation plan, understand the residual extent of the exposure, and plan the steps to bring the building back up to healthy, habitable standards again. Corporate security will want to establish methods to secure the worksite. And, your attorneys will want legal controls to prevent and minimize the exposure from the factory next door.

Nobody knows all the answers, but input from multiple sources will raise considerations you would otherwise overlook. Diverse people forge a thorough solution.

8.5.2 Team Decision-Making Works

Decision by committee – it's almost a punch line to a joke about something that doesn't work very well. But, with effective leadership and project management, good crisis planning balances the perspectives of many in a task-oriented mode. You want a lean, crisp team that is empowered and has a sense of urgency. Together, the team members can tackle the complexity of risks that you will identify – better than even the most brilliant individual manager ever could.

Suppose you try to do all of this planning yourself, and then a disaster strikes. Inevitably, questions will arise about those issues you had never even considered. If you did that work alone, full responsibility for any failure will fall on you. Your work may be criticized and you don't want to be the sole person trying to defend the many decisions and actions taken to plan and prepare.

If you worked with a CPC, you would be able to honestly say: "We brought together the best people we could find. They represented all the important units of our organization, and a wide range of expertise. Every decision we made was the result of an open group process. We did our best." There is effectiveness, safety, and defensibility in utilizing an appropriate number of individuals from varied areas of expertise.

8.5.3 A Daunting Task Demands a Strong Group Effort

A risk manager at an international company – we'll call him Mike – was assigned to put together a crisis management plan. Alone. Mike had a lot on his plate and kept procrastinating. He had no information, no management support, no budget, and no expertise outside his discipline of risk management.

Clearly, Mike felt overwhelmed. Although well meaning, he kept going off on tangents – surfing the Web, reading articles, and trying to figure out what to do and how to proceed. He didn't know enough about business operations, or the human side of crisis, or public relations practice. He knew solely about risk and insurance management. He was in way over his head, and poised to fail.

We met briefly. But Mike's leaders had given him no resources and only a vague mandate, so he lost momentum. Five years later, he still didn't have his crisis management plan in place. It kept falling to the bottom of his to-do list. The company had already experienced one serious incident. If a similar incident occurs again – a high probability in their industry – tough questions would arise regarding their lack of preparedness.

Mike needed help from an executive sponsor, the internal auditor, his own boss, or other person with knowledge and authority to help get him the resources needed. If nothing else, an internal multidisciplinary CPC could be a cost effective way to start the momentum toward preparedness. We worked through the internal auditor and enlisted an executive sponsor to support the crisis planning effort.

Because it was a large, multinational company, with more than 200,000 employees, the firm brought in a senior level group of managers from across the country and around the globe to serve on the CPC.

The scope of the project was daunting, and now that it had sufficient attention, management wanted it done "yesterday." The company had international ground and air operations, distribution centers, facilities where the public was admitted, numerous office buildings, and multiple locations – each with its own inherent risks.

With little standardization in tracking or reporting of issues that occurred and no compilation of occurrences, the various regions were not aware of the critical incidents that occurred in their own areas, much less in the others.

Still, the company was committed to being crisis prepared. We were called in to work with Mike to set up and work with their newly formed CPC. Once the CPC was established and supported, a system to guide the company to a swift and successful completion was in focus. With diligence and collective effort – after five years of inaction – the company had an action plan and an initial response system in place six weeks later. A quality management system was established and, to this day, the company conducts worldwide crisis exercises at all levels of the organization on a regular basis. Lessons-learned at every level of the organization are conveyed to the CPC, and the planning process is a part of the continuous quality improvement system.

8.6 How to Set Up a CPC

Just as important as deciding to have a committee is how you set it up. A number of considerations must be met to ensure the group's ultimate success:

1. Determine the scope.

2. Identify champions.

3. Select the members.

4. Set an agenda.

5. Establish a budget.

6. Make a schedule.

7. Conduct the meetings.

Now, let's examine each step in greater depth.

8.6.1 Determine the Scope

Before you choose your CPC, you should step back and take a large-scale view of your company. Ask yourself these questions to come up with the scope of the project you are undertaking:

▶ What are your objectives and expected deliverables?

▶ Is this a local, regional, national, or international project?

▶ Will the crisis management function be centralized at corporate or distributed throughout the organization?

▶ Will your plan be rolled out company-wide or piloted in selected areas?

▶ Do you have an existing plan that needs improving, or are you starting from scratch?

▶ What areas of foreseeable risks and concerns do you want to address?

▶ How high a priority is this project? How much support does it have from senior management?

▶ How much authority will the CPC have to do its job?

> **The logistical champion will actually lead the CPC through its process. Without the right person in this role, it will be difficult for the CPC to succeed.**

8.6.2 Identify Champions

Champions are leaders, a committee's driving force. Typically, two champions are needed in company crisis planning: a senior-level champion and a logistical champion.

Senior-level champion: The senior-level champion is the visionary. He or she ensures that the right financial and human tools are in place to make the CPC a success, and provides top management support. He or she will delegate to the logistical champion.

Logistical champion: The logistical champion will actually lead the CPC through its process. Without the right person in this role, it will be difficult for the CPC to succeed. A good logistical champion is someone who:

▶ Has the passion and authority to make sure that the CPC's objectives and goals are met.

▶ Understands the scope of the project and agrees with the mission.

▶ Has a deep commitment to the process.

▶ Is able to invest the time to bring it to fruition or guide external consultants to a successful preparedness outcome.

▶ Has deep and wide company contacts, and will be respected by people at all levels in the organization.

▶ Possesses sufficient authority to make things happen.

8.6.3 Select the CPC Members

Getting the right mix of people is critical. Along with a blend of disciplines, you want a blend of personalities as well. It's important to include both task-oriented and people-oriented members. A balance of creative and analytical types is also good.

Depending on your corporate culture, you may either appoint members or invite people to participate. No matter which approach you choose, it would be wise to bring in an attorney (whether on staff or outside counsel) to formalize a defensible process. Besides having a mix of personality types on the CPC, you will want to have a mix of disciplines represented either on the core team or as auxiliary, ad hoc members. Here are some staff positions to consider having on the CPC:

▶ Attorney.

▶ Continuity or contingency planner.

▶ IT manager.

▶ HR manager.

▶ Government relations manager.

▶ Compliance manager.

▶ Risk and insurance manager.

▶ Financial manager.

▶ Medical director.

- ▶ Law enforcement officer.

- ▶ Security manager.

- ▶ Public relations director.

- ▶ Crisis management consultant.

- ▶ Other disciplines according to corporate culture and needs.

How big should your CPC be? I can't give you a definitive answer. In the 200,000-employee company I mentioned above, 50 people participated, which was the largest I've seen, although they broke into smaller subcommittees to handle specific tasks and they wanted it completed in six weeks' time. As a general rule, the smallest CPC contains 5 core members, while 12 is a good maximum number, for efficiency. Anything larger may require breaking into subcommittees. To cover disciplines not included on the core team, you may make use of additional resources on an as-needed, ad hoc basis.

But you must base the size of your CPC on such variables as corporate culture, company size, the scope of the job, budget, and other factors. The key is to balance the effectiveness of a multidisciplinary committee with the efficiency of the smallest possible team.

> **Avoid producing a documented record that could show that your committee knew of weaknesses or gaps in your crisis defense strategy – and failed to address them.**

8.6.3.1 Why You Need an Attorney

Your committee is going to do its genuine best to prepare your company for crises. But after the dust of a calamity has cleared, your preparedness process is likely to be second-guessed anyway. In the worst case, your company and even selected managers may be sued for negligence.

Having an attorney involved in your CPC offers a type of insurance through attorney-client privilege. This confidentiality veil isn't perfect and it won't prevent your being sued, but it will leave you better prepared to defend yourselves if challenged.

Part of the attorney's job on the CPC is to help ensure that the committee does not generate any documentary material that could later be used against you in court. The attorney can supervise the consolidation and approval of any notes produced in the course of the committee's work. By the conclusion of your preparedness process, you want to end up with a single version of what you have done – one that a lawyer has approved. Then, according to the preferences of your attorney, consider shredding everything else as a matter of policy. This approved version becomes the documentation of your committee's work. The attorney would house it under privilege of confidentiality. Some organizations go as far as keeping everything verbal except for the final plan or using a single scribe to document meetings.

Avoid producing a documented record that could show that your committee knew of weaknesses or gaps in your crisis defense strategy – and failed to address them.

8.6.3.2 Select a Consultant

With vast experience, a consultant often serves as a key facilitator at CPC meetings. A consultant is also an invaluable resource to the CPC by bringing expertise and knowledge of other companies to the table. Since crisis planning should include executive level preparedness, the consultant should have experience and comfort dealing with senior executives. So how do you select a good consultant? This person or firm should be prominent in the field of crisis preparedness, and it's even better if they have experience in your industry.

A good consultant will work to identify both weaknesses and positive aspects of your overall crisis management organization within the company. No one consultant has all the expertise you will need, but the good firms fill the gap with affiliations to additional resources. Crisis preparedness consultants tend to charge either project or retainer fees.

8.6.4 Set an Agenda

Determine what topics need to be discussed at each meeting and what "homework" needs to be done before and after each meeting. Consider following the five-step preparedness process of analyzing your foreseeable risks, evaluating new and existing procedures, organizing new controls and drafting the new plan, putting plans and teams in action, and evaluating your results.

For example, in the first CPC meeting, you may want to analyze the vulnerabilities inherent to your organization and examine the existing procedures that correspond to these risks. To facilitate that first meeting, you might ask members to arrive armed with data about the risks each knows about.

8.6.5 Establish a Budget

To run an effective CPC, you will need money. Working with senior management, you will need to outline the costs you expect to incur for such items as hotel accommodations, transportation, meals, materials, reports, consultants, and other needs. As is often usual, budget about 10-20% more than you think you'll need so you aren't stalled midway by lack of funds.

A preliminary budget could pay for expenses to run the CPC. You could make an implementation request later, when you have a better idea of your full crisis preparedness needs.

> We have observed many companies using reverse sequence successfully in planning to create a schedule and a timeline for the CPC – starting with the desired outcome and working backward to see what it will take to accomplish the goal.

8.6.6 Make a Schedule

Before you can decide how often to meet, how long each meeting should last, and the location of each meeting, you will need to consider a number of items:

- ▶ What are your objectives and deliverables?

- ▶ How quickly must the plan be completed?

- ▶ What is the time availability of members?

- ▶ What will it cost to bring the committee together? Would electronic connectivity methods suffice?

- ▶ How much research must be accomplished between meetings?

- ▶ Do you want a minimum number of meetings, or does your culture value the brainstorming that comes from more frequent gatherings?

Optimally, these scheduling questions should be discussed before or during the first planning meeting. We have observed many companies using reverse sequence successfully in planning to create a schedule and a timeline for the CPC – starting with the desired outcome and working backward to see what it will take to accomplish the goal.

Once the preceding steps are in place, you are ready to bring the CPC together. The rest of this book will provide take-and-use guidelines you can apply in order to put a successful crisis management preparedness program into place.

8.6.7 Conduct the Meetings

Once your CPC members are in place, you can determine how, when, and where to meet. The CPC can meet in person, via conference call, or via videoconferencing. My recommendation is that you make a commitment to meet face-to-face, at least periodically. You may have one committee or several smaller subcommittees. You may meet onsite or offsite.

8.6.8 What to Avoid as a CPC

Committees can get sidetracked into nonproductive behaviors. The key is to recognize them, eliminate them, and move on in a positive manner. This will take a strong leader. Some common errors include:

▶ Failing to use an attorney to properly compile committee information and meeting notes; failing to ensure that documentation is written in a legally defensible manner; and failing to protect documentation, to the fullest extent possible, under attorney-client privilege.

▶ Lack of confidentiality by CPC members regarding information that spells out the weaknesses of your company.

▶ Failing to address uncomfortable issues or to give credence to the full range of possible risks. Avoiding questions such as, "If we were terrorists, how would we take this company to its knees?"

▶ Engaging in denial regarding certain foreseeable risks: "It can't happen here."

▶ Alarmism – a "Chicken Little" (the sky is falling) mentality that leads to overreaction.

▶ Failing to prioritize the process enough to complete the project.

▶ Identifying risks without taking any actions to prepare for them.

▶ Failing to monitor your preparedness plan for effectiveness and to update it for new risks that may emerge.

Quick Use Preparedness Guide
Chapter 8: The First Step to Preparedness
Getting Started

The prepared manager:

▶ Balances attention for company growth with attention to foreseeable risks.

▶ Develops a thorough and comprehensive preparedness strategy.

▶ Confronts, rather than avoids, uncomfortable issues.

▶ Takes rational preparedness action on what is in the best interest of the organization even though there may be distractions or gut level resistance to put it off.

▶ Never overlooks the human factor.

▶ Prepares for anticipated needs of all stakeholders who may be involved in the foreseeable risks of the organization.

The five-step preparedness process employs the following steps:

▶ Analyze your foreseeable risks.

❑ What are your foreseeable risks?

▶ Evaluate new controls and your existing controls for enhancements.

❑ What procedures, policies, and controls are in place to address your risks?

❑ What needs to be strengthened?

❑ Identify new controls to supplement existing methodologies.

▶ Organize and draft the new plan.

❑ Plan out and document your crisis response strategies.

▶ Put plans and teams in action.

❑ Execute and utilize your plan according to an implementation schedule that fits your budget, time, and corporate culture.

▶ Evaluate your results.

❑ Initiate an ongoing process to monitor your processes, procedures, and controls for effectiveness.

Setting Up a Crisis Planning Committee

▶ Have you addressed the structure of your Crisis Planning Committee (CPC)?

❑ Multidisciplinary approach.

❑ Team decision-making.

❑ Defensibility.

❑ Senior management support.

▶ Setting up a CPC includes:

❑ Determining the scope.

❑ Identifying a champion.

❑ Selecting members.

❑ Setting an agenda.

❑ Establishing a budget.

❑ Making a schedule.

❑ Conducting meetings.

▶ Have you considered utilizing an attorney for attorney-client privilege?

▶ Have you considered utilizing a consultant to facilitate the process and lend expertise?

▶ What to avoid:

❑ Failing to use an attorney.

❑ Lack of confidentiality.

❑ Failing to address uncomfortable issues.

❑ Engaging in denial.

❑ Alarmism.

❑ Failing to make the process a priority.

❑ Identifying risks without taking adequate actions.

❑ Failing to monitor your preparedness plan.

Chapter 8 – Questions for Further Thought and Discussion

1. Where are places you can look internally and outside the company to determine your foreseeable risks?

2. What are signs of good and poor crisis response in addition to those listed in this chapter?

3. Anticipated issues of stakeholders were listed. What are additional anticipated issues or other stakeholder issues in high-concern situations, such as needs and concerns of customers, shareholders, distributors, suppliers, and others?

4. What are common reasons for not engaging in adequate crisis preparedness? For each, list out rational challenges as to why each excuse is not in the best interest of the organization and its managers.

5. At a minimum, what are the core staff functions that should be a part of your CPC?

6. Think of a crisis situation in a company that you or a friend experienced – or that you read about – and take it through the five steps. How well did management response measure up to what we recommend in this book? How would you prepare for it knowing what you know now?

References

Couric, K. (2009, June). *Capt. Sully worried about airline industry.* Retrieved from: http://www.cbsnews.com/news/capt-sully-worried-about-airline-industry/

Ellis, A. & Harper, R. (1979). *A new guide to rational living.* Hollywood, CA: Wilshire Book Company, p. 37.

Knight, R.F. & Pretty, D.J. (1996). The impact of catastrophes on shareholder value. *Oxford executive research briefings.* Templeton College (University of Oxford).

9

Analyzing Your Foreseeable Risks

In a single moment, your world can change forever. The situations and locations can vary greatly, but tragic and unexpected traumatic events occur with alarming frequency. We are all vulnerable to some degree, in both our personal and professional lives, regardless of where we live or what we do. The challenge for any company is to examine its risks courageously, and move to protect itself, its employees, and its assets with a solid plan of defense.

No one has a crystal ball, or can predict where the next crisis will occur. Someone reading this book will face the next crisis. We just don't know who, what, or when. But if we can begin to look at our organizations and environments with a critical eye, we can discover a door or window that may be open, unwittingly inviting crisis in.

This chapter will help you to:

> ➤ *Understand how societal change has generated risks.*

> ➤ *Observe the ripple effect of vulnerability.*

> ➤ *Identify foreseeable risks for your company.*

> ➤ *See the role of probability and severity in prioritizing your risks.*

9.1 How Societal Change Has Generated Risks

Today's workplace bears almost no resemblance to the one in which our grandparents and parents labored. Colleagues, friends, and connectedness have been redefined through technology. We are a transient society now, less connected to our families and employers in face-to-face ways. Most of us will work with several different organizations during our careers, and change industries as well. People will likely be downsized – often more than once – during their careers. And, we often don't know whom we may be offending. In his insightful book on psychopaths within our society, R.D. Hare (1999) states that "there are at least 2 million psychopaths in North America; the citizens of New York City have as many as 100,000 psychopaths among them." Psychopaths are manipulative, remorseless, cunning individuals without conscience who can often become violent, or at least wreak havoc on those in their paths.

Towers Watson, a global risk management and human resources consulting firm, found in its 2013/2014 *Staying@Work Survey* that stress is "...the number one workforce risk issue, ranking above even lack of physical activity and obesity" (Towers Watson, 2013). Further, it is well established that stress creates accidents, workplace violence, errors in judgment, and an array of other work-related difficulties.

> Societal and workplace diversity has made us more dynamic and well-rounded, providing wonderful opportunities for learning and growth. But it also spawns misunderstandings, some of which explode into accidents or acts of retribution.

High-fatality disasters are occurring with increasing frequency. However, once you consider the changes in the past few decades, this increase in disasters is easy to understand. For example, our formerly agrarian landscape has changed: taller buildings with thousands of people working in them, increased foreign travel, threats of bioterrorism, chemical warfare, more and faster everything. Markets are global, and the pressure to achieve is pervasive. In addition, the workplace is less homogenous than it once was. Societal and workplace diversity has made us more dynamic and well-rounded, providing wonderful opportunities for learning and growth. But it also spawns misunderstandings, some of which explode into accidents or acts of retribution.

These societal changes and others create risks and set the stage for potential disasters.

9.2 The Ripple Effect of Vulnerability

Observing these disasters and crisis situations over the years has driven home the ripple effect of vulnerability that pervades our modern world. One breach of established perimeters or other controls can open up multiple weaknesses. This ripple effect helps to explain why disasters often spiral out of control.

Media spin, demanding customers, government regulators, resistant insurance companies, community outrage, uncontrolled social media, and other accelerants can fan the flames of a small crisis, just as the wind feeds a brushfire. And the crisis can touch off new blazes in places you hadn't expected.

This effect was easy to see during the days that followed the 2013 Boston Marathon bombing. Several blocks of Boylston Street where the bombing occurred remained closed for days following the bombing. Businesses were disrupted, especially retailers that had no access to their worksites. Thousands of law enforcement officers were "on the hunt." Train services in the New England corridor were temporarily stopped as a safety precaution. Washington, DC went on high alert, disrupting business and government alike. The entire city of Boston was shut down by law enforcement directives for all citizens to stay off the streets. The suspects proceeded to kill a police officer, hijack a car, and create serious danger for anyone in their paths as they were pursued by law enforcement. CNBC News reported three weeks after the bombing that the local costs in Boston that could be calculated were US $333 million (Schoen, 2013).

At the workplace, barriers to entry are established with gates, guards, locks, and information technology (IT) passwords. But often, once the initial firewall is breached, the vulnerabilities are exposed that can cause serious damage. Employees, shareholders, customers, and the press – none of these groups is as forgiving as we'd like them to be during a crisis. If we as managers can't deliver on our promises, or are seen as irresponsible, we place our companies in grave danger. Prevention is the best cure, but we can't stop all crises. If your company doesn't have an effective contingency plan in place, your livelihood could be at stake.

9.3 Identifying and Analyzing Foreseeable Risks

Which events would severely disrupt your operations? What are you unprepared for?

By anticipating and analyzing your foreseeable risks and uncovering those incidents that could seriously harm your organization, you can minimize your risk of being blindsided.

Don't wait for a plaintiff attorney, government regulator, investigative reporter, or jury to tell you what risks you should have foreseen – which they *will* do *after* a critical incident has occurred.

If your analysis shows that you have inadequately assessed and prepared for foreseeable risks, your company could be found guilty of negligence or blame in the court of public opinion – or an actual courtroom. More importantly, people can be injured or killed, and blame can be directed toward your company. Core assets, like reputation and your brand, can suffer.

All-hazards planning relates to the establishment of standardized protocol and methodologies that are practiced no matter what the specific crisis incident may be.

9.3.1 Thinking About Likely Scenarios

It is impossible to prepare for every catastrophe your company might experience. This is why we espouse *all-hazards planning* that incorporates the same procedures and protocol within your internal crisis management organization, regardless of your crisis situation. However, you should still consider a hierarchy of likely scenarios.

Sample Factors to Consider

Your company might:

▶ Deal with dangerous equipment.

▶ Work in a tall building for which evacuation is complex.

▶ Have unprotected parking lots at company facilities.

▶ Give tours of your premises to outside visitors.

▶ Have unsecured or easily breached points of ingress and egress.

▶ Experience threats and demonstrations at shareholder meetings.

▶ Send employees to international destinations known for kidnappings, extortions, or political uprisings.

▶ Use tanker trucks to carry hazardous or explosive materials.

▶ Work in an aging building that is not up to code.

▶ Have an internally hostile workforce, and possibly a polarized relationship with the union.

▶ Operate where there are floods, fires, hurricanes, volcanic eruptions, or tornadoes.

Additional foreseeable risks may include:

- ▶ Supply chain vulnerabilities.
- ▶ Product recalls.
- ▶ Substandard foreign manufacturing.
- ▶ Foreign corrupt practices.
- ▶ Being in a targeted industry for terrorism.
- ▶ Communicable diseases such as the bird flu.
- ▶ Criminal or unethical activity by executives or employees.
- ▶ Kidnap and ransom incidents.
- ▶ Regulatory or political interferences.
- ▶ Environmental violations.
- ▶ Activist group obstructions.
- ▶ Indirect damages from associated organizations (by location or industry).
- ▶ Data breaches.
- ▶ Insider trading.
- ▶ Theft of trade secrets.
- ▶ Massive or extended electrical outages.
- ▶ Unexpected death or loss of executives or key employees.

All-hazards planning relates to the establishment of standardized protocol and methodologies that are practiced no matter what the specific crisis incident may be. In addition, by identifying your unique foreseeable risks (like those listed above) and planning for each, required nuances – such as immediate actions and unique considerations – can be anticipated and mitigated.

> # Hurricane Sandy
>
> Most people would not have predicted that the perfect storm conditions of Hurricane Sandy (2012) would cause such catastrophic damage. It was the largest hurricane from the Atlantic Ocean to make landfall and the second most costly hurricane in US history (only behind Hurricane Katrina). According to FEMA, 24 states from Florida to Maine and as far west as Michigan and Wisconsin were impacted (FEMA, 2013).
>
> The confluence was a huge, slow moving storm, colliding with a nor'easter storm coming across New England from the east, and hitting land during high tide. This perfect storm scenario caused massive flooding, deaths, and property damage.
>
> What are the odds that all these variables would come together at the same horrible time? The odds are low, but the incident was foreseeable. Huge storms have historically hit the area in the last century, so it isn't unprecedented.
>
> What about the foreseeability of the future hurricanes? Meteorologists predict much stronger hurricanes in the future. Oceans are reportedly warming measurably, which creates more moisture in the air. The combination of increasing warmth and moisture are the ingredients for stronger hurricanes.
>
> So, if your operations include locations that can be affected by hurricanes or other oceanic windstorms, this would be an increasingly foreseeable risk. It is expected that amplified severity and frequency would lead to sufficient corporate controls to address the manifestation of these occurrences in your crisis preparedness.

> **One way to assess the probability of your foreseeable incidents is to ask yourself, "What is the likelihood that each foreseeable incident we identify would happen within the next decade?"**

9.4 What's Likely to Happen? Analyzing Crisis Probability

One way to assess the probability of your foreseeable incidents is to ask yourself, "What is the likelihood that each foreseeable incident we identify would happen within the next decade?" You may choose a different time frame of course. What's important is to quantify your risks. In general, the more specific you can be about the probability of various events, the more accurate your predictions will become. Specificity is also important when it comes to ranking the events.

Remember to clearly define what you mean by each vulnerability or risk. A fire can be serious or minor. A product defect can result in an easy fix or a reputational catastrophe. It may not be important to pinpoint the exact thing that could go wrong with a product. Probably, it's enough just to plan your protocol and methodologies if there were a seriously disruptive product defect. For example, Toyota had a sudden acceleration problem that made international news, causing massive recalls and serious reputational damages. Battery fires in Boeing's newly launched 787 Dreamliner grounded the entire fleet of 50 jets it had delivered to airline customers at the time. It took months for both companies to come up with acceptable remedies. Neither Toyota nor Boeing could plan for everything that could possibly go wrong with their products. Instead, their foreseeable risk analysis could include well-thought-out procedures for dealing with the disruption caused from a defect and a recall.

Choosing the consequence is also important. For example, you may classify as serious a fire that disrupts operations for more than one day, results in specified damages to facilities and equipment, or causes critical injuries.

9.4.1 Risk Analysis Checklist

Your company's risks can be analyzed in a variety of ways. All of them depend on good information. Look at what has already happened in the past to your company and to others like it. You will want to know about conditions and related risks in all the places where you operate. And consider the political, commercial, and social tensions in the world at large. Here is a checklist to get you started:

▶ **Query your staff.** It's easy to overlook obvious resources. Ask selected managers, supervisors, and employees about vulnerabilities they have noticed. In addition to gleaning information, this approach can uncover employees who have a natural awareness of risks. Later, you might enlist some of these people to help monitor your preparedness efforts.

▶ **Surveys.** Written surveys or questionnaires filled out by employees and other important constituents can help you discover information useful to analyzing foreseeable risks and crisis planning.

▶ **Review history.** What incidents have happened at your company already? Is there a preponderance of a certain type? Have certain locations or types of equipment been involved? Do incidents occur more frequently on certain days or in a certain month? With certain types of personnel, like contracted workers vs. company employees? Or on certain shifts?

▶ **Review near misses.** What near crises have you and others in your industry experienced? These are fertile but often overlooked indicators of pending crises. The FAA reports multiple near misses on runways and in the air near the world's busy airports. One can conclude that the likelihood of two planes colliding at or near an airport in the next 10 years is only moderate since it hasn't happened often in the past – so it's wise to prepare for the aftermath of such a fatal crash today if you have multiple frequent flyers, but it might not be a top priority compared to your high frequency and high severity incidents.

▶ **Review industry mishaps.** Educate yourself on crises that have occurred to competitors and others in your industry. Has the industry suffered a certain type of crisis again and again?

▶ **Assess your locations.** Geography plays a major role in the type of crises your company might encounter. If you have facilities around the globe, each location implies unique threats. Civil unrest, for example, may be more likely in the Middle East or Africa than in the Caribbean Islands.

▶ **Investigate local crime and labor statistics.** A good look at crime statistics can pinpoint relevant trends. For example, if you have a plant in South Chicago, the gang activity there could be a significant risk factor for you.

▶ **Conduct online research.** Internet research services are invaluable. One powerful resource is LexisNexis, which returns full-text articles from 30,000 databases. Unlike some Internet search engines such as Google, it is not free – and subscriptions are relatively costly. However, you can buy short-term access, which could be sufficient.

▶ **Department of Labor statistics.** Study the statistics provided by the government regarding critical incidents in various industries. Review citations given to organizations for health and safety violations, or if there are deaths at the workplace. What could be predictive for your organization?

▶ **Insurer data.** Is there actuarial information that would be relevant to your foreseeable risks? Look for both frequency and financial costs.

> Once you've determined your probable risks, you must analyze which of them could be most damaging to the core assets of the organization.

Other resources you may consider, include reading industry and business journals, attending conferences, benchmarking with other companies, and organizing industry brainstorming groups, to name a few.

9.5 How Bad Could It Be? Analyzing Crisis Severity

Once you've determined your probable risks, you must analyze which of them could be most damaging to the core assets of the organization. Armed robberies may be probable at a bank, but if they do not involve fatalities or large sums, they should not do too much damage. On the other hand, a major fire could devastate an unprepared company, destroying irreplaceable data and possibly costing lives.

Your crisis planning committee (CPC) will have arrived at definitions of your vulnerabilities, as we discussed above. For each identified risk, ask yourselves this question:

If it happened, how severely would it hurt us? Which core assets would be threatened?

9.5.1 Protecting Your Core Assets

A company must protect its core assets in order to survive and grow. Crises tend to threaten core assets. Significant damage to any core assets can cripple a company. As a body needs its heart, brain, lungs, and other bodily systems, a company needs all its core assets to be healthy. I'll address three examples here, but additional core assets include brand, trust, ability to operate, physical and intellectual property, and key relationships.

- **People:** includes all involved stakeholders, such as board members, managers, employees and their expertise, as well as your suppliers, distributors, investors, customers, and more.

- **Finances:** includes overall financial wellbeing, such as cashflow, revenue, expenses, shareholder value, credit rating, capital equipment, and other areas of vital financial strength.

- **Reputation:** the positive feelings people have for your company. This includes how trustworthy, responsive, and sustainable your company is perceived to be.

Let's look at a few of the ways that these integrated company assets affect each other.

People. It is in this area that most companies in crisis are least prepared to cope. Often there are plans to deal with seriously or fatally injured employees. But there is also a pressing need to address all stakeholders who may be outraged or feel harmed. When management actively demonstrates a concern for people's wellbeing, crisis recovery is quicker. Employees are more productive and loyal, and their morale is higher. Customers keep coming or return. Shareholders invest and media is more tolerant.

Finances. Some companies pay the ultimate price after a disaster: They go out of business. Such was the case that I observed with Standard Gravure, in Louisville, Kentucky, a printing company mentioned earlier in Chapter 7. In 1988, a fire diminished the company's operational capacities. A year after the fire, employee Joseph Wesbecker – who was on a leave of absence for a stress-related illness – returned to the workplace and shot 21 people, killing 8. The company remained in business for several months after the shooting, but ultimately succumbed to the disruption of two significant crises within a year. Small- to medium-sized companies are particularly vulnerable, since they are the least likely to be crisis prepared.

Experience and research have demonstrated that prepared companies tend to lose less money during crises than ill-equipped companies. As a general rule, those companies that are prepared and spend the money up front to address their crises adequately tend to spend the least in the long term. Those companies that withhold during the early aftermath of a crisis tend to spend more in the long term. Paradoxical as it may seem to some, this crisis response formula has played true repeatedly.

Reputation. Consider the response following the 2013 Boston Marathon bombing.

Law enforcement responded with immediate effectiveness by remembering to not just address victims and protect the crime scene. They also immediately expanded their reach by checking for additional bombs in trash bins, in manholes under the streets, and more. Their investigation was thorough and included the strategic decision to share with the public the surveillance videos of the suspected bombers in order to gain their identities. Despite widespread complaints, they stopped further public death and injuries (one policeman had been shot and a car and driver hijacked) by enforcing a complete shutdown of the city while in hot pursuit of the suspected bombers.

Once one of the two suspected bombers was killed and the other captured, people throughout the entire city came out on the streets and cheered the thousands of law enforcement officers who all played a part in a very effective crisis response.

Excellent crisis management can serve as an opportunity for reputational enhancement. Skilled crisis managers seek out opportunities to improve reputation, not just to minimize reputational damage. Do the right things in a crisis and the outcome can be greater reputational equity than any amount of public relations and image building could provide during normal times.

9.5.2 Blame Revisited

We discussed the concept of blame in Chapter 6 as a part of reputation management. Blame must also be considered when prioritizing foreseeable risks. The severity of any crisis can escalate significantly if it includes blame toward the company. Blame occurs when management is broadly seen as negligent or uncaring.

> Foreseeable risk analyses most often anticipate situations imposed upon the organization or its leadership, situations that were the fault of neither the organization nor its leadership.

In my experience, being prepared for blame during the aftermath of a crisis is one of the least considered aspects of crisis preparedness. Yet, when crises occur, it is human nature that people affix blame. An easy target is an organization, especially with what appears to be a growing erosion of public trust in institutions and leaders throughout the civilized world.

Foreseeable risk analyses most often anticipate situations *imposed* upon the organization or its leadership, situations that were the fault of *neither* the organization nor its leadership. Correspondingly, the crisis plan addresses response guidelines where the organization is victimized or not overtly blamed. And, as mentioned earlier, the crisis exercise program then rehearses similar situations, such as natural disasters, terrorism, pandemics, workplace violence, fires, and other scenarios where the organization is not the instigator. However, according to the Institute for Crisis Management's *20th Annual Crisis Report* (Smith, 2012), "People with decision making responsibilities are still *responsible* for half of all crises while, on average over the past ten years, 32-percent of all crises were caused by employees, and [only] 18-percent were caused by outside forces, such as activists, disgruntled customers/patients/employees and natural disasters."

Political considerations are one reason for not preparing for crises where there is overt blame toward the organization or its leadership during a crisis. It is hard to go to the executives of the organization and inform them that the crisis preparedness team is making plans in case the CEO or other leader is a crook, negligent, or unethical. You can pretty well expect such an initiative to be rejected. So, crisis preparedness remains mostly at the "faultless" level.

True, crises occur that are clearly not the fault of the organization or its leaders. The Tylenol cyanide poisonings, terrorism in various public transportation systems from Japan to London, Norway bombing and school shooting that killed 77 and injured 319 people, Oklahoma City bombing, 9/11 terrorism, and bombing in the Indonesian island of Bali are just a few examples.

Then a crisis hits. Often, a huge issue is the blame affixed to the organization or its leadership. Questions arise. What did you know and when? Did you take steps to prevent this occurrence? Were people trained? Were proper maintenance schedules followed? Why didn't you respond more adeptly after the crisis hit? Are you telling us the truth? What are you covering up? Is there scandal in any form? The questions go on, all looking for the "smoking gun" that will show the organization or leadership is to blame.

If widespread blame is directed toward the company, then company leadership is likely to take some heavy criticism. Your crisis response just became more complex. The organization can find itself on the defensive. And, the intensity, breadth, and longevity of the crisis will tend to increase.

Man-made catastrophes such as explosions, crashes, fires, workplace violence, terrorism, and large industrial accidents all carry the possibility of high levels of public blame. Even in "acts of God," like weather-related incidents, people will look to man-made causes for the damage they have suffered. Following the devastation caused by Hurricane Andrew in Miami in 1992, a rising chorus of blame emerged. For example, I observed that some people voiced outrage that the South Florida government and the local builders had allowed physical structures to be built without "hurricane straps" on the roofs.

As a general rule, no matter what your critical incident may be, if a chorus of blame is directed toward management or the company, the severity of the incident will increase significantly. You need to be ready to manage outrage just as you are ready to put out physical fires. You will need to do more than putting the correct public relations spin on the incident. Handling potential outrage involves management demonstrating preparedness that includes anticipating blame and being prepared to respond when the company is blamed. It means the corporation is ready to accept responsibility for the incident, if appropriate, and for expertly responding to affected people with corporate caring and concern.

The best time to address the concept of blame is to anticipate its occurrence and severity during the planning process, before a crisis occurs. Even after a crisis hits, the following are good questions that should be included in your response guidelines and considered as the crisis response unfolds:

▶ What is the organization doing or not doing that could be a target for fault-finding following our various foreseeable risks (or situation that just occurred)?

▶ What can we do now to build a more positive reputation and engender stakeholder trust?

▶ What can we anticipate would be the content of fault-finding by various crisis impacted stakeholders?

▶ What are we doing presently that could be perceived as foreseeable, negligent, intentional, unethical, unlawful, or unfair following a crisis?

> **It's important to be specific in naming your risks, so that you can reasonably assess the impact, or severity, each one could have. For example, "workplace violence" is too broad a phrase.**

9.5.3 Plotting Probability and Severity on the Foreseeable Risk Analysis Grid

Consider a simple grid to show the relative likelihood and severity of a company's foreseeable risks. The grid is a tool that allows you to compare identified vulnerabilities to one another, so that you can prioritize efforts to prepare for them.

Table 9-1. Foreseeable Risk Analysis Grid

LOW PROBABILITY *HIGH SEVERITY*	MEDIUM PROBABILITY *HIGH SEVERITY*	HIGH PROBABILITY *HIGH SEVERITY*
LOW PROBABILITY *MEDIUM SEVERITY*	MEDIUM PROBABILITY *MEDIUM SEVERITY*	HIGH PROBABILITY *MEDIUM SEVERITY*
LOW PROBABILITY *LOW SEVERITY*	MEDIUM PROBABILITY *LOW SEVERITY*	HIGH PROBABILITY *LOW SEVERITY*

← SEVERITY

→ PROBABILITY

To fill in the grid in Table 9-1, you first identify your risks through the analytic process we discussed above. Next, you assess their potential severity. Then each one is placed in the appropriate box, according to its low, medium, or high probability and severity. This exercise will help ensure that you identify and prepare most for those crises with the greatest potential impact.

It's important to be specific in naming your risks, so that you can reasonably assess the impact, or severity, each one could have. For example, "workplace violence" is too broad a phrase. A fistfight may be highly probable in a factory setting, but its effect may have low severity. Conversely, a mass shooting by a disturbed employee may be improbable, but its consequences would be severe.

Let's look at a hypothetical list of risks, and see how to assess and plot them on the grid. Your list will probably be somewhat longer, but for now suppose you have agreed that your company faces these six risks:

▶ Domestic violence intruding into the workplace. Past incident: One of your female employees took her children to a shelter to escape battering by her out-of-work husband. Enraged and armed, the man threatened to kill her at work, where he knew he would find her.

▶ Fire or an explosion in your factory, where volatile materials are stored under pressure.

▶ Destructive storms often occur, usually with few consequences.

▶ Biological attack through the mail: Deranged individuals with an anti-capitalist rationale have been sending infectious agents to corporate targets within your industry.

▶ Kidnapping, for ransom of your managers who are located in Nuevo Laredo, Mexico at your manufacturing operations.

▶ Toxic leak from the chemical plant next door, which has a long history of safety problems and incompetent management.

Each member of your CPC should consider these six identified risks individually, to come up with a numerical ranking for the probability and severity for each. You might make this a homework assignment, to be done between meetings using research sources like those suggested above, possibly divided by region or operating location. Or the research could be compiled prior to the initial CPC meeting. This advance work provides the basis for an informed discussion of each risk by the committee.

Have each member of the team assign each risk a simple numeric value, separately for its probability and severity: low=1, medium=2, and high=3. Then, average all the rankings together. Once you have compiled your committee members' best estimates, you can plot them on the grid.

For example, let's assume the average of the scores for the risk of a major fire or explosion was 1.5 in probability, and 2.4 in severity. You would place this risk in the top/middle box in Table 9-1. Let's suppose, just for example, you ranked your risks to the organization as follows:

- Domestic violence (physical assault with serious injuries) intruding into the workplace: probability 1.4, medium; severity 1.9, medium.

- Fire or explosion in your factory: probability 1.5, medium; severity 2.4, high.

- Windstorm: probability 2.8, high; severity 1, low.

- Biological attack through the mail: probability 1, low; severity 3, high.

- Kidnapping of employees traveling to inspect foreign operations: probability 2.6, high; severity 1.7, medium.

- Leak from the chemical plant next door: probability 3, high; severity 2.7, high.

You would place them on the grid like the one shown in Table 9-1.

You want to prioritize your preparedness plans to deal with the most probable and most severe risks you can identify. Those are the ones that fall into the four cells at the upper right. Of course, at your company, some boxes may contain more than one risk.

> **The best crisis management is proactive.
> Preparation helps you respond quickly – and the
> quicker you take the right actions, the more
> likely it is that your intervention will succeed.**

The risks that fall outside those four top-priority boxes should still get attention, but not as much. While you have agreed, for example, that a biological attack on your company through the mail is unlikely, you have also agreed that its severity could be high if your facilities were to be quarantined. You certainly cannot ignore it. But by using the grid in Table 9-1, you have been able to make a rational decision about its relative importance and the amount of resources you will apply to your related preparedness efforts.

9.5.4 Additional Considerations in Assessing Severity

In addition to the threats to your core assets, the wellbeing of your company faces a number of other risks. Some companies are engaged in inherently dangerous operations. Banks and retail operations are often the targets of serious armed robberies. Oil and chemical companies must plan for toxic exposures, spills, explosions, and leaks. Manufacturing facilities could face fatal industrial accidents. Transportation providers suffer accidents that could harm innocent people. Hospitals see emergency room violence and medical staff mistakes that cause harm and death. Companies that do business in politically unstable countries could subject people to kidnapping or emergency evacuations out of the countries. When you are using the grid in Table 9-1 to prioritize your company's actual vulnerabilities, you will want to consider all the factors that could affect severity.

9.5.4.1 Legal Liability

An insurance company was the scene of a tragic triple murder by a disgruntled former employee. It later emerged that the killer's previous managers, at Allstate Insurance Company, had encouraged him to leave his job at that company. Paul Calden had a contentious history. He spoke of aliens controlling his mind, threatened coworkers, and routinely carried a gun in his briefcase. Allstate thought it was ridding itself of the troublesome Calden when it gave him a severance package. It also gave him a letter of recommendation, which helped him get a job at the new company. The letter, which contained no warning or concerns, left Allstate partly liable for his eventual rampage. Eventually, Allstate settled lawsuits stemming from the incident, out of court, for a reported US $50 million. Lack of preparedness and resulting incautious actions can expose you to huge legal consequences.

9.5.4.2 Public Relations

These concerns include costs to protect the hard-won, positive associations your company has built over time, and to deflect negative media coverage that can significantly damage stakeholder trust, your reputation, and brand.

9.5.4.3 Investors

Concerns here include drop in value of stock; the postponement or loss of possible ventures, mergers, or other deals; a drop in a firm's credit rating; and the loss of analyst confidence. The 1984 chemical leak at a Union Carbide plant in Bhopal, India, was an enormous disaster, resulting in an estimated 3,000 deaths and 300,000 injuries including blindness and chronic respiratory disease. Amnesty International estimated that over the next several years 22,000 people died from the exposure. Soon afterward, facing multiple liability lawsuits – including one for $15 billion – the company's stock price had dropped so that Union Carbide had been devalued by $900 million. An otherwise reputable company, Union Carbide and its parent company Dow Chemical experienced the financial costs associated with being unprepared at one point in time.

9.5.4.4 Safety

These concerns include the increased likelihood of watchdogs and government regulators intervening following critical incidents, including pressure from OSHA or similar safety-related regulatory agencies around the world. Following the Chernobyl disaster in Russia, and the earthquake and tsunami in Japan in 2011, the entire nuclear power industry underwent increasing scrutiny by regulators, the media, and citizens in communities throughout the world. Additionally, the air travel industry has experienced similar scrutiny as terrorists have repeatedly used planes and other means of transportation as weapons of mass destruction.

9.5.4.5 Productivity

Issues around productivity include work slowdowns as employees grapple with a difficult situation, downsizing due to a drop-off in business, and accidents because of mental distractions. Lowered morale dampened the Oklahoma Water Resource Board (OWRB) following the Oklahoma City bombing. Located across the street from the Murrah Federal Building, the OWRB building was blown nine inches off its foundation and two people were killed during Timothy McVeigh's terrorist blast. The building was closed and people were relocated. Six months later, despite the efforts of an inexperienced employee assistance program counselor to run psychological group debriefings, productivity remained dramatically depressed, absenteeism was up, employees had quit, the work area was disorganized, and employees were angry.

9.5.4.6 Outrage

Another issue includes outside reactions to the crisis, such as protesters, sabotage by angry employees, and media issues that elicit rage from the public. Laid-off employees can demonstrate this, too. At one unprepared company, a laid-off employee encrypted valuable data on the central server and backup system, rendering only some of it recoverable with estimated costs of over US $1 million.

9.5.4.7 Recruiting

It's difficult to hire new employees at a company associated with a poorly handled disaster and negatively impacted reputation. Although studies show that its workers are at no more risk than other industries, many continue to associate workplace violence with the US Postal Service (USPS). It is safe to assume that this reputation has led to a drop in talented applicants at post offices nationwide, in spite of a comprehensive workplace violence program that was developed and implemented that led to the USPS going without an employee-related shooting for over eight years.

9.5.4.8 Key Relationships

Relationships with customers, suppliers, distributors, stockholders, the media, financial institutions, regulators, and others can be compromised by a crisis, leading to lost revenue and negative publicity. A company is no better than its relationships. The financial services company Cantor Fitzgerald lost nearly 700 employees in 2001 when the World Trade Center was attacked. Cantor CEO Howard Lutnick, shaken with grief, almost immediately announced his intention to "take care of" their families. Days later, though, the company removed the deceased employees from the payroll, angering many of their families. In the ensuing months, the company did offer specific material help, including extending health insurance coverage and promising to distribute a share of partnership profits to them. The company's explanation was that it could not provide such support without a tight focus on its operating budget. While many observers considered this a generous commitment, to others the perceived duplicity felt like a betrayal. Some commentators in the media second-guessed Lutnick's judgment (Gordon, 2011). This is an example of why it's best to use an "external conscience" or trusted advisor who is once removed from the crisis bubble.

Another damaged relationship example was in 2000 when the National Highway Traffic Safety Administration (NHTSA) contacted Firestone (tire manufacturers) and Ford Motor Company about high failure rates of tires leading to Ford vehicle "roll over" accidents (Ackman, 2001). Each company blamed the other for the problem. Ultimately, the close relationship of these two companies, dating back to the early friendship of Harvey Firestone and Henry Ford, was severed. Crises can destroy even the most deeply established relationships, depending many times on how the crisis was managed.

These are just a few of the areas that can ignite in a crisis. They can help you evaluate the severity of your foreseeable risks during your crisis planning process. The best crisis management is proactive. Preparation helps you respond quickly – and the quicker you take the right actions, the more likely it is that your intervention will succeed.

Quick Use Preparedness Guide
Chapter 9: Analyzing Your Foreseeable Risks

▶ Have you brainstormed your possible crisis scenarios?

▶ Have you studied what the ripple effect of vulnerability might be on these entities?

  ❑ Your company.

  ❑ Your industry.

  ❑ Your customers.

  ❑ Your suppliers.

  ❑ Your competitors.

  ❑ Other relevant stakeholders.

▶ Have you further analyzed the likelihood of foreseeable risks using these methods or resources?

  ❑ Query staff.

  ❑ Conduct survey.

  ❑ Review history.

  ❑ Review near misses.

  ❑ Review industry mishaps.

  ❑ Assess your locations.

  ❑ Investigate local crime and labor statistics.

  ❑ Conduct online research.

  ❑ Department of Labor statistics.

  ❑ Insurer data.

▶ Have you analyzed the severity of each of your foreseeable risks?

▶ Have you considered the possible negative effects of various disasters on your core assets, including, but not limited to, the list below?

  ❑ People.

  ❑ Finances.

  ❑ Reputation.

▶ Have you determined if and how your company could be blamed for crises related to each foreseeable risk?

▶ Are the following questions a part of your preparedness and response guidelines to address anticipated blame toward the organization or leaders?

  ❑ What is the organization doing or not doing that could be a target for fault-finding following our various foreseeable risks (or situation that just occurred)?

  ❑ What can you do now to build a more positive reputation and engender stakeholder trust?

  ❑ What can you anticipate would be the content of fault-finding by various crisis impacted stakeholders?

  ❑ What are we doing presently that could be perceived as foreseeable, negligent, intentional, unethical, unlawful, or unfair following a crisis?

▶ Have you analyzed these additional areas of severity for each risk?

  ❑ Legal.

  ❑ Public relations.

  ❑ Investors.

  ❑ Safety.

  ❑ Productivity.

  ❑ Outrage.

  ❑ Recruiting.

  ❑ Key relationships.

▶ Have you used the Foreseeable Risk Analysis Grid to rank your most likely incidents – and those with the greatest potential for creating severe consequences?

Chapter 9 – Questions for Further Thought and Discussion

1. Can you give examples within your own organization or of other organizations where a "ripple effect of vulnerability" caused damage once their perimeter of security was breached?

2. If you were to query individuals and groups during an analysis of crisis probability, what questions would you ask? How would questions differ for the various groups you query?

3. If you were to conduct a similar query with the same individuals and groups, only this time to analyze crisis severity, what questions would you ask? How would questions differ for the various groups you query?

4. How can you qualify and quantify the severity of reputational damage from a crisis poorly handled?

5. If you only have the resources to prepare for one risk, would you prepare for a medium probability/high severity risk, or a high probability/medium severity risk? Why?

References

Ackman, D., editor (2001, June). *Tire trouble: the Ford-Firestone blowout.* Retrieved from: http://www.forbes.com/2001/06/20/tireindex.html

FEMA (2013, April). *6 month report: superstorm Sandy from pre-disaster to recovery.* Retrieved from: http://www.fema.gov/disaster/4086/updates/6-months-report-superstorm-sandy-pre-disaster-recovery

Gordon, M. (2011). Howard Lutnick's second life. *New York Magazine.* Retrieved from: http://nymag.com/nymetro/news/sept11/features/5486/

Hare, R. D. (1999). *Without conscience: the disturbing world of psychopaths among us.* New York: The Guildford Press, p. 1.

Schoen, J.W. (2013, May). *Adding up the financial costs of the Boston bombings.* Retrieved from: http://www.cnbc.com/id/100690046

Smith, L.L. (2012, May). *20th annual ICM crisis report.* Retrieved from: http://crisisconsultants.blogspot.com/2012/05/20th-annual-icm-crisis-report.html

Towers Watson (2013, November). *U.S. employers rank stress as top workforce risk issue.* Retrieved from: http://www.towerswatson.com/en-US/Press/2013/11/us-employers-rank-stress-as-top-workforce-risk-issue

10

Evaluating Your Existing Crisis Procedures

The success of your organization rests, in part, on its culture, policies, procedures, and people. You can build your crisis preparedness on these very same strengths – if you match them to your possible foreseeable risks and start with the existing controls you have in place. Some policies, procedures, and people will apply to more than one area of vulnerability. Other crises may involve executive and managerial teams, with no need for emergency response depending on your culture and the scope and impact of the situation. Accordingly, a well-defined procedure for getting the right people responding effectively is an established control for appropriate situations that will serve the company time and again, no matter what issues arise.

This chapter will help you to:

➢ *Evaluate the existing strengths and weaknesses of your crisis management controls.*

➢ *Determine whether your existing response procedures are sufficient for the risks you identified.*

➢ *Enhance the capabilities you already have in place.*

10.1 Evaluate and Enhance Your Strengths

You can use a computer spreadsheet, or a simple grid like the one shown in Table 10-1, to help maintain a clear picture of your preparedness strengths and your ideas for enhancing them. List your foreseeable risks. Now match them with the policies, procedures, and other controls you have in place, keeping in mind that each one might apply to several of the risks you have identified. Then add the enhancements you can make right now. We will discuss developing entirely new controls and procedures in the next chapter; don't worry about the new controls for now.

Table 10-1. Tool for Evaluating Controls

Foreseeable Risk	Existing Controls	Enhancement of Controls	New Controls
Workplace violence	EAP, guard service	Lower EAP violence warning threshold, etc.	Emergency communication plan
Earthquake	Command center, etc.	Additional monitors and recorders	Off-site command center
Loss of critical information	IT manager, backups, etc.	Retain "hacker consultant," etc.	Periodic hacker testing

10.2 Leverage Your Strengths to Enhance Preparedness

Leveraging – investing the least amount of time, money, and effort in order to yield the greatest possible return – always makes good business sense. That's true of preparation for crises as well.

An effective preparedness strategy will require time, money, and effort, but the best investment you can make is in clear thinking. If you don't have a single extra dollar to spend today, you can still make progress by addressing questions of time, money, and effort.

10.2.1 Time

▶ How soon do you want your preparations to be comprehensive and current?

▶ Who in the organization will champion your plan, and how much time should that person realistically devote to the project?

▶ How many others should be involved, and how much time will the plan demand from each of them?

▶ How often should the crisis planning committee (CPC) meet?

▶ What investment of time can you expect from senior management?

▶ How many people will it take to meet the desired deadlines?

▶ How can you get the greatest result for the least amount of time invested?

▶ Would an outside consultant be needed if there is not enough staff time or expertise to fulfill the preparedness tasks?

10.2.2 Money

▶ What key points of vulnerability in your defense system could be strengthened with minimal, targeted spending?

▶ How much money is needed for full crisis preparedness? Or, for leveraged priority items only?

▶ What can be done before additional financial resources are allocated to improve your preparedness or to make a stronger case for the needed budget?

▶ How will the investment of your company in crisis planning yield quantifiable savings?

If difficult to establish, align your business case with the concerns of senior managers. Research (CFO Magazine, 2012) reported that executives are concerned about reputation and people most, but *protection of core assets of all kinds* is your mantra. Are there cost-justified enhancements that would better equip your organization to face your identified hazards? You can model an analysis of costs and savings from your own experience, or from that of other organizations. Examine company histories (your own and others) for crises that might have been avoided or better contained. On average, how much did these incidents end up costing? Figure in both hard dollar costs (including repairs, business disruption, lawsuit costs, lost customers, etc.) and – as best you can – soft or indirect costs such as lost productivity, turnover, absenteeism, disability and workers' compensation claims, diminished reputation, tarnished brand, and other data available to you. Even if you can't put dollar amounts on the soft costs, at least list them as potentially or actually impacted. What amount of money invested to prevent – or respond better – to events like those would have produced a definable degree of savings?

While we're talking about money, don't forget that well-managed crises can also enhance reputation and company value. For example, look at post-crisis sales and new leadership talent attracted to the business as justification of how a crisis, handled well, increased the value of an organization. How much is the cost of effective crisis preparedness defrayed by an increase in sales following an excellent crisis response? If the company was able to attract a high-value executive following a well-managed crisis, that can also be evidence of crisis preparedness bringing value.

As your justification takes shape, note that the Templeton study (Knight & Pretty, 1996) on increased shareholder value (discussed in Chapter 8) shows how effective crisis response and crisis preparedness can increase the value of the organization.

> **While accepting there are some things you can't change within your organization, what are crisis preparedness actions that are within your influence and control that you could implement?**

10.2.3 Effort

The biggest hurdle is in getting started. Behavior management specialists know the importance of breaking down large projects into small manageable tasks in order to get the job done. While accepting there are some things you can't change within your organization, what are crisis preparedness actions that are within your influence and control that you could implement? Can these advances in preparedness be broken down into manageable tasks that will help you and others overcome the resistance to getting started?

- How much effort will the culture of your company allow for preparedness efforts?

- Will your people tolerate the minor irritations that come hand-in-hand with preparedness, such as participating in writing local emergency response plans, training, and regular evacuation drills?

- Is senior management willing to devote enough talented personnel to develop and maintain an effective crisis preparedness initiative?

- Who is an executive sponsor willing to provide the leadership and authority to push a crisis preparedness initiative through the political bureaucracy of the organization?

> Will individual members of the CPC cooperate and can they depend on their managers and peers to support their involvement?

> What are you willing to do to champion those crisis preparedness activities within your personal control?

10.3 Existing Controls: Where to Look and What to Look For

You can identify several places to benchmark, evaluate, and enhance your existing controls. Most are free or inexpensive and involve only a modicum of inquisitive effort. While going through the following list and digging into what can be found, make a separate list of controls that you don't already have in place. This will give you a head start on the next step of identifying new controls (Chapter 11) that would be appropriate for your organization's crisis preparedness.

Process guardian. Assign a *process guardian* the task of making sure information from post-incident debriefings is properly memorialized. Lessons-learned should then be compiled, agreed upon, and prioritized. The process guardian (discussed further in Chapter 13) will then be responsible for organizing the implementation and following through to make sure your teams, external providers, plan, and processes are improved, as planned.

In-house knowledge. Your company already has a body of experience in responding to and managing unforeseen events that can serve as a guide to the future whether from small crises, real disasters it has weathered, or your crisis exercise program. Possibly, new managers bring crisis management knowledge from another company. In any case, you need to know what your company has done right. Also your management team needs to know its crisis response weaknesses in order to establish a reliable preparedness strategy. A combination of internal and external perspectives can help.

If your company has gone through real crises or you conduct a regular exercise program, but you do not debrief the process thoroughly and follow through on lessons-learned, now is the time to do so. There may still be gems of insight out there among your workers, just waiting to be mined. Now might be a good time to mine them. When your company was hit in the past by unexpected turbulence or participated in a scheduled crisis exercise, did the following happen?

> Were the people who handled your response fully debriefed for lessons-learned? Was the information compiled and analyzed? If not, you can do it now. Better late than never.

▶ Were the conclusions incorporated into your crisis preparedness plan? If not, this is an opportunity for you to capitalize on lessons-learned.

▶ Was your workforce solicited for feedback on what had happened? Sometimes, best ideas come from the grassroots level.

Other Resources for Gathering Knowledge

Internet. This is an obvious place to find helpful crisis preparedness information without requiring management involvement. Support staff with proper guidance can find a wealth of helpful materials and information to assist in your crisis preparedness improvement process.

Electronic newsletters. There are many electronic newsletters available relating to crisis management, disaster recovery, risk management, workplace violence, crisis public relations, and emergency management. Many are free or inexpensive and available by searching online.

Books. Obviously, by reading this book, you are already utilizing this resource. With many books on the market, finding the right books to read are important. Make a habit of asking others with crisis management responsibilities which books have been most helpful. Also, make sure you visit the bookstores at crisis-related conferences that you may attend.

Professional associations and conferences. Other sources you can turn to immediately are the industry and professional associations to which you already belong, or should consider joining. Conferences sponsored by these industry associations are full of materials, knowledgeable members, training courses, and networking possibilities.

International Organization for Standardization (ISO). Several emergent international standards are fully vetted and are great resources for benchmarking and guiding your preparedness in crisis-related areas. ISO 22301 is the business continuity standard. ISO 31000 is the risk management standard that includes guidance on risk assessment. ISO 27001 is the information security management system for protecting data and intellectual property. To a lesser extent, ISO 9001 is generally for quality management systems, but does include guidance for safety.

Local and federal agencies. If you are located in a hurricane or earthquake zone, for instance, you should evaluate your response plans in relation to the latest recommendations of local and state emergency management agencies. What about a general evacuation of the entire area? Also, don't forget benchmarks for facilities evacuations. Your local Office of Emergency

Management could be a helpful resource to help evaluate and enhance your existing capabilities.

Crisis management consultants. During the planning process is a good time to enlist an outside consultant who specializes in crisis management. It shouldn't take a lot of a consultant's time; a good one should have up-to-date information at his or her fingertips. The good ones also tend to be efficient, having completed the process many times. The advantage of considering an experienced consultant is that he or she has seen the inside of many organizations and their preparedness procedures. This cross-section of exposure can help you identify ways to fine tune your existing program.

Insurance broker. Your broker can help you evaluate your existing areas of coverage in light of your risks. In addition, good brokers should have access to external resources to help you be better prepared for managing those risks beyond your insurance coverage. Brokers and insurers they represent have a vested interest in the resiliency of your organization when covered incidents occur. Work in tandem with your insurance broker to come up with enhancements to your existing preparedness program.

> The viability of all oil and gas exploration companies in the Gulf of Mexico was at risk with threatened governmental regulatory restraints. It was in the best interest of all these companies for BP to get the crisis resolved as efficiently and effectively as possible on a timely basis.

Benchmark preparedness plans of other companies. If there was ever an undertaking ideally suited to benchmarking, crisis preparedness is it. Don't hesitate to approach other companies to find out how they are handling crisis preparedness. Even competitor companies are often willing to share crisis management strategies. Because crisis management is not typically considered to be a competitive component between organizations (however, I personally disagree and believe that it is), sharing of preparedness and response strategies is common. You may find that your existing controls could be improved or need to be replaced. Being in the same industry, competitors could all be negatively impacted by a crisis and it behooves the industry for all to be effective at crisis management. An example was the BP Gulf oil spill of 2010. The viability of all oil and gas exploration companies in the Gulf of Mexico was at risk with threatened governmental regulatory restraints. It was in the best interest of all these companies for BP to get the crisis resolved as efficiently and effectively as possible on a timely basis.

Case Study: A Painful Lesson

In 1989, an explosion – the largest in US history – at the Phillips 66 chemical plant in Pasadena, Texas sent a fireball 500 feet into the air (FEMA, n.d.). Debris was reportedly blown for 6 to 10 miles, with 23 people killed, and more than 100 injured. Phillips 66 and local emergency responders did an excellent job of implementing its emergency response plan to address the physical content of the crisis. The fire was extinguished by that evening. The CEO arrived at the site quickly and did a good job as corporate spokesperson and commander in chief, communicating care and compassion to the community and for all employees, including those injured and killed and their families. Insurance programs and contingency plans swung into action. The company and regulators promised investigations.

People were obviously traumatized. The human side of the crisis was promptly addressed through an existing resource the company had identified (existing control). Behavioral health professionals from nearby University of Texas were called in. Once the fire was out, the university reportedly brought in a mobile facility, and positioned it across the street from the explosion site.

Apparently, university personnel were not sufficiently experienced in crisis intervention. Establishing the counseling offices across the street from the site was a mistake. First, employees reportedly didn't want their coworkers or managers to see them on their way into counseling. Second, a known symptom of traumatic stress is "avoidance of reminders" of the incident; thus, having to return to the site for counseling was unacceptable to most. Very few showed up for counseling despite the good intentions of the providers and management. There are better ways to orchestrate a post-crisis intervention, as you should know by now from this book.

Fourteen months later, the company found itself facing more than 200 lawsuits by victims. One employee – who had not availed himself of the offered counseling in the University's ill-fated mobile structure – received a subsequent diagnosis of post-traumatic stress disorder (PTSD). Company attorneys and the insurer settled the claim for $2 million and required the employee not to divulge the terms of the settlement.

But the employee had a hard time keeping the secret. He "quietly" told his friends from work about his newfound fortune. Within three months, the number of lawsuits swelled to over 1,200 claims for PTSD. The exposure from the human side of the crisis, through psychological injury claims, had grown to over $900 million.

Lessons-learned: Had Phillips 66 fully vetted their existing resource for crisis counseling, a landslide of claims – almost $1 billion – might have been avoided. Make sure those controls that are existing are appropriate and effective when you need them. In this case, it would have been appropriate to include the University of Texas personnel into the company exercises and vetted their approach with industry specialists who know the human side of crisis. Lesson learned is to vet your existing controls and if they are not adequate, enhance them or consider new controls that will meet your needs.

10.4 What You Should Look For: Clear Strategy and Good Tactics

When a crisis strikes, you get only one chance to respond. You have to be prepared to do it right – the first time.

> **A valid plan is one that actually accomplishes what it was designed to do. A reliable one can be counted on to work successfully in response to repeated challenges.**

If you critique your plans for clarity as to both strategy and tactics, you'll go a long way toward ensuring that you are ready. You need to keep the differences between them clearly in mind – and not mistake one for the other. This is why we recommend a three-tiered preparedness approach with separate, but integrated, plans and teams at the executive, managerial, and tactical/site levels. Your strategy must be a comprehensive plan, and your tactics must be valid and reliable methods of implementation. A valid plan is one that actually accomplishes what it was designed to do. A reliable one can be counted on to work successfully in response to repeated challenges.

Suppose you have identified workplace violence, from a deranged and armed employee for instance, as a possible risk your company faces. In response, your strategy might be to put in place specific systems, like an employee assistance program (EAP), and controls, like security guards. The EAP and the guards are tactics you have chosen to address your anti-violence strategy.

US Postal Service (USPS) Workplace Violence Strategy

Most people know the huge problem USPS had in the past with employees committing mass murders in postal facilities. Over a 23-year period, USPS experienced shootings mostly by employees or ex-employees in Alabama, Georgia, Oklahoma (2 times), Louisiana, California (5 times), New Jersey and Michigan (2 times each), Nevada, Florida, and Oregon.

Out of necessity, USPS took workplace violence seriously and implemented a comprehensive workplace violence program (United States Postal Service, 2009). With as many as 785,000 employees at the time, the postal service went approximately eight years without another employee-perpetrated shooting.

Lessons-learned: Much like establishing a crisis management program, the USPS strategic decision to implement a comprehensive prevention, preparedness, and response program mitigated the problem in an outstanding manner.

But do the EAP and the guards amount to a comprehensive strategy? No. There is nothing wrong with either of these tools to address workplace violence. However, from a comprehensive standpoint, additional field-tested approaches to preventing workplace violence should also be considered. A workplace violence policy, threat notification system, corporate security department, supervisory training, employee orientation meetings, hostility management training, criminal background checks, drug screening, corporate domestic violence program, and a trained threat response team with a manual that provides standardized response guidelines – these can all help to provide a comprehensive program to address workplace violence.

10.4.1 Assessing Strategy and Tactics: One Example

Let's continue with the example in which the anticipated threat is a violent outburst from a worker and the mechanisms in place for response are an EAP and security guards. This is not nearly as comprehensive as the program USPS put in place. But your existing procedures can be analyzed and enhanced. Surely, there are other controls that could be implemented, but for now let's stick with the two that are presently in place.

> Make sure your EAP coverage includes all your locations and insist that it includes an experienced threat specialist who can supplement its behavioral health capabilities.

10.4.1.1 Validity vs. Reliability

When evaluating your preparedness in this example, your company would need to consider whether its EAP is truly equipped with reliable and valid elements at appropriate levels to address your foreseeable risk of workplace violence. Is the EAP staffed with professionals who are adequately trained and experienced in comprehensively handling threats of violence, for instance? Often they are not, but many offer threat consultations anyway. Does it have a vetted relationship with a competent threat professional? Only some do. Is there a comprehensive and structured management system poised to deal with potentially violent employees who are involved in EAP counseling sessions? They all should have internal protocol that goes beyond the "duty to warn" laws. Does it have the right post-incident skills, such as adequately trained and experienced trauma counselors, with sufficient quality assurance? Most refer out to Crisis Care Network, a national network of crisis responders. Will it be in the right place with sufficient quantity of counselors, and available to you, with the needed threat assessment, threat defusing, and post-incident assistance? Make sure your EAP coverage includes all your locations and insist that it includes an experienced threat specialist who can supplement its behavioral health capabilities.

What about the security guards? Are they trained in how to handle specific incidents that could arise in your workplace? If an employee storms out of a termination meeting and past guards outside the door, do the guards know what action is consistent with corporate policy? What are the primary responsibilities of the guards? Are they to be armed, visible, in uniform, capable of arrest, and on 24-hour watch? How many and where will they be located? Have they passed rigorous background checks and drug testing? What training have they had and what are the qualifications needed to be a guard, as a staff position or through an external provider?

These and other validity and reliability questions should be considered in vetting the resources chosen for your crisis preparedness and prevention program. Let's look at them a bit deeper.

10.4.1.2 Strategy

EAP. Strategically, management must rely on much more than just the EAP. Its counselors are typically skilled behavioral health generalists who provide a very helpful service for employees and families who are experiencing personal problems of daily living. However, these counselors are not trained in issues of threat management and workplace violence.

Threat management goes well beyond the discipline of psychological intervention. Behavioral health assistance might be a part of the equation, but issues can also emerge that relate to human resources, corporate security, law enforcement, legal counsel, facilities management, medical, and supervisory intervention. If you anticipate threats of workplace violence, you will need to establish a multidisciplinary threat response team as well as a threat notification system that encourages employees to voice their suspicions of potential violence to the appropriate managers. Other specialties and components of a comprehensive workplace violence program may also need to be considered as listed above.

A comprehensive strategy for dealing with workplace violence would back up the EAP with broader programs – thus allowing the EAP to focus on the things in which EAP counselors specialize, which is counseling and referrals. This strategy is most effective and builds on strengths of each discipline.

Security Guards. And what about that other control you have in place for preventing workplace violence – your security guards? Maybe you feel better knowing that there are uniformed guards in place. But what kind of skills and capabilities do your guards really have? Is your guard staff thoroughly familiar with your emergency communication and response plan in case a threatening individual shows up unexpectedly at your workplace? Are they familiar with lockdown procedures, shelter in place, evacuation alternatives, and whom to contact immediately in critical situations?

One huge organization that had experienced more than its share of workplace shootings had made a weak attempt to cover workplace violence in instructions to employees. The receptionists and unarmed security guards at the company's various facilities had the following directive listed in their manual regarding how to handle a person with a gun who showed up at the front lobby: "Keep the person occupied and call 911." How many armed perpetrators would sip a cup of coffee and read a magazine while the receptionist or security guard called the police? Even an unskilled plaintiff attorney would have a field day with such a plan.

Whatever your risks, you need a strategy that is clear and comprehensive. The strategy will anticipate the various situations that could emerge. It will provide guidelines that are well thought out and effective for each anticipated situation. The strategy will be benchmarked to ensure it and the tactical directives are appropriate when compared to similar organizations. It will be exercised. And, the strategy and tactical plan will be debriefed after being used, and enhanced to ensure ongoing quality improvement. Ultimately, the strategy will be both valid and reliable.

10.4.2 Leave No Strategy or Tactic Unevaluated

Now let's apply this same kind of thinking to some other aspects of crisis preparedness to see whether they are valid and reliable. This is the sort of thorough and methodical process of evaluation to consider. Phillips 66 would have been well served to engage in this activity prior to their explosion.

As one example, let's say that your organization has designated crisis team leaders to be in charge of crisis response, people who are capable of handling the tasks through adequate training, experience, and crisis leadership coaching. These leaders should be thoroughly familiar with the plans of the company. If a person tasked with crisis leadership is killed or out of the country at the moment of crisis, will an equally qualified backup person be ready to take over? If not, you have an unreliable control.

What if you were to lose your building? It wouldn't take something as horrendous as a terrorist attack. A fire, extended power outage, or natural disaster could make your premises unusable. What would you need to get your operations up and running again in temporary quarters? How soon?

What if your people have destroyed homes and are in no position to help implement your business continuity plan? See if your business continuity plan needs to be enhanced. If your planning has serious weaknesses, then it isn't valid or reliable and needs to be more complete.

> By enhancing your existing controls and procedures, you will leverage your strengths, and you will see positive results. This is what crisis-prepared companies do on a regular basis.

10.4.3 Now Enhance Your Strengths

How can you build on your company's existing policies, procedures, and overall approach to crisis response? You will want to answer the following questions:

▶ Do your preparedness efforts take into account all the probable and severe events we can foresee?

▶ Is there a prevention, preparedness, response, and recovery strategy built into our plans for every significant risk?

▶ Are your crisis prevention and response plans truly valid and reliable? Or, are they "false preparedness" measures that may or may not work?

▶ Have your policies and procedures been thoroughly communicated to all appropriate stakeholders?

▶ Have adequate training and emergency exercises been conducted?

Still not sure of all the answers? A good program of exercises and drills will help. A secret of organizations that are well-prepared is this simple formula.

Once you have your crisis plans in place and the appropriate teams established and trained, exercising is the key to successful preparedness. At that point, for every dollar you have to spend on preparedness, spend approximately 80 cents (80%) on exercising. The purpose of exercising is to test your plans and your teams. A program of regularly scheduled exercises will help ensure that you and your organization will be as good as you possibly can when crises hit. We will discuss more about your crisis exercising program in Chapter 12 on putting your plan in action.

By enhancing your existing controls and procedures, you will leverage your strengths, and you will see positive results. This is what crisis-prepared companies do on a regular basis.

10.5 Common Elements of Preparedness Plans

Every company's situation is unique. But some elements of preparedness planning are appropriate for nearly everyone. Let's go through a few of them, and look at ways they might be enhanced with very little investment. We'll think of it as a brainstorming session. For every example we look at, you can come up with ideas of your own.

10.5.1 Security Risks

Organizations often have security risks that employees tend to ignore. Consider setting up policies and procedures that will encourage employees to comply with security guidelines. It starts by clearly defining and publicizing the desired behaviors and then monitoring compliance.

10.5.2 Cyber Security

Target Corporation experienced a data breach that involved a reported 40 million people nationwide who had shopped in their 1800 stores during the busy 2013 Christmas season. In response, JP Morgan Chase, Citibank, and other banks issued significant restrictions on credit and debit cards that had been used at Target during the breach. Shoppers learned at checkout lanes that their spending limits had been seriously curtailed. Cyber security breaches are modern day risks that can have huge financial and reputational fallout for organizations.

Obviously, your computer systems have virus protection software, firewalls, passwords, and other cyber security controls in place. But are your IT people staying on top of the rapidly changing cyber threats and responding firewall technology? Are you following the standards established in ISO 27001 for information security? Are you sure that every computer used by your people is protected, especially when employees use their own devices for work purposes? What about the devices your employees use when they work from home or when they log onto public Wi-Fi locations?

And how secure are your computers from hackers? Have you considered testing your system by hiring a highly recommended (for obvious reasons) "hacker consultant" to see how easy it might be to get into your system? Or, if it has already been hacked? Data breaches occur with regularity, and many times companies are unaware that the intrusion has taken place.

10.5.3 Public Relations (PR)

Your PR folks probably do a dazzling job of getting out your company's message during normal times. If they didn't, you would have replaced them long ago. But do you know whether they have the right surge capabilities to manage your communications at a time of fast moving, unexpected, high-consequence crises? To find out, you'll want to ask them the right questions and test them during your crisis exercising.

> **Are your PR people experienced in conducting high-stress, post-crisis press conferences, for instance, when reporters might be digging aggressively for information you are not ready to release? Are they skilled in the sensitivities involved when you are blamed?**

Are your PR people experienced in conducting high-stress, post-crisis press conferences, for instance, when reporters might be digging aggressively for information you are not ready to release? Are they skilled in the sensitivities involved when you are blamed? Such a press conference won't be anything like those pleasant events you hold when you launch a product line or announce new members of your board. What high-consequence crises have they helped to manage? Who is their most experienced person that could be available to you on a moment's notice? Take note that the large national PR firms are much stronger in some cities than others. Do they match up with your potential crisis needs? You need a PR professional who will help you take charge of your image and message, from deciding where your spokesperson should stand to what he or she should communicate if hostile questions arise. Your reputation may be dependent on readily having the right PR resource in place.

Seemingly, small mistakes can cause serious damage to your corporate image. Crises demand PR professionals who specifically know crisis management. Some PR professionals are excellent at crisis management, but many are not. An enhancement to your program would be to ensure that your internal and external PR professionals are experienced and skilled in crisis management.

10.5.4 Company Website

Many proactive companies prepare crisis-related "dark sites" for their corporate webpage, keeping the page behind a firewall and out of sight until it is needed during crisis response. Such a site might include appropriate facts about the company during happier times, its products, executive management, work locations, and crisis-specific information. A restaurant chain, for example, may develop background information about exposure to food-borne illnesses. Such a site provides a way for the media, the public, employees, families, and others to access useful, positive information easily about the company and how it is handling itself. When crisis time hits, you can post prepared information quickly for public viewing. Additional capabilities might be built in, such as the provision of daily updates about when and how the company is responding to the crisis. (For more about crisis communications, see Chapter 5.)

10.5.5 Crisis Command Center

Many crisis-prone companies have an existing crisis command center (CCC). But especially if your command center is not a dedicated room that is fully equipped, it's time to reevaluate your capabilities here. If you ever actually have to use such a room, you will need it to be furnished with more than a conference table and chairs.

Does the room contain, for example, Internet capability and satellite or cable-connected televisions with recording capabilities, so that you can monitor and record media coverage? Are adequate landline, cellular, and satellite telephones available? Is there a generator that can withstand a long-term power outage? Are there spare chargers for mobile phones that team members use? Too often, such phones run down during a crisis, while their chargers sit at home.

Your organization may not have the luxury of dedicating a large, accessible space solely to crisis management. Think creatively and match your choices to your foreseeable risks.

Liberty Mutual's Multi-purpose Crisis Center

Your organization may not have the luxury of dedicating a large, accessible space solely to crisis management. However, you can think creatively and appropriately to match your existing procedures and resources to your crisis management needs. Liberty Mutual, the Boston-based insurance giant, provides an example in point. Because it is not a chemical company or other high-risk operation, its need for a CCC was statistically small. Yet, as an existing resource that could be enhanced, this progressive company developed a space that was large, separate, and well-equipped for managing crises. Liberty Mutual's crisis leaders designated a computer training room as their CCC. But, could this room serve as an enhanced resource for crisis management purposes?

The room was extremely well suited to its extra purpose. As a training center, it was already equipped with a bank of networked computers, phone outlets, and plenty of workspace. It was located in an area of the headquarters building without windows or multiple entrances – so it could be readily secured. For easy reference, the company's corporate crisis management team created a schematic drawing of the room in its alternative crisis command center configuration, a drawing that precisely detailed the CCC layout.

As soon as word comes in that a crisis is underway, designated individuals would consult the schematic, and within minutes the room would be transformed. The same room was used for crisis exercises, a practice that is essential if the command center was to be reliable. Part of the exercise program, in fact, involved timing the room conversion to be sure that it fell within an established benchmark.

Despite the large size of the company, Liberty Mutual evaluated an existing resource and converted it inexpensively to meet their crisis management needs. They did not need to overspend to create an excellent CCC that met their crisis preparedness needs.

When considering your CCC, remember that in a crisis, phone lines are likely to be jammed or unusable. Hurricanes, floods, fires, and explosions are just some of the incidents when phone lines tend to be inoperative. Or, maybe an electromagnetic pulse attack will take out computers and phones. Redundant systems are a necessity. Often, text messaging is the only form of communications in the early aftermath of a big crisis. Consider having several lines in the CCC with unpublished phone numbers that do not go through the company's normal switching system. You should be prepared to have those satellite phones charged at all times, and to keep needed phone numbers updated.

10.5.6 Backup Command Center Location

What if your own building cannot be used? That's what happened to Mayor Rudy Giuliani and his team when their World Trade Center CCC was destroyed in the 9/11 terrorist attacks in NYC. He tried a nearby firehouse in lower Manhattan, but the doors were locked with all the firefighters dispatched in the early aftermath. So, he ended up walking the streets and reporting ongoing information to people through the media. Realistically, you and your team will likely need more than a camera man.

Perhaps there is a nearby hotel where you could plan to set up an offsite command center. But what is in place there to enable you to function in crisis mode? You will want to ask the same questions about communications capability and the security systems of the hotel. Will there be reliable access control to keep outsiders away from your crisis management operations? You would not want members of the media, for example, walking in on you unannounced or eavesdropping without your knowledge.

And when a crisis arises, what if the room you expect to use at that hotel is booked for some other function? For example, companies involved in offshore oil extraction in the North Sea off Scotland know that their industry is a risky one, and they keep themselves prepared for the worst. Many of them expect to run their disaster response efforts from Aberdeen, Scotland. So they have signed contracts with hotels there ensuring that the hotels will preempt other functions, if necessary, to give them space for their command centers. The hotels, in turn, include a clause to this effect when they rent function rooms to their everyday clients. While nobody wants to disrupt a wedding reception or retirement party, an oil-platform explosion with casualties deserves precedence.

Keep in mind that any disaster that hits you might hit your neighbors, too. A flood, fire, explosion, or earthquake could affect many companies in your area. What will happen when response teams and out-of-towners from a dozen other companies show up at the same hotel needing space? Why not obtain commitment from the hotel in advance, ensuring that you will get priority?

In this example, your relationship with the nearby hotel represents an opportunity to build upon an existing resource. The new terms you work out with the hotel management, for precedence and priority at a time of crisis, would be an effective, inexpensive enhancement you can make right away. You might have to agree to pay a small retainer, or double at the time, to get guaranteed space during a crisis, but in the big scheme, the cost will be minimal.

> **An integrated notification plan will help you distinguish between people who "need to know" and those who might "like to know." Many managers may wish to be in the information loop, even if they are not essential players in your response.**

10.5.7 Notification Plans

We have discussed earlier how effective communication is crucial in any crisis response – especially immediately after an incident. Communications are existent in all companies. But, can your existing communications, notifications, and team mobilization be improved for effective crisis management? Increasingly, companies are using emergency notification systems for notifications and conference call bridges among crisis team members. In this case, the team is notified and mobilized simultaneously as they are "bridged" into the call. Additional issues now need to be addressed. To do this, consider an *integrated notification plan* in advance. Such a plan would tell you:

▶ Who needs to be notified in each type of incident, and how to alert them.

▶ What they need to know to help them act decisively.

▶ What you and others need to know from each represented staff function in order to effectively manage the crisis.

For example, when you notify and mobilize the attorney on your team regarding a chemical plant explosion, an integrated approach will lead you to ask prepared questions during the conversation, such as whether a legal representative should be present before the incident site is photographed, holding statements are used with the media, or investigations begin.

An integrated notification plan will also help you distinguish between people who "need to know" and those who might "like to know." Many managers may wish to be in the information loop, even if they are not essential players in your response. Your CEO may want to know "immediately, if not sooner" about any calamity – or may be willing to let the senior management team handle most events. Under what circumstances should your board of directors be alerted? Should every member be notified, or only the board chairperson? The plan should also contain instructions about how to make these notifications. Does the CEO wish to be alerted immediately and directly from site management, for example, or only through a senior manager? What if the go-between senior manager can't be located on a timely basis?

How much, if at all, should you investigate before you make notification calls? Senior managers need to define clearly how and when they want to be notified.

Communications and notifications are existing systems that are in all companies at some level. Look to see how you can evaluate these existing tools and enhance them for crisis management purposes. Other systems and resources are already established within your organization that can be applied to your crisis management capabilities. Identify and evaluate them as an efficient and cost effective method for crisis preparedness.

Quick Use Preparedness Guide

Chapter 10: Evaluating Your Existing Crisis Procedures

▶ Leverage your organization's existing tools and resources as you prepare for crises.

▶ Evaluate how your existing plans match up to your foreseeable risks.

▶ Determine the simple enhancements you can make right now for a small expenditure of time, effort, and money.

▶ Establish what your organization is willing and able to invest in preparedness enhancements, in terms of:

❏ Time.

❏ Effort.

❏ Money.

▶ Look in-house for the insights and experience your people already have about the risks you face and the corresponding controls you have in place to prevent them or respond effectively.

▶ Look outside for help.

❏ Check with the Internet, industry associations and conferences, consultants, ISO standards, your insurance broker, and government emergency management agencies.

❏ Benchmark what other companies are doing.

▶ Are the preparedness strategies and tactics presently in place both valid and reliable? Vet them properly.

❏ Validity means that the plan actually accomplishes what it was designed to do.

❏ Reliability means that it will work successfully under repeated applications.

▶ Run a regular crisis exercise program to test your existing preparedness systems against your foreseeable risks. Enhance existing resources to fit your crisis management needs.

Chapter 10 - Questions for Further Thought and Discussion

1. Utilizing and enhancing your existing controls is an economical method to increase your crisis preparedness. What are the strengths and weaknesses of this method?

2. What are examples of existing crisis preparedness controls in your organization (or other organizations) with which you are familiar that are not valid, i.e. false, sense of preparedness? What are examples of controls that are valid?

3. What are examples of existing crisis preparedness controls in your organization (or other organizations) with which you are familiar that appear to be unreliable? What are examples of controls that are reliable?

4. What are 10 resources you have in your organization that could be applied to crisis management capabilities that are presently not being used?

References

CFO Magazine. (2012, August 14).

FEMA (n.d.). *Phillips Petroleum chemical plant explosion and fire, Pasadena, Texas, October 23, 1989*. USFA-TR-035. Retrieved from:
http://www.usfa.fema.gov/downloads/pdf/publications/tr-035.pdf

Knight, R.F. & Pretty, D.J. (1996). *The impact of catastrophes on shareholder value*. Oxford executive research briefings. Templeton College (University of Oxford).

United States Postal Service (2009). *Achieving a violence-free workplace together*. Publication 45. Retrieved from:
http://www.nalc.org/depart/cau/pdf/manuals/PUB_45.pdf

11

Organizing New Controls and Drafting Your New Plans

Your goal at this stage is a crisis preparedness plan and process that is comprehensive and watertight. In this step of identifying new controls, you work systematically to find the leaks and plug them. Once you have completed the analysis of your existing controls (Chapter 10), you should have started already to identify needed new controls to address the foreseeable risks for which you do not have an existing comprehensive prevention, preparedness, response, or recovery strategy. Now that you have evaluated current preparedness and identified new controls, you are ready to establish a comprehensive plan to protect core assets – people, reputation, finances, and more – when they are threatened by a crisis.

This chapter will help you to:

> *Identify new controls that can address preparedness gaps.*

> *Consider how new controls could impact other systems.*

> *Organize and integrate your crisis planning within your organization.*

> *Gain senior management buy-in for your plan.*

> *Create a plan that is implemented and monitored effectively.*

11.1 Addressing Weaknesses Through Controls

A *control* is anything you put in place to deal with a specific foreseeable risk. Policies, procedures, methods, equipment, facilities, and management systems can all be thought of as controls. Some controls can apply to more than one foreseeable risk. Others are custom tailored specifically for a single risk.

11.1.1 Benchmarking New Controls

Mentioned in the previous chapter and highlighted here, one key way to identify needed new controls is by *benchmarking* – that is, investigating the controls that are working well in other organizations. Some new controls have never been put in place simply because no one in your organization brought them forward. Benchmarking with other companies will help you identify new ideas, as well as ensure your preparedness is sufficiently aligned with that of other businesses. However, it is wise to use all the benchmarking resources we discussed earlier: your process guardian and others with in-house knowledge, the Internet, electronic newsletters, books, professional associations and conferences, standards organizations such as International Organization for Standardization (ISO), local and federal agencies, crisis management consultants, insurance broker, and other companies.

You can start by looking at other companies in your industry. Presumably, you have common perils, since you run similar operations. But don't fail to look at other kinds of organizations, too. If you face hazards that are the result of geography, like earthquakes or storms, you would want to benchmark the controls of other companies in your locale. If your executives travel regularly to certain unstable parts of the world, you should find out what controls have been put in place by companies whose people visit the same places, regardless of their lines of business.

Once you have done this research, you will then have to decide whether you want to implement the procedures you uncover, devise your own variations of them – or do neither. (See Sections 11.12.3 and 11.12.4 below for some recommended sources of information for your research.)

> As you brainstorm, consider all the possible responses that could apply to the new risks – even if, at first, some might not appear to fit your culture, bandwidth, or budgetary capabilities.

11.1.2 Brainstorming New Controls

To further identify new controls, consider a brainstorming session with your team. You could have the members of your crisis planning committee (CPC) begin the process individually. First, each will need to know the entire list of existing and enhanced controls that are in use. Then, prepare a list of weaknesses that relate to your previously established foreseeable risks and newly identified risks. Then, have members brainstorm new controls for each one and compile these ideas.

As you brainstorm, consider all the possible responses that could apply to the new risks – even if, at first, some might not appear to fit your culture, bandwidth, or budgetary capabilities. Hopefully, creative ideas and alternatives will begin to flow as you put all options on the table.

11.2 Use a Scenario to Imagine the Worst – and Control It

Use the imagery technique we have discussed before. This time, instead of simply trying to picture disaster or other crisis scenarios as they unfold, add a dimension to the exercise. Picture not only what could happen, but what controls might prevent it from happening, or moderate its impact. You want to come up with concrete ways to prevent the ripple effect. For each new risk, ask yourselves:

> What sequence of events might unfold?

> How might each element of the scenario ripple out to other areas?

> Who are anticipated stakeholders and what would be their needs and concerns?

> What could stop or divert this cascade of related events, at each point in its unfolding?

> What policies, procedures, and controls would offer that protection?

11.2.1 Select a Scenario for Your Brainstorming

Let's take as an example the potential risks that could arrive with your incoming mail. You're certainly aware by now of incidents of terrorism that made use of the mail system. For example, there were the explosive devices sent by Theodore Kaczynski, also known as the "Unabomber," who targeted various corporations for 18 years, starting in 1978, mailing pipe bombs that killed 3 people and wounded 23 others. And there was the anthrax that was mailed to government offices and to Tom Brokaw of *NBC Nightly News* in New York. Similar incidents continued with the 2013 ricin-laced letters sent to President Obama and other public officials. Back when you were conducting the analysis segment of the preparedness plan, you presumably incorporated this awareness into the list of possible risks your company could face.

Suppose you are doing this imagery exercise about a situation in which anthrax gets into your building via the mail. An unknown number of employees are initially infected. A hazardous materials team says your building must be shut down for at least three weeks for decontamination. This may not be as farfetched as it appears.

I happened to be on the *Today* show on NBC one morning in New York City, and the entire staff couldn't go into their offices (across the street from the television studios) for three weeks while the building was decontaminated of anthrax that had been mailed to NBC news anchor, Tom Brokaw. Additionally, everyone was prescribed an antibiotic, ciprofloxacin, as a precaution.

11.2.2 Consider the Stakeholders

Now, think what might different stakeholders want from you if your organization were in this predicament?

▶ Infected employees: continued salaries are needed, along with crisis counseling, reliable medical information about symptoms to watch for, and complete medical care. Expect these employees to ask pointed questions about what management did, or did not do, to prevent this exposure. What will management do to prevent future occurrences?

▶ Their families: they will want information and possibly trauma counseling, especially if there is a concern of exposure for their children at the homes of workers who were exposed, and what to do about items brought home from work that could contaminate them. Family members will also need a way to ask questions of concern.

▶ Other employees: even for those who were not likely exposed, prompt testing for exposure will be warranted; full disclosure regarding management's actions; information and counseling to address fears; continued salary; remote work accommodations, as appropriate; assurance of job security; measures to prevent further contaminations; updates on the law enforcement investigation; guidelines for handling incoming mail; new policies and procedures for incoming mail.

▶ Customers: timely warning about business disruptions; assistance in getting tested, if any exposure is suspected; notification regarding the resumption of normal operations; a response plan to ensure the safety of onsite customers and those who receive materials from your company.

▶ Suppliers: notification of alterations in needed supplies, delivery scheduling; new delivery policies; and the like.

▶ Stockholders/institutional investors: assurance that business continuity preparations and actions are adequate to maintain profitable operations; full disclosure of suspected impact on sales and profitability.

▶ Postal inspectors and law enforcement: full cooperation in protecting evidence and assistance in investigations; access to pertinent records and information that could provide clues.

▶ Other companies in your industry: timely disclosure about the incident; any information or evidence that indicates the possibility of further attacks on related companies.

▶ News media: cooperation and full disclosure about the incident, without jeopardizing the investigation by law enforcement and postal inspectors.

Of course, you will also want to determine what information you want from these stakeholders, as well.

In this scenario, new controls to mitigate the possibility of toxic substances mailed to your facilities might include strict guidelines and supplies if any employee should receive a suspicious package with any type of powder. Supplies like plastic bags and even large trash bags could be readily available. Employees would be directed via policy to bag any suspicious letter or package immediately, contact the appropriate person(s) within the company, and remain in the same location without moving around the facility.

11.2.3 Examine Possible Consequences

Extend this scenario to look for all the possible consequences. For example, stakeholder reactions will vary if the company is an innocent victim versus being blamed in some manner. Looking at your own company, how could this anthrax exposure affect your:

▶ Reputation?

▶ Financial condition?

▶ People?

▶ Culture?

▶ Industry?

▶ Community?

▶ Business operations?

▶ Recruiting efforts?

▶ Insurability?

Within reason, discuss as many possibilities as you can imagine. Of course, in the real event, you can't provide every stakeholder with everything he or she might want. There will be conflicting interests. Your stockholders, for instance, may be concerned with getting operations back to normal and limiting the costs, while employees may be much more interested in staying in the safety of their homes until the building is fully decontaminated and costly mailroom security measures are implemented.

So, what are the new approaches that should be considered to supplement existing and enhanced controls?

> **Good crisis management anticipates the reactions of stakeholders who are impacted and involved....If you wait to establish new controls to address issues after they occur, you will be playing catch up, rather than being proactive and staying ahead of the "crisis curve."**

11.2.4 Anticipate Cascading Effects

Other variables should be considered. What can we reasonably expect might happen in the near- to mid-term following a widely publicized anthrax letter being mailed to your facility?

One expected occurrence could be copycat incidents. Expect anonymous letters that have powder enclosed that may or may not be toxic. Increasingly, your employees will be fearful of opening their mail. People will likely perceive symptoms that they fear are related to exposure. Some employees may consider quitting instead of "risking" working in a building that may have been contaminated with anthrax. At least in the short term, you may want to have all mail opened off site before being delivered internally. Confidentiality of mailed information will be a concern that would need to be addressed. Others may file stress claims. What other things might you expect?

Good crisis management anticipates the reactions of stakeholders who are impacted and involved. Such anticipation permits controls to be established to address these issues in advance and to respond to them if they occur. If you wait to establish new controls to address issues after they occur, you will be playing catch up rather than being proactive and staying ahead of the "crisis curve."

11.3 The Reasonable Person Test

We've discussed the *reasonable person test* in Chapter 6. Again, in sculpting the mix of existing, enhanced, and new controls, you and your team should consider what would appear reasonable if things were to go bad.

The reasonable person test reflects what an informed person would have expected you to do – given what you knew (or should have known) at the time and what you were capable of doing.

Keep in mind that you will be operating in a context that is evolving continually. What is reasonable at one time may appear inadequate and irresponsible if circumstances change. For planning purposes, deem what is reasonable according to what you and your team imagine would be the fallout from any given foreseeable risk if it manifests in (or is related to) your workplace. Then be ready to change your definition of "reasonable" during crisis response, as needed. Most importantly, keep the reasonable person test in the forefront during your planning, exercising, crisis responses, and debriefings.

What if a certain procedure or crisis containment control is used commonly in your industry, neighborhood, or by businesses in general, and you decide not to use it? You should document clearly why you considered it, and why you decided not to use it – in a manner that would pass the reasonable person test. This documentation should be constructed during the planning process. After an incident has occurred, it's probably too late.

Better to take precautionary measures when determining which crisis controls you want to put in place and which to delay or omit. First, any time we are asked to assist an organization with a physical security audit, we recommend that the organization's legal counsel retain us, not the company directly. This puts a bit of protection (but not perfectly) around the findings by making the preparedness process a confidential attorney work product. Also, consider receiving security audit recommendations verbally only with no written report that is discoverable. Too often, well-intentioned security professionals take photos and provide reports that can be used against the organization later if every single recommendation is not implemented.

> **Negligence comes into play if a company's failure to prepare, or to act, does not appeal to be reasonable.**

Consider the situation of All-Tech Investments, the day trading company with offices in CMI's corporate headquarters building in Atlanta, where Mark Barton went on the shooting spree I described earlier in this book. Benchmarking could have told All-Tech that many firms housed in Atlanta's financial district were installing sophisticated swipe card security systems to control access to their offices. But as a regular trader at that office, Mark Barton would have had open access – so such a system would not have stopped him. In addition, a system like that would feel unfriendly to existing and potential day trading customers.

In this case, All-Tech could have documented that it looked at the swipe card entry system as a new crisis prevention control because many offices in its building were installing one, but the company determined that it would be neither practical to use, given the nature of the services the company provides to the public, nor effective against a disgruntled trader or employee. Documentation wouldn't keep the company from being sued, but it could help avoid a costly financial and reputational judgment of negligence. Negligence comes into play if the failure of a company to prepare, or to act, does not appear to be reasonable.

11.3.1 Example: Security Fence

Let's assume a physical security audit report recommends your company erect a fence around your facility to deter intruders. If someone is killed or seriously injured and the uninstalled fence could have stopped the perpetrator, this report, when discovered, will likely cause liability problems and outrage. I have seen this many times during litigation. However, for those new controls you consider but decide not to use, "reasonable" documentation can help your defensibility.

Expense excuse: In the case of not installing the fence, one "reasonable" excuse you don't want to document is that it's too expensive or not a priority in the budget. While it may not be in the budget to put a security fence around your entire facility, you don't want to list that as the reason. Plaintiff attorneys, smelling high dollars, will try to establish willful negligence. You and your company will be accused of having known about the risk, yet placed money over the wellbeing and safety of employees.

Let's assume there was an alleged foreseeable risk in a bad neighborhood, the company knew of the risk and chose to save the money it would cost for a fence to protect its people. The attorneys will compare the annual revenue of the company to the expense of the fence. At this point, the plaintiff's counsel will ask the jury to show the company what "expensive" looks like to the tune of many millions of dollars.

If the fence is considered too expensive, but appropriate, it will help to develop an implementation plan in which the fence is prioritized and phased in over a reasonably scheduled timeframe along with other considered controls. Post crisis, a phased-in program that was not yet fully implemented will show good intent and may seem reasonable to outsiders (like jurors, media, and families) looking at your actions to prevent and respond to the risk of a violent intruder.

Safety rationale: In the case of the fence (a new control that doesn't make it into the budget), it's possible to document the rationale in a manner that passes the reasonable person test beyond money. For example, if your company is in the chemical or nuclear business, or if fire, explosions, or earthquakes are a hazard, a fence could trap your employees within the property. This could create a toxic exposure situation from which they couldn't escape safely. This rationale is about protecting safety of employees, which is much more reasonable and defensible than claiming a fence was too expensive.

Not practical rationale: If you have many railroad cars and large trucks in and out of your property, the fence idea would seem ineffective with gates held open for ingress and egress. Also, if a preponderance of violence in your industry comes from disgruntled employees inside your facilities, the rationale could be made that a fence was not the best control. These "reasonable" justifications for not constructing the security fence will be more defensible than documentation that it was too expensive.

Obviously, you will not implement every idea that emerges. In general, if you consider new or enhanced controls and ultimately decide not to use them, document the rationale (without mentioning expense) of why it is not appropriate to implement these controls. Maintain this documentation in an organized manner, or leave no documentation at all.

11.3.2 Example: Airline Security

Let's apply this reasonable person standard to airline security. Before the first wave of airliner hijackings in the 1970s, there was virtually no control over access to airplanes, other than having a ticket. Neither passenger identification nor luggage was checked. Access to airports was wide open. With no history of terrorism aboard airplanes, this lack of security would have passed a reasonable person's scrutiny at that time.

Once a pattern of hijackings emerged, certain security measures were put in place. Ticket agents silently profiled passengers. Baggage and passengers had to pass through metal detectors to screen for weapons. The general experience in that period was that even if a hijacking occurred, the plane would be diverted to an unintended location, and within a few hours or days the passengers would be free to return home. So, the new security measures seemed adequate. And indeed, hijackings diminished.

Then, the willingness of terrorists to make use of airliners as weapons of mass destruction emerged. First, bombs were hidden in luggage that was stored in a plane's hold, when the perpetrators themselves were not aboard the flight.

That's what brought down the Pan Am flight 103 over Lockerbie, Scotland, in 1988. After that tragedy, the definition for "reasonable" expanded where no baggage was to be on board without its owner. More recently, we have seen terrorists willing to commit suicide in order to turn airliners into missiles – a tactic not fully considered previously. This threat has precipitated many new procedures and controls. With each new circumstance, the measure of what a person would consider as "reasonable" has changed, yet again.

For this reason, it is important that regular reviews of your existing controls take place at least once per year to assure they remain in accord with the present day definition of reasonable. Make use of the methods listed in these last two chapters to benchmark your existing controls. New controls and enhanced controls that were deemed inappropriate in the past may be much more appropriate today.

> **I want you to imagine what might happen if you fail to do what could be considered reasonable.... You identified possible new controls for the areas in which your plans were weak. But then for some reason...you did not follow through and put these new controls in place.**

11.3.3 Value of the Reasonable Person Test

Common Sense: Another way to apply the reasonable person test is to evaluate the plausibility of controls in light of simple common sense. Infectious agents sent through the mail are certainly a risk. But would a reasonable person suggest that the postal service open every letter and package to make sure it's safe before sending it on its way?

Taking the reasonable person test into consideration will assist you in two ways.

 ▶ First, you will make better decisions and your documentation will be more defensible against charges of negligence. It will help if challenged over your prevention, preparedness, and post-crisis response efforts.

 ▶ Second, if your actions seem reasonable to those who are affected, they are more likely to cooperate. For example, prior to the horrendous acts of terrorism of 2001, it would have seemed unreasonable to airline passengers to submit themselves to the intrusive scrutiny that has been implemented since. Today however, these security measures seem inconvenient and there is grumbling, but the measures seem reasonable to the common person.

11.4 The Darker Side of "Reasonable": Pan Am 103

The reasonable person test seems simple and logical, doesn't it? Now allow me to take the gloves off and knock you around for a minute. I want you to imagine what might happen if you fail to do what could be considered reasonable. Suppose you did not conduct a thorough risk analysis, leaving your company vulnerable to risks you should have foreseen. Or maybe you did start to work on a preparedness plan. You identified possible new controls for the areas in which your plans were weak. But then for some reason – cost or lack of commitment from management – you did not follow through and put these new controls in place.

Then, an event you could have foreseen comes to pass – with devastating consequences.

What kind of grilling would you get in court from a plaintiff attorney pursuing a liability claim, if the attorney can show that you knowingly allowed the disaster to occur?

For an answer to this question, I talked personally with James Kreindler. He served as plaintiff attorney in suits arising from such high profile airline disasters as TWA 800, Swissair 111, Egyptair 990, and Pan Am 103 – which blew up over Lockerbie, Scotland, in 1988, after taking off from Frankfurt. "The best example is Pan Am 103," says James Kreindler, partner in the law firm Kreindler and Kreindler.

"Every airline has an Air Carrier Standard Security Procedure, that sets forth the rules for their security system, whether they do it themselves or hire outside contractors," according to Kreindler in our interview. "Pan Am's ACSSP required the positive match of passengers to baggage for interline passengers – those connecting to Pan Am from another airline – at extraordinary security airports, which included Frankfurt. Positive match means making sure that a passenger who has actually gotten on the airplane accompanies each bag.

"The regulation said, 'When you find an unaccompanied bag, the airline must either not carry it, or carry it only if it can be opened and physically inspected.'

"Pan Am, during the time of the Lockerbie explosion, was losing money and cutting costs, "explained Kreindler. "The emphasis in every department was to cut costs. They purchased a few X-ray machines and started X-raying interline bags. Pan Am's security manager in London wrote to corporate headquarters in New York, and said, 'The rules require positive match. We're X-raying interline bags. Do we still have to match them?' And corporate headquarters wrote back, 'No, just load them and go,' thus saving all that money from the cumbersome passenger match." Note that this practice did not pass the reasonable person test that we've been discussing.

Kreindler continued, "So it was this corporate decision that caused the Lockerbie disaster, because the bomb was in an unaccompanied interline bag transferred to the Pan Am plane, in Frankfurt, from Air Malta. That is probably the clearest, classic example of how cutting corners with security or safety is going to cause a disaster. And in fact, in Pan Am's bankruptcy petition in 1990, the first reason they cited for the bankruptcy was the Flight 103 case," and the likelihood that the airline would have to pay enormous damages. Note again that companies that are not crisis prepared are more likely to go out of business after serious critical situations occur.

If you're the plaintiff attorney in a case like this, Kreindler says, "In court, you just rip them to pieces." If you had been in charge of the airline's security during this incident and were cross-examined in court, you would never want to be asked to justify the failure to X-ray the baggage – in a courtroom or by the media. The jury and public would hate you. And what about discussing, but not implementing, a possible control that turns out to have been needed? "That's what makes it intentional wrongdoing or willful misconduct," says Kreindler. "It's that kind of intentional disregard that exposes you to punitive damages."

According to Kreindler, here's how it might go:

Attorney: "You're in charge of security, and that means following the ACSSP to prevent hijacking and bombing?"

Defendant: "Yes."

Attorney: "And those rules are there to help prevent disasters such as Lockerbie?"

Defendant: "Yes."

Attorney: "And prevent the deaths of all your passengers?"

Defendant: "Yes."

Attorney: "And you didn't do a positive match, did you?"

Defendant: "No."

Attorney: "The reason you didn't provide the ACSSP required baggage check is because it was too expensive, correct?"

Defendant: "Yes."

Lessons-Learned: If you do all you can now to prevent disaster, you can go a long way to ensuring that you will never face a courtroom grilling like the one Kreindler gave Pan Am's managers.

11.5 Primary vs. Secondary Prevention: Negotiating Hostage Release

As you identify new controls, you must consider the two types of prevention: *primary* and *secondary*.

Primary prevention: The point of primary prevention is to keep unwanted incidents from happening in the first place. This is the approach commonly taken by safety and security managers. Physical and IT security, safe travel policies, and safety programs all address primary prevention. Primary prevention is essential, but it's not enough.

> Managers many times concentrate on primary prevention so much that they get tunnel vision about what could really unfold in a crisis.

Secondary prevention: In spite of your best efforts, bad things can still happen. Secondary prevention measures are established to stop a critical situation that has already occurred from escalating – that is, to prevent the ripple effect of vulnerability or escalating severity.

Managers many times concentrate on primary prevention so much that they get tunnel vision about what could really unfold in a crisis. That's understandable since we, as human beings, don't like to think deeply about bad things that can threaten our safety and wellbeing. For example, I was involved in a corporate crisis response and rescue mission for seven employees of three oil-related companies who had been kidnapped for ransom in the jungles of Ecuador and Colombia. Because such kidnappings are frequent in Colombia and Ecuador, it's appropriate to focus energy on prevention. However, beyond the services that were provided by negotiators from insurance companies, secondary prevention was inadequate. After existing security measures failed to prevent the kidnappings, secondary prevention was implemented to mitigate the further damage with multiple stakeholders, including:

- ▶ Negotiations for a quick and safe release of hostages. In this situation, one of the original eight hostages was killed; his body was left on the side of a road with a written demand for more money than the negotiators had offered and threats against the others.

- ▶ Assistance for traumatized Ecuadorian employees who were held face down at gunpoint as five Americans, one Chilean, one New Zealander, and one Argentine were taken hostage. In this case, the

Ecuadorian nationals had been threatened with death when they refused to say where two additional Americans had hidden.

- Assistance for those two Americans who narrowly escaped being kidnapped, by running into the jungle, and then observed the kidnappings of their peers.

- Assistance for the employees and managers in Quito, Ecuador, where oil rig workers were hired and dispatched into the field. It is common for these headquarters personnel to feel guilty, and to feel concerned for their own safety, knowing that employees, and possibly family members, of the company are being targeted.

- Support for the families "back home" of those who had been kidnapped. The families felt helpless. These expat employees commuted internationally from their homes with a 3-weeks-on and 3-weeks-off schedule. Families needed ongoing information and qualified trauma counseling as they identified closely with what their loved ones must be going through. Desperate family members could have made the situation worse by arriving onsite, meddling in negotiations, or making public appeals to companies to pay more money. We had to work consistently with one family member who bought a ticket to Ecuador to make a personal rescue attempt. We coached him about the irrationality of that decision and convinced him to leave the rescue to the negotiators, Ecuadorian Anti-Kidnapping Police Force (UNASE), and FBI.

- Then there is the media involvement. In this case, after one hostage was killed, CBS' *The Early Show* twice invited family members of an American hostage to appear on their nationally televised morning program. CBS served as an antagonist leading the cry that the involved companies were valuing ransom money more highly than the lives of the kidnapped employees. There is a delicate balance. An early offer of money often leads kidnappers to raise the stakes. We, again, had to coach family members that a publicly televised appeal for the company to pay additional ransom could, paradoxically, increase the likelihood the kidnappers would hold the hostages longer for more money. Our ongoing trusted relationship with the families during the months of the employees' captivity was the control needed to keep them from complicating the situation inadvertently.

- Upon release, after more than 140 days, the hostages needed personal assistance in many arenas. I met them in the jungle as they were released. They needed medical treatment for malnutrition, tropical diseases, and infestations. Emotionally, they were at risk of posttraumatic stress disorder (PTSD), and the reentry process into their home towns, families, and workplaces would be complicated.

▶ There was a need for a well-planned reentry into society and reintroduction to their families. The released hostages didn't sleep well that first night in Quito, even though they were able to shower and sleep in clean beds for the first time in months.

▶ Other secondary prevention issues emerged to mitigate potential escalating severities. I had the duty of notifying the ex-hostages that the kidnappers had killed their friend, because as we had suspected, they had been led to believe he had been released as a goodwill gesture. It was important to keep the ex-hostages safe following release, given the worldwide attention the situation received. There was also a need for productive reentry back to work for those who chose to stay in their same positions.

▶ Media attention was a complicating factor for a smooth reentry process. As we landed in Quito that night on a private jet with the ex-hostages and disembarked on the tarmac, hundreds of reporters with cameras flashing were everywhere. Security held them back, and we boarded a bus for the prearranged hotel in Quito. We were followed by paparazzi. Reporters had learned of the hotel and masses of them were crowded around it. We had to sneak up a back entry to the arranged hotel rooms. Three floors of rooms were blocked and secured to keep unwanted intruders at bay. Meanwhile, cooperation was needed with law enforcement investigators who had identified the kidnappers correctly and sought verification from the released hostages. Contact with the ex-hostages by phone from the hotel was arranged with family members desperate to hear from them.

▶ Reentry back home was arranged via private jet for each former hostage. We provided experienced crisis consultants to accompany ex-hostages on the flights home. Again, the media was camped out at the intended airports. So, we had to divert at the last minute to remote airports. Customs agents met us on the private jets after we landed. And, discreet ground transportation whisked us to hotels where families had been positioned secretly to meet their loved ones who had been held hostage for months.

These, and additional methods, were all secondary prevention responses that were planned and put into place to mitigate the stakeholders' complications during the months of captivity and post-release situation. Prevention is best, but being prepared to mitigate the secondary implications of a crisis is also paramount. This is the essence of effective crisis response. It's vitally important to establish controls for secondary prevention. Your company and crisis planning committee must continually ask:

- If this foreseeable situation were to occur, how should we respond?

- What could be done to keep an incident from cascading into further stakeholder-related damage?

- Are there new and enhanced controls we should put into place to mitigate potential damage from foreseeable critical incidents? For primary and secondary prevention?

These questions apply both to the tangible content of a crisis, and to the intangible impact it could have on your people, brand, and reputation. Consider these examples of primary and secondary prevention.

Table 11-1. Primary and Secondary Prevention Methods

Type of Incident	Primary Prevention	Secondary Prevention
Kidnapping for ransom in foreign country	All personnel to be routinely escorted by security guards	Evacuation plan for all remaining personnel, in the event anyone is kidnapped
Workplace violence perpetrated by disgruntled former employee	Threat Response Team, and enhanced physical security at premises	Trauma counseling for employees and family members
Fire or explosion at plan	State-of-the-art containment technology, and frequent safety checks for all volatile materials	Sprinkler system throughout building, and evacuation plan with regular practice drills
Earthquake	All facilities to meet or exceed latest earthquake-zone building codes	Backup electrical generation and data storage capacities
Anthrax exposure from incoming mail	Strict mailroom screening of incoming mail, before distribution	Bio-bags available to all employees for use in containing suspected contaminated letters

11.6 Bringing It Down to Earth: Identifying New Controls

By encouraging you to brainstorm, I am not forgetting that you operate in a real world of constraints. In a crisis, you will want to respond to every appropriate need. All of your stakeholders will want you to respond to their needs and concerns. Let's agree that you can't do it all. So in your planning it is up to you, now, to match the range of primary and secondary prevention controls with the answers to these questions:

▶ What is possible, given your budget, time availability, and culture?

▶ What is reasonable, given what you have determined about the probability and severity of your foreseeable risks?

▶ Which achievable controls, taken together, would give you the most comprehensive preparedness strategy?

> **Organizing for crisis preparedness...calls upon you to apply the skills you already use in your business life every day – like prioritizing tasks, communicating intentions, eliciting support, executing actions, and defensibly documenting what you have done.**

Later, we will examine ways to organize and prioritize the elements of your preparedness strategy, how to phase them in over time in a way that does not overwhelm the resources of your company, and how to keep your plans tuned and poised for quick, complete responses as needed.

Organizing for crisis preparedness need not tax you any more than any other project you undertake. It just calls upon you to apply the skills you already use in your business life every day – like prioritizing tasks, communicating intentions, eliciting support, executing actions, and defensibly documenting what you have done.

Before you implement any new control into your plan, ask:

▶ Specifically, what do we want this control to address?

▶ What might be possible intended and unintended impacts (positive and negative) on other systems within and around our organization?

▶ Are there alternatives that would be better suited to address the need?

To answer these questions, clearly envision the sequence of possible events and cascading outcomes.

11.7 No Company Is an Island

Imagine you have a warehouse operation on the Mississippi River in southern Louisiana. On the heels of Hurricane Katrina, you have determined a high probability this region will be hit again by a major hurricane in the next 10 years.

Among your industrial neighbors are oil refineries and chemical and plastics plants, some of which have abysmal safety records. So you have concluded that there is a high probability that there could be a leak or explosion at one of these places, with quite severe effects on your operations, including business disruption, injuries, or even fatalities.

You can't control the weather. But it's relatively simple to minimize its impact. You could move your operations to another location less prone to hurricane damages. You can educate your workers to heed evacuation warnings, which would go some distance toward ensuring that nobody is killed. You can provide or encourage them to keep emergency supply kits in their cars during hurricane season to ensure that if they do have to evacuate, the experience will be less grueling for them and their families. You can make sure your warehouses are engineered to withstand high winds. And you can buy insurance to cover business disruption and storm damage to your property and inventory.

What can you do about the risk from those unreliable neighbors?

You could furnish your own facility with new controls of hazardous materials equipment, like gas masks and decontamination showers, and train your workers in their use. You can install engineering controls that may help, such as a culvert around your perimeter to route away any spilled liquids. Warning sirens could be installed. You can establish good communications with local regulators and the managers of the neighboring companies, to ensure that you will be alerted quickly in the event of any dangerous leak. Other controls could be brainstormed and implemented.

What you *cannot* do is get inside your neighbors' organizations to repair whatever management flaws are responsible for their worrisome safety records. Your company and theirs, after all, are unrelated, except by proximity. And each of you is a player in a free market economic system, in which each entity makes its own decisions within reason.

You could, however, as a corporate citizen of your community – and in your own self-interest – raise the issue of safety. You could do this informally, in conversation with your counterparts from these companies on the golf course. Or you could decide to call on regulators privately or lobby publicly for enhanced regulation, more rigorous inspection, and stricter controls by environmental and industrial regulators.

But meddling in the operations of another company, or encouraging more regulation, may go against your own company's grain and neighborly relations. If you did manage to agree among yourselves to take that sort of step, you would need to develop political skills different from those needed to install hurricane straps to your warehouse roof. And, the regulations you espouse just might end up applying to you in ways that you didn't realize.

It may be more comfortable to move your warehouse to another location, even at great expense. It's a strategic crisis prevention judgment call. But, short of a move out of the neighborhood, if a dangerous leak from a neighboring plant is a probability, you really have to do something to control for it. Alternatively, you could decide to live with the risk and hope for the best. Meanwhile, your plan should reflect reasonable primary and secondary controls for addressing this foreseeable risk.

11.8 New Controls Can Challenge Your Culture

Issues addressed in your preparedness plan can be costly, requiring investments in equipment and hiring extra personnel. Such measures can be a tough sell before they can be incorporated into your planning, especially if your company has always prided itself on a lean-and-mean style. Culturally, senior management may have an overemphasis on growing the value of the company, at the neglect of adequately protecting core assets.

Preparedness may mean sacrificing things of which you are justly proud, such as the architectural qualities of a building. Kansas City International (KCI) Airport is an example of a once great three-building configuration that no longer worked well, simply because times had changed. Planned before the era of airliner hijackings, KCI's layout provided parking and a separate entrance near every gate, allowing travelers to board planes with little wasted time. Sadly, security requirements have long since closed some entrances and necessitated costly screening checkpoints at others. KCI became an unwieldy airport that had to approve a costly $1.2 billion plan in 2013 to convert its three-terminal configuration to a single terminal.

You have evaluated your current preparedness and identified the new controls you must establish in order to have a comprehensive plan. Now, we will look at how to make that comprehensive plan a fixture of your company's culture.

11.9 Consider the Whole System

As a crisis manager, you may be narrowly focused in the silos of emergency response, corporate security, continuity of operations, or similarly focused responses. However, in organizing and drafting your new crisis plans, your role will focus more broadly on protecting all the core assets of the organization. Often, managers in crisis-related fields are oblivious to the contributions they are making (positive or negative) to core assets like trust, brand image, reputation, and even issues like shareholder value. Sure, you must execute with excellence in your silo of responsibility. But, your overarching job in this arena is to help the senior management team to not let any core asset of the organization go down under their watch.

> **Some plans that look good on their own can cause systemic problems. And the system is not limited to what goes on within your organization.**

Protection of core assets is hard to argue against for senior managers. "Core assets" means the organization has to have them or else serious damage or even failure will ensue. These are not "nice to have" assets like a big office, a fancy desk, corporate jet, or overly generous expense account. Core assets are the very foundation that the organization must have to survive. In developing or improving your plan, don't lose sight of this overarching role for you, your team, and the entire crisis management organization within your company.

No action you take, or policy or procedure you establish, will exist in a vacuum. In organizing your preparedness plan, consider how each new and enhanced control might affect and be affected by the system as a whole. Do this by fully socializing your plans with a multidisciplinary group of involved stakeholders. Some plans that look good on their own can cause systemic problems. And the system is not limited to what goes on within your organization. It includes the context and environment in which your company operates, as well.

An example of a systemic problem coming from a preventive control relates to the previously mentioned kidnappings in Ecuador that spilled over from Colombia. Because of increasing guerrilla activity and frequent incidents of violence and kidnapping, oil companies working in Ecuador began hiring units of the Ecuadorian military to protect their sites. In so doing, they enticed poorly paid soldiers away from border patrol duties. That made it easier than ever for guerilla groups to infiltrate Ecuador from Colombia, inadvertently putting the oil companies at greater risk than before. This was especially true when the kidnappers were willing to pay yet even more for inside information and facilitation from the guards (former soldiers), as was the case in the kidnapping of the seven oil workers mentioned previously.

11.10 Integration

In Chapter 3, we discussed the concept of notifying and activating the teams within your three-tiered crisis management organization. Figure 11-1 is a reminder of how the three teams and their plans will integrate. It is recommended that your crisis planning include overarching duties and responsibilities for each of the three levels. While each individual and team will have unique responsibilities, this model serves as a framework for coordinating the component parts into a cohesive whole. Effective crisis response organizations address the interdependent impacts their specific actions have on the other functions within the company and with external stakeholders.

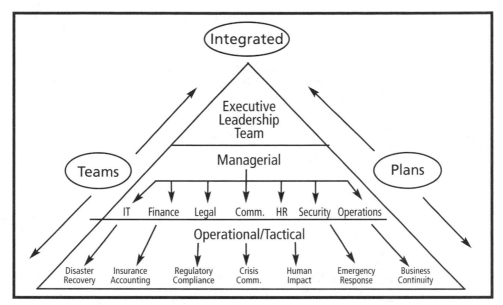

Figure 11-1. Three-tiered Crisis Management Organization: Executive, Managerial, and Operational Teams.

To organize an integrated crisis management process, consider starting with an all-hazards approach. Focus on implementing the same processes for notification and activation, decision-making and actions, all the way through to purposeful disengagement. Additionally, remember to clarify levels of authority, responsibility, communications, and expectations in organizing your plan. Once the all-hazards process is organized, you can supplement your plans with immediate and unique guidelines for specific foreseeable risks. Refer to Chapter 15 for sample checklists of guidelines for specific crises.

11.10.1 Three Tiers Within Your Crisis Planning

The roles of the executive team/crisis management team, managerial team, and operational/tactical teams will obviously vary. At least we hope they do. In order for a full crisis management organization to run smoothly within a company, each level must understand its parameters. If members of various teams drift outside their levels of responsibility, the system can quickly begin to fall apart. This is not good in the midst of a crisis response, but unfortunately it happens regularly for companies that lack response planning that is integrated adequately.

For purposes of organizing your crisis plan, the three tiers of overall crisis responsibility are reviewed below. Refer to Chapter 3 for additional information on each of these three levels.

> Leaders should also consider and integrate their decision-making with the various teams and disciplines within the organization...to ensure decisions and actions in one area of the company do not create unintended negative consequences in another organizational area of crisis responsibility.

Executive Team/Crisis Management Team: Generally, the role of the executive team/crisis management team is to "lead" the crisis response at a strategic level when threshold levels are reached that will mobilize the executives' involvement. Team members are to balance visible leadership, while minimizing their involvement in tactical issues. Their job is to remain once removed from the tactical responses in order to maintain a strategic perspective over the crisis. Every function of the organization should be represented on the executive team.

The crisis plan should include agreed upon guidance for the executive team as to its overarching responsibilities during crisis response. It will be the job of the executive team to lead the crisis through the pre-established guiding principles of the organization. Because crisis leadership is principle-oriented (see Chapter 1 for sample guiding principles), the executive team will assess the crisis fact pattern to define the true nature of the crisis, which core assets of the organization are threatened, and how to manage them. The team will continue to anticipate future developments and decide upon a strategic pathway for an advantageous crisis response. Primarily the focus will be on threatened core assets, monitoring impacted stakeholder needs and concerns, and anticipating how best to stay ahead of the dynamic developments of the crisis.

Leaders should also consider and integrate their decision-making with the various teams and disciplines within the organization. This integration is to ensure decisions and actions in one area of the company do not create unintended negative consequences in another organizational area of crisis responsibility. These considerations should also apply to impacts on external stakeholders.

Managerial Team: The managerial team is positioned between the executive team and the tactical/operational teams. This team has the responsibility of "directing" the crisis response with responsibility over coordinating and resourcing the involved operational/tactical response teams. Typically, it receives leadership input from senior management regarding the defining decisions and actions for how the crisis is to be addressed. The managerial team serves as a conduit of two-way communications with and between the executive team and the tactical/operational teams. Each member of the managerial team should have only one area of responsibility to ensure proper attention is provided to each. For example, a manager who is divided with crisis response duties relating to legal, HR, and external communications – all at the same time – will be unable to attend adequately to all the fast moving needs of each arena. The motto for the managerial team is "one hat, one head." In this example, there should be a legal representative, an HR manager, and a communicator, each with responsibility for one respective area of expertise.

Operational/Tactical Team(s): The operational/tactical responses are "doing" oriented. Most often, these teams are located in the bull's eye of the crisis and address the content of the crisis. This may involve putting out the fire, rescuing impacted workers, or other hands-on duties. Most often, their roles are short-term. After they contain the immediate, time-sensitive critical impacts of the crisis, the longer-term, lingering after-effects (like reputation, legal liabilities, and impacts on key relationships) of the crisis are addressed by the managerial and executive teams.

11.11 Addressing Unique Cultural Issues in Your Plan

In crafting your plan, you may find unique cultural issues that must be addressed and incorporated. Preparedness means recognizing that even highly principled organizations can be in danger. Biases and attitudes can affect the acceptance of the crisis plan from the top of the organization down to site level managers.

In one example of cultural resistance, a large international retailer was led by a CEO who considered himself to be a devout Christian. He firmly stated his belief that God would watch over the company, making crisis preparedness unnecessary. While he did allow some prevention and response measures, he initially refused any personal crisis leadership coaching – an important part of any program. If the CEO and senior management are not personally prepared for crises, the whole organization can suffer. Despite rapid growth, the retailer experienced only moderately severe incidents, but these incidents were enough that the company decided to take crisis preparedness seriously at all levels. Finally, after many years, the CEO and his staff are now very "religious" about protecting the core assets of the organization through preparedness at all levels. It is best not to rely only on luck and God's grace, however divinely inspired.

Cultural resistance also shows up at the field level. One of my companies helped a Fortune 500 company to develop and implement a violence-prevention program similar to the workplace violence program that we helped set up at the US Postal Service (USPS) following their shootings. A few field-level managers didn't want to spend the money in their respective budgets to train supervisors, provide employee briefings, and establish some of the physical security components that were adopted by corporate. We know that a comprehensive program can be effective, evidenced by no employee or ex-employee shootings for eight years following the implementation of the USPS workplace violence program. But, managers within the organization must cooperate.

At this company, one policy required managers to confront employees who make threats. One manager decided that was asking too much. "There is no way I'm going to confront a guy we know about who has made threats," he said. "Corporate can tell us to do it, but they don't have to live in the same neighborhood with this guy after he's fired." (It is important to address the desire of managers to be seen as sympathetic to workers. In this case, we recommended that the manager who does the confrontation explain to the dangerous employee that even though he or she does not want to have this confrontation, it has been forced by an unnamed outside attorney because of a violation of the workplace violence policy.) Expect pockets of resistance as you implement your crisis preparedness program and be ready to address emerging concerns.

11.11.1 Anticipating Resistance and "Smoothing in" New Controls

Even those of us who believe we're surfing the wave of the latest innovations in technology and business can resist change. And if individuals can drag their heels, organizations can sometimes dig in like balky mules. Anticipate the resistance you may encounter.

In organizing your plan, ask yourself:

- Who needs to be brought on board to ensure success?
- Who will be responsible for the ongoing effectiveness of the plan?
- What routines in the organization would have to be modified or replaced?
- Where within the organization can the plan's procedures receive resistance?
- Who in the company will be affected by the plan? Have you gained their acceptance?
- Which decision-makers' active support could smooth the implementation process?

- What support and resources will be required?
- What costs will be incurred? From where?
- What other hurdles do you need to overcome?
- Who would be the appropriate executive sponsor to champion the plan?

11.11.2 Don't Go It Alone

Beware of unilateral implementation of your plan. It might seem quicker and more efficient. But, keep in mind that every member of your management team wants to have a sense of control over how he or she will be affected by the plan. As best you can, bring those who will be involved in the preparedness program into the process of crafting the crisis plan.

If you elicit broad support and participation, your planning will be many times stronger than it could otherwise be. And, key players will be much more likely to accept the implications and involvements that the plan may bring. In fact, with broad support, the crisis management organization becomes a living system within the organization. It can also increase the level of comfort among outsiders who may be watching your approach at managing the risks, such as shareholders, financial analysts, credit rating agencies, board of directors, lenders, suppliers, franchisees, and customers.

> As a person involved in crisis management preparedness and developing crisis management plans in your organization, you would do well to begin to think like a senior manager in your company. Reframe your crisis preparedness initiatives.

11.12 Gaining Senior Management Buy-In

As every manager knows, the culture and tone of an organization are set at the top. When you must challenge or modify that culture in the name of crisis preparedness and writing a crisis plan, securing the active commitment of top leadership is key. Consider some related issues that make sense to senior managers and board members worldwide. *You must meet people where they are before you can influence them*. In general, first strive to understand the beliefs, attitudes, needs, and concerns or those who will be involved in your crisis preparedness program.

As discussed previously, senior managers and board members have two overarching responsibilities: (1) increase the value of the organization; and (2) protect core assets of the organization. Those core assets include people, reputation, trust, brand, finances, shareholder value, ability to operate, intellectual and physical property, and key relationships, such as customers and suppliers.

As a person involved in crisis management preparedness and developing crisis management plans in your organization, you would do well to begin to think like a senior manager. Reframe your crisis preparedness initiatives. Most managers in crisis management visualize themselves as planners and responders who help to minimize recovery time, or who establish an alternative worksite plan if a facility is destroyed, for example. This narrow view doesn't resonate well with senior managers who approve funding.

11.12.1 Reframe Your Role

To escape silo-oriented thinking and to optimize support from your senior management team, reframe your role. Present yourself and the internal crisis management organization as "protectors of core assets." This is a key concern of the leadership of your organization. It aligns your role with the concerns of the senior management team and board of directors. When you are aligned with their concerns, you are in a much better place to influence them positively.

11.12.2 Executive Sponsor

If you are down the food chain from the executive suites, it is important to work your way up to an executive sponsor. Who is the one person with sufficient authority and executive influence to best understand and support your role in protecting the core assets of the organization? There will likely be barriers, and your executive sponsor can offer the ultimate support you need to help you navigate your way through.

11.12.3 Know the Landscape

In order to gain executive support, you must be armed with sufficient knowledge to align adequately with their concerns and needs. The following are some places to garner useful information:

Annual report. Read your organization's annual report, looking for stated preparedness needs, existing risks, and strategies to overcome these issues.

Enterprise risk manager (ERM). If you have an ERM, often he or she is involved in the strategic planning process with executives. The ERM role is to assess risks that are related to the strategic plan. Are you in a position to help mitigate some of those risks?

Internal auditor. As a result of the required internal audit process, internal auditors know and may be willing to discuss risks of the organization and to listen to how you could help address those risks. In many organizations, the internal auditor reports directly to the board of directors. Thus, you may have immediate influence to assist the organization with the risks of most concern at its highest levels.

> It also helps to know what gets any individual decision-maker's attention. Is he or she more convinced by stories about what happened to others in your industry, or is he or she more statistically oriented? A big part of organizing and implementing your plan will involve selling it to senior management.

11.12.4 Additional Resources

Other sources of information to garner support from senior management include:

▶ **Case histories.** Show how critical incidents have affected other companies. Many times, senior managers are unaware of the variety of crises to which the company is vulnerable. A presentation of this real-world information can be compelling. In fact, some crisis consultants maintain a database of information on affected companies, which could be the source of in-depth case histories.

▶ **National Association of Corporate Directors (NACD) and other professional associations.** Attend local chapter luncheons of the NACD (www.nacdonline.org). Typically, you don't have to be a member to attend. Look for luncheon presentations that address crisis management and risk issues of concern to board members. Take this opportunity to discuss crisis preparedness informally over lunch with the various board members in attendance to gain their perspectives. Look for opportunities to attend meetings such as the local chamber of commerce where the program is related to crisis management. Are there professional meetings related to CFOs, general counsel, and other senior executive positions that you could attend? Be a good student. Listen for their interests and concerns to help align with your leadership team's interests.

▶ **Magazines and articles.** Read what your senior leaders are reading. Order copies of magazines that are targeted toward senior executives. chief financial officers, chief risk officers, chief operations officers, CEOs, chief security officers, and corporate counsel all have concerns about protecting the core assets of the organization. Articles are published regularly in the *Wall Street Journal*, *Financial Times*, *Fortune*, Internet, and other sources.

Some magazines like the *Harvard Business Review* provide in-depth articles about how a specific crisis was handled. Get in the habit of sending pertinent articles to people of influence in your organization. Once you know their issues, the doors will open much more frequently than if you are clueless about their pressing concerns.

▶ **History.** What preparedness programs and controls are presently in place within your organization? Does your boss or his/her boss know how these programs and controls are perceived by senior management? Have programs been rejected in the past? Why? These are all important things to know as you pursue your role as protector of organizational core assets.

▶ **Budget.** Establish a budget for your plan, including a cost-benefit comparison to losses suffered by companies that were unprepared for disasters and other crises like the ones you foresee. Make the case that crisis preparedness should be an annual budget item equal in importance to insurance and other entrenched risk management methods.

▶ **Communications.** How do executive communications flow? What is the best format in order to convey information to and from senior executives and board members? While you may or may not have direct access to senior managers, your success in pushing information up the ladder will be improved if it is provided in a format that is regularly used and accepted within the executive ranks.

▶ **Benchmark.** Provide benchmarking data comparing the preparedness of your organization to that of similar organizations. Senior executives are acutely interested in what others at their level are doing.

▶ **Government.** Show the information you have gathered from the Department of Labor or other appropriate government entities about incidents that could affect your organization.

▶ **Insurer.** Your insurer or insurance broker may be willing to share actuarial data that show risks inherent to your industry and locales that need to be managed from a risk management perspective.

▶ **Consultants and security professionals.** Compile and present information from corporate crisis consultants, local law enforcement, former FBI and Secret Service agents, Department of

Homeland Security (DHS), Bureau of Alcohol, Tobacco, Firearms and Explosives (ATF), US Border Patrol (USBP), US Department of State, private security groups, or others in the know.

▶ **Public Relations.** PR firms can compile information about relevant news stories that could be helpful to your cause. The Institute for Crisis Management (Louisville PR firm) provides a free *Crisis Report* annually that compiles the frequency of business crisis stories covered in the media.

▶ **Books.** Use some of the information in this book, such as the positive survey results of the Reputation Institute for companies that effectively handled the September 11, 2001 terrorism or the results of the Oxford University/Templeton study on shareholder value. Organize information from other books that can make your case for crisis preparedness.

It also helps to know what gets any individual decision-maker's attention. Is he or she more convinced by stories about what happened to others in your industry, or is he or she more statistically oriented? A big part of organizing and implementing your plan will involve selling it to your executive sponsor and generally to senior management.

Case Study: Family Received Too Much Assistance

In the early 1990s, CMI was asked to develop the first formal family representative training program for the commercial airlines. The program provided assistance for both surviving passengers and the families of air crash victims through trained employee volunteers for one of the largest commercial airlines in the world. The program quickly spread to other commercial carriers. It has become so successful that it is now mandated by the US Congress for all commercial airlines in the US.

Unfortunately, one airline ran into trouble with its monitoring.

According to public record, the airline assigned a single male family representative volunteer to an unmarried female passenger who had survived a recent crash. Against stated policy, management assigned just one volunteer to work with the victim, rather than two (preferably a male and a female). Obviously, the volunteer received no professional supervision. As you may have guessed by now, the result was that the family representative and the crash victim had an affair.

Subsequently, the airline was sued for negligence and had to pay a multimillion dollar settlement. Proper monitoring could have prevented this incident.

Lessons-learned: Without monitoring, even the best crisis plan can become useless, or worse.

11.12.5 Monitor, Monitor, Monitor

Your process must also include the mechanisms for ensuring that your plan is:

▶ Implemented properly.

▶ Working effectively as planned.

▶ Monitored for quality over time.

Organizing the crisis plan is more than putting guidelines into sequential order. Organizing the plan is a cooperative effort. Politics, cultural issues, potential "turf battles" and priorities will need consideration. Gaining buy-in at all levels of the organization is vital to the crisis planning process. Once organized and facilitated throughout the company, it's time to take your planning efforts out for a "test drive" to verify your plan is reliable and valid, teams are adequately trained, and the program is sufficiently integrated among all involved constituents.

Quick Use Preparedness Guide

Chapter 11: Organizing New Controls and Drafting Your New Plan

Evaluating New Controls

▶ What weaknesses have emerged as you analyzed your foreseeable risks and evaluated your existing capabilities?

▶ What new controls can you devise to address each weakness?

▶ Remembering that crises can also be opportunities, what strengths could be accentuated by incorporating new controls?

▶ Have you benchmarked the need for potential new controls with:

❑ Your own crisis history and near misses?

❑ Others in your industry?

❑ Others in your locale?

❑ Others who share similar risks?

▶ Have you researched current preparedness standards through:

❑ Your process guardian and others with in-house knowledge?

❑ The Internet?

❑ Electronic newsletters?

❑ Crisis-related books?

❑ Professional industry associations and conferences?

❑ International Organization for Standardization (ISO)?

❑ Local and federal government agencies?

❑ Crisis management consultants?

❑ Insurance broker?

❑ Others?

▶ Has your crisis planning committee (CPC) brainstormed new controls and their alternatives?

▶ Have you sufficiently anticipated the ripple effect of vulnerability that could occur with each foreseeable risk? What about anticipated ripple effects from new controls you implement?

▶ Have you considered what each of your stakeholders would want/need/expect in each type of crisis?

▶ Have you considered how each type of crisis could affect your company's core assets, such as reputation, financial condition, business operations, people, trust, culture, industry, and community?

▶ Have you subjected your overall crisis preparedness to the reasonable person test?

▶ If you have withdrawn from consideration some new or enhanced controls for primary prevention or post-incident response (secondary prevention), is your "reasonable person" documentation rational, clear, and defensible?

▶ Have you adequately considered new controls for both primary and secondary prevention?

▶ For each foreseeable risk scenario, have you allowed for controls that would provide crisis prevention and mitigating post-crisis response?

Organizing Your Plan

Before you implement any new control into your plan, ask:

▶ Specifically, what do we want this control to address?

▶ What might be possible intended and unintended impacts (positive and negative) on other systems within and around our organization?

▶ Are there alternatives that would be better suited to address the need?

▶ Have you considered ways that the controls you need may conflict with your company's culture or external environment?

▶ Have you anticipated how each control may be received?

▶ Have you taken steps to build broad support for your efforts?

▶ Have you considered how each control might affect your system as a whole?

▶ Have you determined:

❑ Who needs to be brought on board to ensure success?

❑ Who will be responsible for the ongoing effectiveness of the plan?

❑ What routines in the organization would have to be modified or replaced?

❑ Where within the organization can the plan's procedures receive resistance?

❑ Who in the company will be affected by the plan? Have you gained their acceptance?

❑ Which decision-makers' active support could smooth the implementation process?

❑ What support materials and resources will be required?

❑ What costs will be incurred? From where?

❑ What other hurdles do you need to overcome?

❑ Who would be the appropriate executive sponsor to champion the plan?

❑ Where in the organization can you cultivate the support of other individuals?

▶ Have you reframed your role?

❑ Have you aligned your role with the concerns and needs of senior management?

  ❖ Protector of core assets, rather than the narrow role of data recovery, business continuity manager, etc.

❑ Have you prepared a compelling case for senior management?

▶ Know the executive landscape by focusing on:

- ❏ Annual report.

- ❏ Enterprise risk manager.

- ❏ Internal auditor.

- ❏ Case histories.

- ❏ National Association of Corporate Directors (NACD) and other professional associations.

- ❏ Magazines and articles.

- ❏ History.

- ❏ Budget.

- ❏ Communications.

- ❏ Benchmark.

- ❏ Government.

- ❏ Insurer.

- ❏ Consultants and security professionals.

- ❏ Public relations.

- ❏ Books.

▶ Have you built in mechanisms to make sure new controls are properly implemented and monitored?

Chapter 11 – Questions for Further Thought and Discussion

1. What organizational strengths could be accentuated by incorporating new crisis preparedness controls?

2. In your opinion, what are the top three methods to efficiently learn about new controls from external resources?

3. If a potential, but needed, new crisis control creates a significant conflict between internal staffers (e.g., legal vs. communications, or sales vs. production), what are effective methods to resolve the resistances?

4. How often should your existing, enhanced, and new controls be reevaluated? What is a rationale for why they should be reevaluated at shorter or longer intervals?

5. In establishing a crisis planning committee (CPC) to brainstorm existing controls and the implementation of enhanced and new controls, which of the combinations is best in your opinion? How do you build on the strengths of each and overcome weaknesses of each?

   a. Establish a CPC where there is general agreement among members to increase the likelihood that the crisis planning process will run smoothly toward implementation?

   b. Enlist CPC members who are likely to disagree and throw roadblocks into the crisis preparedness process, but possibly make the program stronger in the process?

6. What are the most likely failure points if crisis response is not integrated among involved staff positions internally? What about with external stakeholders, as well?

7. Where are integration "disconnects" or resistance points for each level between the executive team, managerial team, and operational/tactical teams?

8. What are the roles of the executive team during crisis response? What are the pitfalls that can arise?

9. What are the roles of the managerial team during crisis response? What are the pitfalls that can arise?

10. What are the roles of the various operational/tactical teams (listed below) during crisis response? What are the pitfalls that can arise?

    a. IT disaster recovery.

    b. Insurance.

    c. Accounting and finance.

    d. Regulatory/compliance.

    e. Communications.

    f. Human resources.

    g. Benefits.

    h. Emergency response.

    i. Business continuity.

    j. Other.

12

Putting Plans and Teams in Action

As with any project, you will want to prioritize its elements, and establish a schedule for its implementation. You will want to clearly document the schedule you set. If a crisis occurs before your plan is fully in place and tested, or not yet complete at some locations, this documentation can serve as defensible proof of your intentions. If your company is later accused of negligence, such actions can help you pass the "reasonable person test" that we discussed earlier in this book.

This chapter will help you to:

➢ *Create and train effective crisis teams with the right mix of participants.*

➢ *Exercise and practice the plan using realistic scenarios.*

➢ *Integrate crisis response throughout the organization.*

➢ *Debrief participants in exercises and real crises to improve the plan.*

Some parts of your preparedness program may be relatively quick and easy to put forward. For instance, instructions for building evacuation procedures can be communicated to and exercised by your workforce in a short time. Still, overall, it will take a little more time to put your comprehensive and integrated plans and teams in place. Like the members of a professional sports team, it takes a while to come up with a strategic game plan. Then the players must work together to understand how best to make use of individual and team strengths. This result takes planning, selecting the right team members with diverse skills and strengths, training the individuals and team, and then engaging in sufficient team practices until they develop a smooth, organized, and integrated flow. The process is the same, whether it's a winning sports team or an effective crisis management organization. Putting your preparedness plan in action means executing a series of distinct steps.

1. **Communicate.** First, communicate the plan to the appropriate people throughout the organization.

2. **Train.** The people involved must be trained or at least oriented, as appropriate.

3. **Practice.** Then when you exercise the plan with those who are actively involved, they will be prepared for an actual crisis situation.

4. **Debrief.** To round out the implementation process, debrief the participants involved in exercises or actual crises for lessons-learned.

5. **Refine.** Finally, refine the plan based on experience and what you've learned.

For your plan to transform into decisive action, establish the right teams and leaders for each team. Crisis-prepared companies set up:

▶ **Crisis response leaders** at key levels and locations within the organization.

▶ **Crisis teams** at strategic points in your organization's structure (executive, managerial, and tactical; and centralized or established throughout the organization's regional/divisional areas or business units).

12.1 Setting Up Effective Teams

> **For best results in a large organization, you will need to establish teams at various levels and sites. Each should follow a consistent methodology.**

12.1.1 The Right Mix Makes a Stronger Team

Your teams will be most effective if they are multidisciplinary, not only in terms of staff position and expertise, but also in terms of personality. Include people who are decisive and action-oriented, as well as including analytical and creative thinkers who can generate solutions.

For best results in a large organization, you may want to establish teams at various levels and sites. Each should follow a consistent methodology. In smaller organizations, you may not have the luxury of many teams. But, as a general rule, crisis team members should have only one area of responsibility each. It's obvious that an executive team member who is responsible for leadership during the crisis cannot be consumed with putting out the fire. The old adage that you don't want the CEO driving the fire truck does a good job of getting to this point. Trying to wear too many hats of responsibility and effectiveness will cause a team member to lose focus very quickly.

By now, those people on the crisis planning committee (CPC) who helped to develop your plans will be familiar with your anticipated risks and needs. They may be logical candidates to serve on one of your response teams. But they will now need to demonstrate crisis whisperer qualities other than purposeful planning, such as:

▶ They must be generally available.

▶ They should be able to remain cool under pressure.

▶ They should be capable of decisive action and good judgment – even when information is incomplete.

▶ They need to be skilled at working in a dynamic, fast-moving group.

In addition to an exercise program and depending on your management support and culture, some companies choose to invest in the development of their teams through techniques like group retreats, team-building exercises, wilderness challenges, and the like. In any case, team members must be thoroughly trained in your preparedness and response plans and knowledgeable about the corporate culture, guiding principles of the organization, and their scope and responsibilities.

Crisis team leaders. No matter the team, each of your teams will need a leader and at least one backup leader. Your teams can include emergency response, data recovery, corporate communications, human impact/assistance, legal, security, finance, and more. Each will have a leader who will be responsible for the adequate functioning of his or her respective team. Your leaders will need to integrate their responsibilities, expectations, and authority levels with the other teams and disciplines to ensure competing actions and unintended consequences do not affect other organizational areas of responsibility. These leaders are the people who must provide critical leadership in the event of a crisis, each within his or her own silo of responsibility and integrated strategically with the interests and nuances of the enterprise as a whole.

Team structure. Your crisis team structure will depend on your size, the number of critical incidents you anticipate per year, your geographic locations, and the management philosophy of your company. Some companies prefer to have a centralized command and control structure at the corporate level that may be mobilized often enough to keep its members' skills at optimal levels, or you may opt for a decentralized structure, more at the business unit level with members who know the business, local customs, and people. Clear notification and activation levels would then be established for corporate involvement if the crisis becomes severe or protracted enough to warrant corporate involvement. If you do not anticipate relatively frequent crisis responses, you may be served better with a centralized team. Even with a robust exercise and training program, remote and local level crisis teams that are mobilized, say, once in 10 years will be rusty when the crisis bell rings.

> You cannot afford to assume that each crisis team member – a mature and balanced coworker during the usual workday – is fully capable of functioning adequately during stressful crisis times.

12.1.2 Evaluate Stress Styles

We each have a "stress style" that emerges under times of great pressure. In the business world, the whole idea of human response to stress is one that is often not adequately assessed. You cannot afford to assume that each crisis team member – a mature and balanced coworker during the usual workday – is fully capable of functioning adequately during stressful crisis times. Such an assumption could lead to unexpected negative outcomes. When we first learn of a calamity that is directed our way, most of us have similar initial reactions. Our hearts beat faster. Our palms go clammy. We feel a wave of stress that can cause varied reactions among different people.

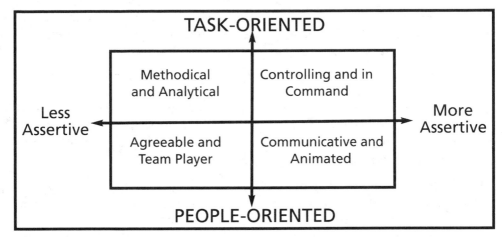

Figure 12-1. Workstyle Response Matrix

Stress Style Matrix

At manageable levels, the daily stressors in our lives can be good for motivation and active life involvement. However, as human beings, we all tend to react differently when the stress level becomes greater than our normal coping mechanisms can withstand.

It is insightful to understand how you and your team members will tend to react during high stress situations. To assess your stress style (and those of team members you know), start by using the matrix in Figure 12-1 to determine your typical behavioral style in normal daily living, social, and professional situations by using this simple two-step process:

1. On the center horizontal line that separates *less assertive* and *more assertive*, plot your common daily living style. The way you operate every day – the way others think of you. If you move toward people easily and have no trouble speaking your mind or promoting your ideas, you would fall somewhere on the more assertive side of the continuum. If you are one who waits to be asked questions, and are less forceful in your dealings with others, plot yourself closer to the less assertive side. Where do you generally rank yourself on the assertiveness line in normal work and social settings?

2. On the center vertical line, plot whether you tend to be more *task-oriented* or more *people-oriented*. For example, does getting the job done tend to take precedence over relationships? People who are highly task-oriented tend to be less interested in those around them and more interested in achievements. Those who are highly

people-oriented consider their relationships with others of greater importance than the tasks themselves. Plot yourself on the people-oriented vs. task-oriented line.

If you rank yourself as *task-oriented and less assertive*, your behavioral style tends to be methodical and analytical. If you are *task-oriented and more assertive*, you tend to be controlling and in command. If you lean toward *people-oriented and less assertive*, your typical pattern is agreeable and a team player. And, if you are *people-oriented and more assertive*, your personality style is inclined to be communicative and animated.

Obviously, this is a broad-strokes exercise, not a precise behavioral profile. No one is completely assertive or completely passive. And, as you know from your own experience, those who move through their personal and professional life successfully tend to strike a balance between all these tendencies. What's useful here is to gain a general insight into your traits or style. For your known team members, you can also estimate their general behavioral styles through the same methodology.

Figure 12-2. Stress Style Matrix

Behavioral Styles and Corresponding Stress Matrix

Now, look at the matrix in Figure 12-2 and notice the "stress style," which shows the tendency for each of the behavioral styles under significant stress.

▶ **Methodical/analytical style.** If you find yourself in the *methodical/analytical* category (less assertive and task-oriented), you are a thorough and dependable worker who makes few errors when you can work at your preferred slower and deliberate pace. Your strengths include the ability to attend to details and work through to accomplish tasks. However, you may tend to avoid quick, decisive decisions under stress. It's a tendency that can cause "analysis paralysis." If the stress gets too overwhelming and the pace is faster than what you find comfortable, your stress style as a *methodical/analytical* is to shut down and avoid. When others are ready to jump at a decision, you may be the individual who will say, "Let's step back and think about this for a moment." Given enough space to gain perspective, you may be the one to come up with some pros and cons and specifics of your action plan that may need to be considered.

If *methodical/analytical* response sounds like a description of you under fire, think about compensating. In a crisis, you may need to push beyond your normal tendency to be methodical, even when you may only have partial knowledge and what seems like too little time to weigh choices carefully. You must purposefully remind yourself that timely decisions are paramount. While more assurance can come by waiting, if the decision and actions are not implemented on a timely basis, you and the team will have a difficult time being effective. In a crisis, there are certainly times when waiting to act can make a situation worse.

▶ **Controlling/commanding style.** If you identified yourself as *controlling/in command* (more assertive and task-oriented), you are one who pushes projects through with speed and determination. You're recognized for your ability to take charge. But your stress style may be become autocratic. Under stress, you (like many top CEOs and other hard-driving, successful types who are also in this category) may find it hard to listen. You feel driven to make something happen, but often without sufficient regard of the possible consequences or reactions.

If this is your penchant, think about tempering it during a crisis by gathering input from a multidisciplinary group before acting. Make it a point to ask for differing opinions and listen to others' viewpoints. While there is little time for deliberation, take the time to gather sufficient information before taking decisive action. Better to pause long enough to include input from others for consideration, rather than to push through your unilateral ideas without useful input from others.

▶ **Agreeable/team player style.** If you are the *agreeable/team player* style (less assertive and people-oriented), you are an all around "nice person" who gets along with others and excels at team building. Your strengths lie in mediating, supporting, listening, and gaining consensus. But when the stress hits the fan, you may tend to give in to others, even when you don't agree. Under stressful conditions you tend to avoid rocking the boat. So your valuable ideas may go unheard or unspoken.

To reduce this possibility of your ideas being ignored, work harder to express your viewpoints. Consider writing down your concerns before expressing them verbally. Go ahead and support other team members, but express your concerns about the reactions of people who may be impacted by a given decision or other issue of concern. Realize that sometimes during crises, conflict and hurt feelings will arise. Expediency will not always allow for ensuring that everyone on the team feels good about the decisions and actions taken. In some situations, doing the right things on time may be more important than arriving at total agreement. Remember, your supportive influence will be helpful and that makes it worth speaking up, but realize that there is often not time to ensure that everyone on the team is pleased.

> By becoming aware of the strengths and stress styles of yourself and others, you can integrate the personalities on your team(s) in a way that will serve you well.

▶ **Communicative/animated style.** If you ranked yourself in the *communicative/animated* category (more assertive and people-oriented), know that your interpersonal strengths are a valuable asset that can be used to motivate others. You readily supply creative ideas and useful solutions to problems. You can be great at selling your ideas and those of your team when you agree with the decisions. But when chaos looms, you may have a tendency to become disorganized, and all aspects of your ideas may not be fully thought out. Also, your motivation may diminish if others don't adopt your ideas readily. As stress mounts, you may become critical and blaming of others.

Remember that not everyone moves as quickly as you do. They may not visualize or buy into your ideas readily. Respect their need to more methodically come up with considerations relating to your visions, ideas, and decisions. If people disagree with you or disregard what you thought was a good idea, your challenge is to work hard not to take it personally. Instead, go with the flow. Take their input into consideration and incorporate it into a creative solution that combines useful input from others.

A team approach that melds all the styles is good. Diverse approaches to problem solving will allow for more effective crisis decision-making. If your team is missing any one of the four styles mentioned above, you may be lacking a balanced perspective for effective crisis response. By becoming aware of the strengths and stress styles of yourself and others, you can integrate the personalities on your team(s) in a way that will serve you well.

12.2 Activating Teams

In many large corporations, you would mobilize the executive team only when an incident hits a defined threshold. For example, expected financial losses of a given value – say, more than $500,000 – would activate the executive team. Any situation that creates reputational risk, trust, or brand image issues should get the attention of the executive leadership team, which would be activated as the corporate crisis management team (CMT). In addition, you need to establish a clear system of defined thresholds to trigger the involvement of different management levels and crisis-related teams. In some cases, you would only notify the executive team for "watchful waiting," but they would not be immediately mobilized.

Vague definitions of crisis severity or expected longevity will leave room for mistakes in notifying and mobilizing the correct teams. Some people in your organization may interpret "media involvement" as pertaining to the traditional media, i.e., television, newspapers, and radio. However, it's important to realize that social media can engage long before traditional media takes interest. Your activation levels for appropriate teams will work best if defined clearly in a concrete manner that could be observed readily (would show up if recorded on a video camera), and could be counted or timed. For example, your mobilization threshold for the executive team might be, "When over 100 negative social media postings are submitted about the organization within a 24-hour period." You would include similar definitions for traditional media.

You may define further specific threshold levels by starting with these general categories:

▶ Financial exposure levels (real or expected).

▶ Serious injury or deaths.

▶ Reputational threats.

▌ Level of media coverage (social, local, national, or international).

▌ Blame or charges of negligence directed toward management or the organization.

▌ Business disruption beyond a defined period of time (real or expected).

▌ Incidents exceeding insurance deductibles or likely not covered.

▌ Recurring incidents.

▌ Anticipated government regulator investigations.

▌ Investor relations concerns, especially with institutional investors.

▌ Harm to contractors, franchisees, distributors, suppliers, or other key relationships, including a defined drop in sales or customers.

▌ Incidents with anticipated claims of negligence or class action legal disputes.

▌ Compromised security and safety of intellectual property, life, and wellbeing.

▌ Unlawful, noncompliant, or unethical acts by or against the organization.

▌ Incidents defined or named by senior management or CPC.

12.2.1 Crisis Manuals and Protocols

With your teams established, you will want to explicitly set out your crisis-response policies and procedures in a manual or checklist of guidelines. Each of your crisis teams will want to be familiar with this information during training and exercises – and, of course, in the event of the real thing.

You have options when it comes to publishing the manual. Should you publish it in hard copy? File it on your company intranet? Put it into an electronic app? Or, is there a commercial software application that best seems to fit your needs?

The physical ways you maintain your plan should fit the culture of your company. Handheld devices, for example, are efficient. They might seem to be just the way to go. But the managers in your factories might find them frustrating in a high-pressure situation, and they might prefer a hard copy for reference. Also, it's sometimes easier to access information in hard copy than on a smart phone.

Nothing says you can't maintain your crisis manuals, checklists, and protocols in more than one format. Distribute your crisis manual in a way that works for your organization, makes the information accessible, is secure, and is optimally usable to everyone who needs it.

Your manual should cover only genuine response items. A common mistake made in the preparation of these manuals is to write them as "training documents." Of course you will use your manual in the course of training. But in a real crisis, your team members will not want to use a manual that is sprinkled with training exercises, unprepared items you should have had in place, or long paragraphs. See Chapter 15 for checklists relating to several crisis events.

12.3 Training...and Practice...and More Practice

In the event of any critical occurrence, the members of your various mobilized crisis teams will have to work smoothly in a group and under pressure. You need to train and exercise them well.

Training and exercising. The crisis plan for each team will be the foundation for training and your exercise program. The training should breed familiarity with the plan for each team member. If team members don't know the plan thoroughly, they will be unlikely to use it effectively during a crisis response.

Training content and exercising should include all the phases of crisis management response, but not necessarily all in the same exercise:

▶ Notification and activation.

▶ Fact finding.

▶ Decision-making.

▶ Prioritizing.

▶ Implementation.

▶ De-escalation.

Crisis leadership, crisis communications, stress management, strategic vs. tactical responsibilities, reputation management, the human side of crisis, and integrated crisis response are all topics that should be addressed with team members and their backups.

> Too often, the primary emphasis in crisis preparedness is on group training and exercising, while individual skill development is an omitted component.

Individual coaching. If a musical band is playing and the guitar player is out of tune, the entire band sounds bad. Likewise, it takes only one errant member to throw an entire crisis team's response off balance. Frequently, one or two individual team players have caused a catastrophic outcome.

For example, in the demise of Arthur Andersen accounting firm, two individuals – a member of the Andersen legal department and an Enron account lead partner – were allegedly responsible for shredding the Enron-related documents that destroyed the firm.

Once senior management has established guiding principles and a strategic plan for crisis management – including cultural, legal, and ethical guidelines – individual coaching for crisis team members will help to ensure that each team member is optimally effective in following the plan. Too often, the primary emphasis in crisis preparedness is only on group training and exercising, while individual skill development is an omitted component. This coaching will help each of your team members overcome those stress style shortcomings we discussed earlier. It will help to fill in for personal "blind spots" and other weaknesses that often occur in the heat of an unexpected, high-consequence crisis response. Effectively prepared crisis teams consist of effectively prepared individuals on the team.

12.3.1 Exercising the Plan

Once your plans are developed and your team members are trained, a crisis exercising program is the next step. Each exercise will test two things: your plans and your teams. In general, a crisis exercise is a learning experience that simulates conditions of a selected critical incident in order to test the effectiveness of the involved plans and teams. Teams and plans will develop in maturity and effectiveness as exercises are conducted on a periodic, but regularly scheduled, basis.

Types of exercises include:

> ▶ **Notification and activation drills.** Team members are notified, activated, and ready to be briefed during notification and activation drills. No further action is taken. The purpose is to breed familiarity with the notification and activation process, measure the time required to muster the various teams, and rehearse the process up to an initial briefing. If you use an emergency notification system, this would be a time to test the ability of the system to contact selected team members simultaneously and bridge them into an initial conference call. This is a critical component of crisis response that tends to be overlooked. Crises can escalate out of control quickly if the teams are delayed in getting assembled for crisis response. Slow or incomplete notification and activation is the first critical crisis response function that can lead to inadequate crisis containment and command of the crisis situation.

▶ **Tabletop exercise.** Leaders provide *injects* (information in a scenario that is added or "injected" by a controller to a player to simulate the details of a real event) in writing periodically during the exercise while the team sits around a conference table. Each inject represents the next development in the crisis fact pattern. Without any external communications (like phone calls or e-mails) or moving about the area, participants address presented issues one at a time. Tabletop exercises typically last 2-4 hours with additional time at the end for debriefing and compiling lessons-learned.

▶ **Simulated exercise.** Participants are subjected to a simulated crisis response within a crisis command center setting and sometimes in additional locations. The crisis fact pattern unfolds in real time via phones, faxes, e-mail, text messages, social networking channels, face-to-face informants, and sometimes simulated television newscasts. Simulators conduct the exercise and are involved to serve as the "universe of resources and contacts" for simulated communications with team members. No *actual* communications go outside the simulators to the real world during the exercise. The intent is to create a realistic crisis response situation that is fast paced, involves all team members, is sufficiently challenging without being overwhelming, and creates a semblance of stress for team members similar to an actual response. Simulated exercises typically last 4-8 hours, but can vary in length. Debriefings are conducted at the end.

▶ **Full-scale exercise.** Real-life scenarios are created, designed to be as close as possible to a real crisis situation. Actors may serve as victims and other roles. Emergency responders, law enforcement, media representatives, and other community resources may be incorporated. Action may take place in several locations simultaneously. The intent is to challenge the entire crisis management organization in a realistic, stress-inducing manner. Multidisciplinary and multijurisdictional debriefings are conducted at the end.

12.3.2 Exercise Outcomes

Strengths and weaknesses of your plans and teams will become apparent with each exercise. Four possible outcomes and follow-up actions can result from an exercise:

▶ **The plans were adequate and the teams were effective.** Action: Next time, exercise a situation that is more complex and difficult.

Possibly, cover an incident that hasn't been previously addressed. It's time to challenge the crisis program to take it to the next level.

▶ **The plans were adequate, but the teams were ineffective.** Action: The teams should be debriefed for lessons-learned. The teams will need additional training and exercising that correspond to identified weaknesses and needs. Individuals on each team may need personalized training and coaching for skill development.

▶ **The plans were inadequate, but the teams were effective.** Action: The plans need to be reviewed for weaknesses, whether it is content, structure, or integration among plans. Revisions to the plans should be made, reviewed by team members, and approved for utilization in future exercises and crisis responses.

▶ **The plans were inadequate, and the teams were ineffective.** Action: The team members need to be debriefed and trained, as a group and individually. The plans should be revised, reviewed, and approved for utilization in future exercises and crisis responses.

If the teams are ineffective, possibly the roles of each member need to be clarified. With additional exercising, crisis response skills should improve. Observations of the team and individual capabilities should be noted to identify areas for improvement. Feedback should be provided in a manner that is correctable and empowering whenever possible. Some team members may need to be replaced.

If the plans are ineffective, the teams utilizing the plans should be debriefed to identify exactly why. Do the plans contain invalid content? Are there omissions, gaps, conflicting information, or overlaps? Do the plans or response guidelines need to be simplified? Is there a problem with the formatting or structure of the plans? Feedback from the teams would then go back to the crisis planning committee (CPC) for improvements.

> **Exercises are critical to your preparedness. Designing them properly takes time, attention to detail, and skilled orchestration.**

Utilizing an external observer is an important component to any exercise program that is often overlooked. Individuals and teams can get too close to their crisis preparedness and response to recognize gaps and weaknesses. An experienced outsider who is not involved in the exercise itself can provide valuable input. This crisis professional would provide no input during the exercise. Instead, the role of this individual (or team of professionals) would be to take note of strengths of the response and areas of needed improvement while the crisis exercise is unfolding. Feedback would be provided in a manner that effectively helps the teams and its members without making anyone look inept.

12.3.3 Developing Scenarios for Exercises and Simulations

Both successful tabletop exercises and simulations require crisis scenarios that are credible and effective. Common design flaws may pose challenges that are insufficiently realistic, too hard, or too easy to hold your team's attention.

None of the participants should learn the content of the scenario in advance. To ensure an engaging scenario, the simulation designers should meet privately with knowledgeable managers who will *not* be involved in the exercise to gather appropriate and realistic content for the exercise. Every aspect of the crisis fact pattern must be appropriately challenging, realistic, and believable. With that said, team members who are participating should be instructed to "suspend disbelief" if they observe that some component(s) of the exercise seem unrealistic or highly improbable.

On the other hand, it is possible to overwhelm a team – especially one that is newly formed – by introducing something that is too elaborate, complex, or fast moving. Designing crisis exercises is an exacting, detailed task. As you prepare one or work with an outside professional, ask yourself these questions:

▶ Does the scenario appropriately use the content of your crisis plan, manual, or checklists?

▶ Are challenges incorporated into the scenario that will exercise and test (but not overwhelm) every discipline represented on your involved crisis teams – such as legal, human resources, security, public relations, and appropriate others, like executives?

▶ Is the scenario sufficiently realistic to engage team members, and thus serve as a real preparation?

Exercises are critical to your preparedness. Designing them properly takes time, attention to detail, and skilled orchestration. Many companies design and conduct these exercises internally, and others find it useful to hire a specialist. In either case, the design, implementation, and debriefing of crisis exercises should be considered expertly and thoroughly during the planning process.

12.4 Planning and Testing Integrated Crisis Response

Less experienced crisis team members and plans tend to focus only on responsibilities within their unique silos. As the sophistication of the organization's crisis preparedness process improves, a need for integrating the crisis response becomes obvious. If you lack knowledge and consideration of the expectations, communication needs, and impacts on other staff positions inside and outside your silo of responsibility, crisis response will tend to be disorganized and inefficient. The same holds true if the needs and impacts of stakeholders outside your organization, such as customers, shareholders, politicians, regulators, insurers, media, and others, are not considered adequately.

> **An integrated approach to crisis management will consider the expectations and concerns of all silos in a manner that addresses the greater good of the company.**

12.4.1 Addressing Expectations

Internally, your people have expectations relating to their silos of responsibility during crises. Not only will they need to address areas of importance to their silos of responsibility, but they will also need to consider the needs, concerns, and implications for other areas of the organization. In many cases, the needs of the different silos of responsibility can have conflicting effects. For example, a common conflict occurs between attorneys and the communications department. Attorneys often want to protect legal liabilities by shutting down communications that could prove damaging in eventual legal proceedings. Meanwhile, the communications department wants to be transparent and forthcoming, mitigating reputational risks and outrage that can bubble up if the company appears to be withholding important information. An integrated approach to crisis management will consider the expectations and concerns of all silos in a manner that addresses the greater good of the company.

An important way to address the integration issue during the preparedness process is to clarify the following two important expectations. By doing so, conflicts can be addressed in the planning process before a crisis hits and synergies established.

▶ **What do leaders within each silo of responsibility want to *receive*** (and from whom) during each foreseeable crisis situation? For example, if there is a fire in a plant, a plant manager will want to know immediately from the insurance or legal department if he or she needs to protect the incident site or if employees can clean up the damage quickly in order to get back to full production as soon as possible. Similarly, until it can be ruled out, corporate security managers typically assume a crime has been involved in situations such as a fire. Once the legal and security departments understand the needs of plant managers as a part of the integrated planning process, they can make preparations to ensure that a plant manager is contacted by legal and corporate security as soon as possible in the case of a plant fire. Likewise, the plant manager would already be aware of the insurance, legal, and corporate security expectations as a part of the integrated planning process that conveys the expectations of each impacted staff function in the company during crises. Meanwhile, the CEO may want to be notified within minutes if a fire breaks out that disrupts operations, even before the plant manager or others are able to take the time to investigate.

▶ **What do leaders within each silo of responsibility plan to *give*** (and to whom) during each foreseeable crisis situation? For example, corporate security may provide prearranged local guard services at any location throughout the enterprise in response to a credible threat of terrorism or workplace violence. The manager at the location will know, as a part of the integrated crisis preparedness plan, that corporate security will provide this service. Meanwhile, HR will need to monitor the rumor mill among employees to address any disruptive fears or misunderstandings. The plant manager will expect ongoing information from HR regarding the status of employees.

If that plant fire in our example has caused a toxic exposure within the neighborhood, the plant manager can expect the legal department to provide immediate dispatch of a local attorney to support the plant manager's investigation. Meanwhile, risk management may want to receive photos of the site from the plant manager to support a claim with the company's insurer. Likewise, your government relations manager will want the plant manager to give timely information that he or she can convey to public sector politicians and emergency responders relating to the toxic exposure within the community. This list goes on. Integrated planning will identify what expected information and responses each staff function will give *and* receive during the various foreseeable incidents that could impact the company.

To integrate your plan, the crisis planning committee (CPC) needs to arrange for an interview or survey to be conducted with the leaders of each staff function (HR, corporate security, legal, finance, business unit heads, etc.) to determine what information and resources they want to receive and what they plan to give during the occurrence of selected identified foreseeable risks. As in the case of the toxic exposure, these interviews would also take place with stakeholders outside the organization, such as local law enforcement, politicians, regulators, neighborhood associations, and emergency responder groups.

Experience tells us that it is best to compile this information within a relational database software program. As the needs and expectations of the various functions change within the organization, it will require a software program to keep track of how each change will affect myriad others throughout the organization. Ask someone from your IT department or a software consultant about applications that would be best to integrate the needs and expectations of your various departments for each foreseeable risk.

> Without clear guidelines about the strategic direction of the response, communication channels, and limits of authority, the crisis response can lose focus quickly.

12.4.2 Integration Failure Points

As mentioned in Chapter 4, over the years of assisting crisis management teams, I have noticed three areas that seem to cause problems repeatedly during crisis responses. The acronym ACE (Authority, Communications, and Expectations) may help you remember these important areas where your crisis teams could run into difficulties.

▶ **Authority.** During a crisis is not the best time to determine who has authority for important decision-making. A common failure point occurs when individuals do not assume authority and responsibility when it is expected. When people are not fully empowered with clear boundaries and guidelines, they have a tendency to back away, especially when important decisions need to be made based on only vague guidelines about what is the best action to take. The default actions are avoidance or delay in order to obtain guidance from an appropriate superior. If authority is not assumed at appropriate levels, precious time is lost, and the effectiveness of the crisis response is compromised.

The converse is also problematic. In this case, individuals assume positions of authority without prior approval. This can result in a crisis response situation where decisions can be in conflict. Without clear guidelines about the strategic direction of the response, communication channels, and limits of authority, the crisis response can lose focus quickly.

It is critically important that appropriate individuals know they are to assume authority at defined levels. Thresholds should be clearly established to enable individuals to know the limits of their authority and at what point they need to garner approvals from superiors.

Prearranged authority is a concern with companies that use the incident command system (ICS) within a corporate setting. ICS is a subcomponent of the National Incident Management System (NIMS), as released by the US Department of Homeland Security (DHS) in 2004. Many companies use it successfully; others end up in a quagmire of conflict. ICS assigns an incident commander with authority over the entire crisis response. However, a problem area emerges because the incident commander is seldom the CEO of the organization and many times the incident commander is not on the leadership team.

The conflict with authority comes when the incident commander orders a response to a higher ranking manager in the company. During normal times, this would never happen. And, if that ranking manager disagrees with the incident commander's decision, a conflict of authority breaks out in the midst of fast-moving, high-consequence crisis events. Such a conflict can slow down the response, create noncompliance, send mixed messages, and undermine the crisis management structure within the organization.

Even without the ICS system, managers need to know the boundaries of their authority. At what point does our plant manager with the facility fire need to defer to business units heads or corporate management for decisions? Often, for example, the plant manager could give prepared holding statements to the press, but any incident-specific statements to the media would have to be approved or provided by corporate.

> ▶ **Communications.** No crisis response is any better than its communications. The most fundamental building block of any relationship is communication (whether crisis related or in daily living).

Engaged crisis teams must receive good information in order to assess the situation and contain the damage. Likewise, they must give out good information to involved stakeholders in order to orchestrate a unified and effective response.

Timely and accurate two-way information should flow between crisis managers and appropriate internal and external stakeholders. Depending on the incident, communications can be compromised with power outages, run down batteries, generators running out of fuel, attorneys with liability concerns attempting to limit transparency, inoperable or overloaded mobile phone towers, overloaded landline phone systems, e-mail that may not work, rumors, misinformation, misunderstandings, fear of disclosure, employees and others speaking without authority, social media, and other impediments. Good planning should include contingencies for these occurrences.

Often, texting is more reliable when other forms of communications fail, but not always. Satellite phones, for the few who have them, can work, but only with recipients who have phone service, or another satellite phone. Even if communications connections are made, then there is the issue of misunderstandings during stressful times that we discussed earlier in chapter 5.

Anticipate communications problems of all sorts in your planning and preparedness efforts. Play the "what if" game to identify communications difficulties and failure points. For example, what if a power outage lasts longer than a week? Come up with as many redundant systems as possible to increase the odds you will not lose this vital communications component of crisis response.

> ▶ **Expectations.** We touched on expectations earlier in this chapter. If people don't know what is expected of them in a crisis, this ambiguity will cause problems. They may do the wrong things. They may not fulfill tasks that should be completed. Your crisis team members are not the only ones who need to know what is expected. For example, your employees should know what is expected of them relating to your "accounting for people system." They should know they are expected to report their location and status, how to do it, and by when.

Likewise, involved stakeholders will want to know what they can expect from you and your organization. During a situation of high concern related to a pandemic outbreak, one Canadian organization with which I worked, purchased and stockpiled CAD $4 million worth of Tamiflu, an antiviral drug that slows the spread of influenza virus. Employees, at least at headquarters, knew that they could expect this medication from the company if a serious outbreak occurred, which created a whole other problem with employees in the field. Who outside corporate would get this medication and why? Where would it be stored and how would it be distributed?

Expectations are high during crises. Your planning process should address this common failure point and iron out as many wrinkles in your system as possible before the next crisis occurs.

12.4.3 Debriefing for Lessons-Learned

No crisis exercise or crisis response should be considered complete until all participants have been debriefed for lessons-learned. Debriefings should be an important component of the crisis planning process. Debriefing has three objectives:

> ▶ Everyone involved should feel increased confidence in his or her ability to function during a crisis, both from active participation and through lessons-learned debriefings.

▶ Leaders should compile information regarding which parts of the plan need more work. Participants should express these observations, such as "We need redundant communications methods," or "We need a much better system to account for our people during a disaster," or "Coordination with other departments would have made it easier for us to function." You will not only find out how to integrate and improve your plan, but you will also build ownership on the part of your team members.

▶ Debriefing should also evaluate the team's functioning. Specific tools for improved performance as a crisis team should be discussed. For example, the use of "time-outs" to help the team remain cohesive and coordinated could be suggested. Possibly, there was "too much telling and not enough questioning and dialogue" for optimal team performance. How can crisis communications be improved? Also, strengths should be identified. What worked well? What did individual team members do that was helpful or effective?

Quick Use Preparedness Guide

Chapter 12: Putting Plans and Teams in Action

▶ Have you established an executive level crisis management team (CMT) with clear guidelines and boundaries for its strategic role?

▶ Is your crisis management organization centralized or decentralized in strategic points and locations? Which is best?

▶ Are team members generally available and able to stay in communication?

▶ Is your team appropriately multidisciplinary?

▶ Is the mix of members conducive to working as a group?

▶ Have you considered the strengths and weaknesses of each behavioral and stress style of team members?

   ❑ Methodical/analytical style.

   ❑ Controlling/commanding style.

   ❑ Agreeable/team player style.

   ❑ Communicative/animated style.

- ▶ Have you trained and exercised your team(s) in the content, procedures, and specific roles they will play in a crisis?

- ▶ Have individual team members been engaged in skills-based one-on-one crisis management coaching?

- ▶ Have you designated crisis response leaders at the key levels and locations of your organization?

    - ❑ Are they capable of providing appropriate levels of leadership during a crisis?

    - ❑ Are backup leaders assigned, trained, and adequately exercised?

- ▶ Have you clearly documented your training and exercise schedule?

- ▶ Have you communicated what is expected of your people (employees and managers)?

- ▶ Have you conducted thorough exercises for the members of your team?

    - ❑ Notification and activation drills.

    - ❑ Tabletop exercises.

    - ❑ Simulated exercises.

    - ❑ Full-scale exercises.

- ▶ Have you implemented methods to integrate your response among various stakeholders (internal and external to the organization)?

    - ❑ Have you identified what expected information *and* responses each staff function will give and receive during the various foreseeable incidents that could impact the company?

    - ❑ Interviews: Compile on relational database software for flexibility with changes over time.

    - ❑ What information and directives does each staff position want *from* others?

    - ❑ What information and directives will each staff position give *to* others?

- ▶ Have you addressed these common failure points of crisis response?

    - ❑ Authority levels defined and assigned.

❑ Communications (two-way) and contingencies established.

❑ Expectations known between internal silos and externally for each foreseeable risk and contingency.

▶ Do you have a debriefing process that captures and implements lessons-learned from every exercise and crisis activation?

Chapter 12 – Questions for Further Thought and Discussion

1. What is the best way to ensure the executive team members will appropriately integrate with the various crisis teams when serious crises occur, e.g., not disrupt established systems; communicate effectively?

2. When a manager within a specific discipline refuses to consider consequences of decisions outside his/her silo of responsibility, what are methods to gain cooperation for the greater good?

3. How can you manage around critical staff managers (including senior executives and others) who are unwilling or unavailable to participate in planned exercises?

4. During assessment interviews, many staff managers and executives don't comprehensively identify the crisis-related information, directives, resources, and services needed *to* and *from* other stakeholders. What are methods to fill in for these gaps in consideration?

5. What questions should be asked during each post-incident/ post-exercise debriefing?

13

Re-evaluating Your Results

The world is not static. Neither is your organization. If you let your preparedness planning stagnate, all the hard work you have done could turn out to be of little use.

Preparedness is like muscle tone. If you stop working on it, your ability to respond will atrophy. You must remain conditioned, poised, and energized for crisis response. You know that the only way to keep your body in shape is to follow a regular regimen of exercise. Likewise, the one way to keep your preparedness planning in shape is through regular exercises and rigorous self-scrutiny.

This chapter will help you to:

➢ Monitor your preparedness.

➢ Revisit the plan regularly.

➢ Make needed ongoing revisions.

➢ Understand the role of the process guardian.

13.1 The Need for a Monitoring Process

For the functions that are vital to its continuing success, we can assume that your company has management systems in place for monitoring on a regular basis. Such functions typically include sales, finance, and productivity. In fact, your executives and managers most likely use customized "dashboards" to monitor the wellbeing of the organization and to identify problems at their earliest stages. It is equally important to have a management monitoring system for your crisis preparedness and response capabilities.

A Real-Life Example

CMI once helped a national retail chain set up a workplace violence response program and threat response team. This company went from being a disorganized accident-waiting-to-happen to having a professional multidisciplinary team with a plan. In the years that followed, though, the company had undergone reorganization. Many people were downsized when a new CEO brought in a number of managers from his previous organization. As a consequence, of the 10 original members of the team we helped to establish, only 3 remained. Meanwhile, during the reorganization process, the company allowed its whole preparedness structure to disintegrate. Does it still have threats and incidents of violence? Yes, at least as many as ever. But responsibility for its corporate-level response capability has fallen to a single security manager, whose job description is overloaded with many other duties.

Lessons-learned: In a few short years, because it lacked the habit of regularly scrutinizing itself and paying sufficient attention to the program, the company was nearly back where it started, back to being an accident-waiting-to-happen.

> Nobody in your company would say that it is enough to purchase and operate a fleet of trucks without ever changing the oil or checking the pressure in the tires. Periodic monitoring and refining is just as essential to preparedness.

It would be best to establish a monitoring system that can give you clues to the need for preparedness. Tracking and compiling a listing of crises will help. What are crises your organization has experienced in the past? What are the small crises situations or near misses that serve as warnings of potential high-consequence crises? Look also at your neighbors and your industry. Are there impacts in the greater environment, like pandemics or issues related to global warming, which could be helpful in justifying crisis preparedness revisions?

Analyzing motives of manmade incidents could also help. Is there a correlation with crime, such as robberies, foreign "knock off" replicas of your products, or bribery? Is there sabotage that is related to attempted union-ization? Are activist groups targeting your industry with reputational smears? Are there new laws or initiatives by regulators that could seriously impact your bottom line? Is the media picking on your industry over sustainability issues or your executives over compensation? These are all harbingers or prerequisites of potential crises that could be included in your monitoring process.

Monitoring should be presented and understood as part of the preparedness process from day one. Nobody in your company would say that it is enough to purchase and operate a fleet of trucks without ever changing the oil or checking the pressure in the tires. Periodic monitoring and refining is just as essential to preparedness. If your preparedness plan is implemented only once – and not revisited or rechecked for ongoing effectiveness – the core assets of your organization could be seriously damaged when threatened by the Grim Reaper of crisis.

13.2 Implementing the Monitoring Process

Scrutiny means revisiting and revising to update your preparedness. Revisit your plan. Walk yourself through all the steps you took to produce the plans you now have in place. That means employing all of the analytical and organizational methods you have gone through in the preceding chapters, and applying them to your new situation. Unless the nature of your organization suggests a different frequency, a defensible policy would be to thoroughly scrutinize your crisis preparedness at least once each year.

Then, bring your plans in line with the new information and insights you uncover. Your goal in each round will be to answer the questions in the Quick Use Preparedness Guide at the end of the chapter.

13.2.1 Who Should Be Responsible for Monitoring?

As with any management information system (MIS), the monitoring methodology for crisis preparedness should be consistent across the company. This way, critical incidents that occur can be defined clearly, so that each location is reporting with the same criteria. Methods for compiling crisis management threats and corresponding controls should be provided in a uniform format.

The prudent company assigns an individual at the senior level with oversight for maintaining the currency of its plan. Of course, he or she may delegate the details. But if the initiative for fresh risk analyses or preparedness exercises comes from senior management, you can expect these efforts to be taken seriously at every other level.

13.2.2 Process Guardian

Someone needs to own the monitoring process. Assign a person or department to be responsible for keeping the internal crisis management organization up-to-date. The responsibility of the process guardian is to ensure that nothing related to the crisis management program falls between the cracks. Just like any other management system, your crisis program will need ongoing attention and someone who is assigned the responsibility to ensure it remains up-to-date. The assignment of a process guardian ensures that "the buck stops" with one individual. When crisis preparedness is not an assigned responsibility on someone's job description, it can easily be ignored. Assign someone to stay on top of the program and hold that person accountable as a part of his or her overall job function and performance evaluations.

Some of the items for the process guardian to monitor could include:

▶ Recurrent training to ensure it is conducted on time.

▶ New team members trained and oriented to the crisis management process.

▶ Phone numbers and other contact information regularly updated.

▶ Plan reviews conducted by the appropriate individuals within the organization.

▶ Compilation of applicable crises and near misses within and related to the organization.

▶ Exercises conducted at defined intervals on various foreseeable risks.

▶ External vendors and their capabilities to supply crisis-related goods and services.

▶ Coordination with internal auditors and corporate strategic planning to identify new risks.

▶ Brainstorming meeting at least annually to identify risks previously unidentified.

13.3 What to Monitor?

Identify key elements for vigilance relating to crisis-related risks of the organization that pertain to your company.

For example, if workplace violence is a concern, it would be helpful to know the number of threats that emerge within the organization and the apparent motives for those threats. When various levels of workplace violence actually occur, the motive again would be helpful to know. By scrutinizing and compiling this information, new controls can be established to mitigate the likelihood of violent occurrences.

Possible motives for threats of workplace violence could be:

▶ Illegal drug-related. (Is there a subculture of methamphetamine abuse within the organization?)

▶ Alcohol-related. (Does your policy on alcohol or benefits coverage have any influence?)

▶ Gang-related. (Are your hiring policies or work locations fostering this problem?)

▶ Domestic violence-related. (Should you implement a corporate domestic violence program?)

▶ Toxic supervisor-related. (Is there a need for training supervisors on managing people?)

▶ Union-related. (Would an alternative dispute resolution program help?)

▶ Employee on employee. (Would hostility management and conflict resolution training help?)

▶ Crime-related. (Is there a need to revisit corporate security measures?)

▶ Ex-employee-related. (Do you need to alter your layoff and termination process when hostility and violence are a concern?)

> **As a general rule, if the desired outcome cannot be objectively counted or timed, then the definition of successful completion will be vague and hard to measure.**

13.4 Desired Outcomes

Your organization can benchmark desired crisis-related outcomes. As a general rule, if the desired outcome cannot be objectively counted or timed, then the definition of successful completion will be vague and hard to measure.

Let's say you set a goal to have appointed family representatives make personal contact with each family of hospitalized or fatally injured employees within four hours after a casualty occurs. You can then measure the actual results.

To get an idea of what else you can measure, let's go back to some of the concepts in this book that denote "good crisis response" and give some hypothetical examples:

- Immediate and decisive actions to address the urgent, crisis-related issues and gain control of the situation:
  - ❑ You can measure how long it takes for the crisis action team (CAT) to assemble in the crisis command center (CCC), for example.
  - ❑ How quickly are notifications completed to identified external stakeholders?
  - ❑ Following initial notification, how long did it take the teams to implement their first response actions?
- Prompt identification of the problems at hand and of the potential for escalation:
  - ❑ How quickly was the compiled list of critical issues provided to senior management in the desired format?
- Willingness to assume responsibility, when appropriate, and to "solve" the problems:
  - ❑ How quickly did the appropriate crisis team come up with a solution to the immediate problem and convey it to defined audiences, such as senior management, employees, customers, impacted stakeholders, or the media?
- Identification and investigation of root causes:
  - ❑ How soon was an investigative team dispatched to identify the cause of the incident?
  - ❑ How quickly were initial communications conveyed to defined audiences regarding the investigation of the root cause?
- An effective crisis communications plan that includes all identified stakeholder groups:
  - ❑ When did the first notifications or organized communications go out to each stakeholder group in accord with established notification goals? For example, to:
    - ❖ Affected employees.
    - ❖ Appropriate government regulators.
    - ❖ Media.

- ❖ Insurance company.
- ❖ Others.

❑ How soon was a hotline established and operational to give and receive communications?

▶ Demonstration of compassion and caring in words and actions:

❑ How soon was contact with family members of casualties attempted or made by a trained family representative?

❑ Was every appropriate communication to various audiences begun with a statement of heartfelt caring and concern about those who have been affected?

▶ Accessibility of management to affected individuals and groups including families of casualties, injured and uninjured employees, and the media:

❑ Did a senior manager make personal contact with the families of serious casualties within the first 48 hours following the incident?

❑ How soon did senior management communicate visibly with impacted groups and the media, as appropriate?

▶ Ongoing steps to make needed short- and long-term changes:

❑ Did the crisis management team (CMT) and crisis action team (CAT) take time-outs at least every two hours to identify any unconsidered or uncoordinated issues that needed to be addressed?

❑ Was a debriefing conducted for lessons-learned within one week of disengagement?

❑ How many changes were identified and appropriately reported?

▶ Little or no evidence of lingering outrage or damaged reputation, business disruption, financial impact, or harm to individuals:

❑ There is no adverse feedback coming to management through the family representatives, surveys, from crisis consultants, or occurrences of negative content reported by the media in the last 48 hours.

❑ Crisis counselors that provided individual or group services for traumatized employees report no indications of lingering outrage.

▶ Stability of sales, stock prices, and other financial indicators:

❏ Maintenance or return of pre-crisis sales levels within three months of the crisis incident?

❏ Stock price remains stable or returns to pre-crisis levels within three months as compared to the overall market?

Again, to monitor the effectiveness of your crisis management plan adequately, you will need to define actions and outcomes that can be counted or timed. Many of the benchmarked outcomes would require a real crisis, e.g., impact on stock price. Others can be measured as an outcome of your exercise program. For example, the benchmark may be for the appropriate crisis team members (and their backups) to meet in the crisis command center (CCC) or on a conference phone line within thirty minutes of notification.

> **Contacting needed persons in the aftermath of a critical incident can be a crisis in itself. It can be especially difficult to contact the spouses of casualties.**

13.5 Taking Internal Inventory

Staying prepared means staying current with changes in your organization. Some relevant changes will be obvious – the opening of a new assembly plant in Monterrey, Mexico where cartel violence and kidnappings are prevalent, perhaps, or the acquisition of another company. Other changes are more subtle, but can still have a big effect. For example, if Greenpeace International targets one of your industry competitors for alleged damage to the environment, this could be worthy of monitoring and preparing appropriately should your organization be next in line.

Contacting needed persons in the aftermath of a critical incident can be a crisis in itself. It can be especially difficult to contact the spouses of casualties. "Phone numbers are one of the hardest things to keep up-to-date," reports a crisis management team (CMT) leader at a major international company that had extreme difficultly accounting for people following the 2011 earthquake, tsunami, and nuclear plant meltdown in Japan. "And in a crunch, you certainly don't want to get sidetracked just because the person you need to reach has a new phone number. We now periodically send out a questionnaire to the people responsible for preparedness at the different levels of the company, with a list of the numbers and other contact information we need verified."

Indeed, the changes in personnel inevitably taking place in a large organization can have profound implications for preparedness. Some examples of personnel considerations that might be part of your periodic monitoring process include:

▌ New company leadership:

❑ Have new individuals in top management been briefed by an identified crisis team member regarding the crisis preparedness plans of the company?

❑ Has each leader been briefed and trained on their specific roles relating to crisis response?

❑ Are new members of the board of directors briefed on emerging new risks to the organization?

▌ Regarding new hires:

❑ Are appropriate preparedness policies and procedures presented to every new employee in orientation meetings?

❑ Has every new employee and manager completed the company's online course and successfully passed the test questions within two weeks of hire regarding what will be expected of them in an emergency?

▌ Promotions and job changes:

❑ Have individuals who had specific roles to play in your crisis response plans been moved to other jobs or given new responsibilities that could prevent them from participating?

❑ Have their roles been reassigned to other people who are fully briefed and trained in what to do in a crisis?

Bottom line: The assigned process guardian within your organization will take responsibility for ensuring that your plan, teams, resources (internal and external), training, exercising, lists, and all other vital components of crisis preparedness are monitored and up-to-date. Just like any other management system, these need to be part of someone's job description, and the resources and authority to make them happen provided. Without this, your preparedness will become anemic over time. It is a false sense of security to develop a manual of checklists or to provide training to a selected team and expect that you are crisis prepared forevermore.

13.5.1 Scrutinizing Your Various Crisis Teams

Every time you monitor your overall preparedness, you should also scrutinize your crisis teams.

Examine each group's cohesion. How well has each team functioned during exercises? How good is each team's leadership? Are there political or personality issues complicating the success capabilities of your various crisis teams? A leader who is too autocratic on the one hand, or too retiring on the other, might have to be replaced. Some companies rotate crisis team leaders on a regular basis to ensure fresh approaches and to establish strong bench strength.

However you address it, there is no room on your teams for halfhearted, sabotaging, or incompetent players.

13.5.2 Taking External Inventory

Your organization doesn't exist in a vacuum. When analyzing your current risks, you must consider not only the changes in your own operations but also changing conditions in the world. And similarly, you would do yourselves a disservice to try to keep your preparedness up-to-date without paying attention to what other organizations are doing to avoid and control crisis situations.

You and your process guardian should continually stay abreast of developments in your industry. How are other companies assessing the risks they face? How are they preparing to cope with those eventualities? Look to industry associations for information on new approaches to preparedness. Other organizations will generally be forthcoming about their preparedness plans. They realize, as should you, that a black eye for any member of your industry can be a black eye for the industry as a whole.

Similarly, you should maintain open communication with the governmental regulatory agencies that are charged with responding to crises, such as the Federal Emergency Management Administration (FEMA), and with local response organizations like fire and police departments and rescue squads, in every place where you maintain operations. Get to know individuals in these organizations. If your company doesn't have a government liaison person or team within your ranks, it might be good to identify a manager to make contact or to identify connected lobbyists or consultants who can establish relationships with government officials and other involved public sector agencies on your behalf.

13.5.3 Ongoing Exercises and Debriefings

It is an important challenge to keep exercises fresh each time, and keep the players engaged. After all, there are a limited number of crisis scenarios you can realistically expect to unfold for your organization. But exercises can be designed to emphasize different aspects of these scenarios. In one exercise you might put emphasis on the first four hours of a response. Focus could also include the speedy analysis of information, while other exercises might focus on opportunities to communicate with the investment community or employees.

It's also important to train for the work that takes place after the immediate response. For example, how do you talk with your customers and employees about any destructive inaccuracies that find their way into the press? What do you do if the community uproar over health and safety does not abate? Blame toward the company can last a long time, and it is wise to incorporate the concept of blame into crisis exercise scenarios.

It's good to vary the timeframe. Start a crisis exercise with the declaration that the physical destruction has been contained, for instance, or stipulate that the pivotal event took place two days earlier. Too often, companies exercise only the early emergency response and first two to 24 hours of a crisis. A lot can happen after 24 hours, and your crisis exercise program should address the medium- and long-term issues that will occur.

> **Just as it may have been difficult to get moving on preparedness in the first place, there is a natural tendency to feel a false sense of security once a plan is in place and not to re-evaluate your crisis response capabilities.**

13.6 De-escalation

We discussed the de-escalation process in Chapter 3, and it's revisited here as it relates to the re-evaluation process. In a real crisis, the end of the crisis management process tends to have a jagged edge. Team members can easily disband and "not have time" to debrief crisis actions for lessons-learned. Also, team members often do not want to dwell on the experience for emotional reasons.

▶ Make it an ironclad policy, with senior management support, that the team will debrief within a defined time period after crisis response, and that everyone involved in the crisis response must attend.

▶ It may be best to employ the services of an outside consultant to orchestrate this valuable process, especially if you detect a need for expert input about the functioning of the teams during the exercise or crisis response.

▶ If you had an external observer take notes regarding strengths and areas of improvement during a given exercise, or involved in helping with crisis response, don't forget to include this consultant or appropriate others from the outside in your debriefings.

▶ Update your crisis response manual and procedures to incorporate the lessons-learned – and to make sure the updates are distributed to everyone who needs them. If it fits your culture and the preference of your attorney, it may be wise to assign someone to generate a report that can be used as a training tool.

Just as it may have been difficult to get moving on preparedness in the first place, there is a natural tendency to feel a false sense of security once a plan is in place and not to re-evaluate your crisis response capabilities. Be a crisis champion to get your people over this illusion. There is no room for complacency or denial. The health and prosperity of your company – and the lives and livelihoods of many – are at stake. The job, life, or reputation you save may be your own or those of people you represent.

Quick Use Preparedness Guide

Chapter 13: Re-evaluating Your Results

▶ Do you have a senior management supported plan for monitoring and re-evaluating your preparedness capabilities at regular intervals, at least annually?

▶ Is someone in your organization's leadership in charge of ongoing monitoring and scrutiny of your crisis management program? Are objectives countable and in a timetable?

▶ Has an individual or department been assigned the function of process guardian with the full responsibility of keeping the internal crisis management organization up-to-date?

▶ Is the process guardian role defined as a part of that individual's job function and performance evaluation?

▶ Have you reapplied the concepts of preparedness to:

❑ Analyze foreseeable risks:

❖ Are the risks you initially considered still threats? Escalated or diminished?

❖ What has changed in your operations, situation, or locations that might expose your organization to new risks?

❖ What has changed in the larger environments that could lead to new risks?

❑ Evaluate current preparedness and controls:

❖ If you have experienced recent incidents (or exercises) that required you to go into crisis response mode, how well were you prepared?

❖ How closely did your policies and procedures match your needs in the real or simulated situation?

❖ How did your various crisis teams function under the pressure of real and simulated events?

❖ Have changes in personnel created gaps in your preparedness or various crisis teams?

❖ Have new employees and managers been oriented as to what will be expected of them during crises?

▶ Identify new controls and refinements:

❑ Based on the answers to the above questions, what revisions and additions should you make to your preparedness plans and capabilities?

▶ Organize your preparedness:

❑ What is the process for incorporating new policies and people into your plans?

▶ Utilize the plan:

❑ How can you utilize your plan to keep it a familiar, living document within your crisis management organization?

❑ What is the best way to test and refine the revisions?

❑ What combination of training and exercises should you use for teams and individuals?

▶ Have you made an internal inventory of your organization to pinpoint changes in:

❑ Personnel?

❑ Emergency contact information?

❑ Places where you operate?

❑ Activities you are engaged in?

❑ New risks?

▶ Have you scrutinized your crisis teams for:

- ❏ Strengths, weaknesses, gaps, insufficient support, inadequate members, strong backup members for each primary team member, or other issues needed for continuous vitality?

- ❏ Efficient operation?

- ❏ Effective leadership?

- ❏ Appropriate assignments?

- ❏ Thorough training?

▶ Have you kept abreast of developments in preparedness on the part of others in your industry and emergency response agencies?

▶ Is it an ironclad, senior management supported policy that your crisis teams will debrief for lessons-learned after every exercise and crisis response?

▶ Have you updated your manuals, team checklists, policies, guiding principles, procedures, resources, and other controls based on your crisis preparedness re-evaluation?

Chapter 13 – Questions for Further Thought and Discussion

1. In your opinion, what are the five most important items to monitor to ensure that your organization remains prepared for emerging risks?

2. How would you define those identified five items in a manner that can be counted or timed?

3. The process guardian is an internal resource who is assigned responsibility for ensuring the organization's crisis preparedness is up-to-date and valid. What are some external resources that could help the process guardian fulfill his or her duties?

4. Once the crisis management system has been fully implemented and tested, what are the roles of the crisis planning committee and process guardian during the re-evaluation process?

5. What are common barriers to expect relating to maintaining the organization's ongoing crisis management capabilities? What are your recommendations on how to overcome those identified barriers?

14

A Look Into the Future

The time to start thinking about crisis management is *not* after a crisis occurs. Often, as a part of my workplace threat-of-violence management services, I am asked to make a prediction of an individual's workplace violence potential. That's a daunting request, but for manmade crises, we know that one of the best predictors of future behavior is past behavior. Likewise, past incidents like natural disasters can help us actuarially predict future crisis situations. This same concept of "looking forward by looking back" applies in general to the world of corporate crises.

This chapter will help you to:

➢ *Understand the contextual changes and risks that can lead to tomorrow's crisis.*

➢ *Meet new expectations of preparedness.*

➢ *Face an uncertain future with effectiveness.*

14.1 Integration

The single greatest "ground swell" in the present crisis management arena is the concept of integration. This is huge, with several large-scale initiatives occurring simultaneously.

In the past, the crisis management issue *du jour* related to foreseeability. Some organizations were successful for a while in claiming that they were unprepared because the crises they endured were "unforeseeable." This reputational and liability defense crumbled following the 9/11 terrorism when commercial jets were transposed into missiles for terroristic purposes. We are now in an era where it is hard to imagine nearly any critical incident that is not foreseeable, even exploding meteors falling to earth from outer space. On February 14, 2013 (Valentine's Day), a meteor the width of a 5-story building exploded over Chelyabinsk, Russia. Twelve miles above the ground, it exploded with a force that was 70 times stronger than a nuclear bomb and created a flash of light that was brighter than the sun. Luckily, the impact of this "Cupid Meteor" was not catastrophic, but the next meteor may not be quite so loving.

Today, the trend is moving quickly beyond foreseeability issues toward an integrated approach to risk assessment, preparedness, response, and recovery. Responsibility for harm to people, communities, and organizations that can be traced back to a narrow "silo approach" will be viewed as negligent by stakeholders.

Integrated initiatives are rapidly becoming "mainstream" within the business community and public sectors. Several developing levels of integration are occurring simultaneously that give us a clear picture of how integration is becoming the standard of the crisis management future.

14.1.1 Enterprise Risk Management

In order to coordinate the various crisis management silos, an "umbrella" or overarching management function is necessary. The disciplines of crisis management, business continuity, emergency response, and disaster recovery are subsets of the overall risk function of an organization. Thus, it makes sense that the responsibilities of risk management are broadening and enterprise risk managers are increasingly assigned the responsibility of coordinating the various crisis-related silos.

Enterprise risk managers are finding a seat at the C-suite and strategic planning tables. As organizations plan strategic initiatives, associated risks are wisely being considered. No longer is risk management only about managing risks through traditional mitigation, acceptance, and avoidance methods. Enterprise risk management (ERM) is included in the facilitation of achieving the upside goals and objectives of the organization. Every strategic initiative can involve new and potentially unanticipated risks. It is the job of the chief risk officer (CRO) or chief risk management officer (CRMO) to help senior management and board members identify and mitigate potential risks of the organization and its strategic plan. In some organizations, the "umbrella" may report up through another channel than ERM, but the integration approach is nonetheless the same.

The overall crisis management rubric needs to be integrated with established controls to help identify and effectively manage unwanted outcomes of the organization. Business continuity, disaster recovery, disaster response, emergency response, crisis communications, the human side of crisis, and strategic crisis management are examples of specific functions that are increasingly being integrated under ERM. By having these various disciplines under a single CRO or other senior manager, the opportunity to integrate and coordinate these important crisis-related responsibilities is magnified.

Increasingly, the various crisis management functions listed above will likely report into the CRO of large organizations.

14.1.2 Software and Apps

When crisis situations are considered in the overarching preparedness and response arenas, the coordination and integration challenges can be massive. For example, the confounding variables of stress, rapid velocity, inadequate information, high consequences, and the hyper-attention of impacted stakeholders collectively create an environment that can easily turn to chaos.

Software and other technology applications are rapidly developing as proprietary and publicly available tools for compiling and accessing needed crisis planning and response information. With handheld, wireless, and mobile technology methods in easy reach of most every business manager, it is easy to imagine every function of future crisis management being integrated through technological advances. For those who embrace effective crisis technology methods, the process of corporate crisis management will become exponentially easier. Foreseeable risk analyses, crisis planning, training, exercising, response, and recovery in the future will all be increasingly integrated and vastly improved through technology applications.

Every organization should assign an appropriate manager, possibly the process guardian (as defined in Chapter 13), to continually investigate the newest technologies within the overarching crisis management arenas.

14.1.3 Emergency Communications Systems

With communications being foundational to successful crisis response, the advent of emergency communications systems has proliferated into organizations of all types. Starting as a capability through simultaneous phone, text, e-mail, and other one-way mass notification, these systems broadened to include two-way communications. The flexibility of these systems allows subsets of any population to be included in selected outgoing and incoming communications on an immediate basis. For example, crisis management team (CMT) members may be contacted simultaneously without including all employees or other managers of an organization.

A notable failure of crisis communications occurred with the 2007 mass shootings at Virginia Tech. Dr. Charles Steger, president of the university, claimed he had no way to warn students of the threat related to the initial double campus homicide. Following the ultimate shooting deaths of 33 people, Virginia Tech established an emergency communications system that allows all students to be notified simultaneously on an immediate basis in the wake of a critical incident. These systems are now a staple in most prepared organizations.

In past years of crisis management, the "golden hour" was considered the acceptable standard for notification and activation of the various crisis teams, with the exception of emergency response that was expected to be more immediate. With the availability of emergency communications systems and ability for crisis teams to bridge into immediate conference calls, the golden hour expectation has changed drastically. The future of crisis notification and activation is transforming into an expectation of immediate response.

With the universal activation of social media communications immediately following crisis situations, any organization that is "late to the table" will run the risk of losing control of their crisis. The ability to notify and muster the team, and brief everyone with immediacy, is a vital crisis management function.

The future of crisis management will have little tolerance for teams that are "late to the dance." Emergency communications systems and future iterations of this technology will be a mainstream crisis management function that well-prepared companies are already using.

> **With some historic false starts, there is a growing trend for public entities and private companies to work together synergistically to prevent, prepare for, and respond to crises.**

14.1.4 Public/Private Partnerships

With some historic false starts, a growing trend has emerged for public entities and private companies to work synergistically to prevent, prepare for, and respond to crises. For example, following the 2010 BP Gulf oil spill, vast amounts of equipment and know-how were combined by public and private entities in order to control the spill and facilitate the cleanup process. Even at the local levels, fishermen were utilized to assist in the cleanup process through privately and publicly funded initiatives.

The response by Wal-Mart following Hurricane Katrina is another example of the post-crisis blurring of responsibilities between government and private industry. Before the government could respond, Wal-Mart provided food, water, and needed supplies in vast quantities to impacted communities. Target Corporation did the same for rescue workers in Minneapolis following the I-35W Mississippi River bridge collapse in August of 2007.

These public/private partnerships are continuing to expand in scope and effectiveness. Private initiatives are integral in emergency management and critical infrastructure protection and are increasing with the US Department of Homeland Security (DHS), Transportation Security Administration (TSA), and port authorities. Corporate physical and IT security professionals are merging efforts with the government sector to synergistically address the relentless threats (such as supply chain breaches, terrorism, cyber security, and others) that are directed toward communities, individuals, nongovernmental organizations (NGOs), public organizations, and businesses. Multiple sales efforts in the private sector are directed toward addressing security needs of individuals and organizations. For example, when TSA decided that laptop computers could remain in selected sleeved bags in order to expedite the airport security screening process, companies were quick to develop compliant bags without metal zippers and other specified features.

The Overseas Security Advisory Council (OSAC) is a very successful and continually growing relationship between corporate security professionals and the U.S. Department of State. Every year, hundreds of corporate security professionals meet in Washington, DC at the annual OSAC briefing to address worldwide security threats to private organizations and the government alike. Ongoing threat information is shared on a daily basis free of charge to all OSAC members.

Corporate crisis managers will want to investigate what public/private resources are available related to crisis preparedness and post-crisis response. Give-and-take relationships are forming and will tend to grow into the future.

14.1.5 International Organization for Standardization (ISO)

Guidelines for preparedness have emerged from various countries and disciplines with struggles for relevance. If you are interested in the single definitive resource now and going into the future, go no further than the International Organization for Standardization (ISO). Internationally-vetted, best-practice standards for services and products are established and integrated through consensus arrived at by over 161 participating countries.

Standards have been established that touch the crisis management arena, such as business continuity, information security, and risk management. Guidance is provided for those interested in developing crisis management preparedness, business continuity, emergency and disaster management, and security-related risk management.

Standards relevant to organizational resilience and crisis preparedness include ISO 22301 for business continuity management systems (BCMS). Information security management systems and compliance are addressed in ISO/IEC 27001 and ISO 27002. Managing risks that can negatively impact a company's performance is covered in ISO 3100 on risk management. Other ISO standards may apply to your organization, such as environmental, food safety, and social responsibility. Refer to the website (www.iso.org) for information on each of the established standards and newly emerging standards that may apply to your crisis preparedness efforts.

14.1.6 R³ Continuum

This concept of integration of prevention, preparedness, response, and recovery capabilities is so important, my companies decided to structure accordingly. R^3 stands for "ready, respond, recover." Crisis Management International (Atlanta) and Crisis Management Latin America (Santiago, Chile) provide preparedness for the many organizational crisis-related plans and readiness initiatives discussed herein. Crisis Care Network (Grand Rapids, Michigan) responds to over 1,000 crises per month with services from crisis management consultations, crisis behavioral health interventions, crisis communications, threats of workplace violence, and other "response" needs. Finally, Behavioral Medical Interventions (Minneapolis and Sydney, Australia) specializes in return-to-work initiatives, management processes to facilitate recovery, and assistance for physically and psychologically injured workers. Recovery strategies are provided to help individuals get off workers' compensation and disability benefits and return to normal life function. Management methods are also provided to business managers (individually and corporately) for accelerating resiliency and recovery after critical incidents.

I suggest that within the culture of your organization, you take a unified look at how the prevention, preparedness, response, and recovery functions synergistically can affect one another. The organizational crisis management industry of the future is increasingly looking at the patterns and connectivity of each and planning accordingly. Through the initiatives listed above and emerging others, crisis management is quickly moving away from the silo approach to a dynamic interplay between all functions vertically and horizontally, internally and externally, as well as individually and corporately. Crisis management of the previous decades is increasingly irrelevant. It is your responsibility to be inquisitive and a fast learner as the overarching field of crisis management is rapidly maturing.

> **Instant social media communications can negatively impact an organization's ability to effectively manage and control crises.**

14.2 Social Media

One of the most influential changes in crisis management opportunities and threats is related to social media. The many applications that allow multitudes of people to immediately share various forms of information are included within the medium of social media. Instant social media communications can negatively impact an organization's ability to effectively manage and control crises. Likewise, those organizations that embrace social media during crisis response have an opportunity to rapidly reach involved stakeholders and provide needed directives. To remain relevant, traditional television, print, and radio media are incorporating social media into their crisis coverage.

Considering the huge power and impact of the rapidly evolving social media, any organization of the future that hasn't fully embraced and participated in social media with expertise will do so at their own peril. It is suggested that every crisis preparedness function within your organization consider the impact and effective use of social media (and whatever comes next) as a critical crisis management tool.

14.3 Crisis Frequency and Severity

In general, nothing is indicating that the world is becoming a safer place. Catastrophes and serious crises are more likely now than ever.

▶ Reputational crises are more likely than ever as stakeholders are armed with blogs, cameras, and more.

▶ The world is more interconnected. Some might call it entangled. We are increasingly more dependent, yet competitive and even hostile, dealing with more different cultures, countries, political figures, and ideologies than ever before.

▶ More people live together in higher densities. Pandemics and disease are increasingly possible as we intermingle through travel and close proximities. Contagious life-threatening antibiotic-resistant infections have emerged.

▶ Business ventures with international suppliers create more supply chain risk than at any time in history. Secure borders are collapsing from immigration issues to data breaches.

▶ Methods of mass destruction are becoming more complex and sophisticated. Nuclear bomb capabilities are increasingly emerging in more countries. The risk of electromagnetic pulse attack is widespread with capabilities in many countries. Destructive data breaches and viruses can destroy systems in every walk of modern life. Electrical grids of most countries are at risk of sabotage, and pandemics can potentially wipe out multitudes of people. The threat of destructive methods coming into the hands of terroristic groups and hostile countries is increasing and can be considered a rising issue into the future. Untreatable medical infections and viruses can be just as damaging, maybe more.

Additionally, disgruntled workers and others have been committing mass murder for decades, terrorists have hijacked airliners, and misfits have slipped poison into consumer products. Carelessness has led to explosions, fires, and toxic leaks since the industrial revolution began. These threats are not going away.

Earthquakes, fires, storms, and floods are, of course, as old as the planet. However, evidence arguably shows that weather-related disasters are getting more frequent and severe. Whether it's about the impact of the alleged climate change, cyclical variations of the earth, or all these, natural disasters are increasingly costly and destructive.

It is harder to pretend that such things can't happen to our own organizations. Damaging incidents are occurring all around us. And no one is immune. I recommend that your organization regularly scan the horizon for foreseeable risks of increasing frequency and severity, especially those that are new and previously unconsidered, and then prepare accordingly.

14.4 Emerging Threats and Change

The good news is that on this day most of us will carry on in our daily lives without a serious crisis. However, the crisis landscape is changing. New threats have evolved over the past 10-15 years that had not been considered previously:

▶ Reputational crises seem to top the list. No longer do the mainstream media control what's said about your organization. Shareholders and NGOs are empowered to exert pressure like never before. Social networking increasingly shapes the reputations of organizations. Investigative news organizations have a global reach 24 hours per day. Serious reputational harm can descend upon an organization in a heartbeat. Reputation management is no longer a unilateral public relations function. It must be multidisciplinary and is rapidly becoming a specialty area of expertise in crisis management that should be prepared to address increasingly sophisticated and informed audiences.

▶ Prior to the 9/11 terrorism, commercial jets were not generally considered to be weapons of mass destruction. Terrorists continue to focus on new and creative methods to exploit commercial airlines for mass destruction.

▶ Pandemic was not on the business disruption radar screen of most organizations.

▶ Anthrax or ricin exposures were not considered in corporate crisis planning.

▶ Tsunamis were of little corporate concern before the Indonesia, Chile, and Japan incidents.

▶ Nuclear power was considered relatively safe with modern structures and methodologies until the Tokyo Electric Company had its post-earthquake meltdown.

▶ Internationally, North Korea, Iran, and others have remained a "hair-trigger" away from outright war.

▶ Global warming is arguably causing an increase in frequency and severity of windstorms, fires, floods, droughts, and other problems.

▶ Before the Boston Marathon bombing, Al Qaeda was considered a greater threat than the domesticated "lone wolf" terrorists. That's now debatable.

▶ Changing US laws are increasingly allowing concealed weapons permits. The sale of guns in the US rose dramatically with the threat of gun control following the Newtown, Connecticut elementary school shooting that killed 20 children and 6 adult staff in 2012.

▶ Pedophiles are targeting churches, scouts, elementary schools, youth sports, and universities.

▶ Companies (too big to fail, like Lehman Brothers) have gone out of business, many times due to unethical and illegal management practices.

▶ Natural resources, like water, are increasingly a cause for disputes and restricted availability.

▶ Government oversight effectiveness is waning in many areas. A 2013 fertilizer plant explosion in Texas killed 15 people and injured over 200 when the company stored 1,350 times the amount of explosive ammonium nitrate allowed by to the DHS. Border security along the Mexican/American border is leaking like a sieve. White-collar crime continues each year to be the most frequent business crisis reported in the media.

▶ Several countries presently have electromagnetic pulse (EMP) simulators and capabilities to produce damaging current and voltage surges that can damage electronic equipment.

▶ Data breaches are commonplace with huge losses of intellectual property and sensitive financial information, like the exploitation of 40 million credit and debit cards used at Target stores in 2013.

▶ Foreign drug cartels are organized throughout target countries in order to streamline their distribution channels and profitability.

14.5 New Targets Are Arising

▶ With new government protections, companies and their executives are increasingly targeted with an unprecedented rapid rise in the number of cases of whistleblowing where employees and others are alleging wrongdoing.

▶ Schools are becoming prime terrorism targets. Even in the most unlikely places schools are targeted, like the school shooting in 2011 that killed 69 children near Oslo, Norway, and injured 110.

▶ A movie theatre in Aurora, Colorado, was another soft target attacked, where James Holmes killed 12 people and injured another 70 during a late night movie in 2012.

▶ A popular nightclub on the Indonesian island of Bali was bombed, killing 202 people and injurying 240.

- The Boston Marathon bombing in 2013 was an example of a target that is hard to protect. Sporting venues with huge concentrations of people are also potential targets.

- Trust in businesses, government, science, media, religious institutions, and politicians has reached all-time lows, resulting in low reputational capital for these entities, making them targets with little "goodwill equity."

- New methods for isolating and hiding ingredients of bombs are emerging, including breast implants filled with powerful explosives. Virtually any organization or community could be targeted.

> **Relying on luck is not a good strategy for protecting core assets of the organization. If you are busy denying risks, you are busy not preparing for them. And excellent leaders of the future are leaders who are prepared.**

14.6 Preparedness Equals Power

It is human nature to avoid danger and uncomfortable thoughts about bad things that could happen, and rightly so. Nobody wants to be at risk. Denial can seem like a way to avoid danger, because it gets the danger off our minds. This is especially true of new risks or incidents that haven't happened to a given organization. But the problem with relying on denial as a strategy for responding to risk is that it isn't good management practice, unless you're lucky. Relying on luck is not a good strategy for protecting core assets of the organization. If you are busy denying risks, you are busy not preparing for them. And excellent leaders of the future are leaders who are prepared.

My companies, Crisis Management International and Crisis Care Network, have discovered firsthand the lessons-learned through our work with literally thousands of organizations in crisis. Responding to over 1,000 organizational crises per month, we see the results every day. Those that are unprepared are far slower to respond and recover effectively. In many cases, when we arrived on the scene, we found companies that had taken inappropriate actions. The responses of these unprepared companies were significantly less organized, and markedly less effective. Every step was unfamiliar to the people involved – they wanted to discuss each one, or impulsively they jumped at insufficiently considered actions, when there was so little time to spare. You can imagine the cascading impact of this lack of preparedness on their personal stress levels and ability to organize, and the lag in getting their companies back up and running.

14.7 So What Lies Ahead?

Increase in defensive strategy. Since so many companies failed or were deeply harmed due to the economic downturn starting in 2008, board directors and regulators have taken a renewed interest in managing foreseeable risks and crisis preparedness. Chief risk officers (CROs) are now included in strategic planning. Internal auditors increasingly report risks directly to the board of directors. Credit rating agencies are focusing on risk and crisis preparedness after being questioned about the validity and value of credit ratings following the 2008 financial crisis.

> **There is no rational strategy that says don't be prepared for crises that can threaten core assets.**

With the interconnected risks of the global market, a balance in strategic focus is emerging with corporate leaders. While growing the value of the organization continues to dominate, there is an increasing focus and appreciation for the defensive side of corporate strategy. Effective protection of core assets doesn't come from impromptu reactions when threatened. Instead, well-managed companies understand that purposeful crisis management systems must be in place to protect core assets like reputation, brand, key relationships, people, and ability to operate.

There is no rational strategy that says don't be prepared for crises that can threaten core assets.

14.7.1 House of Cards

At the risk of sounding like Chicken Little who claimed the sky was falling, large complex systems magnify the significance of small weaknesses. The European Union discovered this after they combined their currency into the Euro. While there may be strength in numbers, there are also unexpected weaknesses (like the economies of Greece, Spain, and Italy that faltered) that manifest when systems combine and become interdependent. In business, supply chains are expanding worldwide. Economies are increasingly entangled. Political pressures are exerted on people and organizations as the disparity of haves and have-nots increases worldwide. Somewhere at some point in time, strategic weaknesses within increasingly complex systems will cascade into serious downturns or even failure. Companies that are vigilant, that anticipate, and that maintain all-hazards preparedness will be the ones that are left standing.

14.7.2 Social Media Revisited

Being able to communicate in real time brings many advantages for people throughout society. Spontaneous mass notifications are the norm when bad things happen. The accuracy of these socially networked messages is often relatively high as people within eyeshot of the incident begin reporting with firsthand information.

On the other hand, social media can serve as a vehicle for planned chaos, as well. Flash mobs are a relatively new phenomenon whereby social media is used to signal a coordinated attack on a target. It is sometimes a store that is quickly overwhelmed and looted, after which the mob quickly dissipates.

Are flash mobs a harbinger of greater spontaneous chaos in the future? For example, there are huge numbers of people dependent on entitlement programs. What happens when a national economic meltdown means these support systems falter? People will have the mechanisms in hand through social networking to take action en masse. The Arab Spring uprising of protests, riots, and civil wars was spawned by social media channels which are not restricted to the Middle East.

Under the right circumstances, violent and coercive uprisings can occur anywhere, fueled by social media and other forces. Who is to say that a distribution center or residential neighborhood couldn't be looted, a company headquarters targeted, or government facilities attacked? If people become desperate enough, sufficiently outraged, or perceive inequities that need "correction," serious and repeated uprisings are not out of the question.

The issue of most concern is how fast these flash mobs, uprisings, and coordinated attacks can surface. With the immediacy of social networking, hostile manifestations could explosively sweep a locale or nation with tremendous velocity.

Hardening of facilities that makes them difficult to penetrate could serve as a primary prevention step. Monitoring and quickly defusing any nefarious focus on your assets through social media could help as a form of secondary prevention before it manifests. And finally, anticipating the worst and establishing policies, procedures, resources, and plans for response and incident mitigation will serve as tertiary prevention that will allow the organization to contain damage once it starts to occur. Even for maturely prepared organizations, now is the time to start thinking outside the historical foreseeable risk box, anticipate new risks and vulnerabilities that will surely emerge, and prepare.

14.7.3 The Internet

The Internet is truly an amazing vehicle. Information about anything imaginable is readily at one's finger tips. As a result, the Internet and electronic connectivity bring out the best of the best. Individuals, groups, and societies can be synergistically connected to increase advancement of worthy causes. The positive outcomes of the Internet are immeasurable.

Unfortunately, not everyone has beneficial intent. The Internet is also being used to bring out the worst of the worst. Pedophiles are sharing photos. Terrorists are training recruits in the art and science of mass destruction. Harmful and reputation-damaging information that is not true and hard to erase is posted about people and organizations. Disgruntled individuals can connect and become emboldened disgruntled groups.

The Internet deserves your attention. Just as there are often warning signs before workplace violence shootings or terroristic acts, the Internet will serve as an early warning system. What's happening to others through the Internet and other connected electronic mediums? How is the information and use of the Internet changing in threatening ways? Assign someone the responsibility for making sure the Internet is scoured regularly for early warning signs of bad things brewing, attacks against your reputation, and other issues that threaten the wellbeing of your organization, locale, and industry.

Outrage about eavesdropping and monitoring of electronic communications of individuals worldwide by the US Government (and no doubt unknown numbers of others) will cause continuing privacy concerns and regulations. Privacy concerns can be at odds with the ability of governments and businesses to electronically monitor for threats. Meanwhile, data breaches and thefts of intellectual property are rapidly increasing. Within the legal parameters available, your organization will be well served to keep a close eye on the Internet and other modalities of information for threats of the future to your company, industry, and communities.

14.7.4 Leverage

Terrorists, just as well as businesspeople, understand the power of leveraging – applying limited resources to strategic points to create enormous effects. With a few airplane tickets and some box cutters, the terrorists of September 11, 2001, exacted a catastrophic price from the world. Soon after, for the price of a few microbes, a stamp, and an envelope, anthrax terrorists were able to close down American office buildings for weeks at a time.

The good news is that companies and government entities also understand how to leverage. Inexpensive protections are emerging. It's now harder for a hijacker to commandeer an airplane. Relatively inexpensive enhancements of flight deck doors, air marshals, and the readiness of passengers to fight anyone trying to overtake an airplane, make a repeat performance much more difficult. You, too, can employ the concept of leverage in your organization to get the most payoff for your preparedness efforts. For example, surveillance cameras are relatively cheap, increasingly sophisticated, provide the potential of early warnings, can serve as eyes and ears in your remote locations, and have tremendous investigative value.

Security professionals know that an effective physical and IT security strategy is to make your organization harder to breach than other organizations. The leverage point is that the protective system doesn't typically have to be perfect, just better than the capabilities of your neighbors. Perpetrators who want to cause havoc will trend toward those organizations that are easier targets. Watch the prevention and preparedness capabilities of others to stay at least one step ahead of the crowd to decrease the likelihood of being targeted.

> **We know from history that individual and group copycats will emerge and jump on the bandwagon when they see bad things happen. But corporations and the government are banding together to come up with controls to combat copycats.**

14.7.5 Copycats

We know from history that individual and group copycats will emerge and jump on the bandwagon when they see bad things happen. But corporations and the government are banding together to come up with controls to combat copycats. Tamper-proof packaging, security systems to impede data breaches, building hardening, supply chain protections, sustainability initiatives, compliance programs, and more are implemented increasingly to prohibit repeat offenses. Just as the criminally-minded copy each other, your company can benchmark and study the methods and lessons-learned from other organizations. In the less secure environment of today, you owe it to yourselves to pay attention to the best practices in prevention, preparedness, response, and recovery. Managers who ignore them open themselves up to the creativity of those who want to copy the bad deeds of psychopaths, criminals, terrorists, saboteurs, and others.

14.7.6 Terrorism

Terrorism is becoming more insidious. Methods of attack are getting bigger and smaller at the same time. On a more global scale, concerns include radiological, nuclear, biological, and chemical exposures. These methods are increasing threats as megalomaniacs in unstable countries gain access to weapons of mass destruction.

As we look at terrorist acts perpetrated upon western countries, we realize the targets are often at the center of democratic power and strength. Corporations are frequent marks. The heart of the world's financial system was attacked twice at the World Trade Center. London and Oslo have experienced bombing attacks. The US military brainpower was attacked at the Pentagon in 2001. Five coordinated sarin gas attacks on a Tokyo subway killed 13 and seriously injured 50. Institutions in the free enterprise system, corporations, schools, religious establishments, public works facilities, and government properties have been targets and will all be targets of the future.

On a smaller scale, domestic individuals (including employees, ex-employees, and other corporate stakeholders) without cohesive affiliations to terrorist groups are executing attacks that can be hard to intercept. An evolving form of terrorism is by the "lone wolf" individuals or close-knit small groups that perpetrate violence on unsuspecting targets. Often these targets are soft with easy access. There are reportedly "at least 2 million psychopaths in North America; the citizens of New York City have as many as 100,000 psychopaths among them." (Hare, R.D., p.1) This prevalence includes corporate employees/managers/executives and psychopaths living in every community. The possibility of continuing lone-wolf attacks is likely and hard to defend. However, threat assessment professionals are becoming increasingly skilled at identifying these individuals who are at increased risk of violence and corporate sabotage.

Generally, the good news is that new methods of defense and response are surfacing. The need for advanced assessment, screening, security, and monitoring will continue to make sophisticated equipment and services available to every organization. Detection equipment and intelligence agencies are becoming much more sophisticated. The shifting balance of good and evil continues on.

14.7.7 Drones

These unmanned aerial vehicles (UAVs) are increasingly coming into prominence. Drones show promise of gleaning highly useful information for law enforcement and security professionals. While there is tremendous potential for surveillance by law enforcement and other legitimate security-related functions, there are strong attempts by invasion of privacy advocates to limit their use.

The problem is that drones are readily available to individuals for purchase. Whether legitimate or black-labeled, drones will continue to become increasingly sophisticated and widely available. People with harmful intent will gain access to them, and if laws prohibit legitimate investigative and surveillance usages, the bad guys will be able to get "one up" on the organizations that are the foundation of our society and economy. In any case, progressively sophisticated controls will need to be implemented to address corporate espionage and other risks related to the proliferation of drones.

14.7.8 Progressive Severity

As soon as the bar is reset to a new height, people strive to jump over it. This holds true as well in the world of terrorism. Adam Lanza shot and killed 26 students and teachers in five minutes in Newtown, Connecticut, in 2013. While unclear about the exact motive, *The Hartford Courant* newspaper reported that Lanza wanted to kill more people than Anders Behring Breivik who killed 77 people in Norway, mostly boys and girls at a youth camp. Police also reported that several articles describing other mass shootings were also found on his computer and in his bedroom (Altimari, D., Mahony, E.H., & Lender, J., 2013).

America progressively went from the Unabomber, to the 1993 World Trade Center bombing, to the 1995 Oklahoma City bombing, to the attacks in 2001. Each was more severe than the ones before. We hate to think about the possibility of nuclear power plants being attacked and making areas the size of New York State uninhabitable. But we have evidence that terrorists have considered this. Possibly the greatest damage done by each of these attacks was the "threshold damage" – the raising of the bar for future incidents.

It is important that you in the corporate world begin to think the unthinkable. Well-prepared companies assign committees of trusted thought leaders to consider unconsidered risks to the organization. The individuals involved need to be trusted because questions are asked, such as, "If we were going to inflict serious damage on this organization in a manner that has never been used, how would you do it?" Other questions might be, "What are threats to this organization that have not been considered?" or "What new and emerging developments could take this organization to its knees?" The bad guys are thinking these things. You should be, too.

> As a corporate leader, the public and your workers expect you to protect them. Rightly or wrongly, your response will be compared to that of other entities that set best standards.

14.8 The Expectation of Preparedness

People everywhere have now watched the way corporate and public crises unfold. They have seen the ways in which organizations were, and were not, prepared. After the widely praised response of New York City's mayor, Rudy

Giuliani, the public expected that the mayor of New Orleans, Ray Nagin, would be equally as effective when Hurricane Katrina descended. It didn't happen. In fact, in 2013, corruption charges were brought against Nagin for money laundering, bribery, conspiracy, and tax fraud. Not all leaders are similarly prepared from the standpoints of skills and character.

On the other hand, the city of Boston firmly established how a coordinated law enforcement response could identify and bring the 2013 marathon bombing culprits to justice quickly. The response in Boston has set the expectations of stakeholders in other major cities, who may be impacted by future incidents of similar magnitudes.

As a corporate leader, the public and your workers expect you to protect them. Rightly or wrongly, your response will be compared to that of other entities that set best standards. For the next hurricane to descend on a city or state, people will expect a Giuliani response, not a Nagin response. Legions of regulators, reporters, and plaintiff attorneys arise to "help" the public make such judgments.

As never before, employees, investors, and others associated with your organization expect you to be prepared. Blame and outrage will surface if involved stakeholders who perceive harm believe that you did not take adequate precautions to *prevent* the damaging occurrence, or if you did not *respond* in an effective manner with sufficient demonstrations of corporate caring.

14.9 Facing the Uncertain Future With Effectiveness

If you were to go to a personal coach because you felt overwhelmed, you might hear advice like this: "You're entitled to feel overwhelmed. The crises coming at you are unpredictable. The reactions of others can be contradictory and confusing. Nothing I can tell you, and nothing you can do, can make life logical, simple, certain, or completely safe. What you can do is to identify your likely risks, prepare to prevent and respond to them effectively, and then do your best if they occur. If you do those things, you won't feel so overwhelmed. You'll have a semblance of control. And, meanwhile, you can even have a good time in other parts of your daily living while knowing you're prepared for the bad things that can happen in one's lifetime."

So, I encourage you to take a deep breath, find the resolve to prepare yourself and the organization that supports you. Then go on living life to the fullest in this world that sometimes seems unexpectedly uncontrollable.

Reinhold Niebuhr's serenity prayer, used universally since 1942 by Alcoholics Anonymous and its derivative groups, seems to apply to the world of crisis preparedness: "God, grant me the serenity to accept the things I cannot change; courage to change the things I can; and the wisdom to know the difference" (The origin..., 1992).

Paradoxically, people and organizations with the greatest sense of peace are those who have openly examined their risks and prepared for them as well as they can. It's not denial or avoidance that brings comfort. It is the calm assurance that you have opened your mind long enough to examine your risks and take action to be *truly* prepared if the unexpected occurs.

Now is the time to increase your vigilance. Risks are not going away. Establish a crisis planning committee (CPC). Review your preparedness plans. Identify your new foreseeable risks and those you may not have considered previously. Address the expectations of your people, and demonstrate to them that you are prepared. Work effectively to prevent incidents from occurring if at all humanly possible.

In addition to internal resources, you will want to identify experienced crisis consultants, prepared peer organizations, and other trusted external advisors from appropriate disciplines to make sure you are appropriately prepared and able to respond effectively. Outside assistance can be very beneficial when bad things happen, whether it's from a trusted peer from another company, a consultant, or a specialist who has expertise related to your specific crisis. Experience has demonstrated that knowledgeable and trusted external resources "outside the crisis bubble" are extremely helpful to those in the center of a corporate crisis.

Identify your risks, procure resources, organize, plan, and train. Exercise your crisis management program on an ongoing basis and regularly enough that you will be prepared with continual quality improvement. Crisis management is like any other management system. Do this and you will be resilient.

If you protect even one person or organization from serious harm, then your efforts will be well worth it.

14.10 Parting Wish

Being in the crisis management business for decades, I admit that I'm a bit heedful and acutely aware of the uncertainties of life. At the end of each calendar year, I think of those unsuspecting people in our world who will experience a serious and unexpected crisis in the upcoming twelve months. Many will be blindsided and unprepared. Others who have taken precaution will thank the day they decided to prepare. If they could unwind the clock, I'm sure those who were blindsided would have taken heed.

None of us know what uncertainties the coming months will bring. With that in mind, whether you are a Bible person or not, there is great wisdom therein that applies to the world of crisis management. In the Bible, Proverbs 27:12 states, "The prudent see danger and take refuge, but the simple keep going and suffer for it."

With over two decades in the crisis business, I feel gratified that I have been able to help so many organizations and their leaders during some of the most difficult times of their lives. It's interesting that I have seen many leaders and organizations that were very well prepared, but bad things happened. I've also seen many companies that were not ready, but they were lucky.

In the many years of my companies assisting worldwide organizations with crisis prevention, preparedness, response, and recovery, I've come to a decision. I have decided that it is better to be lucky than good. Good luck is a really good thing to have. With that in mind, you can increase the likelihood that you will be lucky. Good luck can be influenced. The simple process of paying attention, being prudent, taking heed, and getting prepared will greatly increase your odds. So, I end by personally wishing you all the good luck in the world as you take mindful refuge to increase your odds.

Quick Use Preparedness Guide
Chapter 14: A Look Into the Future

▶ Have you considered new and emerging trends in the crisis management field?

❑ Integrated approach to risk assessment, preparedness, response, and recovery.

❑ Enterprise Risk Management (ERM) as a cohesive umbrella for crisis-related fields.

❑ Software and apps that facilitate preparedness and response efforts.

❑ Emergency communications systems.

❑ Public/private partnerships.

❑ International Organization for Standardization (ISO) best practice methodologies.

❑ Social media as a crisis management tool.

▶ Have you considered what lies ahead?

❑ New areas of crisis frequency and severity.

❑ Emerging threats and changes in the risk landscape.

❑ New targets and methods of those who want to wreak havoc on organizations.

❑ Large complex systems that can magnify the significance of small weaknesses.

❑ Social media that can serve as a vehicle for planned chaos.

❑ The Internet being used to bind people and ideologies for destructive purposes.

❑ Terrorists using the power of leveraging – applying limited resources to strategic points to create enormous effects.

❑ Individual and group copycat acts when they see bad things happen.

❑ Terroristic methods of attack that are getting bigger and smaller at the same time.

❑ Drones of increasing sophistication and wide availability used with harmful intent.

❑ Progressive severity of crisis impacts as nefarious individuals and groups strive to "top" previous critical incidents.

▶ Have you considered assigning a committee of trusted thought leaders to consider unconsidered risks to the organization? Questions to brainstorm could include:

❑ "If we were going to inflict serious damage on this organization in a manner that has never been used, how could we do it?"

❑ "What are threats to this organization that have not been considered?"

❑ "What new and emerging developments could take this organization to its knees?"

There are unsuspecting people and organizations out there right now who will be tomorrow's victims of life altering crises. Please be ready to help them. Your life, their lives, and the wellbeing of your organization can be enriched if you do.

The single greatest obstacle to crisis preparedness is in not getting started. It is not what you read or understand in this book that is useful. It is only what you take and use that counts. I have made an attempt herein to provide as many take-and-use guidelines as possible. Make a commitment to start or enhance your preparedness now.

God's grace and all the best to you and those you help during life's most difficult times.

Chapter 14 – Questions for Further Thought and Discussion

1. What are five new or unconsidered crises that should be on your radar screen for preparedness?

2. What public/private partnerships should be established that would improve your ability to respond to crises and help the communities where you conduct business?

3. Review ISO standards as a template to assess your preparedness. What areas of weakness need attention?

4. In what ways can social media be used to improve your crisis response capabilities?

5. What are creative uses for an emergency communications system within your organization?

6. In considering progressive severity of terrorist acts, what are some likely targets? What incidents might be anticipated as coming next? How could these anticipated incidents affect your organization? What should you do about them?

7. What emerging trends should you consider for the crisis management organization within your company?

8. What are unconsidered risks to your corporation that have not been adequately identified or addressed?

9. What can you anticipate as you look to the future that would merit preparedness action?

10. What are the three primary take-aways from this book that should be prioritized and implemented?

References

Altimari, D., Mahony, E.H., & Lender, J. (2013, March 13). Adam Lanza researched mass murders, sources say. *The Hartford Courant.* Retrieved from: http://articles.courant.com/2013-03-13/news/hc-newtown-lanza-mass-murderers-20130313_1_adam-lanza-nancy-lanza-mary-scherlach

Hare, R. D. (1999). *Without conscience: the disturbing world of psychopaths among us.* New York: The Guildford Press, p. 1.

The origin of our serenity prayer (1992). Retrieved from: http://www.aahistory.com/prayer.html

15

Incident Checklists

The following guidelines and considerations apply to a variety of crisis incidents that could affect your organization. These checklists are designed to supplement the response guidelines provided in the first half of this book. They will supplement your all-hazards planning that will systematize the process of crisis response with consistent protocol, policies, and procedures.

I recommend that you and your crisis planning committee or crisis management team review these guidelines in detail. These checklists should be customized to fit your corporate culture and needs.

This chapter will help you to:

➢ *Respond more effectively when one of the following crisis incidents occurs.*

➢ *Consider immediate actions for specified crises.*

➢ *Supplement your crisis plan to fit your corporate culture and needs.*

To begin, these guidelines assume that emergency responders have already been contacted and that the appropriate alarm has sounded. Items are not listed in any particular order – not chronological, not priority. They are simply lists of things to remember.

15.1 Accidental Deaths

15.1.1 Immediate Action Steps

▶ Have onlookers move away from the area where a deceased person is located.

▶ Ensure that no one else has been injured.

▶ Notify immediate family members once positive identification is established.

▶ Assign family representatives (not the death notifier) to make contact with and assist each family of deceased employees.

▶ Assume all blood and body fluids are infectious.

▶ Do not remove or move the body unless absolutely necessary.

▶ Cover the body to shield it from onlookers.

▶ Keep people away from any areas that may be dangerous.

▶ Get names, addresses, and phone numbers of witnesses.

▶ Do not remove or alter any evidence that could affect the investigation.

▶ Do not ask your own employees to clean up any gruesome areas. Hire an outside janitorial service for this distressing job.

▶ Assure that every object subjected to body fluids is doused with a solution of 1 part bleach to 10 parts water.

15.1.2 Unique Considerations

▶ Determine if the workplace or work area will be closed down following the incident.

▶ Arrange for employees who witnessed the incident or its aftermath to receive professional crisis counseling assistance.

▶ If outsiders, like customers, contractors, etc., are among the dead, determine whether or not to assign family representatives. Coordinate with contractor's employer.

▶ If the fatal accident occurred in the US, Occupational Safety and Health Administration (OSHA) will investigate. Prepare employees to cooperate with the investigation fully. In other countries, be prepared to cooperate with investigations by occupational health and safety authorities.

▶ If a crime is suspected, protect the site for law enforcement investigation, and ask employees not to talk about the incident until law enforcement has interviewed each witness.

▶ Be aware of any persons who appear to be blamed or scapegoated, since they can be severely distressed or even targets of hostility.

▶ Expect questions about safety and fears of recurrence by impacted stakeholders.

▶ Funeral attendance policy and procedures will need to be communicated.

15.2 Aircraft Crash

15.2.1 Immediate Action Steps

▶ If a business jet, verify that it is your jet through positive identification on the tail of the plane.

▶ Obtain the names of the passengers on the manifest.

▶ Verify fatalities vs. injuries.

▶ Notify immediate family members once identities are verified.

▶ Confirm the exact location of wreckage.

▶ Locate hospitals to which victims were sent.

▶ Collect ongoing updates on the injured requiring hospital treatment.

▶ Establish a place where family members can congregate at the crash site, company facilities, or other appropriate location.

15.2.2 Unique Considerations

▶ Send family representatives to families of casualties.

▶ Expect that family members will want to go to the crash site; orchestrate their transportation and travel accommodations.

▶ Consider having family representatives accompany family members en route to the site or meet them there.

▶ Consider possible criminal activity or sabotage.

- ▶ Anticipate the involvement of National Transportation Safety Board (NTSB) and Federal Aviation Administration (FAA) in the investigation.

- ▶ Anticipate Environmental Protection Agency (EPA) involvement if there is a spill of jet fuel.

- ▶ If a serious crash involves senior executives, anticipate a reaction from the investment community.

- ▶ Ensure that an adequate community outreach program is initiated if locals on the ground were affected.

15.3 Chemical/Toxic Exposure

15.3.1 Immediate Action Steps

- ▶ Evaluate the risk of further exposure and consider evacuation.

- ▶ If the worksite is to be evacuated, the evacuation route should be upwind.

- ▶ Identify the source of the fumes and safely stop them if you can.

- ▶ Secure the exposed area. Tape windows and doors to contain fumes, if necessary.

- ▶ Shut off all heating, cooling, and ventilation systems.

- ▶ Identify all persons who need to be decontaminated and start the process as soon as possible with the best method available. Determine which hospitals have decontamination capabilities.

- ▶ Block off and guard the spill area.

- ▶ Ventilate or seal off the area, as appropriate.

- ▶ Call in a specialist in chemical spills, as needed.

- ▶ If in a cafeteria, determine if any food may have been contaminated.

- ▶ Assign an individual(s) to keep people out of the exposed area. If necessary, have someone guard the driveways, facilities, and grounds to prevent people from entering the property.

- ▶ Account for all employees. Get names of affected visitors.

- ▶ Contact neighboring businesses and community representatives if exposure risk exists.

- ▶ Arrange expert cleanup and repair, as needed.

15.3.2 Unique Considerations

▶ Seek specialty medical advice and treatment.

▶ Provide medical education/Q&A for staff, family members, and other affected audiences regarding the effects of the specific exposure.

▶ Prepare for lingering concerns over the potential long-term effects of exposure.

▶ Anticipate the involvement of the appropriate federal and local agencies: US EPA, OSHA, and other regulators. Determine their needs and probable actions.

▶ If the material was delivered, protect all suspicious packages, outside wrappings, stamps, tape, and mailing labels.

▶ If the material was delivered, log the date and time of delivery along with the delivery personnel's name and company.

▶ Notify any delivery services whose personnel could also have been exposed.

▶ The affected area should remain roped or taped off until evaluated thoroughly and any necessary decontamination completed.

▶ Your building may be closed off for several days or weeks. Activate your business continuity plan (BCP) and make plans to continue business in an alternate location.

15.4 Civil Unrest

15.4.1 Immediate Action Steps

▶ Coordinate corporate response with the appropriate embassies, security advisors, law enforcement, and government agencies.

▶ Account for all employees and their family members.

▶ Many times it is better for employees and families to stay where they are behind closed doors.

▶ If evacuation is chosen:

    ❑ Premises only or leave the country?

    ❑ Employees should evacuate to what location(s)?

▶ Organize and facilitate ongoing communications with employees and family members.

▶ Establish a redundant communications source for backup, in case the primary communications source is disabled or monitored.

▶ Coordinate employee and family needs during emergency evacuation.

▶ Stay in close contact with embassies, law enforcement, and government agencies for approval of any statements to the public.

▶ Implement board-up procedures, and secure all facility openings if building is evacuated.

15.4.2 Unique Considerations

▶ Remind evacuees to take needed medications with them in quantities that exceed expected need.

▶ Identify all prescription medication needs of employees and family members and make arrangements to get medications to them if they evacuate without sufficient quantates.

▶ Determine the safety hazards that may occur for communities and returning employees if a worksite is left unmanned over time.

▶ Identify expatriates' homeland family members and establish ongoing communications to and from them.

▶ Assign family representatives to homeland family members, as appropriate.

▶ Anticipate reentry issues and needs for returning expatriates.

▶ If safety was threatened, crisis counseling should be provided after safety and physical wellbeing are established.

15.5 Earthquake

15.5.1 Immediate Action Steps

▶ Assess any significant injuries or damage to the facilities.

▶ Check for structural damage, gas leaks, and electrical hazards. If needed, shut off the gas or electrical supply sources.

▶ If evacuation becomes necessary, exit the building away from windows, shelves, and heavy objects. Expect aftershocks.

▶ Move employees to pre-designated areas well away from the building, exterior windows, and vulnerable objects, e.g., lighting poles in parking lots.

▶ Account for everyone.

▶ Identify and prioritize those in need of medical attention.

▶ Do not move any seriously injured individual unless doing so is absolutely necessary.

▶ Clear driveways of debris to allow emergency vehicles in and out.

▶ Anticipate that emergency medical services may be overwhelmed and streets impassable. If appropriate, consider taking injured persons to the hospital.

▶ Verify that hospitals are in operation. Determine alternative locations for medical care, if hospitals and other treatment facilities are full or not in operation.

▶ Employees will be extremely concerned about their loved ones in the affected area. Assist employees with communications as soon as possible, via telephone, cell phone, text messaging, transportation, etc.

▶ Enlist contractors and suppliers to assist with repairs to the work facility. Contract with them immediately, before they become overwhelmed with other requests.

▶ Quickly secure providers to assist employees with home repairs, motel rooms, rental cars, and other commodities that may be in high demand.

15.5.2 Unique Considerations

▶ Provide security measures to prevent looting.

▶ Do not let anyone go back into the building unless you have confirmed that its structure is sound.

▶ Go to the homes of any employees who are unaccounted for to assess their disposition and needs.

▶ Organize assistance for employee disaster victims whose homes were destroyed, with food, shelter, cash, day care, transportation, etc.

▶ Anticipate that some employees may need shelter if either they cannot reach their homes or their homes were destroyed. Reserve accommodations quickly.

▶ Anticipate requests for leave (time off from work) to address home repairs and meet insurance adjusters, as well as an increase in stress-related absences.

▶ Ensure ongoing communications to and from employees, especially those who have to protect and repair their property.

▶ Organize less-affected employees to assist in humanitarian efforts.

▶ Provide armed guards if cash is provided to employees or if supplies provided to employees are in high demand locally.

▶ Retrieve and secure important records.

▶ Implement the company's business continuity plan (BCP).

15.6 Explosion/Fire

15.6.1 Immediate Action Steps

▶ Move evacuated people away from the building and areas where there could be a secondary explosion.

▶ If a bomb is suspected, keep employees away from areas where additional bombs could be planted, e.g., vehicles, dumpsters, or street manholes.

▶ Instruct everyone to shut down the following electronic equipment, which could inadvertently trigger a bomb that uses a wireless detonator:

❑ Walkie-talkies.

❑ Cellular phones.

❑ Two-way radios.

❑ All other wireless two-way communication devices.

▶ Clear a path for emergency vehicles to enter and exit the premises.

▶ Make sure all building doors are closed and locked.

▶ Do not allow anyone to enter a burning building.

▶ Provide firefighters with a blueprint of the building.

▶ If arson or other crime is suspected, do not move any articles, and protect the incident site.

▶ Establish a receiving area for arriving family members.

▶ If the incident exposes the neighboring community, contact local officials and neighboring companies.

- Have someone locate the nearest fire hydrant prior to the arrival of firefighters.

15.6.2 Unique Considerations

- Account for and assess the status of every employee. Identify any non-employees who were in or near the explosion/fire.

- Once the fire is out:

  - ❑ Beware of electrical, water, and structural hazards.

  - ❑ Elevate valuables off the floor to reduce water damage.

- Be prepared to discuss the (real or perceived) effects of burns or toxic exposures publicly, enlisting a recognized burn unit physician and a toxic exposure specialist.

- Publicly thank fire fighters and other first responders for their assistance.

15.7 Flood

15.7.1 Immediate Action Steps

If a flood is detected in the vicinity:

- Begin sandbagging operations.

- Obtain water contamination procedures from local officials.

- If there is time, elevate valuables to a level higher than the forecasted flood level.

- Cancel all shipments, as appropriate.

- Turn off electrical power, when appropriate.

- Inform people to stay away from dangerous areas, e.g., rapid and deep currents, contaminated floodwaters, unstable structures, and electrical hazards.

- Provide security measures to prevent looting.

- Anticipate and make arrangements for employees who may need shelter if they cannot reach their homes or if homes were destroyed.

- Retrieve and secure important records.

- Put on notice or implement the company's business continuity plan (BCP).

If there is property damage as a result of the flood:

- Enter the building with caution. Snakes or other animals may have entered the building. Electrical hazards may exist. Provide protective equipment.

- Ensure that the electrical service is safe before turning on the power.

- Inspect the building to assess structural damage.

15.7.2 Unique Considerations

- Anticipate and arrange for the supplies, services, and equipment you'll need to reopen the facility.

- Provide typhoid shots for employees who come in contact with floodwaters.

- Assess the personal needs of employees and family members whose homes were seriously damaged.

- Consider organizing assistance for the employees whose homes have suffered severe damage.

- Provide security measures to prevent looting of your facilities.

- Do not let anyone go back into the building unless you have confirmed that its structure is sound.

- Go to the homes of any employees who are unaccounted for to assess their disposition and needs.

- Organize assistance such as food, shelter, cash, day care, and transportation for employee disaster victims whose homes were destroyed.

- Anticipate that some employees may need shelter if either they cannot reach their homes or their homes were destroyed. Reserve accommodations quickly.

- Anticipate requests for leave (time off from work) to address home repairs and meet insurance adjusters, as well as an increase in stress-related absences.

- Ensure ongoing communications to and from employees, especially those who have to protect and repair their property.

- Organize less-affected employees to assist in humanitarian efforts.

- Retrieve and secure important records.

15.8 Kidnap and Ransom

15.8.1 Immediate Action Steps

▶ Do your best to confirm that an actual kidnapping has occurred.

▶ Be cautious: remember the possibility of a false kidnapping notification.

▶ Notify your kidnap and ransom insurer and hostage negotiation firm and follow their lead.

▶ Begin a log of all events.

▶ Set up a kidnap response command center where communications and the situation can be managed over an expected long period of time.

▶ Establish a method to record phone calls if demand calls may come to the company.

▶ Notify kidnapped victims' families.

▶ Obtain current medical history on hostages, including prescription drug information and dates of inoculations.

▶ Obtain statements from witnesses (in conjunction with law enforcement):

❑ Location of the kidnapping.

❑ Vehicle used by kidnappers.

❑ Weapons used by kidnappers.

❑ Any other identifying information available about the kidnappers.

❑ Any ransom note or communication from the kidnappers.

❑ Any other eyewitnesses to the kidnapping.

▶ Determine if there are other potential targets for kidnapping that are accessible to kidnappers.

▶ Identify hostages from other companies, if any, and coordinate your response with their management team.

▶ Monitor ATM withdrawals from hostages' bank accounts, debit cards, personal and corporate credit cards, and the locations where activity took place, to notify authorities.

15.8.2 Unique Considerations

▶ Locate photographs of the hostages for the authorities.

▶ Provide a hair sample sealed in an airtight container for possible DNA matching (obtained from the victims' hairbrushes, if needed).

▶ Identify the specific blood types of hostages.

▶ Maintain law enforcement liaisons and embassy liaisons for two-way communications and information.

▶ Provide the full names, ages, and physical, medical, and mental health conditions of hostages to authorities and negotiators.

▶ Monitor domestic and foreign media and press reports related to the kidnapping.

▶ Protect families from media encroachments. Encourage family members not to accept media requests to discuss the situation, nor to make appeals through the media. Explain that media statements can embolden kidnappers and delay release.

▶ Assign family representatives to family members of hostages.

▶ Provide crisis counseling assistance for family members who will need assistance over the long haul.

▶ Obtain information on kidnap and ransom groups who are active in the area and provide available information to family members.

▶ Explain to family members how negotiations work and why confidentiality by those involved in the release is vital.

▶ Consider this may be an "express kidnapping" (usually released within 24 hours) during which the hostages' bank accounts are raided through ATM withdrawals and other valuables stolen.

▶ Encourage families not to take any unilateral actions or make payments without coordination with negotiators and involved law enforcement.

▶ Prepare for the psychological and reentry (to work and family) needs of hostages upon release.

▶ Plan the actions you will need to take in the event that the hostages are killed.

15.9 Shooting

15.9.1 Immediate Action Steps

▶ If the shooter is suspected to be hiding in the building, give law enforcement blueprints of the building and describe the layout.

▶ Assess if the incident presents a continuing danger and take appropriate safety precautions.

▶ Obtain the identity and physical description of the shooter, including any distinguishing characteristics.

▶ Have someone remain on the line with a 911 emergency operator if the situation is ongoing.

▶ Assign sufficient personnel to keep any arriving individuals clearly away from the scene and out of harm's way.

▶ Have all employees keep their hands visible and to follow law enforcement instructions.

▶ Once confirmed, dispatch company representatives to provide or assist law enforcement with notifications to family of serious injury or death.

▶ After safety is restored, thoroughly search the property and surrounding areas for any employees who may still be in hiding, evacuated to adjacent areas, or sheltered in place.

▶ Identify the location of victims in the hospitals – they may be admitted under an alias (standard procedure for gunshot victims). Ask ambulance drivers to which hospital they are taking victims. Attempt to have a medical person (e.g., company nurse) accompany victims to the hospital in ambulances, if allowed.

15.9.2 Unique Considerations

▶ Identify witnesses for law enforcement investigation. Instruct them not to talk about the incident with others until after the law enforcement interviews with witnesses.

▶ In the immediate aftermath, ask witnesses to write down everything they saw to facilitate the interviews with law enforcement.

▶ Law enforcement officers may give early media statements. Coordinate your messages with theirs.

▶ Protect the crime scene and weapon(s) from any contamination that could obstruct law enforcement investigation.

▶ Call for external cleanup and repair services, as needed. Do not allow any onsite employees to clean up a bloody crime scene. Beware of blood-borne hazards.

▶ Arrange for security personnel to protect victims at the hospital, especially if further violence is possible (as in a gang-related shooting).

▶ Determine what to do with the desks and work areas of fatally injured employees.

Note: Pre-incident active shooter training (such as that recommended by the US Department of Homeland Security), establishment of safe rooms, evacuation routes, and other safeguards may help to minimize inappropriate reactions by employees.

15.10 Additional Crises

In addition to these immediate action steps and unique considerations, I suggest you follow the same format used above (Immediate Actions Steps and Unique Considerations) for other foreseeable risks that may apply to your organization. These might include:

▶ Reputational crisis.

▶ Ethical misconduct.

▶ Pandemic.

▶ Data breach.

▶ Electromagnetic pulse attack.

▶ Defects and product recall.

▶ Facility disruption.

▶ Environmental contamination.

▶ Class action lawsuits.

▶ Consumer activism.

▶ Discrimination.

▶ Unexpected loss of executive.

▶ Hostile takeover.

▶ Labor disputes.

- Sexual harassment.

- Whistle blowers.

- White collar crime.

- Terrorism.

- Supply chain disruption.

Checklists here should not be regarded as complete, since decisions made and actions taken will be the result of a progression of emerging issues. Therefore, it is your responsibility to determine the order of listed actions to take, what to add, and which to omit, according to your crisis planning and the fact pattern of the incident when you first become involved. Consider completing or enhancing a checklist of immediate and unique guidelines and considerations following each crisis response and each crisis exercise. This could be an outcome of each operational debriefing following team activation.

If there are additional checklists of guidelines and considerations (or additions to the checklists provided above), please send them to the author at his e-mail address listed below. Your checklists will be posted on the CMI website with proper attribution for others to utilize. Hopefully, in this manner, we can enjoin to help make the world a little safer and more predictable for those impacted by crisis.

A Final Word From the Author

Please feel free to contact me at:

bblythe@cmiatl.com

404-841-3402

Or, obtain additional information on our continuum of companies at:

www.cmiatl.com (Crisis Management International - Atlanta, Georgia, and Santiago, Chile)

www.behavioralmedical.com (Behavioral Medical Interventions – Minneapolis, Minnesota, and Sydney, Australia)

www.crisiscare.com (Crisis Care Network - Grand Rapids, Michigan)

Permission granted to use the quote from Captain Al Haynes on Flight 232 from the audio narrative *Teamwork in Crisis: The Miracle of Flight 232*, CRM Learning © 2001; Chris Nelson of Target granted permission to use the text describing Target's actions regarding Safeness; permission granted by James Kreindler (partner in the law firm Kreindler and Kreindler, who is quoted about his work in the Pan Am 103 plaintiffs' suit); Jack Cox granted permission to use the information from Liberty Mutual. Permission granted to use the study "The Impact of Catastrophes on Shareholder Value" by Rory F. Knight & Deborah J. Pretty, A Research Report Sponsored by Sedgwick Group, published by Templeton College, University of Oxford; Joy Sever, Director of Reputation Research at the Reputation Institute, granted permission to report on how crises affect companies. Dr. Vincent Covello of the Institute for Risk Communication granted permission to provide information about his studies on "caring" in crisis leadership and crisis messaging restricted to 12 words or less.

Appendix A

Addressing the Families of the Injured

It's been demonstrated time and again that comfort and support is one of the best means to speed the emotional recovery of relatives of a crisis victim. Certainly, natural support systems (to the degree they are available) are typically best. Family members and friends supporting each other, personal relationship with the God of one's faith, religious institutions, and the fellowship of others in the community can all be helpful and comforting to families during very difficult times.

Even when natural support systems are in place, this does not mean that the company has no role in providing assistance. In fact, company assistance is likely to be expected and will be missed if not provided. The organization is in a unique position to provide information about the incident itself and respond to myriad questions that surround critical incidents, such as expediting available benefits and reclaiming personal items at work. Often, companies can assist in such matters as helping extended family members who may need travel accommodations, ground transportation, and much more.

A.1 Bringing People Together

For concerned families of non-injured workers, I recommend you assign employees in the early aftermath to meet any arriving family members and bring them to a designated gathering place.

Use an alternative location for employees and family members to assemble if fires, spewing toxins, or other hazards have rendered your workplace uninhabitable. Hotels are common alternatives and provide a number of advantages, including plenty of meeting space, parking, and the availability of private rooms and communications resources.

Another choice is a community center or place of worship. The latter offers many benefits, not the least of which is the sense of solace that a house of worship brings, whatever the religion or denomination. Consider the possibility that any gathering place you identify might have to serve as a family meeting place for days, especially in a mass casualty situation, as was the case with one church following the Oklahoma City bombing and for families of 12 trapped miners following the Sago Mine explosion in West Virginia.

A.2 Beware of Intruders

In earlier chapters, I touched on the post-event arrival of family members, and outlined key points, including the need for a sentry at your entrances. One purpose is to separate out the families of fatalities. They should be greeted with proper concern and kindness and led to a separate location. The greeter should not, however, share the bad news; this would typically be done by appropriate management or team leaders.

In addition to families of fatalities, anticipate that family members of seriously injured employees may arrive at your workplace following a critical incident. Equip anyone greeting families with the names and hospital locations of injured employees. Then, be ready to identify any arriving family members of hospitalized employees and to provide immediate transportation to the hospital. If at all possible, it is best to have a company representative drive the family members to the hospital immediately following the notification. The intent is to prevent highly-distracted and frantic family members from being behind the wheel.

Another equally important reason to meet and escort all arriving family members is to keep them from the sensation-crazed press. I have no personal prejudice against the media; in fact, they have been very good to our organization. But as a crisis management consultant, I have seen too many insensitive actions justified in the name of "getting the story."

An explosion at a steel company with which we worked caught an employee in a pool of molten steel that flowed onto the floor. Until the steel had cooled, his coworkers could only watch; he died of his injuries a few days later. Families heard of the explosion and rushed to the plant, unaware of the identity of the victim.

Unfortunately, the media got there first. As each family group made its way to the plant entrance, "enterprising" reporters jumped in front of them, stuck a microphone in their faces, and asked their reactions. These poor souls had no idea if their loved one was involved. The offending television reporters used the most emotional clips of this ill-gotten "story" on the evening news. It is in the best interest of your organization and the family members, as well, to protect them from such encroachments by assigning someone to immediately make contact with family members as they converge upon the worksite.

A.2.1 "Legal" Offenders

As stricken families make their way to your facility, members of the press aren't the only ones they need to look out for. An ambulance-chasing lawyer can rival – and even exceed – the zeal of a story-seeking journalist.

Remember the Coca-Cola Enterprises bottling plant in McAllen, Texas, whose delivery truck rammed into a school bus that we discussed earlier? A migrant farm worker family arrived at the site. They had been late in learning about the crash and rushed over to the accident scene to find out if their child had been a victim. A plaintiff's attorney was lying in wait to intercept the family and promise them a ride to the hospital.

En route to the hospital, this smarmy lawyer stopped at his office where he presented the family a contract for legal services, even though his action was against state law. Their English was marginal, their understanding of the documents was vague, and their desire to see the child was overwhelming. They unwittingly signed the documents.

If the incident occurs on your site, you have the right to keep the media and other outsiders off your property. Ask law enforcement to assist you in this effort. If necessary, assign your own personnel, bring in security guards or off-duty police, or do whatever it takes to keep predators away from family members and others, whether at your site, airports, hotels, hospitals, or even quite possibly, at their own homes.

A.3 Assigning Family Representatives

Family representatives – specially trained individuals who are assigned to a victim's family – can play a critical supportive role in compassionately reaching out to families. Their job is an important and difficult one. It is best not to "assign" employees to serve as family representatives because this is delicate and sometimes stressful work that takes the right kinds of individuals to function effectively. Typically, family representatives are either volunteer employees who feel they would be good at providing the caring support needed for impacted family members, or experienced crisis mental health professionals, such as the nationwide network of my company, Crisis Care Network. A good model would be to have a trained company employee/family representative and an external experienced crisis professional serve together. In any case, anyone who serves as a family representative should be adequately trained in the dos and don'ts of their role with families. Contact should be initiated with the family as soon as appropriate, preferably within the first 24 hours of the incident. It is often best to make contact with families while they are still in a state of disbelief and bewildered, rather than waiting until the potential anger and blame stage begins. Depending on the situation, initial family representative contact may be established at the family's home (if the employee is deceased), hospital, airport, or hotel.

Two representatives, ideally a man and a woman, would be assigned to the family of every individual seriously injured or killed. The teams should be trained in advance and should be aware of relevant company policies and the scope of assistance available. It is not necessary that every offering to be provided by the company be anticipated before contact is made. Instead, the family representatives will serve as a conduit of communication between the company and the family. However, levels of authority without having to go back to the company should be established. For example, ground transportation, hotels, and emergency travel arrangements for immediate family members could be within the scope of authority of family representatives without approval from corporate.

Likewise, it is important to know the limits. When employees are killed while working, many countries have workers' compensation laws that will provide limited funeral arrangements. A common reaction of families is to believe that the company is paying for the funeral, leading them to order the most expensive provisions. It is best to brief families on the limitations of benefits provided before they commit to large sums of money and expect the company to cover it all. The company may choose to supplement benefits available, but it's best for the family representatives to know the limits and assist and advise families in decision-making accordingly.

Be sensitive to any language or cultural issues. Make sure each family's representatives speak their language, or that a skilled translator is present who will also know their customs. For example, following the Coca-Cola truck that hit a Texas school bus, killing 23 children, I personally met with multiple families of victims, accompanying company representatives. Everyone spoke a

Mexican dialect of Spanish, except for me. I assumed the role of orchestrating the conversations through briefings with company officials prior to family contacts and answering questions as they would arise during conversations. I learned quickly that it was not appropriate to gaze into the eyes of these family members during the initial greeting. Culturally, there is a belief or superstition that if one looks too long into their eyes, it is considered the "evil eye," which can cause harm to that individual or family. In this case, a show of caring and concern through extended eye contact would have been inappropriate. A quick look in the eye and gazing down was much more appropriate. Also, I learned that it was not appropriate to bring in our Cuban-American consultants from Florida to South Texas. Even though they spoke Spanish, the cultural differences would have served as a hindrance to effective rapport.

A.3.1 The Role of Family Representatives

Family representatives:

- ▶ Serve as the primary point of contact between impacted families and the company.
- ▶ Assist with emergency travel and other arrangements for remote family members.
- ▶ Help with hospital liaison and funeral arrangements, if necessary.
- ▶ Respond to any type of reasonable assistance the family may need.

They also serve as a communication resource between the family and the company. Part of their job includes communicating needs and concerns to the crisis management team (CMT) or humanitarian response team (HRT). Authorization for special requests will also be conveyed through the representatives.

The representatives' ability to act in a sensitive, caring, and effective manner will not only help relatives cope, but will improve the relationship between the family and the company. It will also decrease the likelihood that disgruntled family members, their neighbors, employees, or others will go to the media with their complaints or negative connotations. Possibly, the caring response might even serve as a reputational enhancement as word spreads through various channels about the caring response of the company.

Services provided need not be complicated to be appreciated. Following an American Airlines crash in which everyone was killed, I was involved with a family that had droves of supportive people descending upon the home. There was a large extended family, a large constituent of social and community acquaintances, and membership in a large local church. Caring people collectively brought huge volumes of food. One, much appreciated, task the family representatives fulfilled (upon request) was to make sure there were adequate plastic plates, eating utensils, and paper towels to accommodate the constant flow of food for visitors. We also washed dishes and kept the house picked-up throughout the flow of visitors.

The role of family representatives is not to feign uncomfortable compassion, have stilted sit-down meetings, or try to provide amateur counseling services. It is much better to "go with the flow" of what is needed. In one employee fatality situation, we gained rapport by singing gospel songs with the family and friends by the piano in the living room. Once we became a part of the impromptu choir, we were fully accepted into the inner sanctum of the family. Meanwhile, be sensitive to the family's need for family representative support vs. desire for privacy and some space from outside influences.

Suggest specific areas of assistance as they emerge. A perfunctory statement of "let us know how we can help" will often elicit no response from the family. It is better to remain vigilant for calming and supportive tasks of support that can be provided.

A checklist of general areas of potential assistance is good for family representatives to maintain while working with families. Some areas of general assistance might include:

- Travel arrangements for remote family members, e.g., airfare, flight arrangements, and hotel reservations.
- Meeting arriving family members at airports, train stations, etc.
- Ground transportation or a GPS system for persons unfamiliar with the area.
- Expediting benefits checks to mitigate family cash flow problems created by the incident.
- Information to and from the company or others as appropriate.
- Assistance with funeral arrangements.
- Bring needed supplies and personal items to family members at hospitals or other areas when families may congregate, e.g., nearby church used as a family assembly point.
- Arrange crisis counselors, clergy, or other appropriate external supportive services.
- Identify appropriate professional service providers, e.g., grief counselors, psychiatrists, funeral homes, and medical specialists. (**Note**: Be aware that your company may be subject to claims of negligent referral or of trying to manipulate families through referrals. Thus, if you provide such referrals, it is best to offer a

small number of options and leave the decision-making up to families. Do not provide names of plaintiff attorneys, anyone trying to convert the family to a certain religion, or anyone else with a secondary agenda. Be clear about who will pay for the services that may be recommended before making these referrals.)

▶ Practical errands, clean-up, meals, and other accommodations that will ease routine responsibilities of family members.

▶ Schedule and facilitate a meeting between company management and the family.

▶ Arrange security guards if media, attorneys, paparazzi, or others are encroaching.

▶ Bring personal items of a deceased or seriously injured employee from the worksite to the family.

▶ Arrange for the family to visit the worksite or site of the critical incident, if desired.

▶ Serve as a gatekeeper and conduit of communication between well-wishers and the family during times when they prefer seclusion or only selected visitors.

▶ Facilitate the family's attendance, if preferred, at a company-sponsored memorial service, if provided.

▶ Attendance at funerals.

▶ Taking a "shift" at the hospital where a seriously injured victim is located in order to give the family a break from protracted bedside presence.

A.3.2 A Word of Caution

Be cautious of the emotional attachments that can result. Family representatives should be trained and reminded not to identify "too closely" with a particular family or its problems. Following a commercial airline crash, a family representative asked me to help with a man whose wife, the mother of their children, had died in the crash. The woman and her husband had been the parents of a young son, the age of my daughter at the time. Watching this child begin to grieve, including writing a letter to his mom and burning it in the fireplace so she would get it in heaven, was extremely difficult for me. The youngster reminded me of my own child, and it hit me very hard. This made it difficult for me to let go emotionally when my work was done with this family. Set the expectation with the family and yourselves that the family representative assistance to be provided will be short-term, no matter how strong the emotional ties.

A.4 That Knock on the Door

Following initial death notification, it's likely that family representatives (not the same individuals who gave the notification) will meet relatives at the victims' homes. They should call in advance. If possible, do not park in or block the driveway. Upon arriving, they should identify themselves as representatives of the company, shake hands (or other culturally appropriate greeting), then ask to come in, speaking to each member of the family, including any children present. Get names ahead of time, if possible. If needed, write down names when first meeting family members and close friends to ensure you remember. It's OK to let them know you are doing this.

In such situations, it's generally a good idea to look for a dining room or kitchen chair and say that you prefer a hard chair. This keeps you from inadvertently sitting in the victim's favorite spot. It also permits you to place the chair where you want it, with access to everyone in the room.

A.4.1 Initial Conversation

Speak in a "matter of fact" yet compassionate manner. Do not try to feign empathy or display forced concern. Families don't want "fake." They want the family representative to maintain a state of calm assertiveness and listening in a controlled and caring manner. Achieve a comfort level of conversation. Although the situation is difficult, try to be at ease and natural.

The representative should express concern and intent with words like:

"I first want to express my shock and heartfelt sadness over what has happened. Again, my name is _____. I am an employee of _____ and I want to assist you and your family with any needs, concerns, or communications that would be helpful to you during this difficult time. I will serve as a source of information and communication between your family and the company."

The goal at this initial family meeting is to make "caring contact" and elicit conversation. Company representatives should talk less and listen more, using expressions like, *"What are your concerns at this time?" "What needs to be done right away?" "Do I understand clearly that you would like...?"* and *"Tell me more about that."* The role is to facilitate conversation that is focused on assessing needs and identifying areas of assistance by:

▶ Asking questions.

▶ Discussing and compiling considerations and issues to be addressed.

▶ Confirming the actions suggested would be helpful and desired by family members.

As family members speak, listen very carefully. Some family members may deluge the family representative with needs, problems, and complaints. Others may be reluctant to speak or ask for help and will need prompting with open-ended questions.

Focus *completely* on what each individual is saying as they speak. Write down pertinent items for potential assistance, repeat back what they have said, and come to agreement on what the family representative will do to assist, when appropriate. Tell family members approximately how long it will take to get an answer or action related to their needs. Be absolutely certain to follow up with family members on all promises and responsibilities on a timely basis.

A.4.2 Asking Appropriate Questions

The following questions are provided to help family assistance representatives establish and maintain a rapport with families and obtain actionable items for assistance:

Initial Assessment Questions:

- ▶ *"What are your present needs and concerns?"*
- ▶ *"What needs to be addressed first/immediately?"*
- ▶ *"What are the priorities?"*
- ▶ *"How can we best help you?"*
- ▶ *"Are there any needs that aren't being adequately addressed?"*
- ▶ *"What needs to start that isn't in place? What needs to stop that is presently happening?"*
- ▶ *"What needs to be done to address the situation(s)?"*
- ▶ *"What would a preferred outcome look like?"* (Identify near- and long-term expectations.)

New Information Questions:

- ▶ *"I'd like to hear a little bit about _____."*
- ▶ *"In your opinion, what do you think about _____?"*
- ▶ *"What is not happening that you would like to see started?"*
- ▶ *"How do you intend to approach the problem?"*
- ▶ *"Could you tell me more about the reasons for _____?"*
- ▶ *"When (How) do you envision this happening?"*
- ▶ *"In what areas do we lack information?"*
- ▶ *"How will the decision be made?"*

Confirmation Questions:

▶ *"Do I understand correctly that you want _____?"*

▶ *"Do I understand correctly that you are concerned about/dissatisfied with/satisfied with _____?"*

▶ *"The purpose of our meeting/conversation is _____. Is that your understanding?"*

▶ *"Would you like for me to _____?"*

Attitude Questions:

▶ *"How do you feel about _____?"*

▶ *"What do you think about _____?"*

▶ *"What is your opinion about _____?"*

▶ *"What do you see as the strengths and weaknesses of _____?"*

▶ *"What are your personal reasons for wanting/not wanting _____?"*

▶ *"Are there any other reasons why _____?"* (Questions like this can smoke out negative attitudes and barriers.)

▶ *"What if we _____?"*

▶ *"Would you consider _____?"*

Commitment Questions:

▶ *"Are we in agreement that _____?"*

▶ *"Do we understand that you approve of _____?"*

▶ *"Are you willing to _____?"*

▶ *"Should we set a date/time for _____?"*

▶ *"You agreed to _____, is that correct?"*

Follow-up Questions:

▶ *"The last time we spoke you mentioned _____. Has that situation changed in any way?"*

▶ *"Does _____ continue to be a concern?"*

▶ *"At the present time, are you still interested in _____?"*

▶ *"Have your needs changed in any way?"*

Be careful not to come across as coercive in any manner when asking questions of family members. The role of the family representative is to assist family members with needs and concerns that they want addressed. It is not about getting the family to do what the family representative thinks the family should be doing.

Among phrases to avoid:

▶ *"How are you doing?"*

▶ *"I know exactly how you feel."*

▶ *"It could have been worse."*

▶ *"Everything happens for a reason."*

▶ *"It's God's will."*

More appropriate choices are:

▶ *"I'm here to help."*

▶ *"I can only imagine how difficult this must be for you."*

▶ *"I'll look into that and get right back to you."*

▶ *"I can understand your concern."*

▶ *"Tell me more."*

No matter how carefully the phrases are chosen, it's likely that family members will react with some combination of denial, numbness, anger, remorse, shock, confusion, anxiety, and grief. They do want accurate information, and family representatives should be prepared with management/attorney-approved answers to the "what happened and why" questions. Also, be prepared to be blamed personally, or to receive blame directed toward the organization. Respond by listening intently in a non-defensive manner. Remember the emotional stress they are experiencing and use the appropriate phrases and questions above or others using your best judgment. Family representatives should remain balanced emotionally in all situations.

A.4.3 Appropriate Responses

When questions are asked, it is important to listen. It is also important to respond appropriately. A well-meaning response can cause unwanted reactions if not phrased appropriately. Examples include:

▶ "I can only imagine how difficult this is for you," instead of "I know how you feel."

▶ "I know this has been a huge shock," instead of "It's God's plan."

▶ "I am sorry you're having to go through this," instead of "You shouldn't feel that way."

▶ "There just aren't good reasons for 'why?'" instead of "All things happen for the good and there will be a silver lining."

A.4.4 Dos and Don'ts

Do:

▶ Listen closely in a manner that conveys nothing but total interest in what each person is saying.

▶ Listen more/talk less.

▶ Use active listening techniques, as in: "I hear you saying you're concerned about _____, is that right?"

▶ Ask open-ended questions.

▶ Have pertinent questions and offerings prepared for discussion if the conversation lulls.

▶ Help family members continue talking by acknowledging, nodding, and asking, "Tell me more about that."

▶ Ask them to repeat their request if it isn't understood.

▶ Be honest and only promise what you can deliver.

▶ Make arrangements to accommodate their needs.

▶ Arrange for a baby-sitter (best if known to the family), as appropriate.

▶ Bring an associate or security professional with you if, for any reason, you feel uncomfortable going to the house.

▶ Be compassionate and caring.

▶ Make sure the family knows how to be in touch with you.

Don't:

▶ Don't lie or fake anything.

▶ Don't act like you are "in charge."

▶ Don't ignore anyone.

▶ Don't disagree or argue. Everyone has a right to an opinion.

▶ Don't belittle their experience or situation.

▶ Don't get drawn into religious opinions or political ideologies.

◗ Don't discuss fault or blame. Listen if blame is brought up. Respond by saying, "My job is to provide assistance for you, no matter who or what is to blame."

◗ Don't promise to do something that is not within your authority.

◗ Don't find a lawyer for the family or recommend a financial planner.

◗ Don't personally baby-sit the children.

◗ Don't go by yourself to the family's house (especially at late night, when a family member is alone, or is of the opposite gender).

◗ Don't get overly involved emotionally.

◗ Do nothing that could make a spouse jealous. It's best for each family to be assigned both a male and a female family representative.

◗ Don't become too intimate with family members or show favoritism. Keep a professional and ethical demeanor at all times.

A.4.5 Other Locations, Same Message

Family assistance personnel may also make their initial visits at a hospital. It is not always necessary to make an appointment before hospital visits, but you may want to phone ahead to confirm that it is a good time to meet. Considerations for the initial meeting include:

◗ Before meeting the family, ask a hospital staff member to help you arrange for a private place to meet. Preferably, the hospital will have family meeting rooms. Check the room out before meeting the family.

◗ If family members are in a large waiting room with other people, ask the nurse to quietly point out those you are looking for. If unknown, determine through the nursing staff who in the family appears to be primary contact and quietly approach that person first.

◗ If you are entering a patient room, knock softly, wait, and then enter slowly.

◗ Quietly introduce yourself and confirm that you are speaking with the proper person(s). Shake hands, as appropriate. Use discretion about a gentle touch on the shoulder or other appropriate gesture. Suggest that you all meet "to discuss some issues" in a private place you have arranged. In a patient's room, use discretion whether to talk in front of the injured patient or go to a private place.

▶ Express heartfelt sorrow and clarify your role, with the same questions and statements suggested above.

▶ If extended family members wish to participate in the discussion, welcome them and listen to their input. They can be helpful in interpreting the needs of the immediate family, but they may also express the most anger.

▶ Have a list of pertinent questions you want to ask. Also, list out possible items or services you could provide, such as cell phones, rental cars, hotel or travel arrangements, errands, child care, etc.

▶ Use active listening techniques, as in: "I hear you saying you're concerned about _____, is that right?"

▶ Make sure the family knows how to be in touch with you.

Similarly, if you are meeting with family members at the airport, find a private place to do so. A simple sign to identify the family you're looking for eliminates awkwardness. If members of the press are present, put first names and last initial only on the sign. Don't wear anything that displays your corporate name or logo. Lead family members away from the area, and protect them from intrusive press and media representatives.

If your initial encounter with the family takes place at a hotel, arrange in advance for a private meeting place. Wherever you meet with family members, consider the guidelines above to establish a helpful and caring experience for all involved.

A.5 An Emotional Roller Coaster

The depth of the stress on family members who have recently learned that their loved one is critically injured or dead is unfathomable. The shock and anxiety may be accompanied by an immobilizing numbed state. A refusal to believe what they have heard may be coupled with an urgent need to learn more and take action. The combinations of colliding, even conflicting emotions and needs can be confusing. Do not press family members to accept the reality of the situation. Their denial can be serving a useful purpose of not becoming too overwhelmed. It is not the job of the family representative to push family members through their denial. Instead, meet them where they are emotionally. Respond with statements like, "I can only imagine how hard it would be to accept."

It's also true that different crisis situations elicit different reactions. An airline crash, or other man-made disaster, typically leads to more anger, resentment, and culpability than natural disasters, where there are "no persons" to blame. Multiple reactions can include exhaustion, guilt, an inability to eat or sleep, trouble concentrating, and mood swings. If someone is angry at God, let them be angry. A family representative, turned spiritual counselor, can easily become destined for trouble. Ask a family member if there is a personal spiritual advisor who could help, like a member of the clergy of their choice. Provide assistance in finding a spiritual helper, only at the request of the family members. Consider seeking assistance for the choice through other family members or friends. If they have no religious affiliation, the family representative should not try to convert them to his or her own religion. No secondary agendas should be introduced by family representatives in any manner.

Relatives should be encouraged to express their concerns and issues. Family representative may wish to acknowledge that emotional reactions typically come in waves – they may feel overwhelmed at one moment, and rather numb the next.

Well-meaning family representatives who do the right things in the spirit of caring, concern, and helpfulness should not be surprised if they are the targets of some anger and blame. They must avoid taking it personally. And they should avoid the temptation to take on inappropriate roles, such as medical advisor, family counselor, grief therapist, spiritual advisor, or psychologist. Remember the limits of the family representative's role. Family representatives are provided by the company to assess needs, assist with tasks and arrangements, and serve as a conduit of communication to and from the management. Counseling issues should be deferred to crisis-experienced behavioral health professionals. Or, the family representative may bring in a crisis counselor for the families, if requested. But, confirm the company will pay for these services before making the offer. If the company has an employee assistance program (EAP), they can be contacted for short-term counseling or referrals to needed community resources.

Expect different families to have varying outcomes. It's not uncommon for a selected few family members to be unsatisfied with any level of assistance, no matter how supportive or well-intended. There are often issues of blame that might be directed toward the family representative, as a representative of the organization that killed or injured the family's loved one. If you have any concerns for the safety for family representatives, adequate security should accompany the family representative (such as a plainclothes police officer), all meetings should be in safe public places, or face-to-face assistance should be discontinued. If significant blame is anticipated, the company may want to utilize an external behavioral health professional who is thoroughly trained and experienced to assist the family instead of a representative who works directly for the company.

If issues of getting an attorney come up, the family representative should take the neutral position that the family should do whatever they feel is appropriate with no hint that the family representative believes it's a bad or good idea. Some people have accused family representatives of carrying out their duties in an effort to avoid litigation. While there does tend to be less litigation when family representatives do their jobs well, it is certainly not the role of family representatives to try and influence any legal representation decisions by the families.

The family representative's role is to genuinely assist with family members' needs without any appearances of ulterior motives.

A.5.1 Senior Management Assistance

While we are on the topic of helpful support, let's remember that senior management is not immune from needing assistance during crisis incidents. Many times the blame is directed toward senior managers. The ultimate responsibility of crisis response and decision-making rests on their shoulders. So, there are two areas of potential assistance for senior managers, personal and professional.

On the personal assistance side, employees tend to avail themselves to the EAP or onsite crisis counseling services, but senior managers tend not to participate. For that reason, it is important to identify an external crisis consultant who is adept at personally assisting senior managers during critical times. The critical incident might be a personal issue for a senior manager, like the death or major illness of a family member, substance abuse issues, or significant stress reaction during a time of crisis. In my experience, senior managers won't typically ask for assistance from within the organization or go to the EAP. However, managers who know experienced resources for senior managers often make referrals to that senior manager or the executive committee as a suggested resource.

On the professional side, research at Syracuse University (Schoenberg, 2004) and my experience with executives in crisis has demonstrated the high value for leaders in seeking support from an external resource that is experienced in crisis leadership and crisis response. This external resource may be a trusted peer from another organization or experienced crisis leadership consultant. Why? It is much more difficult to handle the situation when you are inside your own "crisis bubble." An experienced and trusted external resource who is one step removed from the blame and direct responsibility is an extremely valuable senior management resource who can help to maintain a strategic vantage for crisis leadership. This external resource is even more valuable when he or she has been involved in the crisis exercise program and become familiar with the culture, personalities, and nuances of the organization.

Often the needs for senior managers are both personal and professional simultaneously. It's not hard to imagine the distress of having several of the colleagues under your command killed in a natural disaster, terrorism, or explosion. Senior managers can be deeply impacted, especially when they blame themselves in some manner. Additionally, the crisis must be handled at an organizational level. An external resource that can help in both areas is golden. If not one person, then a small consortium of external resources for senior management can significantly increase personal and organizational resiliency.

A.5.2 Time to Disengage

Disengagement can be the hardest part for family representatives, who, by nature, are caring people. There will never be a time when they have done "everything possible" for the family. But there will be a moment when it is time to de-escalate the helping role. Remember, you don't have to solve every problem within the family in order to disengage. It is important to recognize when to disengage and how best to do it. Assistance from an internal management team and a crisis counselor can help family representatives with this disengagement process.

When the lives of family members are permanently altered, it is well beyond the scope of family representatives to remain involved in the long-term until a new normal and adequate adjustment have been established. A part of the family representative's disengagement would be to work toward aligning family members with longer-term care in needed areas. Ultimately, the decisions on choosing service providers should remain only with the family. Especially, if families want assistance in finding an attorney or financial planner, it is best for the family representatives to go no further than discussing generally how to find adequate services and leave all decision-making up to family members.

The expectation of eventual disengagement should be conveyed as early as the initial meeting. It would be good for the family representative to describe the scope of involvement as being "over the next few days or weeks." Make clear that longer-term assistance will be provided as needed, through helping referrals and community resources.

It is time to disengage when:

▶ The scope of initial assistance is completed and the family has an adequate support system of longer-term helpers.

▶ Management and the family representative agree that it is time to discontinue.

▶ An attorney is retained and restricts access to the family.

▶ The family declines further assistance.

▶ Other signs indicate the time is right.

Consider a "disengagement" meeting with the family as agreement is reached that the family representative's role is concluding. Sometimes, family members may resist the attempts of the family representatives to discontinue services. In these cases, it is best that the family representative and your management team problem-solve the situation. How can a proper handoff be provided to other service providers? What are the unfinished needs of the family, or is the resistance mostly about emotional attachment? This is a delicate process to avoid abandonment issues by family members, yet to make a reasonable end to the intended short-term assistance process.

One method to soften the disengagement process for families that become "attached" to the family representatives is called "variable interval disengagement." Rather than being available 24/7 one day, and not at all the next, consider the following approach. Promise to follow up with family members, but make the outreach random and variable. If the family continues to call, the family representatives can make themselves less available as they return to normal work duties. The purpose would be to stretch out the contacts at intermittent times that are unpredictable. In this manner, families aren't expecting contact on any certain day. Exactly when the assistance stopped is not a clear cut line. Also, it can demonstrate caring during the first year to contact the families around holidays, birthdays, and the anniversary date of the incident. Just a note, comment, or other connection that the family representative is thinking about them is helpful.

A.5.3 Family Representative Self-Assistance

During tragic situations, family representatives will need assistance from an experienced crisis counselor or consultant while the family assistance is provided. Family representatives can be deeply impacted as they carry out their duties, especially when assigned to a "difficult family." Or often, the family representative will be resistant to disengaging from the family. A world that once seemed safe may now appear dangerous and unpredictable following an up-front and close encounter with the aftermath of tragedy. Experienced family consultants can provide counseling or very helpful coaching – and onsite assistance – in how to deal with complications and difficult issues that can arise from assigned families.

Being a family representative can be one of the most rewarding experiences of an individual's life. But, it can also be very stressful and family issues may go well beyond the scope and expertise of the family representative. For that reason, it's important for the organization to provide personal crisis counseling and consultation assistance for family representatives during the assignment and disengagement process.

A.5.4 Reentry

The process of going back to normal work life can be an adjustment for family representatives following assignment to a family in the aftermath of a tragedy. When the interaction with the family has formally ended, family representatives who volunteered for this role need to go through a formal disengagement process, as well. This could include debriefings (both operational and psychological) with other family representatives and possibly a crisis counselor individually. Some companies give family representatives a couple days off to get reoriented. Holiday cards may be exchanged with families, but the relationship has served its purpose and is to be deescalated. It's easier said than done.

Everyone has heard stories of heroes (and family representatives can be just that in many cases) who suffer after their mission of mercy is complete. A poignant example is the story of Baby Jessica in Midland, Texas. In 1987, rescuers worked for fifty-eight hours to free the 18-month-old who had fallen into a 20-foot deep pipe drain in the back yard of the family's house. After multiple hours, the world watched as one of the paramedics who hoisted her out became an instant celebrity. But celebrity waned, and he eventually took his own life. According to his brother, the stress of the experience was a cause of his suicide.

This extreme example underscores the necessity of special attention for family representatives and others who care for people impacted by tragic events. Interacting with emotionally wounded, hurting family members is an enormously important part of crisis management. It promises considerable rewards, but it carries risks that should not be ignored.

References

Schoenberg, A.L. (2004). *What it means to lead during a crisis: an exploratory examination of crisis leadership*. Syracuse, NY: Syracuse University.

Glossary

activation thresholds Clearly defined criteria for activating appropriate teams and other resources as they relate to the critical incident that is to be managed and mitigated.

active shooter An active shooter is an individual actively engaged in killing or attempting to kill people, often randomly, in a populated area, such as a workplace. Such situations are unpredictable and evolve quickly.

all-hazards planning A preparedness planning approach involving the implementation of protocol and processes that are the same every time a critical incident response occurs. No matter what the incident, the response team(s) will be notified, mobilized, and structured in the same manner.

anatomy of blame Components of common perceptions and beliefs that constitute blame and outrage by people who are impacted by crises. Usually, this involves perceptions (whether true or not) by involved stakeholders, such as, issues of intentionality, injustice, and foreseeability.

asset Any financial, physical, human, or non-tangible component of an organization that holds value.

be-know-do Holistic components (utilized by the US Army) of an effective leader, involving being a right-minded person with good character traits, knowledge and decision-making skills about how to manage evolving situations, and effective implementation of decisions on a timely basis.

benchmarks Established and best practice standards that are used as points of reference for comparison.

business continuity (BC) A program to prepare for, respond to, and recover from business/organizational disruptions with a minimum of damage to people, systems, operations, and assets.

calm assertiveness During crisis response, a state of being where a person maintains composure while actively engaging in effective activities to address stressful crisis issues, i.e., without unproductive anxiety or aggression.

chief risk management officer (CRMO) or chief risk officer (CRO) An executive accountable for the effective governance of significant strategic, reputational, operational, financial, and compliance-related risks to a business/organization and related opportunities.

CIA Acronym for core assets, impacted/involved stakeholders, and anticipation developed by Bruce T. Blythe as a mental template for assessing, prioritizing, and managing critical incidents.

command center A physical location (although possibly virtual) where crisis managers work to mitigate the response and recovery of a critical incident. Typically, the command center houses the crisis action team (names vary) that serves as an intermediary between tactical/site level responses and executive crisis management team strategic responses.

containing the crisis Assuring the crisis does not escalate in severity in order to restrict the crisis impact to the smallest scope possible.

contingency plan A plan of advanced preparations that addresses an organization's response to critical incidents that involve disruption of operations or systems, unintended outcomes, or other unwanted issues. An often overlooked component is the human side of contingency planning.

control Anything you put in place to deal with a specific foreseeable risk. Policies, procedures, methods, and management systems can all be thought of as controls. Some controls can apply to – or control for – more than one foreseeable risk.

core assets Financial, physical, human, or non-tangible components of an organization that are vital to the viability and survival of an organization.

corporate risk management An area of governance and management responsibility within an organization that identifies and manages existing, new, and emerging risks, typically headed by a chief risk officer (CRO).

crisis A critical incident or situation that threatens the core assets of an organization, e.g., people, reputation, brand, trust, financial wellbeing, shareholder value, ability to operate, physical property, intellectual property, or key relationships. The incident may have occurred, is about to occur, or is perceived to threaten vital components of the organization.

crisis action team (CAT) Also called the managerial team, crisis assessment team, incident management team, or other name designated within a crisis management organizational structure. This team is charged with "directing" the crisis response on behalf of the organization. A primary function of the crisis action team is to serve as an intermediary between the "implementing" operational/tactical responders and "deciding" executive management team. Each member of the crisis action team should have only one area of responsibility to assure proper attention is provided to each functional area of the organization that is impacted or involved in the crisis.

crisis action team leader This designated team leader (typically positioned in the crisis command center) is empowered with broad authority – by policy and by practice – to direct the crisis response actions of the organization. Skills needed include the ability to lead individual and team decisions. Effective crisis action team leaders have the ability to collaborate, integrate, delegate, and monitor progress of the myriad crisis response actions throughout the organization. This leader requires authority, trust, and respect with the executive, crisis action, and tactical/operational teams.

crisis anticipation committee This planning team is established to "consider the unconsidered." In addition to internal personnel, external consultants and other appropriate resources can be included on this committee in order to gain outside perspectives. Committee members should be trusted personnel since brainstorming involves the anticipation and analysis of incidents and situations that could have catastrophic impacts on the enterprise that have not been previously considered.

crisis beyond the obvious This is a method of analyzing the broader consequences of a crisis situation. Rather than simply focusing on the "bull's eye" of the crisis (e.g., putting out the fire and saving lives), strategic perspective is achieved through a broader, longer-term focus. To identify the crisis beyond the obvious, focus should be on core assets of the organization that are anticipated to be impacted, e.g., key relationships/people, reputation/brand, finances.

crisis command center (CCC) The location where tactical assessment, response, and recovery activities are managed. Access to the CCC(s) – possibly more than one, depending on the incident response – by appropriate team members may be through physical presence or remotely. The center is typically well-equipped technologically, with capability for monitoring, sending, and receiving electronic information of all sorts.

crisis communications   The most fundamental and vital component of responding to a crisis situation. Crisis communications includes the ability to receive information, verify the accuracy of incoming information, and send out information to involved and impacted stakeholders in an effective and timely manner.

crisis decision-making Effective crisis decision-making involves the integration of information received, identifying and prioritizing problem areas, anticipation of stakeholder reactions, prudent judgment, calculated risk-taking, courage to take action in uncertain times, and choosing a course of action on a timely basis – typically with only partial information. Crisis decision-making is located somewhere between situational analysis (avoiding analysis-paralysis) and intuition (avoiding impulsivity).

crisis leadership   The US Army's leadership training for combat officers has been applied to corporate crisis leadership. According to this "be-know-do" model, crisis leadership involves high character and demonstrated morals beyond reproach; knowledge about the organization's vision and values with skilled decision-making about how to manage evolving crisis issues; and effective implementation of decisions in a caring manner on a timely basis.

crisis leadership coaching As a specialty within the broader executive coaching that addresses management and leadership issues of daily living and work life, crisis leadership coaching helps individual managers and teams develop skills in managing unexpected, high-consequence situations where high stress, rapid velocity, uncertainty, blame, and outrage prevail.

crisis leadership red zone This paradigm occurs typically when a crisis leader vacillates between passivity/indecision and aggression in managing crises. This is contrasted with a more effective and assertive approach used by the crisis whisperer, one that is inclusive, active, communicative, and decisive on a timely basis.

crisis management The strategic, managerial, and tactical/operational process of minimizing damage to an organization's core assets when threatened by a critical incident or situation, whether real or perceived.

crisis management organization The overarching management system (including internal and external established resources, e.g., people, processes, and equipment) within an organization that is established and maintained to effectively prepare for, respond to, and recover from critical incidents that can or could affect the core assets of the enterprise.

crisis management team (CMT) The body that consists of the organization's executive leadership team, impacted business unit managers, and owners of critical business functions that are strategic-focused on addressing serious threats to the core assets of an organization. This team is activated only when the severity of the crisis situation reaches defined levels, e.g., financial threshold, significant traditional or social media involvement, serious disruption of operations, fatalities or serious injuries, or regulatory involvement. Every business function of the organization is represented on the crisis management team to assure comprehensive coverage of issues.

crisis planning committee (CPC) A multidisciplinary team of internal (and many times including external) specialists who are tasked with analyzing vulnerabilities, evaluating existing plans, and then planning and organizing the comprehensive crisis response capabilities of the crisis management organization within a company.

crisis probability A risk analysis technique to assess the probability of a clearly defined foreseeable incident occurring within a given period of time, e.g., "What is the likelihood that each foreseeable incident we identify would happen within the next decade?"

crisis severity An risk analysis technique to analyze the damage (e.g., mild, moderate, or severe) a clearly defined crisis incident could cause to the core assets of the organization. Crisis severity question: "If it happened, what core assets could be threatened and how severely would it hurt the organization?"

crisis whisperer Like the "horse whisperer" or "dog whisperer" described in the media, this term is adapted to apply to an effective crisis manager who uses rapport, communication with stakeholders, patience, and gentle techniques to control crises while rejecting abusive or coercive methods.

de-escalating crisis team involvement A purposeful process of reducing or ending involvement of the various crisis-related teams once there is agreement (that passes the reasonable person test) among team members.

defensible documentation A compilation of notes that were generated during a crisis response into one official set of documentation. The object is to memorialize crisis-related decisions and actions (or inactions) in a manner that can withstand scrutiny by passing the reasonable person test. A simple documentation format includes a timeline of (1) known facts/situational analysis, (2) decisions made, (3) actions taken, and (4) rationale that supports significant team activities. Defensible documentation methods and maintenance should be approved by appropriate persons in authority within a company.

disaster A natural or manmade catastrophic event that damages one or more core assets of an organization, including the ability to operate for unacceptable or extended periods of time.

disaster recovery The process of reestablishing IT services, including telecommunications, when disrupted by a critical incident, typically a component of a company's business continuity plan (BCP).

disaster response Combined public/private response to address critical needs of people, systems, operations, and assets of a community or area of concern that has been seriously damaged by a natural or manmade catastrophic event.

emergency A critical incident that has caused injury or death, significant damage to property, or other urgent situation that can threaten the wellbeing of an organization and/or people.

emergency communications systems Preplanned and established methods to give and receive timely information with selected audiences during and after critical incidents.

emergency response The immediate response to protect life, safety and wellbeing of people, mitigate physical property damage, and reduce severity of consequences in the immediate aftermath of a critical incident.

employee assistance program (EAP) Confidential services provided by organizations to their employees to address personal problems that may negatively affect job satisfaction or productivity, such as alcohol and drug abuse, marital and family problems, mental health issues, childcare and eldercare, or other problems of daily living.

employee crisis recovery committee A selected grassroots group of employees that provide an advisory function to management relating to addressing employee post-crisis concerns and needs, and suggesting methods to recover from a disruptive critical workplace incident.

enterprise risk management (ERM) A risk-based component of management that includes methods to address risks and capitalize on opportunities in accord with the strategic objectives of the organization. ERM identifies and assesses risks, and then establishes and monitors methods to manage these risks. The objective of ERM is to create, enhance, and protect the value of the organization from a risk management perspective.

escalation This term is used with two definitions in this book: (1) the progression of increasing severity of a crisis; and (2) the process of information and involvement moving up through the organization's chain of command.

evacuation The orderly movement of people from an area that is (or potentially considered to be) dangerous to a place that is safe.

event Used interchangeably with the term "incident," a sudden or slowly developing, expected or unexpected occurrence that leads to a crisis situation.

executive team As it relates to crisis management, senior leaders of an organization who are tasked with the responsibility to strategically "lead" (vs. tactical involvement) the crisis response when threshold levels are reached that will mobilize their involvement. Every function of the organization should be represented on the core executive team.

exercise An activity that simulates a crisis-related situation and tests the strengths, weaknesses, gaps, and limitations of the company's crisis management organization, including the plan(s), team(s), and other preparations.

exercise observer An individual or small team that is not actively involved in an exercise, but has the role of monitoring to assure the objectives are being met and to compile useful information for improvement.

fact finding An ongoing individual and team process during crisis response of receiving, validating, compiling, and prioritizing incoming crisis-related information in order to implement an effective crisis response.

fact pattern Interconnected issues and bits of information that are in context of a crisis situation, including what has occurred, identification of problem areas, stakeholder responses, intended and unintended consequences, and anticipation of upcoming manifestations.

gatekeeper When assigned to secure a crisis command center, this person's sole purpose is to manage traffic in and out of the room. This person should be armed with a list of people who are allowed in the center and assure no one else gains access to the room without authorized approval.

guiding principles Established behavioral and decision-making guidelines for individual and corporate crisis response that are based on undisputable, high-level character traits and social appropriateness.

higher purpose Where the overriding crisis response focus is not on self-serving interests, but on the greater good of the organization, community, and other impacted stakeholders.

holding statements Public statements that are prepared and pre-approved by management prior to a crisis situation for use by appropriate communicators in the early aftermath of a crisis.

human side of crisis The specialty area of addressing the communication, palliative (physical comforting), emotional, safety, wellbeing, and other needs and concerns of impacted crisis stakeholders, including employees, their family members, and others.

humanitarian response team (HRT) The multidisciplinary team that has the single focus on addressing the human side of crisis without distractions of managing other (non-people) components of a crisis.

imagery technique Formation of mental images or mental pictures to visualize the needs and concerns of impacted stakeholders in order to establish empathy and understanding for effective crisis response actions. Sometimes called the "outside-in technique" where crisis managers "look back" at their organization through the imagined eyes and perspectives of impacted stakeholders.

impact The effect a crisis situation or incident has on an organization, whether negative, neutral, or positive.

incident command system (ICS) In this book, a corporate variation of the original ICS system typically used in the public sector that provides a common organizational structure and method for command and control, procedures, communications, authority, equipment, supplies, facilities, and coordination among the various teams involved in crisis response. Typically, an incident commander (IC) is assigned authority over the entire crisis response.

integration Narrowly defined, a collaborative and coordinated approach to address the interrelated components of a crisis response where each individual and team has identified what is expected of other staff functions and other crisis responders during crisis response. This is established by knowing what communications and resources can be expected to and from each internal and external responder for various foreseeable risks of the organization.

International Organization for Standardization (ISO) A group that establishes multiple international standards (including some that are risk- and crisis-related) through a strict standard-setting methodology and participation of technical committee volunteers from 161 participating countries.

isolating the crisis A process to quarantine what is affected from what is not affected through actions and communications, and ensuring the crisis does not escalate in severity in order to contain the crisis impact to the smallest scope possible.

leverage High-influence actions that are used to mitigate and resolve the crisis as quickly and efficiently as possible with the least amount of effort.

logistics The process of acquiring and mobilizing resources and supplies needed for crisis response.

managerial team Also called the crisis action team (and other names) that typically directs the activities of the crisis command center. The managerial team is charged with "directing" the crisis response on behalf of the organization. A primary function of the managerial team during crisis response is to serve as an intermediary between the operational/tactical responders and the executive-level crisis management team. Each member of the managerial team should have only one area of staff responsibility to assure proper attention is provided to each.

mobilization To assemble and put into operation the appropriate teams and resources needed to respond effectively to a crisis situation.

operational debriefing An after-action meeting of respective crisis response teams (operational/tactical, managerial, and executive/strategic), together or individually. The object is to identify needed improvements and new controls that should be implemented to improve response capabilities for the next critical incident or crisis exercise.

operational/tactical team "Doing" oriented response teams that are often located in or near the "bull's eye" of the crisis and addressing the overt content of the crisis. This may involve putting out the fire, rescuing impacted workers, arranging alternative work capabilities, communicating tactical information, securing the incident site, or other hands-on duties.

organizational resilience The ability of an organization to positively cope and adapt itself to the consequences of a crisis.

outside-in perspective The ability to identify and understand the viewpoints, concerns, and needs of impacted stakeholders from their perspectives. This "outside-in" vantage is achieved by imagining the needs and concerns of various stakeholders who are looking in at the organization or management.

primary prevention The process of avoiding a crisis or damaging occurrence before it's onset.

probability The estimate of how likely a crisis event is to happen. Since crisis events can't be predicted with total certainty, probabilities are given a likelihood of occurrence between 0% chance to 100% within a defined period of time.

process guardian A person who is assigned the responsibility for assuring that crisis-related teams, external providers, plans, and processes are up-to-date at all times.

psychological debriefing Typically, one-session group or individual meetings that are intended to reduce the negative and unwanted reactions of people impacted by a crisis situation. Research has demonstrated that the traditional approach of discussing and shared reliving of a traumatic incident may not be clinically helpful. However, there is a social expectation that organizations should demonstrate caring following a distressing crisis incident. Thus, new approaches to debriefing and intervention are focused on supporting issues of post-incident calm, safety, information, interpersonal connectedness, and hope.

psychological first aid (PFA) Assistance provided to impacted people in the immediate aftermath of a traumatic event to reduce distress and to begin adaptive functioning. Components include establishing a sense of safety, allowing a compassionate opportunity to talk, provision of coping information, addressing needs and concerns, establishing social support, referrals for additional assistance, and offer of follow-up.

public relations (PR) consultant Crisis communications may require PR professionals who are experienced and skilled in crisis management. Beyond PR responsibilities during normal times, PR consultants should be fully adept at managing crises.

purposeful disengagement Structured process used to de-escalate the crisis management teams and their active crisis response involvement, based on decision-making that takes into reasonable consideration the disposition of all involved stakeholders.

reasonable person test Reflects what an informed person would have expected you to do, given what you knew (or should have known) at the time and were capable of doing.

recovery Returning an organization to operational stability following a crisis.

reliability An attribute that consistently produces the same results and can be counted on to work successfully in the same manner in response to repeated applications.

resilience The ability for an organization to protect its core assets, including ability to operate at acceptable levels, following a crisis situation.

ripple effect of vulnerability A progressive and unwanted exposure to a threat or damage once primary security measures have been breached.

risk Potential for damage or unwanted outcome relating to a corporate or personal situation, avocation, decision, or action.

runner A trusted person who is responsible to deliver crisis-related messages or items, gather information, or complete tasks in order to help keep team members focused and cohesively working together.

secondary prevention Detecting and addressing crisis issues that are present, but have not yet manifested into critical damage. An example is to effectively address a workplace violence threat before it becomes actual violence.

severity The intensity or seriousness of a critical incident or situation.

SIP-DE A model transposed from instruction in driver's training to a decision-making model in crisis management, i.e., scan the crisis fact pattern, identify problem areas, predict the likely progression of events, decide how to respond, and execute your plan according to priority.

social media Electronic applications of communication that enable users to rapidly create and share information in the aftermath of a crisis in an unfiltered and unregulated manner. It can also instigate crises such as flash mobs or social uprisings.

spokesperson A person selected to speak on behalf of the organization to help ensure that outgoing messages are appropriately provided and through the correct channels.

strategic crisis leadership Overarching leadership during dynamic times of uncertainty, inadequate information, high-stress, expanding list of stakeholders, personal stress, rapid velocity, time limitations, and high-consequence. It involves vision about how the organization will respond, clear understanding of personal and organizational values, emotional stability, defining decisions, getting and giving effective communication with key stakeholders, and a demonstration of corporate caring.

Strategic Crisis Leadership Checklist A quick reference guide provided in this book that was developed by Bruce T. Blythe for persons who are tasked with leading (within their areas of responsibility) during crisis response.

strategic crisis management The focus for managing a crisis is on protecting core assets of the organization. It is principle-oriented and includes defining decisions about what needs to be done, leveraging strengths to mitigate the crisis, commitment to get the crisis resolved, highly-visible and open communications, and an overt display of corporate caring.

strategic preparedness Actions taken to pre-establish the ability in the aftermath of a crisis to effectively lead the mission-critical, vital, broad-term issues as they arise in a principle-oriented manner.

stress style The "go to" reaction of an individual when there is an overload of stress beyond normal coping mechanisms. Reactions can differ among individuals from being autocratic or avoidant, to acquiescence or anger and blame.

tactical crisis management Often involving immediate and emergency response actions, tactics also refer to tangible, "doing" actions taken to address a crisis.

tactical preparedness In the aftermath of a crisis, the ability to react effectively to short-term issues as they arise in a process-oriented manner. Typically the preparedness is narrowly focused on addressing a defined area of damage or threat, in contrast to the broader, principle-oriented focus of strategic crisis leadership preparedness.

tertiary prevention When crisis management actions are directed at damage that has already occurred, in an attempt to prevent further severity, longevity, and subsequent events.

threat A risk-based situation that involves the assessment of severity and probability of occurrence.

threshold damage The raising of the bar for future manmade critical incidents where there is a human tendency to try and outdo previous levels of severity.

tiered crisis management model The overarching structure of a crisis management organization within a company containing integrated executive, managerial, and tactical/operational policies, protocol, plans, and teams.

traumatic stress Reactions of people subjected to traumatic or highly-distressing events, typically involving mental re-experiencing of the incident, anxiety-based reactions, and a desire to avoid things that are reminders of the incident.

valid plan A valid plan is one that actually accomplishes what it was designed to do by bringing about the intended results.

Wall Street Journal test A decision-making test where decision-makers ask themselves whether they would be satisfied or proud if the decision were accurately reported on the front page of the *Wall Street Journal*. This test evocatively captures the idea that a decision may look different once it comes under public scrutiny.

Index

Figures and tables are indicated by f and t following the page number.

Be ready and able to protect, preserve and
recover what is most important:
your people, facilities, assets and reputation.

{ Groundbreaking
approach to emerging
discipline of Emotional
Continuity Management;
proven system/tools
to reduce risk by
proactively managing
workplace emotions.

©2013
300 pages,
glossary, index,
ISBN 978-1-931332-58-3
paperback 6x9
$39.95

©2008
190 pages, illustrations
ISBN 978-1931332-21-7
paperback 8.5 x 11
$49.50

Workbook format
guides managers new
to BCP in developing
a good basic plan and
keeping it updated.
Extensive, easy to-use
downloads including
worksheets, forms
checklists, templates,
and sample plans. }

{ Best practices for
getting everyone
to safety from any
workplace; integrates
EEP and business
continuity for first
time; downloads with
forms, checklists, and
sample plans.

©2013
340 pages, illustrations,
glossary, index
ISBN 978-1-931332-56-9
casebound 6x9
$69.95

Explore and purchase our books at : www.rothsteinpublishing.com
203.740.7400

Credits

Kristen Noakes-Fry, ABCI, is Executive Editor at Rothstein Publishing. Previously, she was a Research Director, Information Security and Risk Group, for Gartner, Inc.; Associate Editor at Datapro (McGraw-Hill); and Associate Professor of English at Atlantic Cape College in New Jersey. She holds an M.A. from New York University and a B.A. from Russell Sage College.

Cover Design and Graphics:	Sheila Kwiatek, Flower Grafix
Page Design and Typography:	Jean King
Copy Editing:	Nancy M. Warner
Index:	Enid Zafran, Indexing Partners, LLC
Title Font:	Nueva STD
Body Fonts:	Sabon and Frutiger

a division of Rothstein Associates Inc
www.rothsteinpublishing.com

Rothstein Publishing is your premier source of books and learning materials about Business Resilience including Crisis Management, Business Continuity, Disaster Recovery, Emergency Management, and Risk Management. Our industry-leading authors provide current, actionable knowledge, solutions, and tools you can put into practice immediately. Founded in 1984 by Philip Jan Rothstein, FBCI, our company remains true to our commitment to prepare you and your organization to protect, preserve, and recover what is most important: your people, facilities, assets, and reputation. Rothstein Publishing is a division of Rothstein Associates Inc., an international management consultancy.

About the Author

Bruce T. Blythe

Bruce Blythe is an internationally acclaimed crisis management expert. He is the owner and chairman of three companies that provide employers with a continuum of crisis preparedness, crisis response, and employee return-to-work services. Crisis Management International (Atlanta-based) is the preparedness arm of the three companies. CMI has assisted hundreds of companies worldwide with crisis and business continuity planning, training, and exercising. CMI also provides workplace violence preparedness programs and threat of violence consultations through a specialty network of threat management specialists, including former FBI and Secret Service agents, and behavioral health specialists. Crisis Care Network (based in Grand Rapids, Michigan) responds to corporate crisis situations 1,000 times per month through a North American network of crisis mental health professionals. Behavioral Medical Interventions (Minneapolis-based) accelerates employee return-to-work for disability, workers' compensation and non-occupational injury cases.

Mr. Blythe has been personally involved in crises such as the 1993 World Trade Center bombing, mass murders at the US Postal Service, the Oklahoma City bombing, 9/11, commercial air crashes, rescue of kidnap and ransom hostages, Hurricanes Andrew and Katrina, earthquakes, fires, floods, and reputational crises. He serves as a consultant and certified coach to numerous Fortune executives and managers in strategic crisis leadership preparedness and response. He has served in the Military Police for the US Marine Corps. He's a certified clinical psychologist and has been a consultant to the FBI on workplace violence and terrorism.

Widely regarded as a thought leader in the crisis management and business continuity industries, Mr. Blythe has appeared on NBC's *Today Show*, CNN, ABC's *20/20*, CBS' *48 Hours*, CNBC, NPR and others. *Fast Company Magazine* published a cover-story article about Blythe's leadership in responding to 204 companies onsite, all within three weeks following 9/11. He provides commentary in *The Wall Street Journal, Newsweek, Business Week, Smart Money, New Yorker, Fortune,* and *USA Today*. He serves as a keynote presenter to 50 national and international conferences per year.

Mr. Blythe is (or has been) a member of:

▶ ASIS International's Crisis Management and Business Continuity Council.

▶ US Department of State's Overseas Security Advisory Council.

▶ Disaster Recovery Institute's Educational Advisory Council.

▶ The Conference Board, as Chairman of the Corporate Security, Business Continuity, and Crisis Management Conference.

▶ Association of Traumatic Stress Specialists, six years on the Board of Directors.

▶ NFPA 1600 Technical Committee's Task Group on Crisis Management.

▶ The International Society for Traumatic Stress Studies.

▶ Association of Threat Assessment Professionals.

Mr. Blythe's areas of expertise include:

▶ Strategic Crisis Leadership (for Senior Executives and Crisis Managers).

▶ Crisis Preparedness and Response.

▶ Workplace Violence Preparedness and Defusing Threatening Individuals.

▶ Human Side of Crisis and Post-Incident Return to Work.

▶ Crisis Decision-Making.

Office: (404) 841-3402 / bblythe@cmiatl.com